German Colonialism Revisited

Social History, Popular Culture, and Politics in Germany
Kathleen Canning, Series Editor

Recent Titles
Imperial Fictions: German Literature Before and Beyond the Nation-State
  Todd Kontje
White Rebels in Black: German Appropriation of Black Popular Culture
  Priscilla Layne
Not Straight from Germany: Sexual Publics and Sexual Citizenship
  since Magnus Hirschfeld
  Michael Thomas Taylor, Annette F. Timm, and Rainer Herrn, Editors
Passing Illusions: Jewish Visibility in Weimar Germany
  Kerry Wallach
Bodies and Ruins: Imagining the Bombing of Germany, 1945 to the Present
  David Crew
The Jazz Republic: Music, Race, and American Culture in Weimar Germany
  Jonathan Wipplinger
The War in Their Minds: German Soldiers and Their Violent Pasts in West Germany
  Svenja Goltermann
Three-Way Street: Jews, Germans, and the Transnational
  Jay Howard Geller and Leslie Morris, Editors
Beyond the Bauhaus: Cultural Modernity in Breslau, 1918–33
  Deborah Ascher Barnstone
Stop Reading! Look! Modern Vision and the Weimar Photographic Book
  Pepper Stetler
The Corrigible and the Incorrigible: Science, Medicine, and the
  Convict in Twentieth-Century Germany
  Greg Eghigian
An Emotional State: The Politics of Emotion in Postwar West German Culture
  Anna M. Parkinson
Germany's Wild East: Constructing Poland as Colonial Space
  Kristin Kopp
Beyond Berlin: Twelve German Cities Confront the Nazi Past
  Gavriel D. Rosenfeld and Paul B. Jaskot, Editors
Consumption and Violence: Radical Protest in Cold-War West Germany
  Alexander Sedlmaier
Communism Day-to-Day: State Enterprises in East German Society
  Sandrine Kott
Envisioning Socialism: Television and the Cold War in the German Democratic Republic
  Heather L. Gumbert
The People's Own Landscape: Nature, Tourism, and Dictatorship in East Germany
  Scott Moranda
German Colonialism Revisited: African, Asian, and Oceanic Experiences
  Nina Berman, Klaus Mühlhahn, and Patrice Nganang, Editors

For a complete list of titles, please see www.press.umich.edu

German Colonialism Revisited

African, Asian, and Oceanic Experiences

Nina Berman, Klaus Mühlhahn, and
Patrice Nganang, Editors

The University of Michigan Press
Ann Arbor

First paperback edition 2018
Copyright © Nina Berman, Klaus Mühlhahn, and Patrice Nganang 2014
All rights reserved

Published in the United States of America by
The University of Michigan Press
Manufactured in the United States of America

A CIP catalog record for this book is available from the British Library.

Library of Congress Cataloging-in-Publication Data

German colonialism revisited : African, Asian, and Oceanic experiences / Nina Berman, Klaus Mühlhahn, Patrice Nganang, editors.
        pages   cm.— (Social history, popular culture, and politics in Germany)
    Includes bibliographical references and index.
    ISBN 978-0-472-11912-7 (cloth : acid-free paper)—ISBN 978-0-472-02970-9 (e-book)
    1. Germany—Colonies—Africa—History.   2. Germany—Colonies—Asia—History.
3. Germany—Colonies—Oceania—History.   4. Indigenous peoples—Africa—Social conditions.   5. Indigenous peoples—Asia—Social conditions.   6. Indigenous peoples—Oceania—Social conditions.   7. Africa—Colonization—Social aspects—History.
8. Asia—Colonization—Social aspects—History.   9. Oceania—Colonization—Social aspects—History. I. Berman, Nina. II. Mühlhahn, Klaus. III. Nganang, Alain Patrice.
JV2035.G37   2013
909'.0971243—dc23

                                                                        2013031519

ISBN 978-0-472-03727-8 (pbk. : alk. paper)

Contents

Introduction   I
    Nina Berman, Klaus Mühlhahn, and Patrice Nganang

Part 1. Interactions

Architecture with a Mission: Bamum Autoethnography
during the Period of German Colonialism   31
    Itohan I. Osayimwese

"The Germans cannot master our language!" or German
Colonial Rulers and the Beti in the Cameroonian Hinterlands   50
    Germain Nyada (Translated by Amber Suggitt)

Sex and Control in Germany's Overseas Possessions:
Venereal Disease and Indigenous Agency   71
    Daniel J. Walther

Ruga-ruga: The History of an African Profession, 1820–1918   85
    Michael Pesek

Bomani: African Soldiers as Colonial Intermediaries in
German East Africa, 1890–1914   101
    Michelle Moyd

Pioneers of Empire? The Making of Sisal Plantations in
German East Africa, 1890–1917   114
    Hanan Sabea

"Zake: The Papuan Chief": An Alliance with a German
Missionary in Colonial Kaiser-Wilhelmsland (Oceania)   130
    Gabriele Richter

**Part 2. Resistance, Anti-colonial Activism, and the
Rise of Nationalist Discourses**

Germany and the Chinese Coolie: Labor, Resistance,
and the Struggle for Equality, 1884–1914   147
    Andreas Steen

The Other German Colonialism: Power, Conflict, and Resistance
in a German-speaking Mission in China, ca. 1850–1920   161
    Thoralf Klein

Nationalism and Pragmatism: The Revolutionists in
German Qingdao (1897–1914)   179
    Jianjun Zhu

Anti-colonial Nationalism and Cosmopolitan "Standard Time":
Lala Har Dayal's *Forty Four Months in Germany and Turkey* (1920)   195
    B. Venkat Mani

Acting Cannibal: Intersecting Strategies, Conflicting Interests,
and the Ambiguities of Cultural Resistance in Iringa, German
East Africa   212
    Eva Bischoff

The "Truppenspieler Show": Herero Masculinity and the
German Colonial Military Aesthetic   226
    Molly McCullers

Part 3. Remembering and Rethinking

Recollection and Intervention: Memory of German
Colonialism in Contemporary African Migrants' Writing   245
    Dirk Göttsche

The Shadows of History: Photography and Colonialism
in William Kentridge's *Black Box/Chambre Noire*   259
    Andrew J. Hennlich

Germans and the Death-Throes of the Qing: Mo Yan's
The Sandalwood Torture   271
    Yixu Lü

The Origins of German Minority Cinema in Colonial Film   284
    Patrice Nganang

    Bibliography   299

    Contributors   333

    Index   339

Introduction*

Nina Berman, Klaus Mühlhahn, and Patrice Nganang

Abdulrazak Gurnah's novel *Paradise* (1994) chronicles the young life of Yusuf and his coming-of-age during the period of German colonialism in East Africa. The Germans, though, do not play a major role in this tale about political, social, economic, and cultural relations between various ethnicities and religious groups. In fact, the novel focuses more on indigenous systems of dependency and oppression than aspects of life related to colonial rule. After his parents give him up to a wealthy merchant as debt payment, Yusuf spends most of his childhood and teenage years as a *rehani*, an indentured slave. Working in the merchant's store on the coast, he learns how to sell goods, becomes aware of the intricacies of the merchant's household, and, once he is assigned to the merchant's caravans, travels back and forth between the East African coast and interior. After Yusuf proves to be reliable and intelligent, particularly during one disastrous caravan expedition, his master offers him salaried employment and improved status within the company and household. But, already, Yusuf has become aware of the net of power relations around him, and resents the merchant for "own[ing] people the way you own us."[1] He has considered his own fate and that of his companion Khalil, a fellow *rehani*. He has gradually come to learn more about the lives of the women of the household and to understand the scope and scale of society's power relations more broadly. He has seen how even those who are set free—such as a gardener, who had been a slave, but was manumitted later, and Khalil, who was forgiven the debt of his father when the merchant married Khalil's sister—are de facto trapped, with no realistic alternative for a different life. As Yusuf slowly grasps the full extent of these dependencies, he begins to consider a different life for himself. But what are his options?

The solution comes one day when a column of *askari*—native soldiers who were recruited by the Germans in East Africa—enters the town in search of more recruits for the impending war with the British. As Yusuf and his friend Khalil watch from within the safety of their boarded-up store, the *askari*, who are led by just one German officer, hunt for young men. They organize the captured men—some frightened, others "appeared happy enough" (246)—into two lines, and then march away. As the column begins to disappear, Yusuf suddenly darts off and joins them.[2]

What Gurnah captures here so brilliantly, namely, the kind of circumstances that may serve as an explanation for the voluntary participation of an East African in the German army, is one of many kinds of colonial encounters that have not received sufficient consideration in scholarship on German colonialism. This multidisciplinary anthology addresses this gap by foregrounding social, economic, political, and cultural practices generated by African, Asian, and Oceanic individuals and groups within the context and aftermath of German colonialism. Recent scholarship has shed new light on our understanding of the relationship between colonizer and colonized; the nature and complexity of "colonial governmentality"; the interplay between the colonial state and local institutions; and the connections between ideology, textual discourses, material dimensions, and social, economic, cultural, and political practices. This anthology is designed to contribute to the ongoing discussion of German colonialism with a fresh focus on the agency of those affected by German colonialism in Africa, Asia, and Oceania. While often postulated, few studies have actually zeroed in on the agency of indigenous actors. By focusing on the history of contact, interaction, exchange, and mutual influence, this volume contributes to current debates on transnational and intercultural processes, and highlights the ways in which the colonial period is embedded in larger processes of globalization, in particular the global expansion of capitalism, technology, and the Western legal framework.

The academic study of German colonialism took form in specific geopolitical and historical contexts, and in various disciplines. Whereas French and British academics engaged intensely with the question of colonialism during and after the period of decolonization, in contrast, West German postwar society and its academics were primarily concerned with understanding World War II and the Shoah. As Sara Friedrichsmeyer, Sara Lennox, and Susanne Zantop point out:

> The German focus on the Holocaust as the central and unavoidable fact of German history may also have occluded Germans' view of European colonialism and their own complicity as Europeans in it. To be sure, various traditions of German thought insist on connections between colonialism and National Socialism. In *The Origins of Totalitarianism* Hannah Arendt explored how imperialism's political self-legitimation laid the groundwork for fascism (and Stalinism), and the German student movement un-

derlined connections between neoimperialism and fascism. . . . Nevertheless, the postulate of the singularity of the Holocaust has been fundamental to postwar West German politics.[3]

East German scholars, however, held a different view of World War II, one in which fascism was understood in the larger framework of capitalism, and colonialism and imperialism were mainly seen as manifestations of capitalism. Helmuth Stoecker and Kurt Büttner, two leading East German historians, made considerable contributions to understanding the colonial period in Africa and Asia.[4] The pioneering work of African historians and fiction writers, dating back to the 1960s (see, for example, the prolific work of Alexandre Kum'a Ndumbe III or the contributions to an anthology edited by B. A. Ogot and J. A. Kieran), received little or no attention outside of Africa.[5] Perhaps the most widely received Africanist historian of the period is UK-based John Iliffe, whose work on German colonialism became canonical.[6] In the United States, several Africanists, Asianists, and Oceanists researched aspects of German colonialism in the 1960s, but many of their master's theses and dissertations were never published.[7] Scholars also examined the continuation of colonial ambitions in the period after World War I.[8] In the 1970s, seminal studies by historians based in the United States, such as the republished work of M. E. Townsend and a groundbreaking study by Woodruff Smith, prepared the way for the next generation of scholars.[9] African historians of the era pointed out the ways in which colonialist policies structured West German foreign policy in the period after World War II, but again, their work saw little reception outside of Africa.[10] Similarly, most of the studies on the German colonies in Asia are from Asian historians or scholars in area studies. Their books and articles have rarely been noticed outside of their fields. This also applies to the voluminous body of ethnographic, biographical, and autobiographical writings produced by former missionaries and missionary societies.[11] While often apologetic, they made available a wealth of information on everyday life and the indigenous populations in the colonies.

After only sporadic publications in the 1960s and 1970s (such as those by Helmut Bley and Karin Hausen), West German historians, including Horst Gründer, Klaus J. Bade, and Jürgen Osterhammel, published seminal studies on German colonialism, most of which shared a focus on political history, diplomatic history, the role of the Christian mission, emigration, and the economic dimensions of colonialism and imperialism.[12] In addition, literary scholars, such as Joachim Warmbold, Sibylle Benninghoff-Lühl, Wolfgang Bader, and János Riesz, began to assess the archive of colonialist fiction and non-fiction.[13] In South Africa, scholars also scrutinized the distinct features of German literary colonial discourse; dissertations and article publications by Ulrike Kistner, Gunther Pakendorf, and Peter Horn, among others, are pioneering analyses in this regard.[14]

A turning point came in the 1990s when German studies, in the United States and, somewhat later, in German-speaking and other countries, paid attention to the colonial period in the context of the institutionalization of the field of postcolonial studies. German colonial studies, as it developed in various disciplines in the 1990s up until only very recently, was characterized by a number of factors that brought a wealth of new information and approaches into play but collectively also generated several lacunae that our anthology is designed to address.

1. Initially, the new interest in German colonialism generated studies that focused primarily on the genocidal dimensions of German colonialism. Studies about the genocide of the Herero and Nama in German Southwest Africa (Jan-Bart Gewald, Jürgen Zimmerer, Joachim Zeller) brought to light the heretofore largely forgotten horrors of that history.[15] The emphasis on the genocidal dimension of German colonialism was also at the core of studies connecting colonialism to World War I, World War II, and the Shoah (Isabel V. Hull).[16] While African and diaspora intellectuals, such as Aimé Césaire, had pointed out the connection between fascism and colonialism for long, the particular parameters of that connection continue to be debated controversially.[17] Overall, scholars began to unearth the multifaceted history of German racism (Pascal Grosse, Fatima El-Tayeb, Tina Campt).[18]

2. Other studies explored colonial discourses, took stock of the literary and cultural archive on colonialism, and related the history of imagination to colonialism. According to this model, and following the Saidian paradigm, cultural discourses were understood as the key factor bringing about colonial and imperial power structures. Susanne Zantop, for instance, highlighted the pervasiveness and specificity of colonial discourse in German culture even before the establishment of the German colonial empire.[19] Various anthologies and special issues refined our understanding of the characteristics of German colonial discourse and the scope of the cultural archive on German colonialism.[20] With their studies on the role of German women in the colonial power structure Martha Mamozai and Lora Wildenthal, among others, brought into focus the complex relationship between issues of race, gender, and nation.[21] In the more recent past, a comparative study by George Steinmetz, in which he investigates the relationship between precolonial discourse and colonial policy, also emphasized the pivotal role of culture in conditioning colonial—albeit

heterogeneous—power structures.[22] The culturalist approach, which has dominated the field for two decades, brought a wealth of material to the fore. For the most part, however, it did not consider African, Asian, and Oceanic sources, material conditions, and agency.

3. The lack of interaction between scholars trained in German history, culture, and literature, on the one hand, and scholars in African, Asian, and Oceanic studies, on the other, proved to be limiting. Until recently, only few Germanist scholars had knowledge of African, Asian, and Oceanic languages. That is, their scholarship did not consider sources in non-European languages. The lack of interdisciplinary work resulted in reductive views of the German colonial period. Scholars based in Africa and Asia or with origins in Africa and Asia, however, made important interventions in the field of literary and cultural studies, and brought comparative knowledge to the table (e.g., Adrian Hsia, Anil Bhatti, David Simo, Zhuang Ying Chen, Shaswati Mazumdar, Patrice Nganang, Adjaï Paulin Oloukpona-Yinnon).[23] But the recent work by Africanists, Asianists, and Oceanists on indigenous agency, for example, is only beginning to have an impact on scholars researching German colonialism in Germany-centered disciplines and fields.

4. For various reasons, only few Africanists, Asianists, and Oceanists focused on German colonialism. The period of formal German colonialism was rather brief; in fact, from today's perspective it might seem like a footnote in history. Germany lost all of its colonies as a result of the Versailles Treaty, and the territories were divided up between France, Britain, Belgium, South Africa, Japan, Australia, and New Zealand. As a result, no colonized country used the German language in any significant way at the time of independence, and postcolonial intellectuals, for the most part, did not publish in German nor did they engage with the German colonial period in ways comparable to the work of their counterparts in, for example, British studies. The impact of British, French, Spanish, and Portuguese colonialism ran much deeper, thus scholars across different disciplines tended to engage with those legacies first. German studies, in large part because of this lack of postcolonial voices, did not come to appreciate the longer history of African, Asian, and Oceanic self-representation.

5. Many Asian, African, and Oceanic intellectuals were inspired by German thinkers, such as Karl Marx, Immanuel Kant, Johann Gottfried Herder, and Georg Wilhelm Friedrich Hegel, yet this connection has remained mostly unexplored, pointing to another largely ignored aspect of intercultural intellectual history.[24] As Valentin Mudimbe shows, the second current of African thought (the first being *négritude*) is Marxism, an aspect that ties German cul-

tural history to the history of African thought.[25] Asian, African, and Oceanic thinkers and theorists both embraced and rejected Marxism, or aspects of Marxism. On the one hand, they formulated a wide range of challenges to Hegel's and Marx's designation of the colonial world as a place at the margins of the world, and as an area waiting for beneficial domination.[26] On the other hand, they developed an array of theoretical alternatives to capitalism. In addition, there is an immense domain of critical appropriations of Marx and Hegel that runs from the beginnings of Asian, African, and Oceanic self-representation to Mao Zedong's sinification of Marxism, Samir Amin's dependence theory, Nkrumah's consciencism, the historiography of C. L. R. James, Third Worldism, Oceanic independence movements, and Fanon's theory of national culture.[27] Similar observations could be made with regard to the reception of Kant, Herder, and other Romanticist thinkers. This rich chapter of intercultural intellectual history (including the stories of the significant number of highly visible African, Asian, African-American, and other intellectuals who studied in Germany) largely remains to be explored, but recent work, especially in the area of German-Indian and Asian-German studies, is charting new ground.[28]

6. The prevalence of the Hegelian and Marxian master narratives as well as of modernization theory or developmentalist thinking is visible in Asian studies, although colonialism in Asia was a very diverse phenomenon. For a long time, Western historians saw East Asia's fall to foreign colonial dominance in the nineteenth century as rooted in a so-called stubborn refusal to abandon the traditional world order and join in free trade and diplomatic exchange. East Asia's resistance to Western demands for trade and diplomatic representation was conveniently dismissed as a traditionalist response to modernity and progress. In the 1980s and 1990s, scholars, such as Paul Cohen, Jim Hevia, Lydia Liu, and others, started to question this view.[29] They argued that conceptually such conventional explanations were essentialist and culturalist, and that instead of illuminating the history of the Asian-Western colonial encounters, these conventional explanations actually concealed it: they interpreted the political strategies implemented by the courts and the official establishment in East Asia as nothing more than traditional reflexes against social change when they could have been understood as contemporary political disputes with the novel phenomenon of global colonial expansion. The conventional view therefore downplayed or ignored contemporary contests outside the predetermined conceptual models of tradition and modernity, backwardness and progress, particular and universal, and so forth. However, and as evidenced in this anthology, responses to German colonialism were never simple answers to a European challenge but creative transfers of knowledge and flex-

ible attempts of resistance (e.g., colonial bases or harbor colonies in China and beyond; the paradigm of semi-colonialism proposed by Chinese historians already in the 1920s).[30]

7. Until recently, and for various reasons, the history of collaborators and intermediaries has been expelled from scholarship. From the perspective of Germanist scholars, indigenous collaboration and interaction was a tricky subject, as studies foregrounding such interactions might be interpreted as exculpatory. From the perspective of Africanist, Asianist, and Oceanist scholars, the topic was threatening for similar reasons.[31] The complexity of the memory of the German colonial past when it is mobilized in former German colonies as an instrument of resistance against subsequent French or British colonialism is equally expelled from German studies. Yet such memories remain very influential, as shown by a practice of the Cameroonian nationalist political party, Union des Populations Camerounaises (UPC), which used to play a prominent role in the struggle for independence and that insists on writing the word *Cameroon* in German, *Kamerun*, and on calling Cameroonians *Kamerunais*.[32]

As a result of these seven factors—the limiting focus on particular aspects of German colonialism; the preponderance of the idealist and culturalist paradigm; the limited archive that ignored African, Asian, and Oceanic sources; the lack of postcolonial voices in German studies and concomitant ignorance of African, Asian, and Oceanic self-representation; the unexplored intercultural intellectual history; the dominance of Eurocentric models of scholarship; and the unwillingness of scholars to explore forms of colonial collaboration and interaction—scholarship on German colonialism lacked, and continues to lack, analyses that pay attention to a wider range of social, economic, and political practices and materiality; the intellectual history of formerly colonized areas; the agency of colonized individuals and societies; and the configurations of colonial and postcolonial transnational and intercultural entanglements.

Our anthology addresses these dimensions and, in so doing, responds to calls from scholars for a more complex line of inquiry—a line of inquiry suggested, for instance, by Jürgen Zimmerer when he argues that "analysing and explaining the dreams of the colonizers is not sufficient for understanding colonialism. It tells us nothing, for example, about the colonized, let alone telling the story from their perspective."[33] By centering on practices of interaction, our anthology contributes to a growing corpus of scholarship in German colonial studies; this scholarship, often inspired by approaches derived from subaltern studies, sheds new light on local power dynamics, agency, and economic, cultural, and social networks that preceded and, as some now argue, ultimately structured German colonial rule. With regard to East Africa, for example, recent studies of this kind (including the work of scholars featured in this anthology) have revised our understanding of the structures of precolonial East African society, slavery in the area, and the agency of various social groups in East Africa. Jan-Georg Deutsch, for example, shows that "the end of slavery, at least in German East Africa, depended only to a minor extent on government policy and the activities of 'enlightened' colonial officials, and to a far greater extent on the persistent attempts of slaves to gain more meaningful control over their lives and day-to-day affairs."[34] This agency has been acknowledged also for the larger working population. Thaddeus Sunseri, in *Vilimani: Labor Migration and Rural Change in Early Colonial Tanzania*, explains that German colonials in late nineteenth-century East Africa faced a substantial labor shortage. As a result, "there were never enough workers for colonial undertakings during this period, and many Africans were able to shape their work environment in response."[35]Building on earlier studies, recent research has significantly refined our view of the East African economy. With regard to porterage, for example, Stephen Rockel explains that nineteenth-century porterage was to a large degree the work of free laborers. This system of a "free wage labor force in East Africa . . . emerged prior to the development of the colonial capitalist economy" and involved large groups of people.[36] According to historian Carol Sissons, "up to 90,000 Nyamwezi males could have worked as porters and traveled to the coast at any time during the second half of the nineteenth century, and perhaps 30,000 actually did so."[37] One question historians have grappled with is how the German colonial state was able to function in East Africa, given the low number of colonizing agents: In 1905, for instance, only 180 German settler farmers lived in East Africa.[38] By 1913, the total "number of Europeans had reached no more than 5,336 . . . as against the indigenous population of some four million,"[39] and 76.9 percent, about 4,100, of these Europeans were Germans.[40] Most surprising perhaps is that the "white strength of the Schutztruppe was 186" in 1913.[41] Here, Michael Pesek's work on the interaction between colonizers and colonized, in particular on the agency of local intermediaries, improved our comprehension of the multilayered interactions that occurred within the space of the colonial state.[42]

These kinds of studies, by bringing new sources to the discussion but also rereading the German colonial archive against the grain, have challenged the image of the enslaved, helpless, and voiceless African by outlining the possible options available to men and women in colonial German East Africa.[43] These studies also confirm an aspect already pointed out by John Iliffe in the late 1960s. He insisted back then that "the very real changes in German behaviour in East Africa after 1906 were not primarily stimulated by new policies devised in Berlin, nor even by regret at earlier immorality, but by the fears engendered by the Maji Maji rebellion of 1905–07 in the south and east of the colony. . . . this rebellion . . . was the African initiative to which the 'Dernburg reforms' were the European response."[44]

The German colonial presence in East Asia, to provide another example, has received little attention by Western historians, because this presence was not only short-lived but also relatively small in size. The few studies that were undertaken mainly focused on the strategies, plans, and motivations behind German foreign policy in the East and stressed the connections between the expansion in East Asia and the buildup of a German naval power. The focus was on the policies designed in the metropolitan center. Only recently has a younger generation of historians started to look at the colonies themselves, and show interest in the complex encounters between German, other European, and indigenous populations.[45] These historians have emphasized the agency of local actors and their role in shaping colonial societies, and have concluded that in East Asia, colonial bases (not colonial territories) were the most typical form of colonial rule. Harbor colonies and colonial bases were small, bordered territories, geographically suited for maritime ship traffic. Ideally, they were also close to resources in the hinterland as well as to important domestic and international trade routes, and also had a small local population that could serve as a workforce. Following the work of earlier Chinese historians, some scholars have argued that the existence of these particular colonial forms are indicative of a special manifestation of colonial rule they called semi-colonialism.[46] Semi-colonialism, for these scholars, described a transitional state in which various forms of hegemony (political, economical, cultural) by a foreign power coexisted with remnants of formal political sovereignty of the dominated country—a situation that was different from that in some African colonies (e.g., German Southwest Africa). The combination of multiple but fragmentary control that characterized China's experience of colonialism created unique "contact zones," sites of asymmetrical relations shaped by the exercise of colonial power on Chinese soil and hosting widely divergent local arrangements.[47]

Our anthology builds on these and other studies and adds new material and dimensions to the discussion in a comparatist and interdisciplinary framework. The recent transnational turn provides much inspiration in this regard, particularly with regard to theoretical and methodological approaches.

Theoretical Framework and Questions of Methodology

By emphasizing social interaction, the essays brought together in this anthology do not make grandiose claims about anti-colonial resistance and subversion; the practices studied here, which mostly originated from conditions and structures that predated colonialism, were often simple reactions and strategies of everyday life that were frequently inconsistent and also changed over time. In this regard, this anthology is informed by central tenets of practice theory, which emerged alongside and in response to three other forms of cultural theory—identified by Andreas Reckwitz as "culturalist mentalism, textualism, and intersubjectivism"—and has produced a rich scholarship in various disciplines, emphasizing the importance of agency, subjectivity, affect, the body, performance, historical change, and experience.[48] Practice theory does not locate the social in the mind (cultural mentalism), discourses (textualism), or interactions (intersubjectivism), but rather in a wide range of practices. According to Reckwitz, "[a] 'practice' (Praktik) is a routinized type of behavior which consists of several elements, interconnected to one another: forms of bodily activities, forms of mental activities, 'things' and their use, a background knowledge in the form of understanding, know-how, states of emotion and motivational knowledge."[49]

The support for practice theory comes from different disciplines. Scholars—the anthropologist Sherry Ortner, the historian William Sewell, and the sociologist Reckwitz, among others—convincingly show that considering practices significantly enhances our understanding of how human beings operate, create meaning, and, through their actions, affect semiotic orders. Sherry Ortner's notion of the "loosely structured actor," for example, illuminates spaces for agency and subjectivity outside of the restrictive conventions of discourse and *habitus*.[50] William Sewell has taken on the question of practice from a different angle and argues that notions of "culture as a system of symbols and meanings" and notions of "culture as practice" are not incompatible.[51] Sewell states that "[t]o engage in cultural practice means to utilize existing cultural symbols to accomplish some end. . . . It [culture] is . . . the semiotic dimension of human social practice in general."[52] Practice theory retains the relevance of the semiotic approach to culture, but foregrounds ideas of thinkers such as Ludwig Wittgenstein, who emphasized the importance of "language use" for establishing meaning. As Reckwitz stresses, "[p]ractice theory 'decentres' mind, texts and conversation. Simultaneously, it shifts bodily movements, things, practical knowledge and routine to the centre of its vocabulary."[53] In analyzing interactions and exchanges in the colonial realm, therefore, the cultural space of symbols is as important as social structures and material conditions. But in the case of colonialism we confront cross-cultural interactions that transcend the boundaries of the sociocultural universe of a given society—a case that social and cultural theory has often overlooked.[54] Colonial interaction takes place in special social and cultural spaces that could be called colonial contact zones. These zones might be actual geographical places, such as colonial cities or treaty ports, or these zones might delineate cultural spaces, such as newspapers, other media, or school curricula in a colonial setting.

Our anthology positions itself not in direct opposition to, but rather as a departure from, concepts that were dominant in the early phase of postcolonial studies. Recent research, especially works informed by subaltern studies approaches, has significantly enhanced our understanding of the economic, social, and political interactions in colonial territories, and has offered new tools to reevaluate cultural expressions that, in light of this new evidence, can no longer be grasped by concepts that have been used in this early phase of postcolonial criticism. Instead of "Manichean allegories" of division, we find interaction that crosses ethnic and racial lines; instead of hybridity, we can identify coexisting cultural forms; instead of mimicry, we see change and the emergence of new sociocultural structures; instead of the silence of the subaltern, we hear a multitude of voices. In this regard, the field of transnational studies has expanded the scope of investigation not only beyond national, but also beyond postcolonial lines of inquiry.[55]

In German studies, the transnational approach was pushed to the forefront of the discussion in the aftermath of the publication of *Das Kaiserreich transnational: Deutschland in der Welt 1871–1914*, a groundbreaking anthology edited by Sebastian Conrad and Jürgen Osterhammel.[56] The much-debated publication opened the field to studies that explore the German presence in the world and German participation in a wide range of economic, social, and political transnational processes by drawing on new sources, reading previously studied material in new ways, conducting multilingual research, and making use of interdisciplinary and comparative methods of investigation. One study that deserves mention here is Andrew Zimmerman's pioneering work, *Alabama in Africa: Booker T. Washington, the German Empire, and the Globalization of the New South*, in which he brilliantly sketches a transnational history involving the German empire, colonized Togo, and the South of the United States.[57] In Zimmerman's account capitalism and modernization emerge as the driving forces that, among other aspects, allowed for cooperation between Germans and African Americans, and also between colonial men and colonized women. In this telling of history, both biological and non-biological racism play a much more complex role than often assumed.[58]

Another work to be mentioned in this context is Kris Manjapra's *Age of Entanglement: German and Indian Intellectuals across Empire*, which brings a host of material about German-Indian intellectual and political history to the discussion.[59] This rich and erudite study contributes in thoughtful ways to the "provincializing of Europe" and is sure to inspire other investigations into transnational histories of entanglement.[60] Recent studies by scholars of literature, language, and thought also stand out as successful inquiries into transnational interactions, including works by Sara Pugach, Natalie Eppelsheimer, Lacina Yéo, and Sai Bhatawadekar.[61] Comparative approaches and innovative research initiatives, such as the Black German Heritage and Research Association, have also enriched the discussion by highlighting transnational interactions and historical continuities and shifts.[62]

The idea of the "transnational," however, is no panacea for the challenge of conceptualizing complex global interactions and histories of entanglement. From a German studies perspective, German interactions with East Africans, for example, may be termed as "transnational," but these same interactions, from an East African perspective, are "non-national," and better described as intercultural and transregional. A note on the idea of the "intercultural" is warranted here: roughly around the same time that postcolonial studies gained currency in the United States and elsewhere, German scholars became interested in the notion of the "intercultural." Alois Wierlacher's numerous publications and activities were foundational for the field of "interkulturelle Germanistik," which is now established across Germany.[63] The field is deeply related to another field, namely, "Interkulturelle Hermeneutik," which is rooted in philosophy, anthropology, and various cultural and social science fields, and foregrounds questions of intercultural *understanding* (see publications by, among others, Bernhard Waldenfels, Wolfdietrich Schmied-Kowarzik, and Munasu Duala-M'bedy).[64] Another important model of intercultural German studies, spearheaded by Leo Kreutzer, emerged at the Leibniz University of Hanover, the École de Hanovre. Here, German studies scholars of sub-Saharan African origin work toward conceptualizing approaches toward an "afrikanische Germanistik."[65] The association "Germanistik in Afrika Subsahara" is another testimony to the growing relevance of intercultural collaborations.[66] Generally, German-language scholarship of the past three decades is informed by debates in these fields (including several essays included in this collection), while philosophical approaches to the study of cultural difference have played only a minor role in postcolonial and transnational studies more broadly.

Recent studies that draw on transnational, postcolonial, and intercultural approaches share methodological concerns that are also brought to the fore by practice theory. These various approaches enable us to understand the actions and interactions of German, African, Asian, and Oceanic people as grounded in materiality and a complex web of factors. They allow us to grapple with the unique colonial world of cities, transit points, and other contact zones where Europeans and local populations both assumed some form or aspect of foreignness and externality. In these colonial terrains, power, accommodation and resistance were construed, misconstrued, adapted, and enacted by actors with very different strategic interests, different perceptions of reality, and different cultures and discourses. What does that mean in terms of methodology? The contributions included here share one or more noteworthy features:

- They are comparative, transnational, and intercultural in scope.
- They draw our attention to texts, intertexts, and other material not studied thus far.
- They expand the archive of German colonial studies by drawing on self-representations by and material evidence about African, Asian, and Oceanic individuals (see contributions by Göttsche, Hennlich, Lü, Mani, Nganang, Osayimwese, Richter, Steen, Zhu).
- They read the archive of German-authored historical sources against the grain (Bischoff, Klein, McCullers, Moyd, Nyada, Osayimwese, Pesek, Sabea, Steen, Walther).
- They include sources and information based on knowledge of non-European languages (Berman, Bischoff, Klein, Lü, Mani, Moyd, Mühlhahn, Nganang, Nyada, Pesek, Steen, Zhu).

The essays in the first part, "Interactions," study various forms of encounters between German colonizers or colonial authorities and colonized groups or individuals. By focusing on interactions, the essays in this part re-conceptualize the relationships within the colonial space as reciprocal processes of exchange and as bidirectional transfers of ideas, symbols, technologies, and goods. Some of the assets transferred and traded belonged to the cultural domain, such as philosophical or political concepts, pieces of knowledge, artistic products, or linguistic forms. But transfers and trades also extended into the realm of peoples and objects: the colonial space was a contact zone where people of various backgrounds and origins met and where various commodities and ideas were traded. Cross-cultural transfers, however, were never a simple, mechanical trade-up, but a complex interactional exchange that modified, adapted, blended, and/or produced that which was transferred.

Itohan I. Osayimwese's essay on the transformations in Bamum visual and material culture in Western Cameroon during the colonial period is a case in point. She demonstrates that architecture was part of a complex set of exchanges and practices that served as a site of negotiation between Bamum autoethnography or self-representation and the representation of the Bamum by dominant colonial discourses. Local actors and elites encouraged the recognition of Bamum cultural forms in colonial discourse and therefore exerted some control over Bamum representation in metropolitan discourses by staging and presenting local culture in distinct ways. Colonial and metropolitan discourses came to be inscribed in local self-representation and thus blended into Bamum culture. As Osayimwese shows, complex processes of cultural exchanges and transfers make it difficult to clearly draw boundaries between indigenous and colonial realms. Germain Nyada focuses on an area most often neglected in studies of colonialism, namely, the investigation of intercultural contact in the sphere of language. His essay investigates the linguistic reaction of Beti people in Cameroon to German colonialism and scrutinizes the multiple linguistic interactions between Beti communities of the Cameroonian area then known as the hinterland and settlers of the center of Cameroon. The study assesses works published by German colonists in Cameroon and oral testimony that records linguistic interactions between the Beti and German settlers. Nyada argues that as a result of German colonial penetration, an autonomous linguistic idiom developed in this part of central Africa (one that is nowadays becoming extinct).

A number of essays in this first part look into the nature, complexities, and contradictions of colonial encounters. Daniel J. Walther's article deals with an aspect that rarely surfaced in the reports of colonial authorities, yet was an intrinsic part of the colonial world. Despite existing racial prejudices, many of the male colonizers desired sexual encounters with local women who worked as prostitutes or served the colonizers. Such encounters brought with them the risk of venereal infection, which ostensibly threatened the colonial order. In combating this perceived threat, colonial physicians attempted to regulate indigenous populations. Walther demonstrates the limits of colonial interventions, since the overall efficacy of this particular aspect of German public health policies fundamentally depended on the cooperation of local populations. For example, some prostitutes chose not to register with local health officials, or chose to migrate from one location to another, while others made conscious choices to submit to health examinations out of their own self-interest.

If prostitution was one established role or channel to support oneself and maintain a certain degree of independence and autonomy, another form was the offering of military services in the colonial markets of violence. Michael Pesek and Michelle Moyd both deal with the important role of mercenaries and soldiers who came from the indigenous populations and, in exchange for money, power, and influence, were willing to provide military services to the colonizers. Pesek's essay explores the history of young men who served as mercenaries to traders and chiefs in East Africa, and who were commonly known as *ruga-ruga*. Their role was ambivalent: In the 1890s German colonial forces encountered the *ruga-ruga* both as their fiercest enemies and as willing allies provided by chiefs in campaigns against their rivals. From the late 1890s until the outbreak of World War I, African fighters were trained by German officers to act as a reserve force. Moreover, they acted as personal guards, police forces, and tax collectors at the courts of local chiefs. Pesek also shows that whereas Germans tried to use *ruga-ruga* for the strengthening of their military and administrative presence, for Africans the opportunity of being a *ruga-ruga* provided a way to embed local knowledge, traditions, and perspectives into a new profession that emerged out of the German colonial project.

A similar ambivalent role of the African soldiers (called *askari*) serving in the German colonial army (*Schutztruppe*) in East Africa comes to light in Michelle Moyd's essay. The German colonial authorities relied on the *askari* for everyday policing and administration of the colony. Consequently, the *askari* became the most visible, and often the most feared, agents of colonial rule. Yet their mobility, relative wealth, and authority over other East Africans gave them a powerful position that they used to further both their interests and those of the colonial state. Moyd understands the *askari* as colonial intermediaries and power brokers who helped shape relationships between the colonial state and East African peoples living around the stations. The *askari* exercised state authority in the interest of accomplishing colonial goals, as well as in the interest of improving their standing as "big men" within East African political, social, and economic contexts.

But not only soldiers could rise to positions of influence. Even the most exploited segment of the local population, the African workers, were able to negotiate their conditions and to challenge colonial owners and entrepreneurs. In her essay, Hanan Sabea describes African workers on sisal plantations as key agents, shaping everyday life on plantations in German East Africa. The everyday practices and negotiations of land and labor relationships also highlight continuities and changes between precolonial and colonial contexts, they crystallize the limitations of colonial desires and rationalities. Sabea's discussion shows that the making of colonial life in German East Africa did not follow the scripts colonial agents imagined and desired.

Gabriele Richter takes us to the German colonies in the Pacific. Her essay, too, deals with the far-reaching role of local brokers, as she focuses on the indigenous reply to the German missionary presence in Kaiser-Wilhelmsland, also known as German New Guinea. Here an alliance was formed by a convert by the name of Zake, a member of the local Kâte people, with the German Lutheran missionary Christian Keyßer. As Richter shows, this alliance served both men, and it increased their influence within their own groups to a considerable degree, thus highlighting the implications of the different strategies employed by the various actors who were engaged in this colonial encounter.

The essays in this first part, then, all emphasize the significant role of intermediaries, power brokers, and middle-men and middle-women in the colonies. In many instances it could be argued that the colonial authorities actually came to rely on local actors for maintaining their colonial presence. Without their support, the colonial rule appears to have been rather limited and weak. Transfers, brokering, and mediating also constantly bifurcated the boundaries that separated the different cultural, political, and social spaces so that both the colonial and the indigenous became mutually inscribed onto each other. While official colonial ideology fundamentally stressed the need to distinguish clearly between races, practices, and ways of living, the reality was more complex, and the colonizers found it difficult to police the demarcation between the different worlds.

The second part, "Resistance, Anti-colonial Activism, and the Rise of Nationalist Discourses," focuses on anti-colonial activities and the formation of nationalist agendas in the colonies and also in expatriate communities. Anti-colonialism and anti-imperialism (understood as a demand for equality and self-determination) were informed by an ongoing transfer of ideas, practices, and forms of protest across fixed boundaries and political forms. For instance, expatriate communities in Europe and the United States were often crucial in organizing agitation against colonial rule and in galvanizing support for the anti-colonial agenda in the colonies. Because self-determination as an ideal loomed large in the controversies surrounding colonialism, nationalism was, from the beginning, an intrinsic element in the demands and arguments of the anti-colonial movement. The goal of anti-colonial agitation from Africa to Asia was to formally put an end to colonial rule, to achieve equality, and to establish nation-states that were controlled by the indigenous people.

Andreas Steen's essay highlights the important role of trans-regional and global connections in the history of German colonialism and the agitation against it. Steen examines the multiple links between the metropolitan center, Berlin, and several colonial spaces dispersed over a large region in East Asia and the Pacific, including China, New Guinea, and Western Samoa. Strong demand and competition for cheap labor in the Pacific colonies prompted the colonial administrations to recruit Chinese workers. Yet the Germans' fear of a negative image internationally combined with their economic dependency on Chinese labor meant that Chinese workers were in an unusually powerful position. Backed by Chinese authorities and their new nationalist policies, the workers fought for better treatment and higher pay. Though only reluctantly, German diplomats and planters met the workers' demands. By 1913—mostly for economic reasons—German authorities granted equal status and other privileges to the Chinese in Samoa, paving the way for similar claims by the local population.

Christian missions were an essential part of the colonial presence. As Thoralf Klein argues, the history of nineteenth- and early twentieth-century missions—like that of colonialism in general—reflects a pattern whereby missionary power was first established and then, later, dismantled. But resistance was not necessarily anti-Christian; often, in fact, it was spurred by local Christians in the name of equality and self-governance. Klein places two cases in a broader perspective: One is the suppression of competing claims of indigenous church leaders by German missionaries; the other is the growth of an indigenous movement for a self-governing church. In telling the story of both, Klein demonstrates the possibilities and the limitations of indigenous Christian agency as well as of missionary authority. At the same time, his essay can be read as a demonstration of the global reach and power of the anti-colonial rhetoric: The sentiments that surface in the case of Chinese resistance to a Swiss society in rural Guangdong closely resemble the critiques of colonial privileges in Samoa, New Guinea, and elsewhere.

The link between anti-colonialism and nationalism is demonstrated in Jianjun Zhu's essay on Kiautschou, a German colony in China. Zhu focuses on a change in German colonial policy that occurred after 1905. From the start, the German occupation of Kiautschou was met with fierce Chinese resistance. Boycotts and protests, as well as violent upheavals in the surrounding areas, all document the resentments against foreign occupation in the first years of German rule. After 1905, relations with the Chinese population improved as the colonial authorities became more willing to accommodate the Chinese population and allow their representatives a say in colonial affairs. After the completion of major infrastructure construction (railway, mines, and a harbor) in the colony and its hinterlands around 1907, an economic upswing began to transform the colony into a busy marketplace, connecting the hinterland to national and international markets reaching from East Asia to Europe. This development was to a considerable degree contingent on the cooperation of Chinese elites and businesses. Segregation and discrimination were practiced in the legal, administrative, and spatial order of the colony, but at the same time contacts, cooperation, and exchanges were beginning to undermine the barriers erected by the colonial state.

B. Venkat Mani turns to another facet of transnational history in his exploration of a dimension of cosmopolitanism. He argues for a mode of conceptualizing cosmopolitanism that adequately accounts for specific moments in European colonial histories when decolonization and/or a modern nation-state was not a readily available future option for colonial subjects. In order to illustrate this point, Mani draws on the example of the Indian (anti-colonial) nationalist Lala Har Dayal (1884–1939) and his critique of Imperial Germany's expansionist ambitions in the early twentieth century. Through a discussion of Har Dayal as a historical protagonist and an analysis of his contestable contentions, this essay sheds new light on the complexities of German colonial and imperial policies and the cosmopolitan critiques of these policies.

The second part concludes with two case studies from Africa that offer insights about social practices of resistance. The first focuses on an event in German East Africa where, in late 1908 and early 1909, twenty-six Africans were sentenced to death by the colonial administration for allegedly practicing cannibalism. Using an analysis of records from the German colonial office as well as reports and letters written by members of the *Berliner Missionsgesellschaft*, Eva Bischoff reconstructs the intersecting strategies and conflicting interests pursued by both African and German actors involved in the court proceedings and the ensuing investigation. In her essay, Bischoff considers recent debates on the role of African dignitaries and clerks as mediators, collaborators, and facilitators of German colonial rule, and argues that denouncing members of their community to the German officials as cannibals was not an act of collaboration on the part of the people of Iringa. Rather, it was an effort to maintain traditional political hierarchies and uphold cultural practices that had been questioned or outlawed by the German colonial government, and is interpreted, then, as an act of cultural and social resistance.

The second case study, by Molly McCullers, examines the impact of German colonialism in South West Africa between 1884 and 1915—particularly the genocide of 1904—on Herero men's notion of masculinity. Differing generational experiences of German colonialism influenced Herero definitions of masculinity, which profoundly shaped Herero societal reinvigoration after the genocide. Following the transition to South African rule in 1915, Herero men took advantage of new opportunities to re-invent their understanding and presentation of masculinity. Herero youths, through their experiences in the German military, formed an organization known as the *Otruppa*, which used German military aesthetics to oppose elders' traditional power and authority. Herero elders in contrast cooperated with the South African regime and used state power to reclaim their authority and power over the youth. By exploring the contentious politics between the Otruppa and the elders, McCullers reveals how the protracted struggle to remake Herero masculinity deeply influenced the reconstruction of Herero society in the wake of German colonial violence. The essays in this part suggest that colonies were terrains where projects of power and concepts of superiority were not only imposed but also engaged, contested, and reshaped by the colonized. Colonialism was also contested in the colonial home country by anti-colonial parties and movements. In fact, this examination of political activism within, about, and against colonial rule has led to reinterpretations and modifications of the meanings of some of the basic colonial concepts, such as race, difference, hierarchy, and nation, both as they were understood in the colonies and in the European metropolitan areas. Circuits of ideas and the rhetoric that upheld or subverted colonialism connected metropolitan society to colonial dominions.

The essays in the third part, "Remembering and Rethinking," consider contemporary responses to and comments on German colonialism, particularly as expressed in the mediums of literature, autobiography, film, and photography. As a group, the articles and the material they study revisit and give voice to the colonial experience from the perspective of Asians and Africans. German colonialism, albeit short in its existence, has had a long-lasting effect on artistic productions both in Germany and in the former German colonies. Whether it lingers because it is a residual of a time past, a remembrance that survives inside structures of other colonialisms, or a traumatic experience that refuses to die, contemporary film, literature and art testify to the complexity of dealing with the legacy of German colonialism. In this part, scholars look at the ways in which written and visual arts engage with German colonialism, and they do so through the lens of African migrant writing, installation, the historical novel, and colonial cinema.

A case in point is Dirk Göttsche's essay on literature of African migrants. It explores the memory of colonialism and its shifting contexts in African migrants' writing in the German language, which emerged in the 1980s as one of the most prominent forms of German postcolonial literature. Following an overview of developments in the (post-) memory of colonialism in such African diasporic writing, Göttsche shares two case studies that focus on the legacies of German colonialism. One is the autobiographical story *Der Blues in mir* (1986) by the Togolese artist El Loko, and the other is the novel *Die Weissagung der Ahnen* (1997) by the Cameroonian diplomat and writer Daniel Mepin. Mepin's novel epitomizes the increasing cross-mapping of colonial memory with other memory discourses, in this case memory of the German Democratic Republic and its demise. In both texts, critical memory of colonialism is inextricably linked to the construction of postcolonial identities and illustrates both Germany's implication in colonial history and the historical dynamic of postcolonial memory in Africa.

Andrew J. Hennlich's essay focuses on the artistic production of William Kentridge, *Black Box/Chambre Noire*, that narrates a melancholic relationship between the Enlightenment and colonialism. Using three references to the black box—the camera's interior, flight data recorders, and contemporary theater spaces—Kentridge constructs a tableau using animation, filmic, and photographic footage, along with robotic puppets to present a number of historical fragments of the Herero genocide in South West Africa (present-day Namibia). By engaging with Kentridge's staging of Mozart's *Magic Flute*, references to Freud's *Trauerarbeit*, and the three black boxes, Hennlich argues that Kentridge's project suggests that history, like melancholia, must be worked through continually. In this approach and proposed constellation, the history of South West Africa links to a number of historical referents, including Nazi Germany, apartheid South Africa and its xenophobic legacies, colonialism, and Cold War violence in Africa. In this regard, as Hennlich argues, Kentridge constructs an important historiographical tool with his multimedia installation.

Yixu Lü's study of a novel by the prominent Chinese author and Nobel Prize laureate Mo Yan connects the form of the historical novel to the very historical events it narrates. In 2001, Mo Yan published *The Sandalwood Torture (Tanxiang xing)*, set in and around his hometown Gaomi in Shandong Province. Drawing on the historical background of the Boxer Uprising of 1900, it promises a Chinese response to German colonialism's negative impact on a place and people with whom the author openly and strongly identifies. Its apparent affinities to the "nativist" school in contemporary Chinese fiction lead to the question of how the colonial era in China is presented to a readership facing the more urgent issues of globalization. This essay also raises the question of whether or not the novel contains a subversive sub-text that is critical of the official Chinese discourse of "national humiliation" in the 1990s. It seeks to resolve this through a close analysis of the novel, in particular of the values its characters espouse or negate.

And finally, Patrice Nganang's essay is an attempt to fashion a theoretical framework that would connect contemporary German minority cinema to colonial cinema. Nganang defines "minority" as exception, and looks at how minorities intervene in the general archive of German cinema from 1919 to the present. He analyzes films about German minorities that were produced after Germany had effectively lost all its colonies. From colonial exoticas to films made about the colonies after the short period of German colonialism, the fabric of colonial films thus reveals structures that survived well into the contemporary era of filmmaking. From specific genres to actors, like Ludwig M'bebe Mpessa, and to the constitutive position of some iconic films, the archive of German film, when analyzed, can expose trends that shed new light on minorities in German cinema by insisting on the origins of German minority cinema in colonial cinema.

The essays of the last part illustrate the relevance of understanding literary, autobiographical, and other artistic expressions as practices that shed light on intercultural contact. Through the use of various media, individuals from Africa, Asia, and Oceania take the initiative to convey their view of the colonial past and to highlight the colonial residue in the present. They emphasize aspects that went previously unnoticed, and they debunk persisting myths. Literary, autobiographical, and other artistic expressions are an integral part of the archive of practices and materialities considered in this volume.

The essays collected in this anthology bring together analyses that study African, Asian, and Oceanic practices during and after the German colonial period in a comparatist and interdisciplinary framework. An anthology conceived as broadly as ours produces its own shortcomings; we hope these lacunae may inspire further inquiries that will contribute to our quest to understand the German colonial period and its repercussions.

NOTES

*The idea for this anthology emerged from a series of panels that Sara Lennox and Nina Berman co-organized for the annual meeting of the German Studies Association in 2008. We would like to thank Sara for her fundamental contribution to this project

1. Abdulrazak Gurnah, *Paradise* (New York: New Press, 1994), 241.

2. For a longer discussion of the novel, see Nina Berman, "Yusuf's Choice: East African Agency During the German Colonial Period in Abdulrazak Gurnah's Novel *Paradise*," *English Studies in Africa* 56, no.1 (2013): 51–64.

3. Sara Friedrichsmeyer, Sara Lennox, and Susanne Zantop, "Introduction," *The Imperialist Imagination: German Colonialism and Its Legacy*, ed. Sara Friedrichsmeyer, Sara Lennox, and Susanne Zantop (Ann Arbor: University of Michigan Press, 1998), 4.

4. By Helmuth Stoecker, see *Deutschland und China im 19. Jahrhundert: Das Eindringen des deutschen Kapitalismus* (Berlin: Rütten & Loening, 1958); *Kamerun unter deutscher Kolonialherrschaft: Studien*, 2 vols. (Berlin: Rütten & Loening, 1960–68); and the edited volume *Drang nach Afrika: Die koloniale Expansionspolitik und Herrschaft des deutschen Imperialismus in Afrika von den Anfängen bis zum Ende des zweiten Weltkrieges* (Berlin: Akademie-Verlag, 1977); for Kurt Büttner, see *Die An-*

fänge der deutschen Kolonialpolitik in Ostafrika: Eine kritische Untersuchung an Hand unveröffentlichter Quellen (Berlin: Akademie-Verlag, 1959); *Neokolonialistische Afrikatheorien im wissenschaftlichen Gewand* (Leipzig: Karl-Marx-Universität, 1969); and with Heinrich Loth, *Philosophie der Eroberer und koloniale Wirklichkeit: Ostafrika 1884–1918* (Berlin: Akademie-Verlag, 1981).

5. See, for example, Alexandre Kum'a Ndumbe III, *Hitler voulait l'Afrique: le projet du 3e Reich sur le continent africain* (Paris: Harmattan, 1980). Kum'a Ndumbe III also published fiction in German. For East Africa, see *Zamani: A Survey of East African History*, ed. B. A. Ogot and J. A. Kieran (Nairobi: East African Publishing House, 1968).

6. John Iliffe, *Tanganyika under German Rule, 1905–1912* (London; Nairobi: Cambridge University Press; East African Publishing House, 1969).

7. Among the unpublished dissertations are Henry Martin Bair, "Carl Peters and German Colonialism: A Study in the Ideas and Actions of Imperialism" (Stanford University, 1968); Arnold Valentin Wallenkampf, "The Herero Rebellion in South West Africa, 1904–1906: A Study in German Colonialization" (University of California, Los Angeles, 1969); Jack Richard Dukes, "Helgoland, Zanzibar, East Africa: Colonialism in German Politics, 1884–1890" (University of Illinois at Urbana-Champaign, 1970). See also the master's theses by, among others, Gary L. Osteraas, "Colonial Enthusiasm in Germany: A Study in the Cultural Background of German Colonialism, 1870–1914" (Columbia University, 1965); Howard Van Trease, "German Colonialism in the South Seas: The Acquisition of New Guinea" (San Diego State College, 1968). Among the published dissertations is John Ernest Schrecker, *Imperialism and Chinese Nationalism: Germany in Shantung* (Cambridge: Harvard University Press, 1971).

8. Wolfe W. Schmokel, *Dream of Empire: German Colonialism, 1919–1945* (New Haven: Yale University Press, 1964). The book was reprinted in 1980 (Westport, CT: Greenwood Press).

9. Mary E. Townsend's 1921 study, *Origins of Modern German Colonialism, 1871–1885*, was reprinted in 1974 (New York: Fertig). Woodruff D. Smith's 1972 dissertation was published as *The German Colonial Empire* (Chapel Hill: University of North Carolina Press, 1978).

10. Kofi Batsa, *West German Neo-Colonialism and Africa: Documentation of the Neo-Colonialist Policy of West Germany in Africa* (Accra: Spark Publications, 1964). See also, from East Germany, Paul Friedländer, *The Neocolonialism of the West German Federal Republic: A Documentation* (Berlin: Afro-Asiatisches Solidaritätskomitee in der DDR, 1965). Publications of this kind on colonialism and neocolonialism were issued in East Germany throughout the 1960s.

11. On this rich body of literature in general, see Albert Wirz, "Missionare im Urwald—verängstigt und hilflos: Zur symbolischen Topographie des kolonialen Christentums," *Kolonien und Missionen: Referate des 3. internationalen kolonialgeschichtlichen Symposiums 1993 in Bremen*, Bremer Asien-Pazifik Studien, vol. 12, ed. Wilfried Wagner (Münster: Lit, 1994), 39–56; Adam Jones, "Ethnographie als 'Nebenprodukt' der Arbeit der Leipziger Mission in Ostafrika," *Auf der Suche nach Vielfalt: Ethnographie und Geographie in Leipzig*, ed. Claus Deimel, Sebastian Lentz, and Bernhard Streck (Leipzig: Leibniz-Institut für Länderkunde, 2009), 95–102; Rainer Alsheimer, *Bilder erzählen Geschichte: Eine Fotoanthropologie der Norddeutschen Mission in We-*

stafrika (Bremen: Universität Bremen, 2010). Examples of missionary writings include Fritz Bornemann, *Der selige P.J. Freinademetz 1852–1908: Ein Steyler China-Missionar; Ein Lebensbild nach zeitgenössischen Quellen* (Rome: Collegium Verbi Divini, 1976); Hermann Fischer, *Augustin Henninghaus: 53 Jahre Missionar und Missionsbischof: Ein Lebensbild* (Kaldenkirchen: Steyler Missionsbuchhandlung, 1946); Christian G. A. Oldendorp, *Geschichte der caribischen Inseln Sanct Thomas, Sanct Crux und Sanct Jan*, kommentierte Edition des Originalmanuskriptes, *Abhandlungen und Berichte des Staatlichen Museums für Völkerkunde Dresden*, ed. Gudrun Meier (Berlin: Verlag für Wissenschaft und Bildung 2000/2002); Karl J. Rivinius, *Weltlicher Schutz und Mission: Das deutsche Protektorat über die katholische Mission in Süd-Shangtung* (Cologne: Böhlau, 1987); Max Schmidt, *Aus unserem Kriegsleben in Südwest-Afrika* (Berlin: E. Runge, 1907); Johannes C. Voskamp, *Aus dem belagerten Tsingtau* (Berlin: Berliner Evangelische Missiongesellschaft, 1915).

12. See, among other titles, Helmut Bley, *Kolonialherrschaft und Sozialstruktur in Deutsch-Südwestafrika 1894–1914* (Hamburg: Leibniz, 1968); Karin Hausen, *Deutsche Kolonialherrschaft in Afrika: Wirtschaftsinteressen und Kolonialverwaltung in Kamerun vor 1914* (Zurich: Atlantis, 1970); Horst Gründer, *Christliche Mission und deutscher Imperialismus: Eine politische Geschichte ihrer Beziehungen während der deutschen Kolonialzeit (1884–1914) unter besonderer Berücksichtigung Afrikas und Chinas* (Paderborn: Schöningh, 1982); *Geschichte der deutschen Kolonien* (Paderborn: Schöningh, 1985); Klaus J. Bade et al., *Imperialismus und Kolonialmission: Kaiserliches Deutschland und koloniales Imperium* (Wiesbaden: Steiner, 1982); Jürgen Osterhammel, *China und die Weltgesellschaft: Vom 18. Jahrhundert bis in unsere Zeit* (Munich: Beck, 1989); Francesca Schinzinger, *Die Kolonien und das Deutsche Reich: Die wirtschaftliche Bedeutung der deutschen Besitzungen in Übersee* (Wiesbaden: Franz Steiner 1984).

13. Joachim Warmbold, *"Ein Stückchen neudeutsche Erd'"—Deutsche Kolonial-Literatur: Aspekte ihrer Geschichte, Eigenart und Wirkung, dargestellt am Beispiel Afrikas* (Frankfurt am Main: Haag + Herchen, 1982); Sibylle Benninghoff-Lühl, *Deutsche Kolonialromane, 1884–1914, in ihrem Entstehungs- und Wirkungszusammenhang* (Bremen: Im Selbstverlag, Übersee-Museum Bremen, 1983); Wolfgang Bader and János Riesz, *Literatur und Kolonialismus* (Frankfurt am Main: Lang, 1983).

14. Ulrike Kistner, *Die kolonisierende Rede: Strukturen eines restringierenden Codes am Beispiel eines Romans von Martin Jaeckel* (PhD dissertation, University of Witwatersrand, 1986); Gunther Pakendorf, "Of Colonizers and Colonized: Hans Grimm on German South West Africa," *Social Dynamics* 12, no. 2 (1986): 39–47; Peter Horn, "Die Versuchung durch die barbarische Schönheit: Zu Hans Grimms 'farbigen' Frauen," *Germanisch-Romanische Monatsschrift* 35, no. 3 (1985): 317–41.

15. See, for example, Jan-Bart Gewald, *Herero Heroes: A Socio-Political History of the Herero of Namibia, 1890–1923* (Oxford: James Currey, 1999); Jürgen Zimmerer, *Deutsche Herrschaft über Afrikaner: Staatlicher Machtanspruch und Wirklichkeit im kolonialen Namibia* (Münster: Lit, 2001); Joachim Zeller and Jürgen Zimmerer, ed., *Völkermord in Deutsch-Südwestafrika: Der Kolonialkrieg (1904–1908) in Namibia und seine Folgen* (Berlin: Links, 2003).

16. Isabel V. Hull, *Absolute Destruction: Military Culture and the Practices of War in Imperial Germany* (Ithaca: Cornell University Press, 2005); Susanne Kuß offers a different perspective in her comparison of three German colonial wars, *Deutsches Mil-*

itär auf kolonialen Kriegsschauplätzen: Eskalation von Gewalt zu Beginn des 20. Jahrhunderts (Berlin: Links, 2010).

17. Aimé Césaire, *Discourse on Colonialism*, trans. Joan Pinkham (New York: Monthly Review, 2000), 36. *German Colonialism: Race, the Holocaust, and Postwar Germany*, ed. Volker Langbehn and Mohammad Salama (New York: Columbia University Press, 2011), focuses in large part on the "continuity thesis."

18. Pascal Grosse, *Kolonialismus, Eugenik und bürgerliche Gesellschaft in Deutschland 1850–1918* (Frankfurt am Main: Campus, 2000); Fatima El-Tayeb, *Schwarze Deutsche: Der Diskurs um "Rasse" und nationale Identität 1890–1933* (Frankfurt am Main: Campus, 2001); Tina Campt, *Other Germans: Black Germans and the Politics of Race, Gender, and Memory in the Third Reich* (Ann Arbor: University of Michigan Press, 2004).

19. Susanne Zantop, *Colonial Fantasies: Conquest, Family, and Nation in Precolonial Germany, 1770–1870* (Durham: Duke University Press, 1997). A range of theoretical trajectories guides the studies by, among others, Sander L. Gilman, *On Blackness Without Blacks: Essays on the Image of the Black in Germany* (Boston: Hall, 1982); John K. Noyes, *Colonial Space: Spatiality in the Discourse of German South West Africa 1884–1915* (Chur, Switzerland: Harwood, 1991); Russell A. Berman, *Enlightenment or Empire: Colonial Discourse in German Culture* (Lincoln: University of Nebraska Press, 1998); Peter Martin, *Schwarze Teufel, edle Mohren: Afrikaner in Geschichte und Bewusstsein der Deutschen* (Hamburg: Hamburger Edition, 2001).

20. *The Imperialist Imagination: German Colonialism and Its Legacy*, ed. Sara Friedrichsmeyer, Sara Lennox, and Susanne Zantop (Ann Arbor: University of Michigan Press, 1998); *German Colonialism: Another Sonderweg?*, ed. Marcia Klotz, special issue of *European Studies Journal* 16, no. 2 (Fall 1999); *Germany's Colonial Pasts*, ed. Eric Ames, Marcia Klotz, and Lora Wildenthal (Lincoln: University of Nebraska Press, 2005); *German Colonialism, Visual Culture, and Modern Memory*, ed. Volker Langbehn (New York: Routledge, 2010); Michael Perraudin and Jürgen Zimmerer, *German Colonialism and National Identity* (New York: Routledge, 2011); *Postkolonialismus und Kanon*, ed. Herbert Uerlings and Iulia-Karin Patrut (Bielefeld: Aisthesis, 2012); *Deutsch-afrikanische Diskurse in Geschichte und Gegenwart: Literatur- und kulturwissenschaftliche Perspektiven*, ed. Michael Hofmann and Rita Morrien (Amsterdam: Rodopi, 2012).

21. Martha Mamozai, *Herrenmenschen: Frauen im deutschen Kolonialismus* (Reinbek bei Hamburg: Rowohlt, 1982); Lora Wildenthal, *German Women for Empire, 1884–1945* (Durham: Duke University Press, 2001); *Frauen in den deutschen Kolonien*, ed. Marianne Bechhaus-Gerst, Mechthild Leutner, and Hauke Neddermann (Berlin: Links, 2009).

22. George Steinmetz, *The Devil's Handwriting: Precoloniality and the German Colonial State in Qingdao, Samoa, and Southwest Africa* (Chicago: University of Chicago Press, 2007).

23. Adrian Hsia, *Hermann Hesse und China: Darstellung, Materialien und Interpretation* (Frankfurt am Main: Suhrkamp, 1974); Anil Bhatti, "Utopie-Projektion-Gegenbild: Indien in Deutschland," *Zeitschrift für Kulturaustausch* 37, no. 3 (1987): 388–525; David Simo, *Interkulturalität und ästhetische Erfahrung: Untersuchungen zum Werk Hubert Fichte* (Stuttgart: Metzler, 1993); Zhuang Ying Chen, *Asiatisches Ge-*

dankengut im Werke Hermann Hesses (New York: Lang, 1997); Shaswati Mazumdar, *Feuchtwanger, Brecht: Der Umgang mit der indischen Kolonialgeschichte—Eine Studie zur Konstruktion des Anderen* (Würzburg: Königshausen & Neumann, 1998); Alain Patrice Nganang, *Interkulturalität und Bearbeitung: Untersuchung zu Soyinka und Brecht* (Munich: Judicium, 1998); Adjaï Paulin Oloukpona-Yinnon, *Unter deutschen Palmen: Die "Musterkolonie" Togo im Spiegel deutscher Kolonialliteratur (1884–1944)* (Frankfurt: IKO, Verlag für Interkulturelle Kommunikation, 1998).

24. Among the pioneering studies in this regard are Liang Zhixue and Shen Zhen, "Fichtes Philosophie in China," in *Der Grundansatz der ersten Wissenschaftslehre Johann Gottlieb Fichtes* (Tagung des Internationalen Kooperationsorgans der Fichte-Forschung in Neapel 1995), ed. Erich Fuchs and Ives Radrizzani (Neuried: Ars Una, 1996), 287–98; Joachim Kurtz, "Selbstbehauptung mit geliehener Stimme: J. G. Fichte als Redner an die chinesische Nation," in *Selbstbehauptungsdiskurse in Asien: China—Japan—Korea*, ed. Iwo Amelung et al. (Munich: Iudicium, 2003), 219–42; Susan Buck-Morss, "Hegel and Haiti," *Critical Inquiry* 26, no. 4 (2000): 821–65; Sai Prakash Bhatawadekar, "Symptoms of Withdrawal: The Threefold Structure of Hegel's and Schopenhauer's Interpretation of Hindu Religion and Philosophy" (PhD diss., Ohio State University, 2007).

25. Valentin Y. Mudimbe, "African Gnosis—Philosophy and the Order of Knowledge: An Introduction," *African Studies Review* 28, no. 2/3 (1985): 149–233; *The Invention of Africa: Gnosis, Philosophy, and the Order of Knowledge* (Bloomington: Indiana University Press, 1988). For an English translation of select writings on colonialism by Karl Marx and Friedrich Engels, see Karl Marx and Frederick Engels, *On Colonialism: Articles from the New York Tribune and Other Writings* (New York: International Publishers, 1972).

26. Wolfgang Bauer, Peng Chang, and Michael Lackner, *Das chinesische Deutschlandbild der Gegenwart: Eine Bibliographie, vol. 2: Karl Marx und Friedrich Engels im chinesischen Schrifttum, 1970–1984* (Stuttgart: F. Steiner Verlag Wiesbaden, 1989).

27. On Mao Zedong's sinification of Marxism see Nick Knight, *Rethinking Mao: Explorations in Mao Zedong's Thought* (Lanham, MD: Lexington Books, 2007). For a study of the Mau movement, see Michael J. Field, *Mau: Samoa's Struggle for Freedom* (Auckland: Polynesian Press, 1984). For a recent cultural analysis that is informed by Marxist approaches, see Akinwumi Adesokan, *Postcolonial Artists and Global Aesthetics* (Bloomington: Indiana University Press, 2011).

28. Douglas T. McGetchin, Peter K. J. Park, and Damodar R. SarDesai, eds., *Sanskrit and "Orientalism": Indology and Comparative Linguistics in Germany, 1750–1958* (New Delhi: Manohar, 2004); *Mapping Channels between Ganges and Rhein: German-Indian Cross-Cultural Relations*, ed. Jörg Esleben, Christina Kraenzle, and Sukanya Kulkarni (Newcastle upon Tyne, England: Cambridge Scholars Publishing, 2008); Mechthild Leutner and Klaus Mühlhahn, eds., *Deutsch-chinesische Beziehungen im 19. Jahrhundert: Mission und Wirtschaft in interkultureller Perspektive* (Münster: LIT, 2001).

29. Paul A. Cohen, *Discovering History in China: American Historical Writing on the Recent Chinese Past* (New York: Columbia University Press, 1984); James L. Hevia, *Cherishing Men from Afar: Qing Guest Ritual and the Macartney Embassy of 1793* (Durham: Duke University Press, 1995); Lydia H. Liu, *Translingual Practice: Litera-*

ture, National Culture, and Translated Modernity—China, 1900–1937 (Stanford: Stanford University Press, 1995); *The Clash of Empires: The Invention of China in Modern World Making* (Cambridge: Harvard University Press, 2004).

30. Bryna Goodman and David S. G. Goodman, "Introduction: Colonialism and China," in *Twentieth-Century Colonialism and China: Localities, the Everyday and the World*, ed. Bryna Goodman and David S. G. Goodman (London: Routledge, 2012), 1–22.

31. Monika Albrecht highlights the double standards of a postcolonial criticism that remains rooted in generalizing dichotomies. See "Doppelter Standard und postkoloniale Regelpoetik: Eine kritische Revision Postkolonialer Studien," *Postkolonialismus und Kanon*, ed. Uerlings and Patrut, 67–111.

32. See Thomas Deltombe, Manuel Domergue, and Jacob Tatsitsa, *Kamerun!: Une guerre cachée aux origines de la Françafrique, 1948–1971* (Paris: Découverte, 2011).

33. Lora Wildenthal, Jürgen Zimmerer, Russell A. Berman, Jan Rüger, Bradley Naranch, Birthe Kundrus, and Maiken Umbach, "Forum: The German Colonial Imagination," *German History* 26, no. 2 (2008): 253.

34. Jan-Georg Deutsch, *Emancipation without Abolition in German East Africa c. 1884–1914* (Oxford: James Currey, 2006), 3.

35. Thaddeus Sunseri, *Vilimani: Labor Migration and Rural Change in Early Colonial Tanzania* (Portsmouth, NH: Heinemann, 2002), xxi.

36. Stephen J. Rockel, *Carriers of Culture: Labor on the Road in Nineteenth-Century East Africa* (Portsmouth, NH: Heinemann, 2006), 5–6.

37. Quoted in Rockel, *Carriers of Culture*, 33.

38. Juhani Koponen, *Development for Exploitation: German Colonial Policies in Mainland Tanzania, 1884–1914* (Helsinki: Lit Verlag, 1995), 254.

39. Koponen, *Development for Exploitation*, 562.

40. Koponen, *Development for Exploitation*, 567.

41. Koponen, *Development for Exploitation*, 566–67.

42. Michael Pesek, *Koloniale Herrschaft in Deutsch-Ostafrika: Expeditionen, Militär und Verwaltung seit 1880* (Frankfurt: Campus, 2005). See also, among other studies, Andreas Eckert, *Herrschen und Verwalten: Afrikanische Bürokraten, staatliche Ordnung und Politik in Tanzania, 1920–1970* (Munich: Oldenbourg, 2007); Stefanie Michels, *Schwarze deutsche Kolonialsoldaten: Mehrdeutige Repräsentationsräume und früher Kosmopolitismus in Afrika* (Bielefeld: transcript, 2009); Thomas Morlang, *Askari und Fitafita: "Farbige" Söldner in den deutschen Kolonien* (Berlin: Christoph Links, 2008).

43. Jakob Zollmann provides another intriguing example of probing German sources with regard to the interaction between colonizers and colonized; see *Koloniale Herrschaft und ihre Grenzen: Die Kolonialpolizei in Deutsch-Südwestafrika, 1894–1915* (Göttingen: Vandenhoeck & Ruprecht, 2010). On new methodological and analytic ways to read the colonial archive from the nineteenth-century Netherlands Indies see Ann Laura Stoler, *Along the Archival Grain: Epistemic Anxieties and Colonial Common Sense* (Princeton: Princeton University Press, 2008).

44. John Iliffe, *Tanganyika under German Rule, 1905–1912* (Cambridge: Cambridge University Press, 1969), 7.

45. Klaus Mühlhahn, "Negotiating the Nation: German Colonialism and Chinese Nationalism in Qingdao, 1897–1914," *Twentieth-Century Colonialism and China*, ed. Bryna Goodman and David S. G. Goodman (London: Routledge, 2012), 37–56; Mechthild Leutner, ed., *"Musterkolonie Kiautschou"—Die Expansion des Deutschen Reiches in China; Deutsch-chinesische Beziehungen 1897–1914—Eine Quellensammlung* (Berlin: Akademie, 1997); Fu-teh Huang, *Qingdao: Chinesen unter deutscher Herrschaft 1897–1914* (Bochum: Projekt, 1999); Klaus Mühlhahn, *Herrschaft und Widerstand in der "Musterkolonie" Kiautschou: Interaktionen zwischen China und Deutschland, 1897–1914* (Munich: Oldenbourg, 2000).

46. Rebecca E. Karl, "On Comparability and Continuity: China, circa 1930s and 1990s," *Boundary* 32, no. 2 (2005): 169–200. On the cultural dimension of semicolonialism see also Shu-Mei Shih, *The Lure of the Modern: Writing Modernism in Semicolonial China, 1917–1937* (Berkeley: University of California Press, 2001).

47. Mary Louise Pratt, "Arts of the Contact Zone," *Profession* 91 (1991): 33–40.

48. Andreas Reckwitz, "Toward a Theory of Social Practices: A Development in Culturalist Theorizing," *European Journal of Social Theory* 5, no. 2 (2002): 244.

49. Reckwitz, "Toward a Theory," 249.

50. Sherry B. Ortner, *High Religion: A Cultural and Political History of Sherpa Buddhism* (Princeton: Princeton University Press, 1989), 198–99.

51. William H. Sewell Jr., *Logics of History: Social Theory and Social Transformation* (Chicago: University of Chicago Press, 2005), 162–64.

52. Sewell, *Logics of History*, 164.

53. Reckwitz, "Toward a Theory," 259.

54. See Mühlhahn, *Herrschaft und Widerstand in der "Musterkolonie" Kiautschou*, 28–34; see also Mechthild Leutner and Klaus Mühlhahn, "Interkulturelle Handlungsmuster: Deutsche Wirtschaft und Mission in China in der Spätphase des Imperialismus," in Mechthild Leutner and Klaus Mühlhahn, eds., *Deutsch-chinesische Beziehungen im 19. Jahrhundert: Mission und Wirtschaft in interkultureller Perspektive* (Münster: Lit, 2001), 9–42.

55. For explorations of categories and modes of inquiry central to the investigation of transnational phenomena, see, among others, Steven Vertovec, *Transnationalism* (London: Routledge, 2009); Michael C. Howard, *Transnationalism and Society: An Introduction* (Jefferson, NC: McFarland, 2011); Michael Geyer and Charles Bright, "World History in a Global Age," *American Historical Review* 100, no. 4 (1995): 1034–60.

56. Göttingen: Vandenhoeck & Ruprecht, 2004. See also the contributions to the h-german forum on "Transnationalism," January 2006, http://www.h-net.org/~german/discuss/Trans/forum_trans_index.htm.

57. Andrew Zimmerman, *Alabama in Africa: Booker T. Washington, the German Empire, and the Globalization of the New South* (Princeton: Princeton University Press, 2010).

58. For an exploration of biological racism and cultural racism, see Michael Schubert, *Der schwarze Fremde: Das Bild des Schwarzafrikaners in der parlamentarischen und publizistischen Kolonialdiskussion in Deutschland von den 1870er bis in die 1930er Jahre* (Stuttgart: F. Steiner, 2003).

59. Cambridge: Harvard University Press, 2014.

60. Dipesh Chakrabarty, *Provincializing Europe: Postcolonial Thought and Historical Difference* (Princeton: Princeton University Press, 2000).

61. Bhatawadekar, *Symptoms of Withdrawal;* Natalie Eppelsheimer, "Homecomings and Homemakings: Stefanie Zweig and the Exile Experience In, Out of, and Nowhere in Africa" (PhD diss., University of California, Irvine, 2008); Lacina Yéo, *Die Rehabilitation "Schwarzafrikas" in ausgewählten literarischen und publizistischen Schriften deutschsprachiger Autoren seit 1960: Paradigma eines deutschen Beitrags zum internationalen postkolonialen Diskurs* (Frankfurt: Lang, 2011); Sara Pugach, *Africa in Translation: A History of Colonial Linguistics in Germany and Beyond, 1814–1945* (Ann Arbor: University of Michigan Press, 2012).

62. *Hybrid Cultures—Nervous States: Britain and Germany in a (Post)Colonial Word,* ed. Ulrike Lindner et al. (Amsterdam: Rodopi, 2010); Andrew Sartori, "Beyond Culture-Contact and Colonial Discourse: 'Germanism' in Colonial Bengal," *Modern Intellectual History* 4, no. 1 (2007): 77–93. For the Black German Heritage & Research Association, see http://blackgermans.us/new/about-2/

63. One of Wierlacher's earliest pertinent publications is *Das Fremde und das Eigene: Prolegomena zu einer interkulturellen Germanistik* (Munich: Iudicium, 1985).

64. Bernhard Waldenfels, *Studien zur Phänomenologie des Fremden,* 4 vols. (Frankfurt am Main: Suhrkamp, 1997–99); Wolfdietrich Schmied-Kowarzik, ed., *Verstehen und Verständigung: Ethnologie, Xenologie, interkulturelle Philosophie* (Justin Stagl zum 60. Geburtstag) (Würzburg: Königshausen & Neumann, 2002); Munasu Duala-M'bedy, *Xenologie: Die Wissenschaft vom Fremden und die Verdrängung der Humanität in der Anthropologie* (Freiburg im Breisgau: K. Alber, 1977).

65. Leo Kreutzer, *Goethe in Afrika: Die interkulturelle Literaturwissenschaft der "École de Hanovre" in der afrikanischen Germanistik* (Hannover: Wehrhahn, 2009).

66. See the website of the organization, http://www.gas-verband.org/home/index.php/content/view/13/21/lang,de.

PART I
Interactions

Architecture with a Mission

Bamum Autoethnography during the Period of German Colonialism

Itohan I. Osayimwese

The Bamum Kingdom of western Cameroon held a prominent place in the German colonial imagination from the first official encounter between the two groups in 1902 until the expulsion of German nationals from Cameroon in 1915. Western scholarly knowledge of Bamum history has been the result of focused research by a small group of scholars starting in the 1920s. These scholars have investigated Bamum art, political systems, religion, linguistics, cartography, textile production, and military culture. They have paid particular attention to situating the Bamum Kingdom in relation to the changing regional politics of western Cameroon throughout the nineteenth century, and in the context of the profound reorganization of established ways of life brought about by European colonialism.

In this essay, I argue that the Bamum leadership took advantage of the receptiveness inherent to a dynamic tradition of artistic production in order to stake claims of agency within the colonial order. In particular, I discuss transformations in Bamum architecture as part of a larger collection of innovative forms of cultural production promoted by the Bamum leadership. Invoking the term *collection* and its standard association with uniquely modern practices of categorizing the world, writing teleological history, and the development of the Western museum as an institution of nationalist unity, is particularly appropriate here.[1] It is precisely within this constellation of practices that we should place Bamum forms and policies. From their transformation of sculptural programs and mastery of acquired construction methods and materials, to their pursuit of strategies to publicize their innovations, I show that the Bamum leadership and its artists masterfully manipulated visual and material culture for the purposes of self-representation. I propose that we read this phenomenon through the concept of autoethnography.

Autoethnography is elaborated here as both a conceptual framework that

Fig. 1. "Parade in front of the old palace, which later burned down."
Note the figural and non-figural columns, frieze, and squared doorframes. Photographer: Anna Wuhrmann, 1911/1915. (Source: BMA E-
30.31.060.)

encapsulates a complex multivocal historical experience and a heuristic device
that produces a balanced contemporary historiography. Rather than the traditional focus on the 'Other' as the subject of anthropology, autoethnography
frames the ethnographic gaze dialogically, and makes the ethnographer the
"subject-object of observation."[2] Autoethnography has been applied to describe a number of critical ethnographic practices ranging from self-reflexive
work where researchers examine their own transformation as a result of cultural encounters to indigenous ethnography in which cultural insiders construct
and present their own cultural stories.[3] The cultural forms and processes that I
discuss meet all three conditions for autoethnography described by Mary Louise Pratt: (1) they were concerned with forms of self-representation that engaged with the colonizer's own terms, (2) they eschewed autochthonous forms
in lieu of new ones that collaborated with the idioms of the dominant culture,
and (3) they were received heterogeneously by metropolitan observers.[4] My
reading of Bamum history explores the mobility of ideas, objects, and persons,
within the context of a self-conscious construction of identity by the Bamum
elite.

Bamum in Cameroonian-German Colonial History

The Berlin Conference of 1884 served as the German state's entry into the intra-European competition for global political and economic dominance through colonial power. After years of internal wrangling Germany declared South West Africa, Cameroon, Togo, and East Africa to be protectorates. Cameroonian colonization followed a by-now-familiar course when the dominant Douala regent, King Ndumbe Lobe Bell, under pressure from French and British incursions, signed a treaty with German representatives in July 1884.[5] Since the predominant aim was economic exploitation with minimal metropolitan investment, German influence spread inland haltingly, requiring numerous small-scale campaigns to subjugate polities that stood in the way of German interests. Consequently, the German administration did not reach Bamum territory until 1902.[6]

Sultan Njoya, the young ruler of the Bamum, chose a different approach to the incursion than the unsuccessful defensive stance taken by other regional leaders. He welcomed the German expedition and agreed to cooperate with its economic and military endeavors. One advantage of this strategy, which Njoya appreciated, was that becoming a German ally would strengthen his position vis-à-vis regional polities with antagonistic relationships to Bamum.[7] Bamum had become a major regional power in the sixteenth century under King Nsare. The kingdom underwent a second phase of development in the early nineteenth century under the leadership of King Mbuembue (ca. 1820–40), who successfully led military campaigns against neighboring states whose inhabitants, territories, and artistic traditions were integrated into Bamum society.

German administrators immediately perceived Njoya and members of his court to be different from other West Africans. Many reports describe Njoya as warm, intelligent, elegant, aristocratic, modest, and tactful. Lieutenant Hirtler's report of the 1902 colonial government's reconnaissance mission to Bamum set the tone: "The caliber of this man in person, [and] his proportionally great education and power of comprehension, elevate him far above the other chiefs of this district."[8] These character traits, together with the high material and cultural standards in which the Bamum appeared to live, contributed to the development of what art historian Christraud Geary has described as a "Bamum myth." This myth celebrated the Bamum as one of the fabled "paradisiacal and wealthy kingdoms in the interior of Africa."[9] The myth was underscored by the discovery that the Bamum had a dynastic history that they actively preserved. "Historicity, wealth, Bamum superiority, and the emphasis on the exotic" were thus ingredients of the Bamum myth.[10]

I make two contentions in response to Geary's admirable corpus. First, I propose that there was no "myth" about the Bamum that German observers misread or mystified. One interpretation of myth in everyday parlance concerns an erroneous belief that preempts the truth. Myth in the context of Geary's discussion thus presupposes an autochthonous narrative of identity that is yet to be told. Maintaining this conviction about a Bamum myth disregards poststructuralist critiques that dispel claims about either outsiders or insiders attaining positions of objectivity necessary for "authentic" knowledge. Another interpretation of myth describes it as a purely fictitious representation or an outright fabrication with no referent in reality. This definition is equally inapplicable to the Bamum case, as both the colonial archive and Njoya's self-authored history, *Histoire et Coutumes des Bamum* (1952), indicate the existence of narratives about the Kingdom, albeit narratives in a state of becoming.

Second, I argue that this non-myth was not exclusively, nor even primarily, a German creation. Rather, the Bamum leadership played as important a role in its articulation as any German agents. As I argue below, Bamum involvement in the production of this narrative was so extensive as to suggest that it was autoethnographic, if not in intention, then certainly in effect.

Authentic and Hybrid Palaces

Admiration for the imposing Bamum palace was a leitmotif in much that was written in German publications of the period. On closer analysis, however, the palace turns out to have been the product of an evolving artistic and technical practice. Though it was touted as a representation of a timeless culture, the Bamum palace did not actually meet colonial standards of authenticity—a fact that was resolutely ignored.

The sheer material presence of the Bamum capital, Fumban, contributed to its mystique. One of the larger cities encountered by Europeans in the region, Fumban had a population of 15,000 to 20,000 inhabitants and was surrounded by a multi-layered system of moats and walls. Fumban's palace (Figure 1) provided a literal and metaphorical focal point in the city. Both Germans and the Bamum elite represented the palace repeatedly in various mediums. Contrary to the impression provided by historical descriptions and photographs portraying partial views, the "palace" was a complex of over one hundred individual buildings in close proximity to each other. Two to three thousand people resided in this royal complex that encompassed more than 70,000 square meters.[11] Individual buildings were arranged around large courtyards and joined to create a continuous façade. Periodic fires destroyed the palace and necessitated communal rebuilding. This was the case when a 1909 fire destroyed the new palace that Njoya had commissioned in 1904–5, which was a fifteen-minute walk away from the dilapidated court of his father. In response, he embarked on a project to renovate his father's palace.[12]

New architectural elements were integrated into the renovated palace including rounded doorways and pillars carved with humanoid figures. Photographs indicate that palace doorframes had been rectangular and veranda pillars unadorned prior to this point. Njoya himself explained that he appropriated the rounded doorways from an image he had seen in an illustrated magazine.[13] Clearly, the long arm of European print culture had reached Bamum. Difficulty of construction or Njoya's growing antagonism to colonial rule may account for the subsequent return to rectangular doorways from 1912.[14] With few exceptions, scholars have ignored the indirect mode of colonial cultural influence represented in Njoya's appropriation of rounded doorways. Though little information is available on the circumstances surrounding Njoya's engagement with this particular magazine, the incident suggests a critical opening for future scholarship. The use of rounded openings can be traced to European print sources, but the shift to figural pillars between 1908 and 1911 may be explained by the integration of artists from annexed regions and competition with other powerful Grassfields kingdoms, notably the Bamileke, whose palace sculpture displays a significant affinity with Njoya's.[15]

The length of the façade of the palace became the subject of speculation by colonial observers and was reported to lie somewhere between 81 meters and 150 meters.[16] Whatever its actual length, it was considered unexpectedly large for an African building. Njoya's audience courtyard, located immediately inside the palace, was greatly admired. The king received visiting dignitaries in this space and staged receptions calculated to impress by displaying emblems of Bamum power like his two-headed beaded throne. It is the most photographed section of the palace and likely one of the few areas accessible to German visitors. Verandas supported on carved posts in the new style surrounded the courtyard. A polychromatic frieze above calls attention to the exceptional height of the buildings. In a travelogue published in 1914, the artist and amateur anthropologist Marie Pauline Thorbecke commented on the "ancient lizard motif" on the frieze.[17]

Thorbecke verbalized what seems to have been a common perception of Bamum culture.[18] This perception of historicity contradicted the image that Njoya conveyed of himself and his culture as modern and progressive. Indeed, as I argue subsequently, some German observers came to the same conclusion.

These two perceptions of the Bamum—as authentic and timeless on one hand and modern and progressive on the other—existed in a productive tension with one another. Njoya himself challenged the assumption of historicity in his *Histoire*. Here, he described roofs decorated with "drawings of dogs" that "nobody had ever seen."[19] Directly contradicting the notion that he had been swayed by European precedent, Njoya proclaimed the primacy of his intellectual imagination. With this, he proved his awareness of the peculiarities of Western epistemologies that emphasized independent intellectual achievement.

Thorbecke's claim about the great age of the palace was tantamount to a statement about its authenticity. Colonial architects frequently framed the architecture of colonized populations in terms of authenticity and hybridity. They concerned themselves with evaluating the veracity of current architecture in relation to authentic forms. Authentic forms were those that were ancient and bore no resemblance to modern forms. Most importantly, authentic architecture showed no signs of hybridity.[20] As scholars of postcolonial studies have argued, the purpose of such discourse was to police the boundaries of hegemonic colonial culture. The problem with hybridity was that it proved that colonial difference was an unstable construct.[21] From its integration of regional forms to its uncertain chronology (old palace, new palace, renovated palace, Mbuembue's palace, Nsangu's palace, Njoya's palace), the Bamum palace embodied a degree of dynamism in its production and hybridity in its formal expression that makes claims about its timeless character and representative authority problematic.

Hybrids in the Palace

To compound matters, Njoya commissioned at least three explicitly hybrid buildings during his reign. When mentioned at all, comments about these hybrids were either denigrating or ambivalent. One such house was built in 1908–9.[22] An archival photograph (Figure 2) shows a three-story house. Its plastered three-story core is surrounded by verandas. In contrast to the slender, carved, wood posts of more conventional palace buildings, the rectilinear piers holding up the first-floor veranda are of bulky mud-brick. Skeletal wood columns define the veranda and support steep hipped roofs on the second and third floors. Though carved from wood, the columns show no figural decoration like that included on the façade of the main palace. Despite their height from the ground, the second and third floor verandas have no balusters or safety railings in between their

Fig. 2. "New palace in Fumban." Photographer: Martin Göhring, 1905/1912. (Source: BMA E-30.31.074.)

columns. Doors and windows pierce the thick walls beyond the verandas on all floors. A wood framework sits above the ribbed sheets of the hipped roof.[23] At the apex of each roof ridge sits a finial. Though the photographic evidence of these finials is limited, they bear a certain formal resemblance to the pyramidal structure of conventional Bamum raffia stem roofs. There is, however, no photographic evidence of roof finials in Bamum architecture.

Njoya's hybrid house shared several elements with structures built by the Basel Mission Society, which opened a station in Fumban in 1906. Figure 3 depicts one of the first buildings erected by the mission.[24] This simple rectilinear two-story building has a frame built from sawn and planed boards. A shallow hipped roof extended into deep eaves that shaded verandas on the front façade. Slender, bracketed wood columns connected by simple wood balustrades defined these outdoor living spaces. Whitewashed plaster formed a smooth finish on the wattle and daub walls, and contrasted with the brown wood of the frame to endow the structure with the stereotypical *Fachwerk* (half-timbered) aesthetic promulgated by the Basel Mission.[25] Mission buildings, including those built during subsequent phases of Basel Mission construction in Bamum, were frequently elevated on masonry piers as a prophylactic against tropical diseases.[26]

Fig. 3. "Mission outhouse in Fumban." The two-story half-timbered
form was typical of mission buildings. Photographer: Martin Göhring,
1906/1912. (Source: BMA E-30.28.012.)

Njoya's new building behind the palace utilized bracketed wood posts that
resemble those on Basel Mission buildings. On their own, however, wood posts
were not a novelty in Bamum architecture, as the figural and non-figural columns on the main palace buildings demonstrate. Njoya's hybrid house also had
a masonry foundation (Njoya used mud-brick instead of stone), though Njoya's
building remains grounded in the site in a way that distinguished it from the
mission buildings' deliberate disengagement from the ground. However,
Njoya's layered pyramidal massing and sprawling cross-axial floor plan contrasted with the simple rectilinear form of the Basel Mission structures.

Njoya's house also bore similarities to colonial buildings that he may have
seen when he visited the coast in 1907 or 1908.[27] He may have been particularly impressed by the governor's palace in Buea (Figure 4), whose layered
massing, large size, heavy masonry walls, and neoclassical details were calculated to express the power of the regime. The governor's palace as well as
many planters' residences in the city displayed complex rooflines with roof
ridge ornamentation reminiscent of Njoya's finials in Bamum (Figure 2).[28]

Another important building that Njoya likely saw on the coast was the
palace of the Douala regent Rudolf Manga Bell (Figure 5). Arguably a visual
and material riposte to German presence in Doula, the extreme layering of the

Fig. 4. "Governor's House in Buea," built ca. 1902. (Source: Colonial Picture Archive, Frankfurt University Library, 041–0243–32.)

massing of Bell's house was echoed in Njoya's new buildings. It seems unlikely that similarities between these two buildings were happenstance. Njoya and Bell were political rivals whose relationship may have extended to competition in the arena of architectural representation.[29]

Other potential sources can be identified for Njoya's hybrid house. Njoya commissioned mission-trained carpenters and sought advice directly from Eugen Schwarz, the Basel Mission architect, for this building project.[30] It is important to note, however, that Njoya challenged the prevailing view that his building was influenced by "white" examples: "the king had never seen any of their houses at the time he built this one."[31] Geary and others have also suggested that elements of the new Bamum architecture were borrowed from other regional traditions.[32] The range of identifiable sources for Njoya's building make it an exemplary structure that deepens our understanding of hybridity.

In her travelogue, Marie Pauline Thorbecke praised Njoya's European-style house as one of the best houses in the colony. Beneath her protestations of beauty lay ambivalence, however. She insisted on reading essential racial characteristics into the house: "Despite the European influence they [these

Fig. 5. "The palace of Paramount Chief Manga Bell in Duala (Cameroon)." Photographer: Johannes Immanuel Leimenstoll, 1900/1903 (Source: BMA E-30.06.009.)

houses] remain African and give testimony of an innate artistic taste that the Africans could not have acquired from Europeans."[33] Likewise, mission architect Schwarz felt conflicted about the results of the project: "In this way, a house arose that arguably brought honor to the king of Bamum, but on the other hand, one must look again at the impressive building with black eyes in order to find it satisfactory."[34] As Pratt has explained, this kind of ambivalent reception is typical of autoethnographic texts. Despite these comments, racial and cultural difference were not embodied in Njoya's house, which could have easily passed for the home of a new settler.[35] Njoya himself was satisfied with his experiments. He reported that "everyone said that his intelligence far surpassed that of all other men, because they had never seen anything quite like this house."[36] He described his house in glowing terms: "The walls were covered with fabrics and the floor with mats, the hearth was coated with a type of varnish."[37] He filled it with "rarities and ornaments" and showed it off to visiting dignitaries.[38]

Njoya's experiments culminated in the 1917 construction of a mud-brick, arcaded palace that integrated Bamum, regional, German, Islamic, and other influences.[39] His architects' increasing adeptness with new forms, materials, and techniques is on display in this building.[40] Nevertheless, the new palace was again rejected by colonial observers: the Basel missionary, Anna Wuhrmann, admired Njoya's enterprising spirit but noted that "white guests might not approve" of the "unfortunate" European-style building.[41]

Njoya's motivations for commissioning these buildings likely ranged from intellectual curiosity to a desire to control the Bamum visual and material environment in order to generate, express, and maintain cultural capital and political power. Pratt contends that autoethnographic texts rely in part on hybridity for their effects. Rather than being "autochthonous forms of self-representation," they entail "partial collaboration with and appropriation of the idioms of the conqueror."[42] Njoya's architectural interventions, including changes to the main structures of his palace complex and multiple freestanding hybrid houses built to its rear, met this condition.

Bamum Innovations from Photography to Military Dress

Between 1902 and 1915, German observers came to know Bamum primarily through photographs. The first German expedition to Fumban took photographs of the city—images that the Leipzig Museum of Ethnography immediately requested. Not only did photography shape early representations of Bamum, it also brought together disparate interest groups.[43] The Basel Mission produced the most comprehensive body of photographs of the Bamum. Its missionaries had been using the new science to depict conditions in the West African mission field and generate metropolitan support since the 1890s.[44] Importantly, however, Bamum individuals were not always passive photographic subjects. In several documented cases, they adopted strong positions about poses, accoutrements, or settings.[45] These photographs circulated through mission, trade, and professional networks, and made Fumban a destination for other Europeans intent on photographing, painting, studying, and collecting Bamum. As they raised the profile of the Mission and increased the cultural capital of missionaries, these images exported representations that were produced by all actors—Bamum, German, and otherwise.

Another unambiguous case of innovation in the service of self-representation is illustrated by Njoya's invention of a written script between 1895 and 1900.[46] The script was taught at schools in Fumban and was used as a tool for communication between disparate groups within and outside the kingdom, for the translation of the Bible, and by German officials communicating with locals.[47] The colonial community was impressed by Njoya's innovation, which they perceived as a sign of his openness to modernization and colonialism. The script was also used to document Bamum history and customs. By translating older forms of Bamum historiography into this modern medium, Njoya and his courtiers made it more accessible and initiated its incorporation into metropolitan discourse in a characteristically autoethnographic manner.

Njoya soon turned from mapping history to mapping geography. He may have made maps before 1902, but he found new inspiration in the work of missionaries and of the cartographer Max Moisel. Western influence is evident in the documentation of distances and topography in the large-scale survey that Njoya undertook between 1912 and 1920. His map depicts Bamum as a totality but does not locate it in a global context—a gesture that can be read as a self-conscious dismissal of competing territorial claims. By masking international, regional, and internal power struggles, Njoya's maps imagined a community in the manner of the modern nation-state.[48]

Among the most telling of Njoya's institutional reforms were changes he made to Bamum military culture. Njoya and his soldiers adopted Hausa clothing and appropriated elements of Islam around 1895 in honor of the Fulbe who had helped repel a challenge to his throne.[49] By 1905, they had exchanged these garments for German-style uniforms. Colonial administrators facilitated the transition with gifts of flags, firearms, uniforms, and portraits of the Kaiser. Njoya not only accepted the uniforms but also transformed them by accessorizing them with Bamum iconography, which made them legible to both metropolitan and regional observers. He also commissioned palace tailors to make new uniforms according to novel designs.[50] He had rescinded these policies by 1909, however. His change of heart was influenced, as Geary has argued, by Germany's response to the growing power of the Bamum army, namely, a ban on Bamum possession of firearms. Germans also derided Bamum adaptation of Western dress as something that emphasized rather than erased racial difference. Perhaps Njoya became aware of these metropolitan responses. This is a clear case of colonial mimicry or the production of the colonial subject as "the same, but not quite."[51] That this transformation was captured on camera, presented, and represented in visual imagery and written commentary emphasizes the impact of the autoethnographic act.

Njoya developed a range of other institutional reforms.[52] By his own evaluation, his most important contribution was to the judicial system, where he eased the use of capital punishment and limited the power of the nobility.[53] Scholars have too easily accepted colonial reactions to Njoya's panoply of innovations as unthinking "acts of friendship and emulation."[54] In this essay, I have tried to analyze Njoya's activities as a series of self-conscious and related actions if not a unified strategy.

Gift Exchange as a Tool for Self-Representation

It was one thing for Njoya to mold Bamum into a modern nation, but it was quite another to convince others of the transformation. One strategy that Njoya used effectively in this regard was gift exchange. Though the practice among Grassfields kingdoms is well understood, the theoretical dimensions of gift exchange have not been interrogated as a framework for interpreting Bamum-German relations. Like several essays in this anthology, this one therefore reads against the grain of the colonial archive and contemporary historiography.

Njoya gave many gifts to visitors, including a map he gave to Göhring in 1906; a pipe he gave to Captain Glauning, the head of the German military in the region; a beaded life-size figure he gave to the colonial administration on Glauning's death; and a large, beaded, two-figured throne he sent for the Kaiser.[55] Scholars have attached great import to the release of this symbol of kingship. Its release should not be overemphasized, however, since its provenance has been questioned and since old thrones were usually replaced after the coronation of new kings.[56] Njoya's gifts were also partly a response to market forces since the ethnographic museums in Berlin and Leipzig regularly requested Bamum artifacts.[57] Njoya received gifts from the colonial administration in return. Indeed, gift exchange was a form of diplomacy practiced by Grassfields leaders and the European elite alike in the late nineteenth and early twentieth centuries.[58]

Since Marcel Mauss's seminal work, a vast body of scholarship has emerged that theorizes gift-giving in relation to economic self-interest, the materialist-spiritual significance of reciprocity, and the construction of social order.[59] In the second of these interpretations, the material properties of the gift are implicated in its ability to "transform social actors and relations."[60] For the donor, the gift is an "objectified form of their own identity" that continually evokes their presence in the imagination of the receiver.[61] Gift-giving is thus fundamentally concerned with identity construction and self-representation. Finely balanced hierarchies were embedded in the gift-exchange systems of different societies. In some colonial contexts, these balanced systems became distorted under pressure from alternate systems of exchange.[62] Taken together, gifts given by Njoya and his court to representatives of the metropolitan culture can be said to constitute a "collection" whose plausible aim and effect was to shape the representation of Bamum. This collection anticipated the emergence of modern museums—conscribed spaces for the public management of bodies and objects curated by the state and its agents to socialize the emergent public of the modern nation-state into self-awareness and self-regulation—in 1920s Bamum.[63]

Representing Bamum in Twentieth-Century Germany

Given the existence of this collection, it is no coincidence that Bamum was included in two important exhibitions in early twentieth-century Germany— the 1914 German Werkbund Exhibition in Cologne and Leipzig's 1914 International Exhibition of Book Trades and Graphic Design (BUGRA). New ideas about the role of art and industry in modernity were articulated at these exhibitions. Architects at the Werkbund Exhibition erected a model colonial house with a photographic display of "worthy" colonial buildings in order to modernize architecture in the German colonies.[64] They largely excluded current architecture by colonized populations but included some archaeological and ethnographic images in their display.[65] Thus, in architecture as in other spheres of cultural production, the colonized were conscribed to anachronistic time and space. Photographs of Fumban, its palace, and Njoya of Bamum were included in this exhibit.[66] Given the ambivalent reception of the hybrid palace buildings, it is more likely that the "authentic" palace was displayed. That this seemingly ancient building was included in an exhibit intended to modernize architecture in the colonies exemplifies the ideological inconsistency of colonialism and modernism alike. Even more noteworthy is the fact that Njoya's palace was one of few representations of the architecture of the colonized within the colonial pavilion, and one of the rare ones to include detailed identification information.[67]

Similarly, Njoya was the only African named in a display of "native literacy" in the colonial pavilion at BUGRA in Leipzig. The display included samples of his "independently-invented" script, his portrait, as well as examples of student work from colonial and Islamic schools in Cameroon.[68] Here, the ability to write distinguished Njoya and allowed him to rise above the nameless hordes of ethnographic discourse. Importantly, the exhibit managed to reconcile contradictory perceptions of Njoya's accomplishment as a personal feat that illustrated a modern outlook, as proof of essential Bamum qualities, and as a product of German influence.[69] Through the act of naming, his pictorial likeness, and the material presence of Bamum script, Njoya was present at an exhibition whose specific existence he may not even have been aware of. BUGRA and the Werkbund are doubtless only two among other as yet undiscovered instances of Bamum representation in Germany.

Afterlife of Autoethnography

Today, Njoya's final hybrid palace is home to the Bamum Palace Museum where local historians have continued the work of cultivating the Bamum nation for domestic, regional, national, and international consumption.[70] They have paid significant attention to documenting and preserving the Bamum script.[71] Bamum art has also played an important role in the contemporary construction of Cameroonian national identity.[72] The palace itself has been the object of collaborative local and international preservation efforts since the 1960s.[73] More recently, these kinds of efforts have been challenged on some of the very same grounds discussed in this chapter: What is authentic? What is hybrid? Who decides? What is the relationship between object and culture? From Bamum to Berlin and Paris to New York, Bamum art and history continue to be the subject of European and American scholarly interest through the very same autoethnographic forms devised at the turn of the century. Eighty years of scholarship on both sides of the Atlantic has clarified the active role that Njoya and his court played in representing Bamum.

NOTES

1. Tony Bennett, *The Birth of the Museum: History, Theory, Politics* (New York: Routledge, 1995).

2. Paul Atkinson, Review of *Auto/ethnography: Rewriting the Self and the Social*, by Deborah Reed-Danahay, *Journal of the Royal Anthropological Institute* 5, no. 1 (Mar. 1999): 152–53; James Buzard, "On Auto-Ethnographic Authority," *Yale Journal of Criticism* 16, no. 1 (2003): 73.

3. Carolyn Ellis, Tony E. Adams, and Arthur Bochner, "Autoethnography: An Overview," *Forum Qualitative Sozialforschung / Forum: Qualitative Social Research* 12, no. 1 (2010), Art. 10, http://nbn-resolving.de/urn:nbn:de:0114-fqs1101108; Brian Gregory, Review of *Auto/Ethnography: Rewriting the Self and the Social*, by Deborah E. Reed-Danahay, *Journal of American Folklore* 113, no. 449 (Summer 2000): 329.

4. Joel Martineau, "Autoethnography and Material Culture: The Case of Bill Reid," *Biography* 24, no. 1 (2001): 243.

5. Ralph A. Austen, *Middlemen of the Cameroons Rivers: The Duala and Their Hinterland, c.1600–c.1960* (New York: Cambridge University Press, 1999), 96.

6. Claude Tardits, "The Kingdom of Bamum," in *Kings of Africa: Art and Authority in Central Africa*, ed. Erna Beumers and Hans-Joachim Koloss (Maastricht: Foundation Kings of Africa, 1992), 43.

7. Christraud Geary, "Impressions of the African Past: Interpreting Ethnographic Photographs from Cameroon," *Visual Anthropology* 3, no. 3 (1990): 300; Karin Schestokat, *German Women in Cameroon: Travelogues from Colonial Times* (New York: Peter Lang, 2003), 57.

8. Oberleutnant Hirtler, "Bericht des Oberleutnants Hirtler über eine Expedition nach Bamum," *Deutsches Kolonial Blatt* 14, no. 18 (1903): 491.

9. Geary, "Impressions of the African Past," 300.

10. Christraud Geary, *Images from Bamum: German Colonial Photography at the Court of King Njoya, Cameroon, West Africa, 1902–1915* (Washington, DC: Smithsonian, 1988), 38; Geary, "Impressions of the African Past," 307.

11. Suzanne Preston Blier, *The Royal Arts of Africa: The Majesty of Form* (New York: Adams, 1998), 176–77, 194.

12. Geary, *Images from Bamum*, 64–74.

13. Geary, *Images from Bamum*, 69.

14. Geary, *Images from Bamum*, 69.

15. Geary, *Images from Bamum*, 70; Christraud Geary, "Art and Political Process in the Kingdoms of Bali-Nyonga and Bamum (Cameroon Grassfields)," *Canadian Journal of African Studies / Revue Canadienne des Études Africaines* 22, no. 1 (1988): 15–17.

16. Geary, *Images from Bamum*, 70; Passarge-Rathjens, "Bamum," in *Deutsches Kolonial Lexikon*, vol. 1, ed. Heinrich Schnee (Leipzig: Quelle & Meyer, 1920), 126, http://www.ub.bildarchiv-dkg.uni-frankfurt.de/Bildprojekt/Lexikon/lexikon.htm; Ernst Vollbehr, *Bunte Leuchtende Welt: Die Lebensfahrt des Malers Ernst Vollbehr* (Berlin: Ullstein, 1935), 116.

17. Geary, *Images from Bamum*, 70.

18. See, for example, the description of the "precious old beadwork" on Njoya's throne in the caption of BMA QE-30.017.0005.

19. Sultan Njoya, *Histoire et coutumes des Bamum rédigées sous la direction du Sultan Njoya*, Mémoires de l'Institut Francais d'Afrique Noire, Centre du Cameroun. Série Populations no. 6 (Dakar: pl. A-E, 1952), 111.

20. C. G. Büttner, "Ueber das Erbauen von Haeusern fuer Europaer im inneren Afrikas," *Deutsche Kolonialzeitung* vol. 1 (1887): 18–19; Itohan Osayimwese, "Colonialism at the Center: German Colonial Architecture and the Design Reform Movement, 1828–1918" (PhD diss., University of Michigan, Ann Arbor, 2008), 59–74.

21. Homi Bhabha, *The Location of Culture* (New York: Routledge, 1994).

22. Geary and Adamou Ndam Njoya, *Mandu Yenu: Bilder aus Bamum, einem westafrikanischen Königreich, 1902–1915* (Munich: Trickster, 1985), 58, 70–71; Schestokat, *German Women*, 61. BMA E-30.32.018 depicts another house that bears no formal similarities to the one discussed in my previous paragraphs. Additionally, Njoya is said to have commissioned a European-style house for his mother (Geary, *Mandu Yenu*, 95, 99).

23. The material composition of the roof is unclear in these photographs.

24. Soon after their arrival in his city, Njoya graciously provided the mission with

accommodations constructed out of conventional Bamum raffia palm and thatch. See BMA E-30.28.006.

25. Peter A. Schweizer, *Mission an der Goldküste: Geschichte und Fotografie der Basler Mission im kolonialen Ghana* (Basel: Chr. Merian, 2002), 108.

26. Wolfgang Lauber, *Deutsche Architektur in Kamerun 1884–1914: Deutsche Architekten und Kameruner Wissenschaftler dokumentieren die Bauten der deutschen Epoche in Kamerun/Afrika* (Stuttgart: K. Krämer, 1988), 49. Also BMA D-10.4,18, "Ueber Afrikanisches Bauwesen," 1895.

27. Catherine Coquery-Vidrovitch, *The History of African Cities South of the Sahara* (Princeton: Markus Wiener, 2005), 263. BMA E-30.32.006 provides the 1908 date for Njoya's visit.

28. Lauber, *Deutsche Architektur*, 68, 80.

29. Jean-Pierre Felix Eyoum, Stefanie Michels, and Joachim Zeller, "Bonamanga: Eine kosmopolitische Familiengeschichte," *Mont Cameroun* 2 (2005): 14.

30. Geary and Njoya, *Mandu Yenu*, 74.

31. Njoya, *Histoire et coutumes*, 109.

32. Geary and Njoya, *Mandu Yenu*, 71.

33. Schestokat, *German Women in Cameroon*, 61.

34. Geary and Njoya, *Mandu Yenu*, 71.

35. Franz Baltzer, "Hausbau der Europäer," in *Deutsches Kolonial Lexikon*, vol. 1, ed. Heinrich Schnee (Leipzig: Quelle & Meyer, 1920), 47, http://www.ub.bildarchiv-dkg.uni-frankfurt.de (accessed May 13, 2009); Büttner, "Ueber das Erbauen von Haeusern," 18–19.

36. Njoya, *Histoire et coutumes*, 111.

37. Njoya, *Histoire et coutumes*, 109.

38. Geary and Njoya, *Mandu Yenu*, 58; Geary, *Images from Bamum*, 76; Schestokat, *German Women in Cameroon*, 61.

39. Blier, *The Royal Arts of Africa*, 167–68; Geary, *Images from Bamum*, 73–74; Marc Robert, *La restauration du palais des Sultans de Bamoun à Foumban* (Paris: UNESCO, 1980), 4.

40. Blier, *The Royal Arts of Africa*, 168.

41. Schestokat, *German Women in Cameroon*, 60.

42. Mary Louise Pratt, *Imperial Eyes: Travel Writing and Transculturation* (New York: Routledge, 1992), 7.

43. Geary, *Impressions of the African Past*, 300.

44. Christraud Geary and Paul Jenkins, "Photographs from Africa in the Basel Mission Archive," *African Arts* 18, no. 4 (1985): 56.

45. Geary and Jenkins, "Photographs from Africa," 62; Geary, *Images from Bamum*, 40. This assertiveness also applied to other artistic mediums purveyed by Europeans: the German painter, Ernst Vollbehr, reported that Njoya wanted to sit for a portrait but specified that the portrait include a mustache "like the Kaiser's" (Vollbehr, *Bunte Leuchtende Welt*, 116).

46. John Mbaku, *Cultures and Customs of Cameroon* (Westport: Greenwood Press, 2005), 55.

47. Blier, *The Royal Arts of Africa*, 166; John Hegglund, "Modernism, Africa, and the Myth of Continents," in *Geographies of Modernism*, ed. Peter Brooker and Andrew

Thacker (London: Routledge, 2005), 49; Schestokat, *German Women in Africa*, 47, 94; Tardits, "The Kingdom of Bamum," 55; Konrad Tuchscherer, "The Lost Script of the Bagam," in *African Affairs* 98, no. 390 (1999): 57.

48. Hegglund, "Modernism," 50; Thomas J. Bassett, "Indigenous Mapmaking in Intertropical Africa," in G. Malcolm Lewis and David Woodward, ed., *The History of Cartography: Cartography in the Traditional African, American, Arctic, Australian, and Pacific Societies*, vol. 2, book 3 (Chicago: University of Chicago Press, 1998), 41.

49. Geary, "Patterns from Without," 7; Mbaku, *Cultures and Customs*, 55.

50. Geary, "Patterns from Without," 8–11.

51. Bhabha, *The Location of Culture*, 86.

52. Mbaku, *Cultures and Customs*, 54–55, 104.

53. Njoya, *Histoire et coutumes*, 128–33. Since they lacked direct implications for German interests, Njoya's activities in this area were not widely discussed in colonial literature.

54. Steven Nelson, "Collection and Context in a Cameroonian Village," *Museum International* No. 235 59, no. 3 (2007): 25.

55. Christraud Geary, *Things of the Palace: A Catalogue of the Bamum Palace Museum in Foumban (Cameroon)* (Wiesbaden: F. Steiner, 1983), 13; *Patterns from Without*, 9.

56. Geary, "Bamum and Tikar: Inspiration and Innovation," in *Cameroon: Art and Kings*, ed. Lorenz Homberger (Zurich: Museum Rietberg, 2008), 49; Mbaku, *Cultures and Customs*, 105.

57. Geary, *Things of the Palace*, 46–53.

58. Geary, *Patterns from Without*, 9.

59. Jacques T. Godbout, *World of the Gift* (Montreal: McGill-Queen's University Press, 1998), 118–27.

60. Michael Graydon, "Don't Bother to Wrap It: Online Giftgiver and Bugchaser Newsgroups, the Social Impact of Gift Exchanges and the 'Carnivalesque,'" *Culture, Health & Sexuality* 9, no. 3 (2007): 278.

61. Ibid. (italics mine). Also see Godbout, *World of the Gift*, 122.

62. Lorraine V. Aragon, "Translating Precolonial into Colonial Exchanges in Central Sulawesi, Indonesia," *American Ethnologist* 23, no. 1 (Feb. 1996): 50.

63. On museum collecting see Bennett, *The Birth of the Museum*, 66. Nelson suggests that it was only in the 1920s that Bamum royal objects broke the binds of "closed storage" to make their way into the arena of public viewing in the spirit of modern museums and their ideological economies. I am arguing that these objects were already being manipulated (in the German period) in ways that overlap with the more formalized frameworks of the later period (Nelson, "Collection and Context").

64. Osayimwese, "Colonialism at the Center," 306.

65. BArch R 1001/6374, *Allgemeine Angelegenheiten, Ausstellungen: Deutsche Werkbundaust. in Koeln 1914, 1913–1916*, "Verzeichnis der für die Werkbund Ausstellung Kolonialhaus-eingegangenen Photographien, Baupläne, gg.," 194–207.

66. Four Bamum photographs are listed in the exhibition inventory: "Two drums in front of the palace of the Lamido of Bamum," "Some Bamum plantation workers in Douala," "Street in the Hausa city district in Bamum," and "The Palace of the Lamido

of Bamum" (BArch R 1001/6374, 194–207). However, no photographic record of the actual display has been located.

67. The only other case of this among the hundreds of items listed in the inventory of photographs also comes from Cameroon—the palace of the Douala regent Manga Bell.

68. BArch R1001/6348/1, *Allgemeine Angelegenheiten, Ausstellungen: Ausstellungen, 1911–1912.* "Letter from BUGRA to Dr. Solf, June 3, 1912," 69; *Internationale Ausstellung für Buchgewerbe und Graphik Leipzig (BUGRA), Amtlicher Katalog* (Leipzig: BUGRA, 1914), 524; LC Lot 3884G Box 2 of 5, *Weltausstellung für Buchgewerbe und Graphik, Leipzig, 1914.*

69. Schestokat, *German Women in Cameroon*, 59.

70. Cf. Nelson, "Collection and Context."

71. See http://www.bamumscript.org/ cited May 18, 2009.

72. Steven Nelson, *From Cameroon to Paris: Mousgoum Architecture in and out of Africa* (Chicago: University of Chicago Press, 2007), 145.

73. Robert, *La restauration du palais.*

"The Germans cannot master our language!"

or

German Colonial Rulers and the Beti in the Cameroonian Hinterlands[1]

Germain Nyada (Translated by Amber Suggitt)

Language as an Instrument of Power

In July 1884 a treaty was signed between German and local leaders in "Cameroons." This led to the territory being placed under German "protection." The treaty dealt only with the coastal area that was under joint control of local agencies. The leaders Jim Ekwalla (alias King Dido), Bell (alias Ndumb'a Lobe), and Akwa (alias Dika Mpondo) planned to continue the trade monopoly with the hinterlands despite the signing of the treaty. Prior to the treaty the German consul Emil Schulz had already pledged in writing to respect, among other things, the trade monopoly of the Duala.[2] The first demand stated in the *Wishes of the Cameroonian People* is that the trade monopoly is to stay in the hands of the Cameroonians. Furthermore one reads: "Our wishes is [*sic*] that white men should not go up and trade with the Bushmen, nothing to do with our markets [. . .]."[3] The Bushmen were ethnic groups living inland who supplied the coast with goods. Despite the colonists making direct contact with the hinterlands, the leaders of the coastal area did not want to relinquish this trade advantage that played an important role in their sovereignty. As Kum'a Ndumbe III explains, the Cameroonian signers of the "Protectorate" were attempting to prevent a possible splintering and weakening of their economic power.

In spite of the efforts of the Cameroonians, three years after the seizure of the region the German explorers Richard Kund and Hans Tappenbeck reached the hinterlands in the center of Cameroon due to a breach of contract.[4] The location they reached, which was originally called Ongola, had never before come into direct contact with Europeans. Following their arrival the place was

given the name "Yaunde-Land." It was established as the first stop in the hinterlands and renamed after its four ethnic groups: The Bene, Eton, Ewondo (or
Jewondo), and Mwelle. Although these people were actually called the "Beti,"
they received the name "Yaunde-People." The word "Yaunde" appeared in
print for the first time as a heading in the monograph written by Georg Zenker
(1855–1922) during his term as supervisor of the "Yaunde"-Station. The
monograph dealt with customs, architecture, and rituals of the area. Philippe
Laburthe-Tolra explains that the name "Yaunde" symbolizes and subsumes a
series of ambiguities and errors.[5] According to him such ambivalent approaches
were typical of the first Germans who governed what is today the capital of
Cameroon. Laburthe-Tolra points out that Zenker took up the name "Yaunde"
from his predecessors and that it is really a mispronunciation and false transcription of the word "(J)Ewondo," the name of the Ewondo people.

This originally erroneous pronunciation and orthography of the name
"Jewondo" has hardly been changed since German colonial rule and is used
today still in Cameroonian institutions. This suggests that the same mistakes
and miscomprehensions in pronunciation and transcription were reproduced
by the Beti themselves. It is therefore important to determine why the local
population, as well as hired translators and language assistants, repeated
such errors so uncritically that mistakes such as "Yaunde" exist even today.
There is the hypothesis that an independent dialect called Mongo Ewondo
("Yaunde-language" during the German colonial era) developed in the Beti
language area[6] out of contacts made at that time and as a result of language
errors arising in communication situations. Before discussing the Mongo
Ewondo situation it is necessary to give a brief introduction to the Beti languages. Jean-Paul Kouega defines this language group as follows:

> Beti is the group name of a cluster of mutually intelligible ancestral lan-
> guages spoken in the south of Cameroon and in the north of Gabon, Equa-
> torial Guinea and Congo. These languages include Bebele, Bulu, Eton,
> Ewondo, Fang and Mangisa [. . .]. Although the languages of this group
> share a high proportion of linguistic features, their speakers view them-
> selves as sharing a common culture but not a common language.[7]

Kouega's definition allows for a detailed insight into the Beti languages as
conceptualized today. During the German colonial era most attention was paid
to those languages that were spoken in and around Cameroon's capital city:
Bene, Eton, Ewondo, and Mwelle. Mongo Ewondo developed out of these four
languages. It was even spoken by the colonists, their foreign porters, and sol-

diers who acquired Beti languages, as well as by the Beti themselves. Its original use by the Beti is ambivalent: on the one hand they wanted to alleviate the language burden for the foreigners and make it easier to be understood; on the other hand the use of this new language contained a self-affirming dimension.

In order to comprehend this second dimension concerned with the use of Mongo Ewondo we should turn to Robert McColl Millar for support and consider the prestige that accompanies standardized languages. He postulates that every language features a "High variety" and a "Low variety." As a result of these varieties inherent in every language McColl Millar speaks of diglossia and of a diglossian relationship that exhibits two characteristics: function and prestige.[8] Function indicates that use of the language made by the speaker of one or the other linguistic varieties. It encompasses both linguistic varieties and is dependent on context. Prestige, in turn, emerges in light of the disposition toward the distinctive linguistic variety. Regarding linguistic prestige John Earl Josephs writes that "[i]ndividuals learn standard languages in order to increase their personal standing. And 'eloquence' in the use of language almost universally functions as a mantle of power."[9]

In the colonial context this assertion retains its validity. According to colonial thought new regions could only be controlled by a linguistic approach and appropriation of these regions and their inhabitants. Thomas Stolz et al. describe the German colonial context as follows:

> Linguistic communication with the colonized was [. . .] essential; in the absence of a sufficient base of German language skills among the indigenous peoples in the protected areas, because of the unwillingness to acquire language forms that established the relationship with the languages of other colonial powers, and due to the almost total ignorance of the colonized peoples' native languages on the part of the Germans, colonial communication proved to be a problem of massive proportions that had surely not been reflected before.[10]

The distribution of power associated with colonization is put into perspective in this quotation. With regard to the language use during the colonial era, it could be inferred that colonial rulers also learned local languages in the colonies because they sought to attain prestige. Proper acquisition of a distinctive linguistic variety could have been viewed as a demonstration of strength, not only in the metropolis but also in the colony. This is because "[s]omeone may have limited ability in H[igh variety], but still regard it as a more fitting and prestigious variety."[11] It is easy to understand, then, that the colonial rulers would never have wanted to allow their dominant position vis-à-vis the native peoples to be diminished as the result of a low linguistic variety. Colonial authority could be strengthened through the instrument of language. The fact that "language [is] a condition for the exertion of power, indeed it is itself a power"[12] proves quite true in the German "protectorates." From this it is reasonable to reach the conclusion that any colonized person who confronted this instrument of power through an indirect course of action was acting "subversively," that is to say, self-affirmingly. In this manner the colonized attempted to torpedo the colonial power.

Linguistic, self-aware, and self-affirming forms of actions were not rare on the part of the colonized. In order to elaborate on the actions that led the Beti to repeat the linguistic errors of their foreign conversation partners, I will engage with the writings of Zenker and Dominik on the one hand, as well with some songs that arose at that time. Zenker and Dominik were the most important administrators of the so-called Yaunde-Station, in that they both managed the area from 1889 to 1910. Many statements that are discussed in my article stem from their writings. The testimony of a person who has been told the experiences and adventures of the German colonial era by eyewitnesses will also be presented in this article. Finally, I have integrated the former system of communication with talking drums.

The Lingua Franca of the Cameroonian Hinterlands

Brigitte Weber writes that Cameroon is ninth out of 218 countries of the world on a list ranking linguistic diversity from highest to lowest.[13] Because of this multilingualism, communication between Europeans and indigenous peoples, as well as among the indigenous peoples from different territories within the colonial context, was unimaginable without a lingua franca. Whereas Pidgin English was a lingua franca in and around Douala, other languages such as Hausa or Wandala were used in various regions of the hinterlands. At that time Mongo Ewondo was the lingua franca in the Beti language area. Bernd Heine calls this language *"Bulu bediliva* [. . .], or *pidgin Ewondo* or *Ewondo populaire* [and explains that] the evolution of this language is linked to travel, urbanization, and commerce."[14] Mongo Ewondo is still spoken today on occasion among the Beti. Its usage occurs exclusively in multilingual groups and under the abovementioned conditions. As a general rule, use of this language does not lead to significant social relationships between the participants. In order for a conversation to take place in this dialect, at least two of the conditions mentioned by Heine must be fulfilled, conditions that are requisites for any pidgin language. This means that the relationships between the participants must deal with commerce, travel, and/or urbanization. Kouega also explores the question of when Mongo Ewondo is used. In doing so he differentiates between native speakers and second-language speakers of the Beti languages:

> [. . .] Beti speakers [are] found in Cameroon in the forest zone in the southern half of the country [. . .]. Second language users of Beti, who are mainly immigrants who reside in—or people who visit—the East and the South provinces [regions], speak a simplified variety of the language commonly referred to as *Petit Ewondo* or *Mongo Ewondo*.[15]

We can see that Mongo Ewondo is not a native language for any speaker. Although Kouega explains by whom, how, and where Mongo Ewondo is spoken today, he remains unsure of the conditions under which this lingua franca evolved. The excerpt furthermore demonstrates that Mongo Ewondo is indeed a means of communication, but that it has no written component. Its transmission occurs therefore orally. It also seems beyond a doubt that the oral transmission of Cameroonian languages is decreasing in everyday use due to the ever increasing prominence of the official languages (English and French). As a result, Mongo Ewondo appears to be dying out much faster than local languages that are still transmitted orally. During the German colonial era, however, Mongo Ewondo was very widespread. Ewondo, which is one of the three most commonly spoken Cameroonian languages today, was one of the Beti languages suggested by colonizers for the national language. The reason for this has to do with the fact that the Ewondo language was spoken by the Pallottines (members of a Society of Apostolic Life within the Roman Catholic Church), the protection forces, and by the leaders of the German expeditions.[16] Ewondo acquired this status with the help of the Pallottines' translation of the Bible. The remaining Beti communities had to make do with this translation of the Bible, as all Beti languages are mutually comprehensible.

Communication of the Duala and Beti with the Germans and their foreign porters was difficult. The colonists had to learn the local languages as well, despite the services of their translators. One of these colonists is Hans Dominik.

In 1895 Dominik (1870–1910) replaced his predecessor Zenker as manager of the "Yaunde"-Station. During his fifteen-year term he wrote two books depicting his Cameroonian adventures and experiences. In *Kamerun*, a variety of languages are present that serve either to facilitate or to alleviate the communication among the various protagonists. These are English, or rather Pidgin English,[17] German, Arabic, and Mongo Ewondo.[18]

Mongo Ewondo served as the typical language of communication for conversational and contractual purposes between Dominik and local leaders. Like his predecessor Zenker, Dominik endeavored to acquire the local languages in order to interact better with the Beti and to eliminate the need for an interpreter. Beti languages were very important, as the local leaders spoke neither German nor English as a result of their limited contact with the coastal area and Westerners. In this context a modified variety of local languages emerged. During the process of acquisition of the Beti languages, errors occurred in the Germans' and soldiers' use of the language, errors that could have been corrected by native speakers. Instead, linguistic mistakes made by the colonizers and their foreign assistants were knowingly repeated by native speakers in their interactions with the nonnative speakers. Two significant motivations are at the root of this deliberate repetition of mistakes. Looking at the modern use of Mongo Ewondo it seems that, on the one hand, there was the desire to facilitate communication with the "stranger." McColl Millar suggests that, regarding the deliberate use of the low variety, "preachers [. . .] might use a 'folksy' tone in order to get their point across, employing the low variety to make them appear closer to the people" (3). It is incontrovertible here that the Germans wanted to approach the local populations through language, albeit not via the low variety. The low variety and the lingua franca accomplish the same function. On the other hand, however, the local population ridiculed the colonizers by deliberately repeating their linguistic errors. This indicates a contemptuous attitude toward the colonizers. Through various interactions the parlance of Mongo Ewondo was established, without limiting the Beti languages to native speakers. This lingua franca developed out of linguistic contact.[19] As a result of this, Mongo Ewondo contains all the characteristics of those lingua francas that, as Peter Mühlhäusler explains, "emerge as vehicles of intercommunication between speakers of many different languages."[20] In other words, pidgin languages or lingua francas arise out of the confluence of people with different origins and native languages. Regarding the emergence of a lingua franca during the colonial era, Carl Meinhof writes in the year 1920:

> Because of the great linguistic fragmentation that prevails in our colonies, the use of commercial languages is indispensable if one wants to interact beyond tribal boundaries. The European is understandably neither capa-

ble nor willing to learn the languages of each individual tribe with which he wants to do business. As a result he makes use of these commercial languages and even helps them to develop and proliferate further.[21]

Europeans were not always aware of the linguistic nuances in the colonies, where participants developed a simplified language with an often limited lexicon. This language resulted from their respective native languages and the various relationships (work, commerce, travel, etc.).

In Dominik's *Kamerun*, numerous aspects of linguistic modifications can be found. For example, during an encounter the local leaders recount to Dominik the horrors and atrocities they experienced at the hands of the second-in-command during Dominik's vacation. Dominik attempts to duplicate their complaints in his book in both the original language as well as directly reproduced with the accent.

"'*Ah, Dominik, commander abě*' (Oh yes, Dominik, the commander is an evil man)."[22]

In Dominik's rendition the staging of a personal communication situation shows through, one which, on the one hand, illustrates the features of Mongo Ewondo; on the other hand Domonik's level of comprehension is made clear. The author himself translates the reproduced words into German and employs the faulty language in doing so. The English substantive *commander* functions in the "Yaunde" sentence as a loanword. What is also striking about this sentence is that a predicate is missing. The adjective *abě* comes right after the subject. In Ewondo the sentence would read: "*Ah, Dominik, commander a ne abě.*" Not only the sentence structure of the resulting spoken "Ndjobi-Ewondo" but also its translation is worth of research. A verbatim translation of this pejorative compound word is indicative of the incorrect terminology used by non-native speakers; "Ndjobi-Ewondo" could be understood as "*ripped* Ewondo." Further excerpts from *Kamerun* provide insight into this dialect:

"'Kata kata, madinge wa abui' (I love you)." (176)

[Kata kata, ma ding wa abui][23]

This sentence is characterized by a conjugation error, for the personal pronoun is combined with the finite verb form. The same mistake is made in the next sentence:

"'*Mawuo, mawuo*' (I died)." (200)

The proper form is as follows:

[*mə wuo (Help! Help!)*)]

Aside from the conjugation error the reader is also confronted with a misunderstanding, since the sentence was translated literally. The transcribed distress signal would normally be translated as "Help!" A similar error arises in this next sentence:

"*'Dominik, wasu'* (are you back)." (239)

[*Dominik, u bad ye so?*]

This phrase is more of a statement ("you're coming") that has nothing to do with the question indicated, even if the author did understand the meaning of the posed question. In this respect the reader is faced not only with an erroneous translation but also with a divergence from the Ewondo. Another sentence more worthy of investigation is the following:

"Amba stood still, turned halfway around and pointed his hand forward towards the elephants: '*Massa, wajene?'* (Master, do you see?)" (265)

[*Massa, u / wa jɛni?*]

It is interesting to find in this sentence the word "Massa," which originates from Pidgin English. The use of this word reveals how languages enrich their vocabularies through borrowings. The author claims to be citing the words of his colleagues. It is difficult to say, however, which of the abovementioned sentences were really formulated as such and which were misunderstood and incorrectly transcribed by Dominik. Nevertheless we can be fairly certain that the reproduced quotations serve to illuminate the dialectal varieties of the Beti languages that were already suggested. For example, it is typical of such reduced linguistic forms to omit predicates from some sentences. The complaint already cited above by the local leaders illustrates this:

"*'Ah, Dominik, commander abĕ'* (Oh yes, Dominik, the commander is an evil man)" (173).

[Ah, Dominik, commander <u>a ne</u> abĕ mot]

If there is a verb in a sentence it is not always properly conjugated to match the subject, when the subject is plural. The following sentences serve as examples:

"*'Jaunde adinge fianga, adinge abok, beta abĕ abĕ abui.'* (We Yaunde love playing and dancing; war is very bad.).*"* (173).

[*Jaunde ba ding fianga, ba ding abok, bita bi ne abĕ abĕ abui.'*]

Instead of *bita* Dominik writes *beta*, a word that doesn't exist in the Beti languages. We can verify that Dominik's transcription is not the result of pronunciation by looking to Martin Heepes' *Jaunde Texte*[24] and Hermann Nekes' *Language of the Yaunde in Cameroon.*[25] Likewise the iterative use of the adjective *abĕ* before the adverb *abui* is evidence of a lower linguistic level, since the iteration in elevated speech does indeed make use of the superlative but excludes the use of an adverb. The next two sentences reveal a similar problem:

"*'Kata kata asú'* (Dominik is coming)" (180)

[*Kata kata a zù*]

"*'Bissimbi asú'* (The soldiers are coming)" (180).

[*Bəsimbi ba zù*]

The word "bissimbi," which is rendered as "soldiers," actually means "bad omen." "Besimbi," the proper word for "soldiers," sounds very similar but is quite different. Furthermore the verb is conjugated in the third person singular. Dominik remains unaware of the hybrid nature of the "Yaunde language." We can see from his transcription that there is no differentiation between the personal pronoun and the finite verb form. Both are combined together in every instance. Regarding Cameroon's already quite complex linguistic situation of the colonial era, Brigitte Weber explains that the local linguistic fragmentation throughout the entire colony was very difficult for the colonizers to master.[26]

It is also noteworthy that there are untranslated sentences and phrases in Dominik's transcriptions and translations, whenever he was evidently unsure of their meaning. In light of this the following sentence can be mentioned: "The man [Zumbeganti] 'handed me the palm wine-filled gourd with the words

Awou maha'" (242). In this sentence the reader must deal not only with a mispronunciation—or rather an incorrect transcription—but also with an untranslated sentence. Instead of "Essomba-Ngonti" Dominik writes "Zumbeganti." *Awou maha* can be translated as "very dry, mister!" Additionally, the Beti's pet name for Dominik "Kata-Kata" (the unseizable) remains unexplained in the text for his target German readers. Moreover there is absolutely no commentary in the text. Although the name "Kata-Kata" sounds positive we cannot ignore the fact that it could contain a derisive dimension, especially if we consider the general context.

Interpreters and Language Mistakes

Considering the fact that the colonists could not work without the aid of interpreters, it is reasonable to conclude that the Germans did not overestimate their language abilities. Dominik confirms the important role played by the interpreters: "Often the success of an entire expedition relies on a reliable interpreter" (189). Due to their important role, I will present here both of the interpreters who were active in this area. This will make clear that the linguistic errors were avoidable.

When the first German expedition reached the Cameroonian capital city, it transpired through contact with the Beti that the Beti languages were intelligible to the porters and soldiers from the Southern Cameroons. Because of this, these soldiers and porters were very helpful during early negotiations with Chief Essono Ela, the first leader in the Beti language area with whom the Germans made contact. Among them was Martin Paul Samba (1875–1914), who was also from the Southern Cameroons. Samba is regarded as the first significant Cameroonian interpreter in the Beti area. Curt Morgen introduces him as such: "I was followed [on the way to Yaunde] by my servant Zampa, an approximately eighteen year-old strapping young fellow who, during later trips with me, proved himself to be a most dependable person thanks to his dauntlessness, devotedness, and care."[27] If Samba did become a "respected and important figure during the expedition" (30), as Morgen claims, this is not just a result of his reputedly evident loyalty but also because of his role as an interpreter. This role is even clearer in Dominik's book where he writes: Samba "went with the commander to the coast because he was proficient in the Yaunde languages and was to serve as an interpreter in the negotiations with the natives."[28] It is interesting that both Morgen and Dominik refer to Samba as "Zampa." This is how Dominik describes his colleague:

Incidentally, the good *Zampa* is [. . .] chiefly to thank for the fact that I have settled into Cameroon so quickly. *Zampa*, [. . .] was brought to Germany by Morgen, where he became a soldier of the Garde Fusilier in Berlin. He then returned [. . .] to Cameroon and was appointed as sergeant in the army, where he improved his excellent language skills and knowledge of the country thanks to the occasional use of them.[29]

It is easy to see that "Zampa" is a mispronunciation of Samba.[30] Equally incorrect are the transcriptions of Chief Essono Ela and Chief Ombga Bissogo's names, referred to by the colonists as "Zonu" and "Mbasamsoko," respectively. Regarding Essono Ela Dominik writes: "I received an especially warm reception from the old Chief Zonu of Voghe-Da, an approximately 70 year-old, yellow, rather sunken-in old man" (71). Even the family name of this man, who is presented as an "honest man" (72), is pronounced differently than by the Beti. Instead of "Mvog-Ada" Dominik hears "Voghe-Da." In the process Dominik repeats a transcription by Zenker (34). The colonist claims, however, to have had very good contact with Essono Ela. The following was written regarding the resistance leader Omgba Bissogo:[31]

> *Mbasamsoko* would ostentatiously drum to him [the French assistant Rabischung] every evening that he would cut *fufuge*'s hair (they called Rabischung "elephant skin" because he looked a little wrinkled), would make him into a slave and would send him away naked with a cutlass in the hand with which to cut grass for the horses every morning. (174)

Reproduced in the drum language, the degree of aggressiveness, and especially the degradation of the German representatives at the hands of Ombga Bissoga, is very obvious. From these passages we can conclude that the linguistic errors of the colonists concerned not only the names of locations but also the vocabulary, grammar, and proper names. Like her husband, Samba's wife Meta took over interpretation for some of the negotiations carried out under Dominik's leadership. Samba's successor was Karl Atangana (1876–1943), referred to by Dominik as *Attang*.

The Colonial Exposure to Language Deficiencies

The various strategies developed by the colonists in communication situations with the local population indicate that the Germans were not entirely unaware of the Beti's persiflage. Nonetheless the colonists remained inferior to the colonized in the area of communication. The statements of the colonizers also demonstrate that they mistrusted the Beti. Zenker writes, for example: "The character of the Yaúnde deviates little from that of the average negro character. They are superstitious, deceitful, greedy, and at every opportunity they steal and lie."[32] The stereotypes in Zenker's statement will not be discussed here. What is relevant about it is that it reveals a series of insubordinate reactions of the local populace toward the colonists. It also seems most likely that the colonists attempted to thwart the Betis' conduct. For example, due to the linguistic difficulties that accompanied the Beti languages, the colonists arrived at the idea of combining Mongo Ewondo with nonverbal forms and resorted to the use of the talking drums, envoys, or Cameroonian partners of the colonial rulers.

As already explained above, talking drums served to transmit news and information across relatively far distances. In the opinions of those interviewed this method of communication was supposedly quite mysterious to the colonists at the beginning of the occupation of the area. Eyewitnesses of the time also confirm that the language drums were quite popular with the colonists. As part of a field study from September 2008, older residents of the current-day district of Mvolyé were interviewed as eyewitnesses to events of the colonial era. They affirm that the first station leaders liked this method of communication for corresponding with local leaders. It can be assumed that the colonists' interest in the drum is due to the fact that they initially did not understand it. For this reason they reportedly increased the opportunities for such drumming in order to better acquaint themselves with the meanings of the drum sounds. The prerequisite for comprehending the drum message, however, was an understanding of the local languages. This is because the drum sounds were codified cultural and linguistic signals. In light of the only approximate mastery of the local languages, this attempt to understand the drum signals appears very ambitious today. Those interviewed were also in agreement that envoys were only employed in order to transmit information, especially if one of the Europeans needed credible or confidential news from a leader, or whenever it was a matter of conveying an unofficial order. Conveying such information by means of the talking drum, whose sounds were understandable to most of the Beti, would have negated the confidentiality of the messages. In all other cases the envoys were not used.

Some of the interviewees affirmed that envoys were employed in particular for personal matters of superiors—for example, love affairs.[33] Regarding the female Cameroonian partners of German administrators in the Yaunde area, it is important to note that local women played an ambivalent role in the German-Cameroonian cultural encounters. In addition to their "official" position as partner they also, according to Laburthe-Tolra, acted as spies for their German partners. He explains that they were supporters of colonization in that they revealed secrets of their community to the colonial rulers. With regard to Zenker, the anthropologist writes:

> An Ewondo girl played an important role in Zenker's life, pursuant to a tactic later authorized by the governor von Putkammer [*sic*]. She served him as a political "antenna" by explaining the intentions of the local populace and the *drum sounds* to him, and by helping him to learn the *language* and customs of her people.[34]

From this excerpt we can see that the colonial administration acknowledged the political relevance of relationships with local women and employed these strategically. Relationships with the native women were especially promoted by von Puttkamer. Thanks to female Cameroonians' service as spies, the colonizers were able to achieve political advantages: They discovered and thwarted conspirators, thereby sustaining an unbridled and successful occupation and management of the hinterlands. The Cameroonian women were also reported to have been most helpful in decoding the drum signals. In order to understand the content of such messages, several colonists became involved with Cameroonian women since they did not consider male language aids to be as trustworthy. After all, the security and advancement of the colonial undertaking depended on being able to control the ongoing information, making knowledge of the drum language vitally important.[35] The drum language accounted to a certain extent for the relationships between the Cameroonian women and the Germans. In addition to Embolo, Zenker's second wife, Laburthe-Tolra mentions another woman whose role at the station was rather significant: "Ngoso, Onambele Ela's daughter, also played the role of intendant and informant at the 'station'" (8).

We can see that the Beti had precise knowledge of the function of every woman. It would be misguided, however, to assert that the local female partners of the colonizers were defenseless subjects who submitted in everything to the will of their partners. It would also be incorrect to believe that the colonial rulers conceived their relationships with Cameroonian women from this perspective only.[36] The example of Zenker, who didn't leave either of his wives until his death in 1922, is rather illuminating. The interviewees also tell that Cameroonian partners of German colonizers spoke Mongo Ewondo in conversations with Europeans. This is a likely assumption if we consider that the Beti could not speak any European languages due to their limited contact with the coast.

From a purely Eurocentric perspective, which is lacking the pragmatic and largely dependent aspects discussed above, relationships with local women were viewed as a contemptible by-product of colonization. The uneducated views of those in the metropolis are indicated here with words such as "tropicalization" or "indigenization." From a racist perspective it was presumed that every German who maintained a relationship with a Cameroonian woman was, in this way, adopting local customs. With the help of this inevitable process, however, Zenker, as one example, was able to broaden his knowledge regarding the customs of Beti communities. At every opportunity the colonists attempted to appropriate local customs. For this reason, the so-called tropicalization included changes in eating habits as well. The colonial administrators made strategic use of such actions to gain sympathy from the Beti, as well as to avoid potential conflicts before they occurred. Officer Puttkamer, for example, demanded a princess from the Sultan Njoya in western Cameroon, one whom he presumably wanted to marry. Instead of a princess the sultan deceitfully provided him with a young woman from the neighboring vicinity. Puttkamer, clueless about this, went on to produce a daughter with the woman.[37]

Further communicative actions were carried out between the colonists and the Beti in an attempt to supplement or strengthen the fragmentary communication. One example of this is the various items exchanged by the Germans and Beti in order to please one another. The more excited one was for a meeting, the greater and more valuable the gifts. The gift exchange had a political dimension by allowing each party to exert a certain pressure on the other. In this context, gift giving was also a means of establishing trust. It is precisely for this reason that the leaders practiced an old custom with the Germans that still prevails in the Beti communities today. It had long been tradition in the Beti area to assign one's children to trusted friends. This practice was extended to the colonizers as well; the interpreters Samba and Atangana were handed over first to Kund, then Tappenbeck, and finally to Dominik. In this article such actions that demonstrate friendship are also viewed as diplomatic actions.

In addition to these symbolic arrangements manifested through gift giving, everyday signs helped to fill in the language gaps whenever a communication failure was anticipated due to cultural reasons. The desire for "tropicalization" and the conspicuousness of certain cultural aspects of life forced one to be creative.

In order to demonstrate further how the Beti interacted with the German colonizers as self-aware and self-serving agents, I will look at three things. First, I will show how Mongo Ewondo was perceived by the Germans. Second, I will explain why the language aids for the colonists did not correct linguistic errors in this context. Finally, I will discuss how the local population took advantage of the colonists' linguistic deficiencies as a way to ridicule them.

Zenker describes the Beti languages as follows: "Those tribes of the Yaúnde that are known as the Fang people are broken into many smaller divisions; they differ from one another in name, though they have the same language, customs, and traditions."[38] This is an astonishing viewpoint when one considers how lacking Zenker's understanding of the Beti languages was. At any rate it shows how the Germans disregarded the native perspective of differentiating the Beti languages from one another.[39]

In languages with no distinct writing system, standardization—or rather the acquisition of a distinctive language variety—occurs deliberately in institutions that have pedagogical or didactic functions. These errors had obviously not occurred to Dominik due to his external perception—as was the case with other colonists, for even after living among the Beti for seven years he continued to marvel at Zenker's approximate language skills. Referring to his reception at the station by his predecessor, Dominik writes: "Zenker [. . .] instructed the porters in the Yaunde language where to place their loads."[40] In 1913, Günter Tessmann looked into Zenker's transcriptions of the Ewondo language. He came to a rather negative conclusion:

Much of what he [Zenker] says is completely unintelligible. Zenker did attempt to clarify things through native designations, but the attempt failed. Disregarding the fact that one must first translate the Yaunde words from the Saxon dialect into standard German (*ngu* instead of *nku, infoun* instead of *mvum*), they are frequently so inaccurate that it's not even possible to guess what he meant.[41]

What is interesting about this excerpt is that Tessmann, who is amused at Zenker's transcriptions—since it's not even possible to "guess" what is meant—also fails to properly correct the word "Yaunde." This is not surprising, however, when we consider that the native speaker Karl Atangana, who was employed as an informant, allowed such errors to slip past.

Atangana's actions seem paradigmatic of the interpreters' actions toward the colonists, though this was not necessarily the case for all of the colonized. Due to his term as a language assistant in Hamburg (1911–13) and his collaboration on the publication *Jaunde Texte* with Paul Messi—his successor at the Colonial Institute—Atangana is regarded as one of the most important transmitters of the Ewondo language aside from the missionaries.[42] He was successful at establishing the Ewondo language as a lingua franca, making it far more widely used than the languages of the other communities in his region. In light of the linguistic errors that enabled the development of Mongo Ewondo, Atangana's legendary devotedness and faithfulness to the colonists is somewhat dubious. The erroneous word "Yaunde" is even reproduced without question in the title of the work (*Jaunde Texte*), although at that time the Europeans understood the "Yaunde language" to refer to both the Beti language as well as the hybrid language that developed out of it. Even though every native speaker could differentiate between the Beti languages and their own dialectical variety, the foreign speakers remained unaware of the nuances.

A sentence taken from Morgen's *Durch Kamerun* provides insight into the interpreters' method of operations at that time. Referring to his first arrival in "Yaunde" Morgen copies down a stanza from a song that was sung in his honor:

> "'*Ntangani, Ntangani tellesen'* etc., 'The white man is coming, the white man is coming and is good' etc."[43]

This stanza from the song allows for two possible interpretations. On the one hand we could assume that the content was simply mistranscribed. Even when there is a subject, there must still be a personal pronoun after the conjugated verb (*"telle"*). Furthermore the preposition before the adverbial locative (*"u"*) is missing. In this case the proper transcription would be the following:

> ["'*Ntangani, Ntangani u telle a zen'* The white man is coming."]

On the other hand it is possible that the sentence was transcribed properly, but only if it were glossed over in translation. The actual meaning of *"Ntangani, Ntangani tellesen"* is "the white man is at a dead end." Depending on his interests, the circumstances, and his own understanding of what was said, it is possible for an interpreter to relate something either correctly or incorrectly. On occasion, overconfident colonizers were ridiculed by their colleagues without being aware of it. In *La Marseillaise de mon enfance*,[44] a book by Jean-Martin Tchaptchet describing his childhood years during the 1930s and 1940s in Cameroon, there is an illuminating example. The reader encounters a case where the father of the narrated "I," due to his official intermediary function as interpreter for the French colonial administration, represents himself as being much more powerful than the colonizers who believed themselves to be so superior. The assumed power of the French colonial rule is trivialized and undermined when the father of the narrated "I" depicts one of the French administrative officials as inept while translating his speech into the local language (*Mend'umba*), which the official did not understand. Meanwhile the interpreter directed his audience to applaud the speaker. Without a doubt the colonial administrator perceived the applause as general agreement with what he was saying. This approbation, however, was only for the interpreter who denigrated the administrator. From this we can see that Mongo Ewondo, which developed during the colonial era, contained a self-affirming dimension at least in the face of the German colonial dehumanization.[45] This hypothesis is even more plausible when we examine the statements of the locals toward the colonists. The latent self-assertion of the repeated linguistic errors occasionally appears here even more distinctly. These words furthermore reveal the actual disposition of the colonized toward the German representatives.

During an informal discussion in 1995 Mevengué Ntsama (1928–96), the son of one of Dominik's porters, shared with me an inspiring song that is relevant for the self-assertion of the colonized people's language. It was sung by his father Ayissi Etah (1890–1967)[46] and his father's comrades during their military education in "Yaunde land." These armed porters, who occasionally had to fight as soldiers, were able to make fun of the clueless German instructor with this song. During drills the colonist gave them orders in Mongo Ewondo:

Mina ke yo tétélé!	You sleep standing!
Mina dja dzá!	You join in song!

After the first order the porters who were standing would close their eyes and pretend to sleep, tottering and staggering around. After the second order the following song was often sung in Eton:

Zá kán y mô bezimi nâ	You're a strange soldier!
Téh ngál, téh ikpa!	You have neither musket nor helmet!
Á má nung medjòk á tób'li	After all that palm wine at lunchtime
Á ze wéh bôt l'ibòb y!	You surround us as if possessed!
Zá kán y mô bezimi nâ	You're a strange soldier!
Téh ngál, téh ikpa!	You have neither musket nor helmet!

Á mádi mbòk esómló	You greedily devoured termites
Á ze wéh bôt é minsuli!	Now your ass makes disgusting popping sounds!

The German instructor, who wanted to become more knowledgeable of the "Yaunde language," apparently never grasped the ridiculing content of the song. We could therefore assume that the standard languages were not completely intelligible to the colonists and their foreign colleagues. Consequently, it is not surprising that the Beti incorporated foreign expressions in order to communicate with nonnative speakers. As already indicated, porters were given a military education. If we consider how important and crucial discipline is in the army, the scope of the porters' self-assertion in the song by referring to the colonists' language deficiencies becomes much clearer. The extremely pejorative and degrading meaning of these stanzas proves that the colonized people were not passive, helpless, and powerless subjects; under colonial administration they defended their own interests and thereby positioned themselves socially (see Michael Pesek and Michelle Moyd in this anthology). The song even attempts to move in an opposite course on the symbolic level.

Conclusion

In this article I have shown two things: First, that the confluence of the Beti communities with the German colonists resulted in the development of an independent dialect, Mongo Ewondo, in and around the Cameroonian capital city due to an increase in trade relationships and a rise in communication situations. The variety of Beti languages, which appears to be decreasing nowadays, emerged as a result of native speakers knowingly repeating mistakes made by nonnative speakers. The German representatives, despite their various attempts and their goal-oriented approach, did not manage to master the variety of the Beti languages. Second, I have shown that this dialect was spoken by people in the local communities for two very different reasons. On the one hand they wanted to alleviate comprehension for nonnative speakers, and on the other hand they degraded the colonists and nonnative speakers and trivialized the colonial rule. On a purely linguistic level, the colonial rulers with their foreign porters and soldiers did not manage to comprehend and internalize the nuances of the Beti languages. For this reason the colonists regarded the language family of the Beti languages as a single language. For the Beti the use of this dialect, which had arisen during interactions with the foreigners, was therefore ambivalent. Through the use of this pidgin language they developed a subtle method of self-affirmation that revealed individual interests vis-à-vis the colonial rulers, such that their apparent submission was really only the means to an end.

NOTES

1. I would like to thank my friends Julia Boger and Bakpa Mimboabe for their extremely valuable assistance in revising this article. They spared no effort in sending me literature from Germany.

2. Kum'a Ndumbe III, "Les traités camerouno-germaniques 1884–1907," in *Africa and Germany: From Colonisation to Cooperation 1884–1986 (The Case of Cameroon)*, ed. Kum'a Ndumbe III (Yaounde: AfricAvenir, 1986), 44.

3. Kum'a Ndumbe III, "Les traités camerouno-germaniques 1884–1907," 59.

4. Frederic E. Quinn, "Rain Forest Encounters: The Beti Meet the Germans 1887–1916," *Introduction to the History of Cameroon in the Nineteenth and Twentieth Centuries*, ed. Martin Njeuma (Hong Kong: Macmillan, 1989), 88.

5. Philippe Laburthe-Tolra, *Yaoundé d'après Zenker (1895). Le plan de 1892. L'article de 1895. Reproduction du texte allemand et des 6 planches originales, avec un portrait de l'auteur* (Dijon: Presses Universitaires, 1970), 14.

6. The people who live in that area are part of the Beti communities.

7. Jean-Paul Kouega, *A Dictionary of Cameroon English Usage* (Oxford: Lang, 2007), 33.

8. Robert McColl Millar, *Language, Nation and Power: An Introduction* (New York: Palgrave Macmillan, 2005), 3.

9. John Earl Joseph, *Eloquence and Power: The Rise of Language Standard and Standard Languages* (London: Frances Printer, 1987), 43.

10. Thomas Stolz, Christina Vossmann, and Barbara Dewein, "Kolonialzeitliche Sprachforschung und das Forschungsprogramm Koloniallinguistik: Eine Einführung," *Kolonialzeitliche Sprachforschung. Die Beschreibung afrikanischer und ozeanischer Sprachen zur Zeit der deutschen Kolonialherrschaft*, ed. Thomas Stolz, Christina Vossmann, and Barbara Dewein (Berlin: Akademie Verlag, 2011), 10. All renderings of German citations into English are, unless otherwise noted, produced by the translator.

11. Robert McColl Millar, *Language, Nation and Power*, 3.

12. Josef Klein, "Sprache und Macht," 16.2.2010, http://www.bpb.de/apuz/32949/sprache-und-macht?p=0, last accessed 19.7.2012.

13. Brigitte Weber, "Deutsch-Kamerun: Einblicke in die sprachliche Situation der Kolonie und den deutschen Einfluss auf das Kameruner Pidgin-Englisch," *Kolonialzeitliche Sprachforschung*, ed. Stolz et al., 113.

14. Bernd Heine, *Pidgin-Sprachen im Bantu-Bereich* (Berlin: Dietrich Reimer, 1973), 58.

15. Kouega, *A Dictionary of Cameroon English Usage*, 33, emphasis in original.

16. Jean Tabi-Manga, *Les politiques linguistiques du Cameroun. Essai d'aménagement linguistique* (Paris: Karthala, 2000), 30.

17. A dialectical variety of the English language.

18. Literally: "Little Ewondo."

19. Gunther von Hagen, *Kurzes Handbuch zum Negerenglisch an der Küste Westafrikas unter besonderer Berücksichtigung von Kamerun* (Berlin: Dingeldey und Werres, 1913).

20. Peter Mühlhäusler, *Pidgin and Creole Linguistics* (London: University of Westminster Press, 1997), 2.

21. Carl Meinhof, "Handelssprachen," *Deutsches Kolonial-Lexikon*, vol. 2, ed. Heinrich Schnee (Leipzig: Quelle und Meyer, 1920), 33.

22. Hans Dominik, *Kamerun. Sechs Kriegs- und Friedensjahre in deutschen Tropen* (Berlin: Stilke, 1911), 173.

23. Bracketed sentences are corrections provided by the author.

24. Karl Atangana and Paul Messi, *Jaunde-Texte. Experimentalphonetische Untersuchungen über die Tonhöhen im Jaunde und einer Einführung in die Jaunde-Sprache*, ed. Martin Heepe (Hamburg: Friederichsen, 1919).

25. Hermann Nekes, *Die Sprache der Jaunde in Kamerun* (Berlin: Reimer, 1913).

26. Weber, "Deutsch-Kamerun," 114.

27. Curt Morgen, *Durch Kamerun: Von Süd bis Nord. Reisen und Forschungen im Hinterlande 1889 bis 1891* (Leipzig: Brockhaus, 1893), 30. Curt Ernst von Morgen (1858–1928) was a German officer and explorer.

28. Dominik, *Kamerun*, 175.

29. Dominik, *Kamerun*, 42, my emphasis.

30. Cf. Victor Julius Ngoh, *History of Cameroon since 1800* (Limbe: Pressbook, 1996), 107. Despite the significant recognition he had received, Samba was executed in August 1914 with other Cameroonian leaders under the allegation of treason.

31. Ombga Bissogo was one of the leaders in the area who took up arms against German colonialism. In 1895 he led his soldiers into a battle against the German colonists. He won the battle but was later betrayed by his wife during a German attack on his village of Mvog Betsi. Ombga Bissoga was deported to the Yaunde-Station where he was arrested and later executed.

32. Georg Zenker, "Yaúnde," in *Yaoundé d'après Zenker (1895). Le plan de 1892. L'article de 1895. Reproduction du texte allemand et des 6 planches originales, avec un portrait de l'auteur*, ed. Philippe Laburthe-Tolra (Dijon: Presses Universitaires, 1970), 41.

33. On September 1, 2008, the author met with two of the interviewees in Yaoundé: J.-J. Atangana (age forty-nine), grandchild of the leader Karl Atangana, and J. E. Mbarga (age fifty-four), curator of the Karl-Atangana Library.

34. Laburthe-Tolra, *Yaúnde*, 7, my translation and emphasis.

35. Germain Nyada, "Deutsch-kamerunische Kommunikationssituationen: Unterhaltungen mit den 'Jaunde' im Regenwald (1890–1910)," *Jahrbuch für Europäische Überseegeschichte*, vol. 9, ed. Markus A. Denzel et al. (Wiesbaden: Harrassowitz, 2009), 225–34.

36. Cf. Dag Henrichsen, "'. . . undesirable in the protectorate . . . not completely without morals.' 'Mischehen' und deren Nachkommen im Visier der Kolonialverwaltung in Deutsch-Südwestafrika," *Frauen in den deutschen Kolonien*, ed. Marianne Bechhaus-Gerst and Mechthild Leutner (Berlin: Ch. Links, 2009), 80–90.

37. Peter Heller, *Deutsche Kolonien. DVD 1. Mulattin Else oder Eine deutsche Art zu lieben* (Munich: Multimedia, 2007).

38. Zenker, *Yaúnde*, 36.

39. Kouega, *A Dictionary of Cameroon English Usage*, 33.

40. Dominik, *Kamerun*, 65.

41. Günter Tessmann, *Die Pangwe. Völkerkundliche Monographie eines westafrikanischen Negerstammes. Ergebnisse der Lübecker Pangwe-Expedition 1907–1909 und früherer Forschungen 1904–1907* (Berlin: Wasmuth, 1913), xvi.

42. Jean Tabi-Manga, *Les politiques linguistiques du Cameroun*, 29.

43. Morgen, *Durch Kamerun*, 44.

44. Jean-Martin Tchaptchet, *La Marseillaise de mon enfance* (Paris: L'Harmattan, 2004), 37.

45. Albert Memmi, *Portrait du colonisé précédé de Portrait de colonisateur* (Paris: Corréa, 1957), 107.

46. The protagonist and his son are from the village of Melik, which is located 63 km (39 miles) north of the Cameroonian capital city.

Sex and Control in Germany's Overseas Possessions

Venereal Disease and Indigenous Agency

Daniel J. Walther

After Germany gained territories in Africa and the Pacific in the 1880s, the introduction of colonial rule brought political, economic, and social disruption to the populations directly and indirectly under German rule. One area where this was particularly evident was in the spread of sexual transmitted diseases (STDs) and in the public health campaign to stop their spread. Colonial physicians saw the proliferation of these diseases as undermining German attempts to establish and maintain colonial order. The efforts to combat their spread further justified German colonial rule and hence provided opportunities for Germany to extend its domination over its colonial subjects. However, much to the frustration of these doctors, the success of their policies largely depended on the actions of those at whom the various measures were directed.

Indeed, the decisions and behavior of non-elite indigenes directly impacted the efficacy of these programs. Some autochthons did not comply with German regulatory requirements for prostitutes; compulsory health examinations for indigenous laborers, soldiers, the wives of soldiers, and prostitutes; enforced medical treatments for those found infected; and educational programs. Their tactics and motivations varied, but collectively their non-violent, non-confrontational actions contributed to limiting the success of these various measures aimed at reducing spread of STDs, at least according to German health officials. Simultaneously, some indigenes did willingly register as prostitutes, allowed themselves to be examined for STDs, underwent treatment until cured, and heeded the health advice shared by German colonial physicians. Like those who did not conform to German expectations, they had their own motivations, but nonetheless they did contribute in part to the success of these measures.

In both types of responses, their actions do not necessary need to be viewed exclusively as either resistance to or compliance with German requirements and expectations. Rather, those who took a particular action also did so in accordance with their own agendas.[1] Consequently, this study examines how everyday indigenes responded to German public health measures to stop the spread of STDs, how their actions caused colonial authorities to adapt their approaches to combating this health concern, and ultimately how their practices impacted the efficacy of these measures. Moreover, it will also suggest the reasons that motivated individuals to pursue a particular action and, in doing so, will provide a glimpse into the impact colonialism had on the everyday lives of autochthonous peoples and the various ways they responded to these changes. Thus, this essay will give voice to those who experienced German colonialism every day, and further our understanding of the extent and simultaneously the limitations of German colonial hegemony throughout its overseas empire.

Overwhelmingly, the literature on indigenous responses to German colonialism explores the more obvious forms of opposition, namely, armed and collective. Moreover, those that do explore the actors also tend to focus on the elites.[2] These approaches are readily apparent in the burgeoning historiography of the Nama and Herero Wars in German Southwest Africa.[3] Thus, most do not examine the everyday encounters of commoners with their colonial interlopers. Andreas Eckert does do this to a degree in his *Die Duala und die Kolonialmächte*, but ultimately he focuses on elites within society.[4] In a case study, Philipp Prein explores non-violent opposition to German colonialism in Southwest Africa, yet it too focuses on collective action.[5]

As the works of James Scott and Detlev Peukert have shown, opposition to a hegemonic power manifested itself in a wide array of often apparently insignificant ways.[6] Obviously, outright resistance did take place in the colonial setting. However, there were also actions taken that were often non-violent and individualistic, usually amounting to nonconformity and not outright opposition or resistance. Even if there was an act of outright protest, it may not have been directed at the colonial system per se, but rather at a particular policy or action on the part of the authorities. However, when viewed collectively, these individual acts had a substantial impact on the colonial enterprise and revealed the degree to which the objects of control accepted or rejected the values being imposed upon them by colonial authorities. Moreover, "[w]hatever the response [of the colonized], we must not miss the fact that [their] action[s] . . . changed or narrowed the policy options available to the state."[7] Scott called these acts *"everyday forms of resistance."*[8]

The study of colonialism is of course not merely the story of the elite among both the colonized and the colonized. However, it is extremely difficult to access the voices of indigenous commoners, individuals who often had more regular contact with colonial authorities than elites did, and hence more opportunities to be influenced by them and to shape colonial policy. Generally speaking, historical documents that directly record their experiences often do not exist. Rather, their lives and experiences are recorded in the writings of others, often their colonial rulers. As Subaltern Studies has demonstrated it is possible to discern "fragments" or "traces" of suppressed narratives, the stories of the subaltern, in the records of the ruling elite.[9] Thus, in the case of German public health policies, in particular the fight against the spread of venereal diseases, the actions and behavior of indigenous commoners is found in the reports and essays of German colonial physicians. These documents provide a window into the colonial contact zones.

According to colonial doctors, STDs were widespread throughout Germany's overseas possessions and undermined German attempts to maintain viable colonies.[10] In describing the situation, colonial doctors often used apocalyptic language, such as "plague," to describe the impact of STDs.[11] First, STDs were seen as reducing the efficacy of colonial military personnel, both German and autochthonous and, hence, weakening one of Germany's vehicles for protecting its possessions from potential internal and external threats.[12] Second, officials noted that sexually transmitted diseases not only reduced productive capacity of existing labor force,[13] but they potentially also undermined future productivity by ostensibly contributing to declining birthrates among indigenous populations.[14] Finally, in some territories, STDs apparently threatened the health vitality of the German population as a whole, including those who were rulers in the colonies.[15]

While numerous factors contributed to the spread of STDs, including the introduction of aspects of European culture, such as promiscuity, colonial physicians placed primary responsibility for their dissemination on the behavior of indigenes.[16] Admittedly, colonial physicians did hold whites accountable for their spread.[17] Nonetheless, for these doctors, autochthonous attitudes and comportment played a salient role in the dissemination of STDs.[18] Consequently, most policies pursued to stop their spread focused on non-European populations. Particular attention was given to prostitutes because, as in Germany,[19] many colonial bureaucrats saw the body of the prostitute and these infectious diseases as synonymous.

In order to control the spread of STDs, colonial physicians pursued a variety of measures. These included education, the regulation of prostitution, and the regular examination of high-risk groups. These groups included not only prostitutes but also indigenous soldiers and laborers as well as the wives of these soldiers. If found infected, they underwent mandatory treatment until released by a physician. In several instances, the treatment required forced internment in specially designed buildings to prevent the escape of infected individuals.

Though much energy went into preventative educational activities, most physicians saw regular medical examinations as the primary vehicle for identifying carriers of STDs, that is, those responsible for their spread. Thus, in the colonies, indigenous soldiers and laborers were subjected to requisite health examinations.[20] Because medical officials quickly noted that these measures were essentially useless without an examination of women, prostitutes were required to report for regular medical examinations.[21] In places like East Africa and Cameroon, this also included soldiers' wives, whom German physicians viewed also as prostitutes.[22] The required registration of prostitutes facilitated the control of their health.[23] The obvious goal of the examinations was to identify infected individuals. If diagnosed with an STD, the individual underwent mandatory treatment until healed.[24]

According to various reports, it appeared that these measures contributed to limiting the spread of STDs. For instance, Dr. Heuermann noted that for 1902/03 "through the implemented measures it appears that in the past few months a reduction [in the cases of STDs] has taken place, at least in Duala."[25] Similarly, Dr. Steuber reported that "through these measures a considerable reduction in the number of new cases of venereal illnesses among Europeans and coloreds has been achieved at least in Dar es Salaam."[26]

Nevertheless, despite some apparent successes, most colonial physicians viewed their efforts as unsuccessful. For instance, though Steuber noted advances in Dar es Salaam, his report also indicated that on the coast the number of cases was still high, despite the "regular doctoral examination of soldiers and above all prostitutes."[27] Physicians elsewhere reported that their efforts failed to dampen the spread of STDs.[28]

In explaining the lack of success, colonial doctors reported the extreme difficulty they had in registering, examining, and treating all those suspected of prostitution or of spreading STDs. In Atakpame, Togo, for instance, the only way colonial officials could determine who was engaged in prostitution was by periodic sweeps through the town. Only those found would be registered by the police, be subjected to medical examination, and, if necessary, undergo medical treatment. On the February 16, 1914, sweep, seventy-three women were picked up. Forty-two of them were diagnosed with an STD.[29] No reports existed on how many avoided the sweep. Authorities did, however, complain that it was increasingly difficult to register all prostitutes because many engaged in what is known as opportunity prostitution.[30] In Lome, Togo, one doctor reported "through the expansion of opportunity prostitution the often pursued campaign [to stop the spread of STDs] was unfortunately unsuccessful."[31]

Physicians also noted that prostitutes often avoided medical control by simply leaving the area. As one physician in Cameroon, reported, "an earlier attempt to put all prostitutes in Duala under police control failed as a result of fluctuation of the population."[32] Similarly in Lome, Togo, another doctor wrote that prostitutes simply left the region.[33] Meanwhile, in Southwest Africa, a colleague stated that many prostitutes either did not register or moved from one area to another.[34] In the Marshall Islands, one medical official noted that the population there was always on the go, which made it impossible to regulate prostitution and hence the spread of venereal disease. He added that the only way to prevent the spread of STDs was to eliminate their freedom of movement, but this would most likely reduce the economic output of the colony.[35]

Moreover, even those who were diagnosed with an STD often left treatment before it was completed. For example, of the 468 indigenous cases initially treated for gonorrhea in East Africa in 1904/05, 56 were reported as "elsewhere" (*anderweitig*), implying they were no longer under German supervision. With regard to syphilis cases, five of the initial twenty-six cases were also reported as "elsewhere."[36] In response to this situation and similar behavior in the colonies over the years, colonial officials increasingly resorted to imprisoning behind fences or under armed guard autochthonous patients undergoing treatment.[37] Nevertheless, as Dr. Born in German New Guinea reported, this was still no guarantee that patients would complete their treatment.

> After the previous experience it would not be appropriate to treat all the sick in the Jabwor hospital. Despite all supervision the venereally infected from Ebon have had the opportunity to have sex both amongst themselves as well as with those outside [the hospital]. It has even transpired that a women infected with gonorrhea has dug under the fence in order to get outside.[38]

For most physicians, the main reason for their limited success was the behavior of the autochthonous populations. From their perspective, indigenes' "lax morals,"[39] "indolence,"[40] "ignorance,"[41] and even "indifference"[42] contributed significantly to spreading STDs.

These were obviously the perspectives of the colonizers, individuals who viewed autochthonous behavior through their own cultural lenses. But conspicuously absent from these reports were the voices of indigenes. Admittedly, it is difficult to know exactly their motivations, because their voices were usually not recorded unless they constituted a part of an official, that is, European, act, such as a court case or a formal meeting with colonial authorities. Consequently, their actions were only noted by colonial officials, most often either as statistics or in medical reports. As Alexandra Widmer has demonstrated, such documents legitimized the colonial presence because writing documents was an attempt by colonial authorities to assert their "superiority and gave [colonial] agents a chance to make sense of the reality around them as they remapped the world through their words."[43]

Nonetheless, indigenes did speak through their actions. They were the ones who decided not to register, to leave the region, to avoid or even escape from treatment. And through the use of other studies examining prostitution and the economic and social dislocations that accompanied colonialism in other colonies one can make conjectures.

One of the most obvious explanations for such behavior on the part of prostitutes was the desire to maintain their source of income. Registration and the possibility of forced treatment interrupted their livelihood. As several scholars have demonstrated, the introduction of European rule and the concomitant changes to the local economies opened up new possibilities for indigenous women to earn an income. Indeed, the disruption of preexisting economies, the proletarianization of indigenous societies, and the introduction of migrant labor either provided women with opportunities to attain financial independence or required them to support their families.[44] One of the easiest ways to earn money was through prostitution, especially because of the presence of a disproportionately higher number of men.[45]

According to White, women in East Africa engaged in prostitution for three reasons: out of necessity (survival), to support fathers, and to gain independence. She also wrote that at times these different types overlapped and even merged into one another, though rarely in the case of women working for their families.[46] Bozzoli, Mair, and Little noted similar reasons for other parts of Africa.[47] Thus, "women saw prostitution as a reliable means of capital accumulation, not as a despicable fate or a temporary strategy."[48]

In German Africa, there were several examples of women turning to prostitution in order to earn an income for themselves. One observer in Southwest Africa noted that African women preferred not to share their income with their male relatives.[49] Missionaries there also reported that imprisoned Herero during the years of war in the early twentieth century apparently preferred to earn money by prostituting themselves to white men rather than to have a husband.[50]

The acquisition of wealth through prostitution often enabled them to support themselves or to acquire land or livestock for themselves.

Income from prostitution could also be used for similar purposes to help their families. This was often necessary as a result of European colonial policies that disadvantaged indigenous owners of land and livestock. Hence, prostitution could become a vehicle for fathers for restock their herds[51] or for families to improve their economic situation. In the German reports, colonial observers took a more negative view of women working to support their families. For instance, in Cameroon one physician wrote that among the Ngumbas and Bulus around Grossbatanga, "the women [were] rented or lent out so that the husband [could] satisfy his need for rum."[52] In Southwest Africa, one settler insisted that many African families nourish themselves through prostitution: "Many men prefer not to work but rather to lead a comfortable life from the money which their wives and daughters earn through their filthy business."[53] The Chinese and Japanese prostitutes operating in the German overseas empire, the majority of whom worked in Qingdao and in the German Pacific territories, were often forced into prostitution through some type of contractual arrangement. These contracts were usually entered into either by families or through deception. Indeed, some families escaped economic hardships by selling their daughters into prostitution, and many daughters willing went out of a sense of familial obligation.[54] Meanwhile, other women, lured by ostensible promises of good wages, found themselves abducted and pressed into prostitution either at home or quite often overseas, such as in German New Guinea. In such situations, they often worked for a madam.[55]

Admittedly, as the German sources indicated, some women in their African colonies engaged only in opportunity prostitution. Luise White noted a similar experience in British East Africa.[56] The two main reasons tended to be either to supplement one's income in a financial emergency or to get one through a period of poverty. Once the crisis or situation passed, there was no reason to continue to engage in prostitution.[57] However, as one colonial physician in Cameroon commented, such behavior was often the result of local chiefs using them "as a source of income,"[58] that is, they supported the income of someone who exercised authority over them. A different German observer noted that African women in Southwest Africa preferred it "if their men or relatives did not know of their side employment (*Nebenerwerb*) so that they did not have to share the earnings with them."[59]

Another possibility explaining autochthonous actions was mistrust of German authorities, a view supported by colonial doctors themselves.[60] Indeed, according to one missionary report, indigenes in Southwest Africa believed that their examinations and treatments "were merely undertaken in the interest of white men."[61] Other reports indicated that physicians often mistreated or were unfriendly toward patients[62] or that female patients felt extremely uncomfortable being examined by male doctors.[63] One report from Southwest Africa suggested health measures were often too aggressive, especially in those instances when entire communities were subjected to medical examinations against their will.[64] In Cameroon, one physician commented that because examinations took place in a prison, many indigenes were disinclined to seek medical assistance.[65] In all these instances, the comportment of male German medical professionals and colonial authorities contributed to indigenes' attitudes and behavior that often resulted in avoidance of public health measures.

This mistrust of German authority could also have been related to indigenous understandings of disease and cultural practices that differed from those of the Europeans. Prior to the arrival of Germans, indigenes had their own understanding of diseases and how to treat them, beliefs that carried into the colonial period. For example, at a meeting in Windhoek with the German colonial government, leaders of the Herero, Nama, and Bergdama declared that "venereal diseases and their treatment are known to them for a long time; therefore, they are in the position to formulate an opinion about the different methods of treatment and [determined] that those of the whites are wrong." For them, syphilis was a "blood disease and had to be treated accordingly." "Gonorrhea was healed by them by removing the infectious material from the body through an internal means."[66] Not surprisingly, Dr. Scheller, the chief medical officer in the colony, stated that these perceptions lacked any knowledge of the foundational sciences and therefore could not be taken seriously.[67]

Such quick dismissals of indigenous views most likely compounded the already at times tenuous relations between German physician and autochthonous patient. Not only did German doctors practice medicine differently, but they often also refused to try to approach their patients through the local perspective. Quite plausibly, this inability to understand the worlds of their patients could have resulted in frustration on the part of the doctors, perhaps explaining some of the unfriendly, even aggressive behavior toward their non-European patients. Thus, doctors' inability to understand the others' culture may have contributed to an even greater mistrust on the part of some local populations. However, it should be noted that the comportment of some colonial doctors actually led to an increase in the number of people they treated. For example, Dr. Born, the successor of Dr. Meyer on Truk in the Pacific, reported that "Dr. Meyer paved the way exceptionally well, the people have trust in the doctor and follow willingly all directions."[68]

The most common ways indigenes responded to these intrusions was through migration. As scholars of British and French Africa have noted, autochthons often responded to colonial policies they disliked by moving from one region to another and even from the colony of one European power to that of another.[69] As colonial physicians indicated, many simply did leave, and this certainly constituted one response of some Africans to German efforts to control the spread of STDs. Moreover, in the Pacific the migration of peoples was a common occurrence, even before the establishment of European colonies.[70] Hence, inhabitants of the Marshall Islands may have consciously used migration as a means to avoid treatment, or it may have simply been a regular part of their life (or both).

Monitoring and even prohibiting the movement of those individuals who decided to avoid health controls was an extremely problematic task because of insufficient personnel. Indeed, colonial doctors repeatedly argued that a lack of resources hindered them considerably in controlling indigenous behavior. Hence, due to financial limitations there were not enough personnel, material, and facilities to cover a population and territory significantly larger than Germany itself.[71]

However, not all indigenous behavior undermined or hindered German measures intended to stop the spread of STDs. In fact, autochthons also pursued actions that supported German efforts. Without a doubt, the measures employed by German health officials, namely, health education, the registration of prostitutes, and the introduction of regular health exams, did contribute to the reported successes. In fact, German medical authorities argued that their efforts contributed to indigenes seeking medical treatment for STDs. But it should also be pointed out that this success depended on the compliance of indigenes.

Consequently, some indigenes allowed themselves to be examined and treated. As the statistics indicated, most autochthons completed their treatment; those who left were always a minority.[72] One health official in Cameroon explained this situation by noting that "because the danger of infection from gonorrhea appears to be known, a certain amount of protection is exercised by the natives themselves."[73] His remarks were supported by a colleague in East Africa who wrote that "the people had great trust in the 'new remedy' and came in great numbers in order to receive the Salvarsan injection," a trust that apparently did not exist before.[74] In some cases in Cameroon, a physician reported, "father in-laws bring their son-in-laws before the wedding to the physician to have them examined for venereal diseases."[75]

While once again their voice was absent from colonial records, indigenes did make decisions to ostensibly conform to German expectations. Quite plausibly, they recognized the dangers of STDs and saw the advantage in seeking medical assistance. Hence, they pursued such actions not necessarily in open support of German public health agendas but rather out of their own self-interest.

Conclusion

For German colonial authorities, the spread of STDs was a serious issue that threatened the vitality and hence future of the territories as German possessions. On a regular basis, colonial doctors reported on the number of infected according to the type of venereal disease and the number of days they were treated. For instance, according to the 1907/08 report for German East Africa, 207 Europeans (out of a population of 2,734, or roughly 8 percent of the white community) were treated for venereal diseases for a total of 541 hospital days and 3,755 clinical days. For the indigenous population, the number treated stood at 1,708 with 24,632 days spent in the hospital and 15,565 days in the policlinic.[76] And, as late as 1911, Governor Theodor Seitz in Southwest Africa expressed grave concern over the threat posed by venereal diseases to the economic development of the colony and the future of white rule there.[77]

Therefore, colonial doctors pursued measures to limit the spread of these diseases. As in Germany, these efforts focused primarily on the body of the prostitute. In both the metropole and the colonies, the prostitute represented both the "sexualized female body" and the "diseased body."[78] Because the prostitute in both places was the outlet for male sexual energy, she posed a threat to the existing order and hence had to be controlled through public health policies.[79] Ultimately, though, the efficacy of these measures depended in no small part on the actions of autochthons.

For instance, due to conditions in the colonial environment, indigenes could avoid the type of control colonial officials wanted to exercise. Thus, by working against or avoiding public health measures, some indigenous women and men did not conform to German notions of health and order. Most did this by not registering, by avoiding examinations, or by leaving treatment, often-times by moving from one location to another. Most likely the women did this because German policies often deprived them of their source of income, whether it was for their own capital accumulation or for someone else. Others may have avoided examinations because of the way they were treated by colonial authorities. Regardless of the reason, through their actions they undermined the overall effectiveness of these measures, a fact pointed out by colonial officials, albeit through a decidedly negative view of indigenous behavior. Equally important, some members of the colonial population contributed to the success of the German campaign to stop the spread of STDs. Some willingly allowed themselves to be examined and treated for STDs. In one recorded case, fathers even sent their future sons-in-law to be examined. Therefore, they contributed in part to the efficacy of public health programs in the colonies. Many did so most likely to further their own agendas, not necessarily that of colonial physicians.

In the end, then, though impossible to discern precisely their motivations, indigenes through their actions clearly impacted German colonial health policies that were directed toward controlling the proliferation of STDs. Though their actions may not have been conscious attempts to resist, or even to support, German colonial rule per se, their individual decisions, taken collectively, influenced the policies physicians implemented. Indeed, their behavior caused German officials both to develop a friendlier attitude toward autochthons, in order to convince them to seek out European medical assistance, and simultaneously to resort to more coercive measures in order to ensure that indigenes completed their treatment. Ultimately, according to colonial doctors, their efforts to curb the spread of STDs failed in large part due to indigenous comportment and attitudes. This was certainly true, but not exactly for the reasons German physicians imagined. Indigenes had their own agendas and rationales for their behavior that were quite different from how Germans constructed them.

NOTES

1. Andreas Eckert, *Die Duala und die Kolonialmächte: Eine Untersuchung zu Widerstand, Protest und Protonationalismus in Kamerun vor dem Zweiten Weltkrieg* (Münster: Lit, 1991), 8.

2. John Illife, "The Effects of the Maji Maji Rebellion of 1905–1906 on German Occupation Policy in East Africa," in *Britain and Germany in Africa: Imperial Rivalry and Colonial Rule*, ed. Prosser Gifford and Wm. Roger Louis (New Haven: Yale University Press, 1967), 557–76; Peter Hempenstall, *Pacific Islanders under German Rule: A Study in the Meaning of Colonial Resistance* (Canberra: Australian National University Press, 1978); Peter Hempenstall and Noel Rutherford, *Protest and Dissent in the Colonial Pacific* (Suva: Institute of Pacific Studies of the University of the South Pacific, 1984); Eckert, *Die Duala und die Kolonialmächte*.

3. See Gesine Krüger, *Kriegsbewältigung und Geschichtsbewußtsein: Realität,*

Deutung und Verarbeitung des deutschen Kolonialkrieges in Namibia 1904 bis 1907 (Göttingen: Vandenhoeck & Ruprecht, 1999); Jürgen Zimmerer and Joachim Zeller, ed., *Genocide in German South-West Africa: The Colonial War (1904–1908) in Namibia and Its Aftermath* (Monmuth, Wales: Merlin Press, 2008); Andreas Bühler, *Der Namaaufstand gegen die deutsche Kolonialherrschaft in Namibia von 1904 bis 1913* (Frankfurt am Main: IKO, Verlag für Interkulturelle Kommunikation, 2003).

4. Andreas Eckert, *Grundbesitz, Landkonflikte und kolonialer Wandel: Douala 1880 bis 1960* (Stuttgart: Franz Steiner, 1999).

5. Philipp Prein, "Guns and Top Hats: African Resistance in German South West Africa, 1907–1915," *Journal of Southern African Studies* 20 (1994): 99–121.

6. James Scott, *Weapons of the Weak: Everyday Forms of Peasant Resistance* (New Haven: Yale University Press, 1985); Detlev Peukert, *Inside Nazi Germany: Conformity, Opposition, and Racism in Everyday Life* (New Haven: Yale University Press, 1987).

7. Scott, *Weapons of the Weak*, 36.

8. Scott, *Weapons of the Weak*, 36.

9. Gyanendra Pandey, "Voices from the Edge: The Struggle to Write Subaltern Histories," *Mapping Subaltern Studies and the Postcolonial*, ed. Vinayak Chaturvedi (London: Verso, 2000), 281–99.

10. *Medizinal-Berichte* (hereafter *MB*) *1905/06* 1907: 293, 356, 389; *Arbeiten aus dem kaiserlichen Gesundheitsamte* (hereafter *AkG*) 1897: 74; *AkG* 1904: 584, 585.

11. *MB 05/06* 1907: 293.

12. *MB 1907/08* 1909: 311; *AkG* 1904: 73, 74.

13. *MB 1907/08* 1909: 125–26, 132.

14. BArch R1001/6040: 15–16; BArch R1001/5788: 30; BArch R1001/5764: 5–9.

15. BArch R1001/6042: 70.

16. *ASTH* 4 1900: 104–5; *ASTH* 6 1902: 233.

17. *AkG* 1904: 100; *MB 1906/07* 1908: 171.

18. *AkG* 1898: 634; *MB 1905/06* 1907: 157, 198, 359; *MB 1907/08* 1909: 77; *MB 1908/09* 1910: 282; *MB 1909/10* 1911: 397.

19. Regina Schulte, *Sperrbezirke: Tugendhaftigkeit und Prostitution in der bürgerlichen Welt* (Frankfurt am Main: Syndikat, 1979), 7; Mary Spongberg, *Feminizing Venereal Disease: The Body of the Prostitute in Nineteenth-Century Medical Discourse* (Washington Square, NY: New York University Press, 1997), 6, 35.

20. *AkG* 1897: 34: *AkG* 1904: 46; *MB 1909/10* 1911: 329; Margit Davies, "Das Gesundheitswesen im Kaiser-Wilhelmsland und im Bismarckarchipel," in *Die deutsche Südsee 1884–1914: Ein Handbuch,* ed. Hermann Hiery (Paderborn: Ferdinand Schönigh, 2001), 425.

21. *MB 1906/07* 1908: 172; *MB 1908/09* 1910: 261; Dr. Podesta, "Entwicklung und Gestaltung der gesundheitlichen Verhältnisse bei den Besatzungstruppen des Kiautschou-Gebietes im Vergleich mit der Marine und unter besonderer Berücksichtigung von Örtlichkeit und Klima in Tsingtau," *Deutsche Militärärztliche Zeitschrift* 38 (1909): 576, 589.

22. *MB 1908/09* 1910: 510–11; *MB 1905/06* 1907: 364, 391, 404.

23. BArch R1001/6040: 136.

24. *MB 1905/06* 1907: 392; *MB 1909/10* 1911: 328; *AkG* 1898: 634.

25. *MB 1905/06* 1907: 404.

26. *AkG* 1902/03: 388.

27. *AkG* 1902/03: 388.

28. *MB 1905/06* 1907: 80, 199, 293; *MB 1908/09* 1910: 511.

29. BArch R150F/FA3: 10–12, 36–37.

30. *AkG* 1904: 576; *MB 1907/08* 1909: 201.

31. *MB 1905/06* 1907: 199.

32. *MB1907/08* 1909: 201.

33. *MB 1904/05* 1907: 121.

34. *AkG* 1902/03: 407.

35. BArch R1001/5787: 188–90.

36. *MB 1904/05* 1906: 74.

37. See, for example, *MB 1905/06* 1907: 392; *AkG* 1898: 634; *AkG* 1904: 53, 54; BArch/R1001/5762: 317.

38. BArch R1001/5788: 30.

39. *AkG* 1898: 634; *MB 1905/06* 1907: 198.

40. *MB 1905/06* 1907, 359; *MB 1907/08* 1909: 77.

41. *MB 1905/06* 1907: 157.

42. *MB 1909/10* 1911: 397.

43. Alexandra Widmer, "The Effects of Elusive Knowledge: Census, Health Laws and Inconsistently Modern Subjects in Early Colonial Vanuatu," *Journal of Legal Anthropology* 1, no. 1 (2008): 97.

44. Luise White, *The Comforts of Home: Prostitution in Colonial Nairobi* (Chicago: University of Chicago Press, 1990), 20; Eckert, *Grundbesitz, Landkonflikte und kolonialer Wandel*, 205; Phil Bonner, "'Desirable or Undesirable Basotho Women?' Liquor, Prostitution and Migration of Basotho Women to the Rand, 1920–1945," in *Women and Gender in Southern Africa to 1945*, ed. Cheryl Walker (Claremont, South Africa: David Philip Publishers, 1990), 250.

45. Lucy Mair, *African Marriage and Social Change* (London: Frank Cass, 1969), 33; Emmanuel Akyeampong, *Drink, Power, and Cultural Change: A Social History of Alcohol in Ghana c. 1900 to Recent Times* (Portsmouth, NH: Heinemann, 1996), 63.

46. White, *The Comforts of Home*, 48–50.

47. Belinda Bozzoli, *Women of Phokeng: Consciousness, Life Strategy, and Migrancy in South Africa, 1900–1933* (Portsmouth, NH: Heinemann, 1991), 81, 91; Mair, *African Marriage*, 43, 55, 65, 141; Kenneth Little, *African Women in Towns: An Aspect of Africa's Social Revolution* (Cambridge: Cambridge University Press, 1973), 76.

48. White, *The Comforts of Home*, 1–2.

49. Franz Seiner, *Bergtouren und Steppenfahrten im Hererolande* (Berlin: Wilhelm Süsserott, 1904), 165.

50. Wolfram Hartmann, "Urges in the Colony: Men and Women in Colonial Windhoek, 1890–1914," *Journal of Namibian Studies* 1 (2007): 62.

51. White, *The Comforts of Home*, 1, 15, 37; Mair, *African Marriage*, 55–65.

52. BArch R1001/6012: 1.

53. BArch R151F/G.iv.D.2: 77d–77e.

54. Ronald Hyam, *Empire and Sexuality: The British Experience* (Manchester: Manchester University Press, 1990), 140; Gail Hershatter, *Dangerous Pleasures: Pros-*

titution and Modernity in Twentieth-Century Shanghai (Berkeley: University of California Press, 1997), 182, 191; D. C. S. Sissons, *"Karayuki-san*: Japanese Prostitutes in Australia, 1887–1916—I," *Historical Studies* 17 (1977): 323–41.

55. Christian Henriot, *Prostitution and Sexuality in Shanghai: A Social History, 1849–1949*, trans. Noël Castelino (Cambridge: Cambridge University Press, 2001), 185, 188–91; Sissons, *"Karayuki-san."*

56. White, *The Comforts of Home.*

57. Mair, *African Marriage*, 43, 141, 147; White, *The Comforts of Home*, 20, 34.

58. *AkG* 1904: 576.

59. Seiner, *Bergtouren und Steppenfahrten*, 165.

60. *AkG* 1904: 576.

61. BArch R151F/H.ii.h.i: 75–76.

62. For example, BArch R1001/5671: 127.

63. BArch R1001/5962: 143–44.

64. BArch R1001/6010: 61–62.

65. BArch R1001/5764: 91.

66. BArch R1001/6040: 25–28.

67. BArch R151F/h.ii.h.i: 54–58.

68. NAA G2/U17: 61–63.

69. M. C. Musambachime, "Protest Migrations in Mweru-Luapula, 1900–1940," *African Studies* 47 (1988): 19–34; A. I. Asiwaju, "Migration as Revolt: The Examples of Ivory Coast and Upper Volta before 1945," *Journal of African History* 14 (1976): 577–94.

70. Stephen Castles, "Migrant Settlement, Transnational Communities and State Strategies in the Asia Pacific Region," in *Migration in the Asia Pacific: Population, Settlement and Citizenship Issues*, ed. Robyn Iredale, Charles Hawksley, and Stephen Castles (Northampton, MA: Edward Elgar, 2003), 3–26; B. Malinowski, "Kula: The Circulating Exchange of Valuable in the Archipelagoes of Eastern New Guinea," in *Peoples of the Pacific: The History of Oceania to 1870*, ed. Paul D'Arcy (Burlington, VT: Ashgate/Variorum, 2008), 261–70; Dorothy Shineberg, "The Sandalwood Trade in Melanesian Economics, 1841–65," in *Peoples of the Pacific: The History of Oceania to 1870*, ed. Paul D'Arcy (Burlington, VT: Ashgate/Variorum, 2008), 359–76.

71. For example, NAA G2/U17: 61–63; NAA G2/U24: 8. At the start of 1914, there was approximately one physician per 100,000 indigenous patients distributed over territory roughly 5½ times larger than imperial Germany. Eckert, *Grundbesitz, Landkonflikte und kolonialer Wandel*, 120–21.

72. For example, *MB 1904/05* 1906: 74, 218.

73. BArch R1001/6012: 1.

74. BArch R1001/5747: 254.

75. BArch R1001/6012: 1.

76. *MB 1907/08* 1909:132.

77. BArch R1001/6040: 15–16.

78. Spongberg, *Feminizing Venereal Disease*, 6, 35.

79. Daniel Walther, "Sex, Race, and Empire: White Male Sexuality and the 'Other' in Germany's Colonies, 1894–1914," *German Studies Review* 33, no. 1 (2010): 45–72.

Ruga-ruga

The History of an African Profession, 1820–1918

Michael Pesek

The caravan trade, to a certain extent, anticipated the responses of African societies toward the establishment of colonial rule. Germans often traveled along the same routes that were used by the caravans; their expeditions considerably relied on the infrastructure of that trade.[1] Following this line of argument I investigate here how Africans, who served as armed guards in coastal caravans or for chiefs who participated in the trade, reacted toward the establishment of colonial rule. These young men were commonly called *ruga-ruga*, and they were, roughly speaking, mercenaries. Their role in the caravan trade and in social transformations of African societies in its aftermath is well documented by historians.[2] Nevertheless, what is rarely analyzed is their role during German colonial rule. Most authors have focused on the *askari*, the regular soldiers of colonial troops, or on chiefs as intermediaries of colonial rule. Like the *askari*, the *ruga-ruga* played a major part in German military expeditions as temporarily hired mercenaries. But unlike the *askari*, the *ruga-ruga* were only temporarily recruited by the Germans and thus less integrated into the military machinery.

Historians of nineteenth-century East Africa have suggested that many peoples of the region did not maintain stable patterns of belonging because they experienced cataclysmic demographic and social changes. Two major events caused East Africans to migrate at the time: the *Ngoni* invasion that forced thousands of people in the south to move from their home villages, and the inter-regional caravan trade that went hand in hand with civil war and the enslavement of many East Africans. With this demographic change new patterns and ideas of belonging evolved in which locally defined patterns coexisted with other forms of belonging, such as the participation in the caravan trade and the working culture that materialized as a result of it. One of the best examples in this regard is the emergence of the *Wanyamwezi*. Before the arrival of traders from the coast, the population of the central plateau was divided into many little chiefdoms, and, despite a common language, people defined their belonging in terms of a particular chiefdom rather than a larger ethnic group. When inhabitants of the central plateau began to participate as petty traders or porters in the caravan trade it became common among the Zanzibari and coastal traders to speak of them as people from the western mountains, or *"Wanyamwezi."* Those who went to work in the caravans increasingly adopted this term. Porters from the central plateau had earned a good reputation, and belonging to the *Wanyamwezi* promised young men higher status and wages in the caravans and later in European expeditions.[3]

The focus on occupational patterns of belonging rather than ethnicity may help us to direct our view toward a wider range of contexts and motivations of African responses toward colonial rule. Moreover, it takes into account that many East Africans were not confined to the constricted world of their home villages but were moving through different places. This essay not only discusses African responses toward colonial rule; it also seeks to explore German responses toward African realities. It would be a rather limited perspective to assume that colonial rulers had not had to adapt to local contexts while establishing their rule. Notwithstanding the implications of precolonial conditions, Germans tried to manipulate and transform these realities. This history of the *ruga-ruga* illustrates that it was neither a one-dimensional and unambiguous process nor one that was exclusively authored by the Germans.

The Emergence of the *Ruga-ruga*

In 1881, at a time when the region was in turmoil, the German traveler Hermann Wissmann reached the eastern shores of Lake Tanganyika. Some forty years before his arrival, traders from the East African coast had arrived at the lake. With their large caravans, which often included several thousand porters and armed guards, they had become powerful players in the making of the political landscape of nineteenth-century East Africa. Notably at the central plateau they became makers of kings either by military power or by forming alliances with local chiefs.[4] Nonetheless, African chiefs, who began to engage in the caravan trade, gradually demanded a share in the trade and contested the hegemony of the traders from the coast. The second half of the nineteenth century was mainly characterized by the struggle for control over the caravan routes. One of the most powerful pretenders was Mirambo, who had risen to the throne of the small chiefdom of Uyomba with the help of young armed followers who called themselves *ruga-ruga*.[5] When Wissmann reached Miram-

Fig. 6. A group of ruga-ruga in the 1880s. (Source: Paul Reichard. Deutsch-Ostafrika. Das Land und seine Bewohner, seine politische und wirtschaftliche Entwicklung. Leipzig: O. Spamer, 1892.)

bo's residence in 1881, the chief was at the height of his power, controlling most of northern Unyamwezi. He had clashed several times with strong forces of traders from Tabora and their allies from Unyanyembe and had remained victorious.[6] The German traveler was deeply impressed by the military design of Mirambo's empire and the high standards of military discipline and skills among his *ruga-ruga* (Wissmann 1889: 89).[7]

The *ruga-ruga* were an African response to the social and political upheavals that came along with the caravan trade. Moreover, they were also a product of the trans-local cultural transfers of that time. The *ruga-ruga* adopted cultural practices from a wide range of origins. Their clothing was shaped by local as well as coastal patterns. They usually wore the *kanzu*, the long cotton shirt of the coast, and long red capes. Moreover they decorated their heads with colorful feathers or with turbans. They sometimes adopted the Muslim faith of the traders and were known to believe in all sorts of magic, as it was common in Unyamwezi. Some sources hint at an extensive consumption of hemp.[8] Many were of humble origins: they were former slaves or prisoners of war or people who had either served in caravans of coastal traders or were from Unyamwezi. They came mostly from the central plateau, but among them were also some *Nguni* from the South, who introduced their knowledge of military organization into Mirambo's forces.[9] Many were teenagers who had lost their families during the civil wars ravaging Unyamwezi during these years. They were known to show no mercy to civilians when they raided villages. To a certain extent they were the predecessors of today's child soldiers.

The Colonization of the *Ruga-ruga*

In 1889 Wissmann returned to East Africa, this time as commander of the colonial troops, with the order to quell East African resistance against the Germans. Five years before, Carl Peters had concluded protection treaties with chiefs from Nguru that became the basis for German claims to Eastern Africa. The following years, Peters tried to expand the influence of his German East Africa Company (DOAG) to the coast. With the help of German gunboats he pressured the Sultan of Zanzibar, who had established some authority over the coast, to entrust his DOAG with the administration of several coastal towns. The agreement resulted in a rebellion against the Sultan and local elites as well as against Germans. Within a few months Wissmann subdued the resistance of the coastal towns and took over the administration from the DOAG.

Although his superiors in Berlin had issued orders to confine himself to these achievements, Wissmann had far wider schemes in mind. From his point of view the control over the trading routes from Lake Tanganyika to the coast was essential for Germany's future in East Africa. His interpretation of the resistance of coastal towns as an uprising of "Arabs" hinted at his intentions to break the dominance of traders from Zanzibar and the Swahili coast.[10] Wissmann had only few resources available to execute his advance into the interior. With his thousand troops he was hardly in control of the coast. Therefore, he placed all his hopes into an alliance with the powerful *ruga-ruga* empires of Mirambo and Nyungu-ya-Mawe.[11] Already in 1890 Wissmann headed an expedition toward Mpwapwa, which was then an important commercial center along the caravan route to Tabora. To demonstrate his enmity toward the "Arabs" and to win popular support from Africans, he forced some coastal traders to walk chained in front of his expedition.[12] Wissmann's hopes for an alliance with Mirambo quickly faded. Already in Mpwapwa, news reached him that the ruler had died some months before and that his empire was in dissolution. Shortly after his return to the coast, Wissmann himself was recalled to Berlin by his superiors, who were disappointed with his unauthorized actions.

But what survived Wissmann's departure was his influence over the first generation of German colonial officers whose admiration for him came close to worship. One of the lessons Wissmann taught his adepts was the importance of African warriors for military expeditions.[13] When Germans advanced further into the interior they encountered *ruga-ruga* both as their fiercest enemies and as willing allies. This was the case in Unyanyembe. In the late nineteenth century, chief Iseke of Unyanyembe had emerged as a powerful rival to the community of coastal and Zanzibari traders, who had founded the town of Tabora in the 1820s and dominated the surrounding chiefdoms for more than fifty years. With the arrival of the Germans in July 1890, the local power balance was reshaped, although the beginnings of the German presence were rather shaky. The first German officer in the area, Emin Pascha, left Tabora after only a short stay. One year later, a second German expedition arrived at Tabora, but the commanding officer had merely twenty-three *askari* at his disposal. This was not enough to challenge either the Tabora traders or Iseke, the ruler of Unyamyembe. In 1891, after a series of skirmishes between local rivals, the situation had developed into a stalemate: Neither Iseke nor the traders had the power to dominate the region and its trading routes. The Germans were therefore seen as potential allies, notably by the Taborians. There was a sharp divide among the Tabora traders as to how to respond toward the arrival of the Germans. An influential group around Said b. Salim, the *liwali*, or representative of the Sultan of Zanzibar, voted for cooperation, and their main argument was to use the Germans to get rid of Iseke of Unyanyembe, who threatened to block the caravan routes. Another faction that was headed by the powerful trader Muhammad b. Khalfan al-Barwani (better known by his nickname Rumaliza) regarded the Germans as a far greater threat and suggested an alliance with Iseke to expel them from Unyamwezi. Nevertheless, Said b. Salim decided to support the Germans against Iseke, whereas Rumaliza sent some of his *ruga-ruga* to help Iseke.[14]

From the perspective of most *ruga-ruga* it mattered little for whom they risked their lives. Tabora, as a commercial center, was a central marketplace for hiring *ruga-ruga*, and, according to German officers, there were plenty of them ready to fight for either side. Nevertheless, according to the historian Michael Singleton many Muslims in Tabora and elsewhere in the interior were attracted to millenarian ideas, notably to Madhism spreading from the Sudan toward Unyamwezi as early as the late 1880s. It is probable that many *ruga-ruga* converted to Islam while serving coastal traders or new warlords, and were therefore receptive to such ideas. What Singleton is stressing is that millenarism served as a means to form alliances against the German occupation.[15] Rumaliza was a member of the *Quadiri* Sufi order, and it is likely that many of his followers, including the *ruga-ruga*, were *Quadiris*, too.[16]

After two unsuccessful attempts of the Germans and their allies from Tabora to storm the fortress of Iseke, the chief was eventually defeated and killed in January 1893. In the aftermath of the battle, Unyanyembe was pillaged and plundered by the *ruga-ruga* allied to the Germans. In the following campaigns to quell the resistance of chiefs in Unyamwezi and Usukuma this pattern was employed over and again. In a punitive expedition against the Sukuma chief Serengema, for instance, only twenty *askari* but three hundred *ruga-ruga* of a neighboring chief participated, which was the rule rather than the exception.[17] This overall pattern caused John Iliffe to speak of early German rule as bearing resemblance to the *ruga-ruga* empires of the 1870s, as Germans used "bands of gunmen to maintain authority over compliant local leaders much as Mirambo had done, and its conquest was often an extension of tribal war in which the Germans shared the plunder."[18] But the *ruga-ruga* also fought on the side of resisting chiefs. According to German reports, Rumaliza sent some of his *ruga-ruga* to support the Hehe Chief Mkwawa when he was under siege by colonial troops. As experts in warfare, the *ruga-ruga* had helped to fortify Mkwawa's residence against German artillery.[19]

Despite the importance of the *ruga-ruga* for the successes of the German colonial military, most officers had a rather low opinion of their African allies. Some regarded them as no more than brigands.[20] According to one officer who had participated in the storming of the fortress of Iseke, they lacked any form of military discipline. "They cause high expenses for all the ammunition they squander and for all the gifts and food they demand, but if it becomes critical they quickly pull back behind the lines and thus impede the movements of regular troops," lamented another officer.[21] However, some officers appreciated certain aspects of the military behavior of the *ruga-ruga*, in particular their uniforms and their admiration for drilling. Despite all reservations, German officers highly praised the use of the *ruga-ruga* in scorched-earth tactics: "The ruga-ruga are of use if one likes to destroy entire regions. In that they are top-notch."[22]

When Wissmann returned to the colony in 1896 for a second term as governor, he devised a plan to form auxiliary troops mainly made up of *ruga-ruga*. His main goal was to strengthen the strategic reserves of colonial troops. During this period, Germans were in desperate need of new recruits and a reliable but cheap reserve of auxiliaries. Between 1891 and 1896 the *Schutztruppe* had constantly been in action against resisting Africans and had paid with a high toll of lives. In 1891 the *Schutztruppe* had lost nearly two-thirds of its soldiers in the battle of Rugaro against warriors of the Hehe-Chief Mkwawa. Wissmann made the final subjugation of Mkwawa, who after five years was still not beaten, one of his main priorities as governor, and for this task every soldier of the *Schutztruppe* was needed.[23]

Wissmann's model for his auxiliary force was the Prussian *Landwehr*. In nineteenth-century Prussia the *Landwehr* had been the nucleus for the intro-duction of a compulsory military service, and Wissmann hoped a similar force would be the first step toward this goal in the colony as well.[24] The initial basis of the auxiliary force was to be recruited from among *ruga-ruga* provided by loyal chiefs. The volunteers were obliged to come to the *boma*, or governmen-tal station, regularly for military training. According to Wissmann this training had to be less perfect than that of regular colonial troops. In particular, conces-sions in terms of discipline had to be made. Moreover, he suggested that uni-forms had to be reduced to a minimum to ensure that no confusion with the uniforms of the *askari* were possible. He recommended khaki shorts, blouses, and sailor's caps as appropriate uniforms for the *ruga-ruga*. Their weapons and equipment were to be modern firearms, leather belts with cartridge pouches, hatchets, knives, and some tools.[25] This list indicates that the *ruga-ruga* units were designed to be more than a strategic reserve. For Wissmann, their training served a significant (if not primary) function in the process of creating colonial subjects. The regular presence at the *boma* helped to tie the *ruga-ruga* to the German district officer. At colonial ceremonies, such as the emperor's birthday, which often included lengthy speeches, the officers presented the *ruga-ruga* with food and gifts of cloth. These events ended with oath ceremonies in which the *ruga-ruga* had to swear allegiance to the Emperor. For their willingness to serve, the *ruga-ruga* were rewarded with privileges, such as exemption from certain taxes and access to basic medical care.[26]

Although Wissmann's second period in office ended abruptly after one year, his scheme was introduced all over the colony in the following years, primarily in the regions of Unyamwezi and Usukuma where the *ruga-ruga* had previously been known. There are no figures available that indicate how many Africans were recruited into the system, but it seems that it remained up to the individual officers whether to implement the system in their district or not. Moreover, it was left to their individual taste how to handle and equip their *ruga-ruga*. In some places, the *ruga-ruga* were regularly paid, in others they were only exempted from taxpaying. Some officers equipped them with modern firearms; others gave them simple muzzle-loaders. The officers themselves displayed some creativity in staffing them with uniforms that ranged from *Schutztruppen*-like uniforms to red ribbons and to motifs on ordinary clothes.[27]

Notably those chiefs who had enhanced their power with German help developed a taste for colonial uniforms and representations. One of the prime examples was the Haya-Chief Kahigi of Kianja, who, with German support, rose from a little chief to one of the most powerful figures in the interlacustrine region. The Haya kingdoms had been relatively little affected by the caravan trade of the nineteenth century, and the *ruga-ruga* were widely unknown in the region until the arrival of the Germans. Nevertheless, the introduction of the *ruga-ruga* scheme gave Kahigi both the possibility to satisfy German demands for some sort of colonial design of his office and, at the same time, to strengthen his power by hiring soldiers whose loyalty was bound only to the chief himself. Kahigi's alliance with the Germans was based on his ability to present himself as a powerful and at the same time loyal chief. For German colonial officials highly ceremonial meetings with the chiefs were an important occasion to introduce their vision of colonial politics in local contexts. Their reception by the chiefs became a tool for measuring the loyalty of the chief and his ability to perform the orders of the *boma*. Kahigi knew this very well. He had built his residency after the model of the *boma*: a stone house with two floors filled with pieces of furniture imported from Europe. He owned gramophones, clocks, and even a picture of the German Emperor. He himself was dressed in the uniform of a cuirassier with a sun helmet or a turban on his head. His *ruga-ruga* were armed with guns and clothed in uniforms that resembled those of the *Schutztruppe*. They were trained after Prussian rules and marched on parade when a German official visited the court of Kahigi.[28]

In Kahigi's chiefdom the *ruga-ruga* were engaged in various duties. First of all they served as personal guards of the chief. Moreover, they enforced the chief's orders notably with his sub-chiefs, who often had fallen under his regime as a result of the restructuring of the political landscape by Germans. Some *ruga-ruga* served as tax collectors, postmen, and court ushers. For Kahigi, the *ruga-ruga* became a means to adapt local political structures to the new conditions that accompanied colonial rule. To some degree this gave him the autonomy to create his own vision of colonial rule and to keep a certain distance from colonial rulers. The Germans, on the other hand, saw in the *ruga-ruga* a means to successively transform local politics without major commitment. Moreover, the *ruga-ruga* helped them to overcome their notorious shortcomings of military resources. The *ruga-ruga* were not only employed at their place of origin but, in cases of emergency, in other areas as well.

Fig. 7. *Chief Kahigi with his ruga-ruga while he was waiting for the arrival of Count of Mecklenburg in 1908.* (Source: J. Czekanowski, ed. **Wissenschaftliche Ergebnisse der deutschen Zentral-Afrika-Expedition 1907–1908 unter Führung Adolf Friedrichs, Herzogs zu Mecklenburg. Vol. III: Ethnographisch-Anthropologischer Atlas: Zwischensee-Bantu, Pygmäen und Pygmoiden, Urwaldstämme. Leipzig: Klinkhardt & Bierman, 1911.**)

The Return of the *Ruga-ruga*

With the outbreak of World War I, East Africa became a bitterly contested theater of war, involving some 100,000 troops on the side of the allied British and Belgians, and nearly 20,000 troops on the German side. With the war looming, the Germans were in desperate need of new recruits. Some 2,500 *askari* served in the *Schutztruppe* in 1914; one year later the Germans had raised more than 10,000 new recruits. It can be assumed that this success was based mainly on the recruitment of the *ruga-ruga*. Most of the new recruits came from regions where Wissmann's scheme had been implemented before the war, notably Unyamwezi and Usukuma. Moreover, the Germans continued to rely on African auxiliary troops as they had done during the colonial conquest. Especially at the northwestern and southwestern borders only few regular troops were available to German commanders, and the *ruga-ruga* became an important part of the German troops. They often made up the majority of the fighting troops. According to estimates of the British War Office more than 12,000 African auxiliaries fought on the German side during the war.[29] Numbers are hard to access because the involvement of African irregulars in German war efforts was rather volatile, and reports only occasionally mention the *ruga-ruga*. In Rwanda alone there were around 700 *ruga-ruga* and only a few hundred *askari*. When, in January 1915, the German officer Max Wintgens attacked Anglo-Belgian positions at Lake Kivu, his troops comprised 11 German officers, 46 *askari* and more than 60 *ruga-ruga* who had been provided by the King of Rwanda.[30] Overall, the *ruga-ruga* fought many battles, and their role within regular troops varied. They took part in the battle for Tanga, which was one of the major battles of the war, and in the positional warfare at the northwestern front, where most German and British forces were concentrated. Here they served mainly as scouts and salient guards. When German forces attacked the British garrison at Jassini some hundred *ruga-ruga* were among the attackers. Official German reports of the battle mention a regular company of *ruga-ruga* that was led by a German officer and equipped with modern guns and maxims.[31] Much less connected to German forces were those *ruga-ruga* who were commanded by their own chiefs, as was the case at Lake Victoria, where local chiefs had recruited their warriors for the defense of their villages against raids from Massai and Baganda. These local vigilantes were partly supported by German local officials, who provided local chiefs and their warriors with arms to fight against the Massai and Baganda, who were supported by the British.[32]

Whatever caused Europeans to fight on African soil, Africans developed their own visions of the war. The German commanding officer at Lake Nyassa, Konrad von Falkenhausen, in the south of the colony relied heavily on the support of African chiefs for his war efforts. Provided with only few regular troops by Lettow-Vorbeck, the *ruga-ruga*, supplied by local chiefs, became his main fighting force. With his few *askari* and hundreds of *ruga-ruga* he occasionally raided villages and positions on the British and Belgian side of the border. His main goal was to capture cattle that he later divided among his allied chiefs to ensure their willingness to support him with *ruga-ruga*, food, and information about enemy movements.[33]

This was the case in Rwanda as well. When Wintgens attacked Anglo-Belgian positions at Chahafi he was accompanied by dozens of *ruga-ruga* who were given to him by the Rwandan king Musinga. Whereas Wintgens's goal was to capture the post of Chahafi, the *ruga-ruga* preferred cattle. Wintgens's attack failed, but the *ruga-ruga* went home with hundreds of cattle, goats, and some prisoners of war. Musinga's rationale for support of the German commander had little in common with German military aims. The region around Chahafi had been regarded by Rwandan kings as their very own sphere of influence since the mid-nineteenth century. With the partition of East Africa by the Belgians, the British, and the Germans, the northern region had slipped out of the king's control, and had become home to his rivals and dissenters. Musinga obviously hoped to renew his influence in the region with the help of the Germans.[34]

The relationships between German officers and their African allies were far from harmonious. The officers' judgments on the usefulness of their *ruga-ruga* ranged from words of praise to wholehearted damnation. For most part, their trust in the loyalty of their *ruga-ruga* was limited. A German officer who commanded nearly 300 *ruga-ruga* along the River of Rumi faced the desertion of 50 of them on the first day of battle. On the second day he was left with only 80 *ruga-ruga*. To prevent further desertions of the *ruga-ruga*, another officer divided the ammunition among his *ruga-ruga* only at the very beginning of battles.[35] For nearly two years, Wintgens had been successful in defending the borders against superior Anglo-Belgian forces. His success was mainly based on his ability to tie the *ruga-ruga* of the Rwandan king into his war effort. When, in 1916, Belgian and British troops crossed the borders for a major offensive, the German resistance quickly disintegrated. In view of the overwhelming enemy forces, the more than 700 *ruga-ruga* of the Rwandan king simply returned home.[36]

In the chaos that followed the withdrawal of the Germans, local warriors developed their own interpretation of the war, and the loyalties of the *ruga-ruga* became even more precarious. In Unyamwezi the shifting loyalties turned into a real war between different *ruga-ruga* factions. The Usaramo-Chief Manati offered the services of his *ruga-ruga* to the arriving British troops. Neighboring *Nyaturu* warriors, who acted on behalf of the Germans, had occasionally raided his villages.[37] Europeans were confronted with raiding parties of African warriors as well. In September 1916, German missionaries at Kitunde, a small missionary station in Unyamwezi, were attacked by warriors of a neighboring chief, who claimed to be part of the British forces in the region. As they began to plunder and pillage the station, the missionaries demanded an official document legitimating their actions. The *ruga-ruga* responded by shooting one of the missionaries.[38]

In the final two years of the war, the difference between regular troops and irregulars blurred increasingly. From 1916 onward, Lettow-Vorbeck's troops were constantly on the run, and with him thousands of porters, the families of the *askari*, and hundreds of the *ruga-ruga*. In late 1917, German forces es-

Fig. 8. *Ruga-ruga in the First World War. (*Source: **Walther Dobbertin,**
ed. *Die Soldaten Lettow-Vorbecks. Ein Buch von deutschem Wehrwillen
und deutscher Waffenehre.* **Wiederhof-Buchholz: W. Dobbertin, 1932.)**

caped across the Rovuma River into the territory of Portuguese East Africa.
Along with 1,900 regular troops, some hundred *Yao ruga-ruga* crossed the
river. The Germans still continued to recruit *askari* from these *ruga-ruga* units,
as they faced shortages in troops from desertions and combat deaths of their
own soldiers. But many *Yao ruga-ruga* accompanied German troops only for a
limited time. Having satisfied the hunger for looting, they packed the booty
onto the backs of their porters and prisoners of war, and finally left the Germans to return home.[39] By then, Lettow-Vorbeck's troops had already lost any
resemblance to a regular army. The difference between his companies, maraud-
ing groups of deserters, and local *ruga-ruga*, had dissolved. The British officer
Edward Northey, who hunted Lettow-Vorbeck's troops, reported in a clearly
frustrated manner to his superiors that he was observing a constant coming and
going among the German forces. Deserting *askari* and porters daily reduced
the German troops, only to be replaced with local warriors who, for one reason
or another, accompanied the Germans for a while.[40]

In some places the war revived the old *ruga-ruga* empires. Deserted
askari, various African government officials, and traders from the coast used
the power vacuum left by the Germans and gathered the human flotsam and
jetsam of the war to found their small private empires. In 1919, a British ad-

ministrator reported that a former slave had ascended to the throne of the chiefdom of Massasi. The old chief had moved away and never returned. With the help of deserted *askari* and *ruga-ruga* the new chief had brutally imposed his will onto the local population. A similar picture was drawn in another report from the Kilimanjaro region, where former *askari* had imposed little *ruga-ruga* empires, and plagued and pillaged locals.[41]

Epilogue

World War I and its aftermath saw the last significant appearance of the *ruga-ruga* in the history of Eastern Africa. British sources rarely refer to them after the war. During the hundred years of their history, the *ruga-ruga* served many different masters, from the warlord Mirambo and the trader Rumaliza to the traveler and colonizer Hermann Wissmann and the Prussian general Lettow-Vorbeck. Predominantly, however, they fought for their own profit. To become a *ruga-ruga* opened up opportunities for young African men at a time when most Africans were exposed to violence and exploitation by people who were invading the country from various directions. The line between being a victim and becoming a culprit was notwithstanding fine. The *ruga-ruga* were responsible for atrocities against civilians during the nineteenth-century slave trade, colonial conquest, the everyday life of colonial rule, and, last but not least, during World War I. Yet, beyond their military actions, they were also important agents in pre-colonial and colonial state-building. The transformation of the political landscape of Unyamwezi in the second half of the nineteenth century would have been impossible without the *ruga-ruga*, who enabled ambitious Africans to become powerful chiefs and to break the dominance of coastal traders.

The *ruga-ruga* were intermediaries in various ways. They were the product of the often cataclysmic transformations of the nineteenth and twentieth centuries, and they were important agents in these processes. In the late nineteenth century they adapted cultural patterns from coastal traders and military knowledge from *Nguni* societies. Colonial chiefs, like Kahigi of Kianja, used the *ruga-ruga* to introduce and experiment with new patterns of governance. The *ruga-ruga* became an arena of negotiation between Germans and Africans over how Africans were to be integrated into the colonial state. To work as a *ruga-ruga* offered young male Africans the possibility of a career within the framework of colonial rule but beyond the colonial state. Their integration into the colonial world remained unstable and ambiguous.

NOTES

1. Michael Pesek, *Koloniale Herrschaft in Deutsch-Ostafrika: Expeditionen, Militär und Verwaltung seit 1880* (Frankfurt am Main: Campus, 2005).

2. Edward A. Alpers, "The Nineteenth Century: Prelude to Colonialism," in *Zamani: A Survey of East African History*, ed. B. A. Ogot and J. A. Kieran (Nairobi: East African Publishing House, 1968), 229–48; Ralph A. Austen, *Northwestern Tanzania under German and British Rule; Colonial Policy and Tribal Politics, 1889–1939* (New Haven: Yale University Press, 1968); R. W. Beachey, "The East African Ivory Trade in the Nineteenth Century," *Journal of African History* 8 (1967); Norman R. Bennett, *Mirambo of Tanzania, 1840?–1884* (New York: Oxford University Press, 1971); John Iliffe, *A Modern History of Tanganyika* (Cambridge: Cambridge University Press, 1979); Aylward Shorter, "Nyungu-ya-Mawe and the 'Empire of the Ruga-Ruga,'" *Journal of African History* 9 (1968): 235–59.

3. Jonathon Glassman, *Feasts and Riot: Revelry, Rebellion, and Popular Consciousness on the Swahili Coast, 1856–1888* (Portsmouth: Heinemann, 1995), 59; Pesek, *Koloniale Herrschaft*, 69; Steven J. Rockel, *Carriers of Culture: Labor on the Road in Nineteenth Century East Africa* (Portsmouth: Heinemann, 2006), 123.

4. R. G. Abrahams, *The Political Organization of Unaymwezi*, (Cambridge: Cambridge University Press, 1967), 37; Bennett, *Mirambo*, 27.

5. Shorter, "Nyungu-ya-Mawe," 240.

6. Bennett, *Mirambo*, 54; Hamed bin Muhammed el Murjebi, "Autobiographie des Arabers Schech Hamed bin Muhammed el Murjebi, genannt Tippu Tip," *Mitteilungen des Seminars für Orientalische Sprachen* 3/4 (1902/03): 176.

7. Hermann von Wissmann, *Unter deutscher Flagge quer durch Afrika von West nach Ost, 1880 bis 1883*, 2nd ed. (Berlin: Walther & Apolant, 1889), 89.

8. Wilhelm Blohm, *Die Nyamwezi. Gesellschaft und Weltbild* (Hamburg: Friederichsen De Gruyter, 1933), 58; Emin Pascha and Franz Stuhlmann, *Die Tagebücher von Dr. Emin Pascha* (Hamburg: Westermann, 1927), 409; Henry M. Stanley, *Through the Dark Continent, or, The Sources of the Nile around the Great Lakes of Equatorial Africa and down the Livingstone River to the Atlantic Ocean*, 1 ed. (Toronto: General Publishing, 1988 [1899]), 67.

9. In the 1840s, Nguni migrants from Southern Africa reached the Southern shores of Lake Tanganyika. Initially the Nguni evaded the pressure by Shaka Zulu but later turned into peripatetic societies that combined the military organization of the Zulu Empire with local cultures of war.

10. According to Glassman's analysis of the uprising, the rebels were mainly people from the interior, who had come to the coast as caravan porters (Glassman, *Feasts and Riot*, 2).

11. Report of the Imperial Commissioner for East Africa, Dar-es-Salam, July 27th 1889, in *Reichstagsakten 1889/90*, 7. Legislaturperiode, Volume 127, No. 11; Musée royal de l'Afrique centrale, Tervuren, Diaries of Wissmann, 7.8.1891; Stuhlmann, Franz, *Mit Emin Pascha ins Herz von Afrika*, vol. 1 (Berlin: D. Reimer, 1894), 58.

12. Rochus Schmidt, "Die Mpapua-Expedition—Wissmann, Emin und Stanley," in *Hermann von Wissmann—Deutschlands größter Afrikaner. Sein Leben und Wirken un-*

ter Benutzung des Nachlasses dargestellt, ed. Carl von Perbandt, Georg Richelmann, and Rochus Schmidt (Berlin: Schall, 1906), 257.

13. This lesson is to be found in a small booklet written by Wissmann that was part of the library of every military station in German East Africa. Hermann von Wissmann, *Afrika: Schilderungen und Rathschläge zur Vorbereitung für den Aufenthalt und den Dienst in den deutschen Schutzgebieten* (Berlin: E. S. Mittler, 1895).

14. Deutsches Kolonialblatt (henceforth DKB) 1894, "Bericht des Leutnants Prince über die Niederwerfung und Vernichtung des Häuptlings Sike von Tabora, 2. 1.1893," 200.

15. Michael Singleton, "Muslims, Missionaries and the Millennium in Upcountry Tanzania," *Cultures et Développement* 9, no. 2 (1977): 261.

16. B. G. Martin, *Muslim Brotherhoods in Nineteenth-Century Africa* (Cambridge: Cambridge University Press, 1976), 159; Michael Pesek, "Islam und Politik in Deutsch-Ostafrika, 1905–1919," in *Alles unter Kontrolle: Disziplinierungsverfahren im kolonialen Tanzania (1850–1960)*, ed. Albert Wirz, Katrin Bromber, and Andreas Eckert (Hamburg: LIT, 2003), 106.

17. Ibid.; DKB 1893, "Bestrafung des Sultans Sengrema in Usukuma," 330.

18. Iliffe, *Modern History*, 117.

19. DKB 1893, "Bericht des Leutnants Prince über den Rückmarsch der Tabora-Expedition vom 3. Januar bis 18. April des Jahres," 266; "Bericht Sigls vom September 9, 1893," DKB 1893, "Verlegung der Station Ulanga," 381; Bundesarchiv, "Berichte Leue an AA/KA," February 2, 1896.

20. Rochus Schmidt, *Kolonialpioniere. Persönliche Erinnerungen aus kolonialer Frühzeit* (Berlin: Safari-Verlag, 1938), 64; C. Waldemar Werther, *Die mittleren Hochländer des nördlichen Deutsch-Ost-Afrika: Wissenschaftliche Ergebnisse der Irangi-Expedition, 1896–1897 nebst kurzer Reisebeschreibung* (Berlin: H. Paetel, 1898), 53; C. Waldemar Werther, *Zum Victoria Nyanza: Eine Anti-Sklaverei-Expedition und Forschungsreise* (Berlin: H. Paetel, 1894), 62.

21. Bundesarchiv R1001/1030 Schwessinger to Soden, November 26, 1892.

22. Ibid.

23. Tom von Prince, *Deutsch-Ostafrika Gegen Araber und Wahehe. Erinnerungen aus meiner afrikanischen Leutnantszeit 1890–1895* (Berlin: Mittler & Sohn, 1914), 195.

24. DKB 1896, Runderlass des Kaiserlichen Gouverneurs an die Stationen und Bezirksämter, 367; Bundesarchiv R1001/1030: Berichte Leues an Auswärtiges Amt, Kolonialabteilung, 17.2.1896.

25. DKB 1896, Runderlass des Kaiserlichen Gouverneurs an die Stationen und Bezirksämter, 367.

26. Tanzania National Archives G 2/4 Besichtigungsreise des Hauptmanns Johannes, 4.4.1902, 17.4.1902.

27. Ibid., Bundesarchiv R 1003FC/1141: Runderlass Gouvernement Dar es Salaam, 26.8.1910.

28. For a detailed description see Michael Pesek, "Praxis und Repräsentation kolonialer Herrschaft: Die Ankunft des Staatssekretärs Dernburg am Hofe Kahigis von Kianja, 1907," in *Die Ankunft des Anderen: Empfangszeremonien im interkulturellen und*

intertemporalen Vergleich, ed. Susann Baller et al. (Frankfurt am Main: Campus, 2008), 214.

29. NA WO 106/258 "German Administration and the attitude towards natives."

30. "Bericht über das am 1. Januar 1915 stattgehabte Gefecht gegen den englischen Uganda-Posten am Tschahahfi," in *Zusammenstellung der Berichte über die in den Monaten November, Dezember 1914 und Januar 1915 stattgefundenen Gefechte der Kaiserlichen Schutztruppe für Deutsch-Ostafrika nebst Nachtrag über die in den Monaten August bis Oktober stattgefundenen Gefechte*, ed. Deutsch-Ostafrika, Kaiserliches Gouvernement (Morogoro: Regierungsdruckerei, n.d. [1915]): 278; National Archives WO 106/259, "District Commissioner's office an den Provincial Commissioner, Western Province, Kabale, Kigezi District," 26.6.1919.

31. Von Boemcken, "Bericht über die Vorgänge an der Grenze bei Jassin von Mitte Dezember 1914 bis Mitte Januar 1915," in Deutsch-Ostafrika, Kaiserliches Gouvernement, *Zusammenstellung*, 234.

32. Austen, *Northwestern Tanzania*, 125.

33. "Bericht über den Marsch am 3. und 4. 12.1914 im Gebiet der belgischen Watualen Ujinjiri und Kabuika," in Deutsch-Ostafrika, Kaiserliches Gouvernement, *Zusammenstellung*, 227.

34. Bericht über das am 4.10.1914 stattgehabte Gefecht gegen die Belgier bei Kissenji, in Deutsch-Ostafrika, Kaiserliches Gouvernement, *Zusammenstellung*, 30.

35. Bericht über ein Gefecht am Rumifluss, 11.9.1914 in Deutsch-Ostafrika, Kaiserliches Gouvernement, *Zusammenstellung*, 17.

36. Musée Royale de l'Afrique Centrale, Mémoires du Colonel honoraire Scheppers, Vétéran de l'Etat Indépendant du Congo, n.d. [ca. 1918]; Belgique, Ministère des Affaires étrangères, Direction des Archives, FP 1129/2657 Tombeur, Rapport du mois d'avril 1916, Kibati, 15.5.1916.

37. J. C. Bagenal, "The East African Campaign: Written from a diary at Maneromango 1917" (Rhodes House Library, Oxford: C. J. Bagenal Papers, 1915–17 MSS Afr. s. 2351, n.d.), 87.

38. Th. Bechler, *Zur Kriegszeit in Deutsch-Ostafrika, im Kongo und in Frankreich Kriegserlebnisse und Gefangenschaft der Unyamwesi-Missionare der Brüdergemeinde in den Jahren 1914–17* (Herrnhut, 1918), 29, 79.

39. National Archives CO 691/5 War Diary Northey, 1.-30. April 1917.

40. National Archives CO 691/15 War Diary Northey, 1.-30.3.1918.

41. National Archives CO 691/ 29 Report of the Civil Administrator, Occupied Territory, GEA, Milow Sub-District. 30.1.1919; F. J. E. Bagshave, Personal Diaries, unpublished manucript (Rhodes House Oxford, Bagshave, F. J. E. Papers, n.d.), 2.2.1917.

Bomani

African Soldiers as Colonial Intermediaries in German East Africa, 1890–1914

Michelle Moyd

Between about 1890 and 1900, African soldiers (*askari*) of the German colonial army (*Schutztruppe*) in East Africa carried out the conquest of German East Africa. Once established at colonial military outposts (*bomas*) across the territory, *Schutztruppe* officers, non-commissioned officers (NCOs), and civilian administrators relied on the *askari* for everyday policing and administration of the colony. Their presence as uniformed messengers, guards, executioners, and meters-out of corporal punishment made them the most visible agents of colonial rule.

Historians have described literate colonial employees, such as clerks, translators, and teachers, as intermediaries. They were the agents of colonial rule who "bridged the linguistic and cultural gaps that separated European colonial officials from subject populations by managing the collection and distribution of information, labor, and funds."[1] This essay argues that *askari* also acted as intermediaries between the centers of colonial authority and the peoples who lived in proximity to the *bomas*. Everyday colonial life in the *bomas* reinforced the processes that helped consolidate colonial rule. German military strength resided in the *bomas*, but the *askari* also carried colonial state authority with them, ready to strike against those who resisted German rule. Beyond the obvious military roles of the *bomas* and the *askari*, the movement of many different kinds of people in and out of the *bomas* activated colonial authority on several levels—economically, socially, and culturally. *Askari* moved in, around, and between administrative stations in their everyday work, and East Africans who lived in proximity to the *bomas* also incorporated the colonial centers into their lives in various ways. Despite the everyday violence and coercion that the *askari* practiced in the name of the colonial state, their lives were full of face-to-face interactions and negotiations that blurred the boundaries between colonizers and colonized.

Askari and other colonial intermediaries might easily be understood as colonial "collaborators," and indeed, past scholarship has tended to label them this way.[2] They should, however, be understood as military intermediaries who fulfilled German colonial interests, while also creating new opportunities for East African men, women, and children to improve their access to status, wealth, and security. *Askari* negotiated the terrain between their roles as practitioners of everyday colonialism and their roles as community members in ways that tied local East Africans to the *bomas* through violence, but also sometimes through attraction and cooperation.

The Kiswahili word *bomani* is a useful way of thinking about the dynamics set in motion by the presence of colonial stations throughout German East Africa. *Bomani* can mean either "in (at) the *boma*" or "to the *boma*," depending on the context of its usage. Thus, it connotes both the *bomas'* fixity and the mobility that enabled colonial rule. The *bomas* were the beginning and end points for the *askaris'* day-to-day itinerant practices of colonial rule. They thus make useful analytical sites for situating the *askari* as colonial intermediaries, whose daily duties, family ties, and social connections brought them face-to-face with colonial officials, other Europeans, and East Africans living in and around the stations. The routine patterns of work and rest that characterized garrison life, the duties and activities that took the *askari* out of the *bomas*, and their travels between *bomas* all connected them to existing social networks and economies that enriched them materially, socially, and psychically. Violence and coercion inhered in these everyday duties and ultimately contributed to their ability to fashion themselves as respectable men with clients, land, livestock, and cash wealth. *Askaris'* self-fashioning as respectable men required the tacit or forced participation of other East Africans, since it was their reactions to the *askari* that reinforced soldiers' understandings of themselves as men of means.

The *bomas*, where *askari* worked and often lived, were multipurpose spaces visited frequently by African colonial subjects, both voluntarily and involuntarily. They went to the *bomas* to pay taxes, to buy and sell goods and services, to attend juridical proceedings and community meetings known as *mashauri* (sing. *shauri*), to witness spectacles such as public executions, and to attend festivals and celebrations for major events. In other instances, the *askari* brought the *boma*'s authority to local residents in their daily duties of tax collection, delivering messages, or escorting dignitaries. In all of these activities, East Africans experienced *askari* in their roles as colonial intermediaries, viewing them as representatives of the *boma* and as men of some social standing. Young men and women whose kinship ties had been severed in regional violence during the 1880s and 1890s often came to the *bomas* hoping to gain personal socio-economic security through incorporation into *askari* households. Many of them ultimately became *askari* dependents.[3]

The degree to which East Africans came into contact with the *bomas* was not the same across the colony, and colonial authority was far from total. But most residents of German East Africa recognized that the uniformed and armed *askari* carried the *boma*'s authority with them, however far away from a physical *boma* an *askari* might be. This recognition contributed directly to the *askaris*' ability to present themselves as "big men." East Africans who experienced the *askari* in their capacities as police, guards, and soldiers often feared them. But just as Africans understood the *bomas* as spaces of both oppression and possibility, many viewed the *askari* with mixed feelings reflective of the soldiers' simultaneous positions as colonial oppressors and men with access to socio-economic possibilities that could benefit those willing to see the *askari* as potential patrons. Such dependent relationships trapped people in subordinate positions in local socio-economic hierarchies, but they also provided a modicum of protection from lack of kinship ties or economic means.

This essay offers three glimpses into *askari*'s everyday lives as colonial intermediaries. The first section explains how *askari* and others lived and worked in and around the *bomas*. The second and third sections provide two examples of how *askari* practiced what I call "itinerant colonialism" in their roles as tax collectors and messengers for the multipurpose colonial proceedings known as *mashauri*. The essay shows how the *askari* exercised state authority in order to accomplish colonial goals, while simultaneously improving their status as "big men."

Bomas as Nodes of Authority

The *bomas*' ability to represent German authority rested to a large degree on the "theatricality" of the spaces themselves.[4] The imposing forts, made of whitewashed stone, clay, or brick, were built primarily to provide effective defense against attacks by African armies. But they also played a central role in helping German colonial officers perform their claims to authority over surrounding areas. German officers designed the *bomas* to be architecturally impressive, as well as to provide a space within which the *Schutztruppe* could perform technological displays and military drill exhibitions. German imperial flags flew over the forts, and the *askaris*' guard boxes, painted in a bold striped pattern using the imperial colors black, red, and white, stood right outside the gates. These structures housed the personnel, technological, and visual markers that rendered German military strength formidable to observers.

The trappings of German colonial strength resided in the *bomas*, but in order to be effective as centers of colonial life, they also required a wide range of quotidian relationships with people who came from the areas around the *bomas*.[5] Each station depended on a local economy that provided station members with vital goods and services such as food, laundry, and transportation. The German fantasy of achieving self-sufficiency for its stations required a sizeable and diverse African labor force. African laborers, traders, and others came to the stations to look for employment opportunities.[6] For example, African men and women worked in the station gardens and tended the station's herds. Some of them later became *askari* themselves, or members of *askari* households.[7] Market halls were often located on the stations, drawing sellers and buyers from the surrounding countryside.[8] Traders also set themselves up on the stations' fringes to target *askari* and other colonial employees, especially on paydays. Literate Africans worked as clerks in the station post and telegraph offices, teachers in government schools, and scribe-translators for judicial proceedings.

Construction, renovation, and expansion of station buildings, which was ongoing throughout the colonial period, relied on African labor.[9] Colonial officials soon adjusted their construction expectations to local practices, materials, labor practices, and aesthetics.[10] Efficiency in procuring laborers was best achieved by asking local leaders, known as *majumbe* (sing. *jumbe*), to provide them. To secure the German levies, *majumbe* mobilized their slaves, clients, and household members, with or without compensation. The *majumbe* were generally men of means who had abundant access to labor resources. *Majumbe* could draw laborers from the dependents in their households or from people who had been judged guilty in local judicial processes. Compensation thus depended on the status of the particular laborer and the degree of reciprocal obligation that featured in the *majumbe*-client relationship. Of course, the *majumbe*'s ability or willingness to pay for labor also played a role. *Majumbe* acted as middlemen in filling station labor requirements, allowing *Schutztruppe* officers to avoid negotiating individual contracts with people who saw German rule as illegitimate. Local workers reported to the *bomas* early in the morning with their tools, split up into work groups under *askari* supervision, and were put to work on station construction and upkeep.[11] *Askaris'* garrison duties included constructing station buildings, including their own homes. They also worked as craftsmen.[12] This work scheme kept construction costs low, and kept otherwise idle *askari* occupied. It also allowed them to supervise station laborers, who could include "tax-laborers" or chain-gang prisoners.[13]

The communities surrounding the *bomas* thus developed, or were forced into, social and economic ties to the stations reflective of the fluidity between "colonized" and "colonizer" milieux. Some of these work relationships turned into other kinds of relationships, including marriages, domestic servitude, or other forms of dependency. The *askari* translated their roles as supervisors of workers into *babas*, or "fathers," to vulnerable young men, women, and children who sought protection and community membership.

The stations attracted large numbers of people to their gates despite their imposing exteriors. Labor, whether voluntary or involuntary, was one reason Africans came to the *bomas*. But they also came to participate in or witness special European-sponsored events, such as festivals, parades, and public executions. Dance competitions known as *ngoma* occurred on major festive occasions, and smaller ones also routinely took place in the *askari* villages just outside of the *bomas* and elsewhere in the wider *boma* communities.[14] The contexts where such activities occurred conveyed *Schutztruppe* desires to project power through theatricality.[15] The *Schutztruppe* staged spectacles such as parades and shooting contests, particularly on special occasions like the Kaiser's birthday, openings of railway lines, and visits from high-ranking officials.

During these festivities, the *askari* paraded for the dignitaries and the rest of the crowd in spectacular ceremonial expressions of colonial power. East African men and women who came to the *bomas* on such occasions thought of the German parades and drilling sessions as their particular style of *ngoma*.[16] One of the prevalent forms of *ngoma* in East Africa, the *beni*, incorporated elements of European-style brass-band music and military drill. East African spectators at events like these could have easily associated *beni* with *Schutztruppe* parading sessions. The precision of *askari* parades and drill invariably impressed European observers.[17] On the parade grounds, the *askari* reportedly reflected the highest standards of Prussian military tradition as they performed the colonial government's key rituals of authority. East African onlookers recognized that the Germans were engaged in displays of authority on these occasions, but they also interpreted *Schutztruppe* drill and ceremony through the lens of local modes of dance and performance, such as *ngoma*.[18]

Askari parades marked the beginning of festivities that lasted for the rest of the day and into the night. In honor of these occasions, *askari* also received small cash gifts or goods such as tobacco. They had good reason to celebrate once they were released from parade duties and could begin dancing *ngoma* and consuming intoxicants.[19] The transition from Prussian-style parade to post-parade revelry allowed the *askari* time to celebrate, but that time was also laden with the potential for mischief and violence. The competitive nature of the *ngoma* themselves could easily exacerbate already heightened tensions between the different ethnic sub-groups among the *askari*.[20] The variety of dance styles performed by *askari* who came from places as distant as Cairo attracted large audiences who were entertained by the novelty of the performances and the chance to see new modes of dance that originated outside of East Africa.[21]

Ngoma were "total social phenomena"—overwhelming aural and visual spectacles in which crowds gathered to dance, sing, and drum into the wee hours.[22] The mood was heightened by liberal and widespread consumption of palm wine and hemp.[23] *Ngoma* might occur inside or outside of the *boma* proper. Either way, they were opportunities for all kinds of people to intermingle, with the competitive aspect helping to reinforce different "communities of commitment" among participants and to create a dramatic scene.[24] German observers usually viewed major *ngoma* as expressions of adoration for the European dignitaries involved, and "an approval of colonial rule."[25] But *ngoma* were also occasions for participants to demonstrate their level of satisfaction (or lack thereof) with German patronage and fulfillment of their "duties of reciprocity."[26] Thus, such occasions could be quite tense. The "loosening" of social restraints on such occasions made "uninhibited mockery of authority" a common feature of *ngoma*.[27] Such mockery included giving Germans nicknames that poked fun at particular physical or behavioral traits. Dancers might even perform these characters during *ngoma*.[28]

German authorities organized public celebrations as a way to reinforce a sense of *Heimat* for themselves, but these occasions also allowed them to demonstrate their largess and patronage by relaxing the rules, providing food and drink, and distributing gifts. East Africans translated these occasions into expressions of strength within a framework of mutual obligation or reciprocity. Along with other public spectacles such as *mashauri,* German-sponsored festivities shaped new *bomani* sociabilities. These contributed to the expression of German authority, but also to expressions of local identities, values, and hierarchies that operated under the surface of German fantasies of state control. As *boma* community members, the *askari* were central to the creation of *bomani* colonial cultures.

Itinerant Colonialism I: *Askari* as Tax Collectors

Askari carried out a number of duties in the name of the colonial state. These duties allowed them to travel from place to place, armed and in uniform, to perform the state's authority. One such everyday duty was collecting taxes. Tax collection gave the *askari* abundant opportunities to abuse anyone who resisted. A Lutheran missionary working in the Kilimanjaro region in 1904 witnessed the fear provoked among his congregation by an *askari* tax collection visit:

Recently in Mbaa Masi, as I tried to start the sermon, the people saw a few soldiers appear in the distance. Immediately, everyone fled, the elderly in front, the women with the children and infants behind. I asked them if they had not paid their taxes; when they said yes [they had], I said to them, that they then had no reason to flee. 'But the soldiers harass and beat us,' they replied, running away.[29]

This and other reports from the period show widespread fear of the *askari* in East African communities.[30]

Tax collection occurred in two ways, both conducted by intermediaries. First, *majumbe* collected taxes from the people under their purview and delivered them to the stations. Second, tax collectors, including *askari* and other trusted agents such as clerks, traveled through the tax districts "to urge delinquents to make their payments, thereby preventing too many from escaping taxation." Taxes were paid in cash, livestock, and other goods (such as cereals and wax).[31] Colonial authorities mobilized a mixture of civilian and military intermediaries to collect taxes because of their different skills, such as literacy or language facility, which made tax collection possible. The high-ranking *askari*, described as "temporary personnel," provided the coercive and security element that backed up the other intermediaries in their efforts to make people pay taxes to an alien government.

Numerous tax collection interactions escaped German officers' supervision, which left open many possibilities for *askari* to expropriate local residents.[32] Nor were colonial officials especially concerned with *askaris'* bullying tactics. Colonial government officials elevated the "prestige of the state" and enforcement of colonial order over any other competing interests, and thus paid little attention to complaints about *askari* abuses. The *askari* thus continued their activities unchecked, believing they were entitled to their "illegal exactions."[33] Indeed, these sources of additional income directly contributed to their abilities to fashion themselves as men of standing in the *boma* communities.

Itinerant Colonialism II: *Askari* as Agents of *Mashauri*

Local residents often came to the *bomas* to participate in recurring events called *mashauri*. These were forums for "public deliberation of issues concerning the administration of a district and its population, including legal matters and problems brought to the meeting by the audience."[34] Or, as colonial judge Hans Poeschel put it,

> The shauri can mean anything. Shauri is the court session, shauri is every deliberation and every gossip session[.] [. . .] Having a shauri is the greatest enjoyment that the black knows. For him, it replaces the newspaper, theater, and cinema. [It] is to him what playing skat and drinking beer [are] for the Germans, [what] boxing and football [are] for the English.[35]

Poeschel's emphasis on the *shauri* as a form of entertainment for African attendees captures the element of spectacle the *shauri* embodied. But it downplays the graver aspects of people's attendance at *mashauri*. Colonial officials often handed down harsh sentences at the end of deliberations. The standard punishment for most infractions was either the *hamsa ishirini* (twenty-five strokes with a hide whip) or a period of confinement on a chain gang. Most stations had a special hall or other space designated for conducting the *shauri*, which occurred regularly and handled all manner of local government affairs, judicial matters, private disputes, and public complaints.

Mashauri featured prominently in the everyday affairs of colonial officers and other colonial functionaries, including the *askari*. They took place on a regular basis, even daily in some locations.[36] Colonial officers sometimes complained that conducting *mashauri* took up inordinate amounts of their time, even as they also acknowledged the institution's necessity for colonial governance.[37] Alongside their bureaucratic purposes, they served as sites where colonial authority was enacted, and spaces where colonial sociability played out. Streams of people showed up on *shauri* days to present their complaints, to make requests, to respond to summons, or just to observe the day's events. Michael Pesek argues that *mashauri* were a form of "colonial choreography," in which "the bureaucratic patterns of the colonial state were transformed into a theatrical spectacle."[38] Colonial officers presided over *mashauri* at the *bomas*, and also conducted them on an ad hoc basis during their periodic district tours. *Mashauri* instantiated state authority through paternalistic, face-to-face exercises designed to foreground the ideals encompassed by the German civilizing mission.[39] Yet the German decision to use the Kiswahili word *shauri* to refer to these multipurpose proceedings indicates that at least to some degree, East African notions of community space, justice, and conversation influenced colonial practice.

Askari or ex-*askari* participated in *mashauri* in several ways. They often served as "native" observers of the proceedings.[40] *Askari* also spread word about *mashauri* to surrounding areas.[41] To record complaints against specific individuals, German officials completed a form known as a *Schaurizettel* authorizing plaintiffs to summon the defendant to a *shauri*. *Askari* were sent to arrest those who did not appear. The *Schaurizettel* served as *askaris'* authorization to arrest the accused and escort them back to the *boma*. The pre-printed official form featured bold black, white, and red diagonal stripes with a picture of the imperial eagle in its center. Spaces on the form indicated who was being summoned, when and where they should report, and other details as required. These "well-known and feared" documents had a Kiswahili nickname—"*bendera*-notes" ("flag-notes")—because of their resemblance to the flags that flew over all the stations in German East Africa.[42] According to one German memoirist, "[e]ven if [the recipient] did not command the art of reading, he still knew what the black-white-red piece of paper [with the] strange bird with tattered feathers in the middle meant; it was the unmistakable official order to follow the askari."[43] After locating the accused offenders, *askari* escorted them back to the station. Back at the *boma*, *askari* also carried out punishments for non-compliance with the *Schaurizettel*, along with any additional punishments handed down by the colonial official administering the *shauri*.[44]

    Askari carried out the will of the colonial state independently, often traveling alone or in small groups without German officers present. Their presence incited fear among civilians, but *askari* also abused people to demonstrate their strength through violent threats and acts. In 1905 a German lieutenant at Marangu gave an *askari* a *Schaurizettel* stipulating that he should pick up a Chagga man named Msaba, who was living at a Lutheran mission station in Mamba. Upon arrival the *askari* located Msaba's wife Salime, but not Msaba himself. Believing that Salime was hiding Msaba, the *askari* struck her. Upon learning of the incident, the German lieutenant promised that the *askari* would be punished, since he had overstepped his bounds in striking Salime.[45] This incident is unusual inasmuch as it was documented by a *Schutztruppe* officer, but there were many more such cases in which the *askari* practiced similarly abusive behaviors with impunity.

    Documents like the *Schaurizettel* proved to other colonial officials that the *askari* had reason to be under way with specific people, valuable items, or dangerous materials. In conducting the affairs of the colonial state, individual *askari* routinely traveled great distances as escorts, messengers, and guards. They were entrusted to move people and goods expeditiously and safely, notwithstanding the security and environmental challenges they faced when traveling. Another official document, the *cheti cha rukhsa* (*Erlaubnisschein* or permission slip) was pre-printed in German and Kiswahili, and included spaces for officials to enter information such as the number of women and children accompanying the traveler; number of weapons; pounds of gunpowder and/or lead; and numbers of fuses the traveler carried. Such documents explained clearly why the *askari* was traveling, and they recorded the instructions given to the *askari*. German authorities imagined that they were controlling their soldiers through these documents, and to some degree perhaps they were. As the *askari* transited back and forth between the *bomas*, however, they visibly conveyed the state's authority through their uniforms, their weapons, the bits of paper they carried, the people and goods they guarded.

In carrying the *Schaurizettel* and other similar documents that authorized them to move unimpeded through the colony on colonial business, *askari* carried state authority with them. The documents also conferred legitimacy on their actions as they performed their duties, which reflected the itinerant nature of German colonial administration. These bits of paper expressed the *boma*'s authority, emboldening *askari* to carry out coercive and violent acts against those they encountered in their everyday duties, and whom they considered beneath them. *Askari* acted with impunity because their superiors usually had no oversight over them, and their victims feared repercussions if they reported them. *Askari* benefited greatly from the colonial state's reliance on itinerant practices of power. These practices gave them freedom to perform their superiority complexes, and to wrap their abusive actions in state authority. Colonial practices of governance served both state and *askari* interests. The *bomas*, uniforms, documents, and weapons made them appear invulnerable, even if this was not always the case.

Conclusion

Interactions between *askari* and East Africans who lived around the *bomas* were more complex and diverse than existing portrayals of the *askari* have led us to believe. *Askari* set themselves apart from those around them through their uniforms, their relative wealth, and their privileged status. The authority vested in them by their German superiors marked them as different from others in the colony, and they acted on this difference, often with impunity. Thinking of them as spatially isolated, however, makes it difficult to see the multiple levels of their participation in everyday colonialism. Even within the space that most defined them as a recognizable group—the *boma*—they participated in smaller spaces of appearance that brought them into routine contact with others both inside and outside the *bomas*. The *bomas* were thus less exclusively military than their formidable external facades, and German idealized representations of them, would indicate. The *bomas* became nodes of authority because of their relationships to surrounding communities and the movement back and forth across their boundaries that people undertook every day. At the same time, the *bomas* radiated strength outward through the *askari* and other intermediaries, who wielded it as part of their own self-understanding as men of influence. In some ways, the everyday practices that enabled colonial rule made the state appear stronger than it really was. In the everyday lives of East Africans who experienced the *askaris'* coercive methods, or who experienced the *boma* as a space of oppression, the colonial state seemed quite formidable indeed. But *askari* also created possibilities for East Africans to participate in local colonial economies and their socio-cultural offshoots, if they so desired. In these ways, the *askari* and the *bomas* helped tie diverse East African peoples to the colonial state, setting in motion new modes of self-fashioning, ways of making a living, and social relations.

NOTES

For support while revising this essay, I am most grateful to the Institute for Historical Studies, University of Texas, Austin.

1. Benjamin Lawrance, Emily Lynn Osborn, and Richard L. Roberts, ed., *Intermediaries Interpreters, and Clerks: African Employees in the Making of Colonial Africa* (Madison: University of Wisconsin Press, 2006), 4.

2. Ibid., 7.

3. Marcia Wright, *Strategies of Slaves and Women: Life Stories from East/Central Africa* (New York: Lilian Barber, 1993), 185–87, 206; August Leue, *Dar-es-Salaam: Bilder aus dem Kolonialleben* (Berlin: Wilhelm Süsserott, 1903), 158–67, 213–26.

4. Michael Pesek, *Koloniale Herrschaft in Deutsch-Ostafrika: Expedition, Militär und Verwaltung seit 1880* (Frankfurt: Campus Verlag, 2005), 191.

5. Ibid.; Brian Siegel, "Bomas, Missions, and Mines: The Making of Centers on the Zambian Copperbelt," *African Studies Review* 31, no. 3 (1988): 61.

6. Wright, *Strategies*, 185–87.

7. M. Hildebrandt, *Eine deutsche Militärstation im Innern Afrikas* (Wölfenbüttel: Heckners Verlag, 1905), 12; Otto Stollowsky, *Jambo Sana! Lustige Geschichten, Plaudereien und Schnurren aus dem Leben in Deutsch-Ost und Zanzibar* (Leipzig: Anger-Dachsel, 1921), 123; Wright, *Strategies*, 179–223.

8. Juhani Koponen, *Development for Exploitation: German Colonial Policies in Mainland Tanzania, 1884–1914* (Helsinki: Lit Verlag, 1994), 186; *Militärisches Orientierungsheft für Deutsch-Ostafrika* (Dar es Salaam: Deutsch-Ostafrikanische Rundschau, 1911).

9. Hildebrandt, *Eine deutsche Station*, 23.

10. Hildebrandt, *Eine deutsche Station*, 23; Tom von Prince, *Gegen Araber und Wahehe: Erinnerungen aus meiner ostafrikanischen Leutnantszeit, 1890–1895* (Berlin: Mittler, 1914), 114.

11. Hildebrandt, *Eine deutsche Station*, 20.

12. Ibid.

13. Ibid., 19–20. See also Sperling to *Gouvernement*, 1 March 1911, Tanzania National Archives (hereafter TNA), G 7/42, no folio number; TNA, G 7/12, p. 66.

14. In Kiswahili, *ngoma* can mean a drum, a dance performance involving drumming, or a party.

15. Pesek, *Koloniale Herrschaft*, 262–63.

16. Ibid.

17. "Was Prinz Adalbert in Tanga gesehen hat. Bilder vom Prinzenbesuch am 13. Februar." *Beilage zur Usambara-Post*, 18 February 1905. See also Missionary Raum, "Eröffnung der Usambara-Eisenbahn in Neu-Moschi am 7. Februar 1912," *Evangelisch-Lutherisches Missionsblatt* 67 (1912): 208–9.

18. Gudrun Miehe et al., eds., *Kala Shairi: German East Africa in Swahili Poems* (Cologne: Rüdiger Köppe Verlag, 2002), 458–70.

19. "Gouvernement Befehl," 8 October 1891; and Schmidt to Soden, 24 October 1891, TNA, G 1/4.

20. Terence Ranger, *Dance and Society in Eastern Africa 1890–1970: The Beni Ngoma* (Berkeley and Los Angeles: University of California Press, 1975), 19.

21. Leue, *Dar-es-Salaam*, 187–89.

22. Jonathon Glassman, *Feasts and Riot: Revelry, Rebellion, and Popular Consciousness on the Swahili Coast, 1856–1888* (Portsmouth, NH: Heinemann, 1995), 161.

23. "Was Prinz Adalbert in Tanga gesehen hat," *Usambara Post*, 18 February 1905; *Anzeigen für Tanga (Stadt und Bezirk)*, May–July 1903.

24. Ranger, *Dance and Society*, 19.

25. Pesek, *Koloniale Herrschaft*, 262.

26. Glassman, *Feasts and Riot*, 245–46; Jane Parpart and Marianne Rostgaard, eds., *The Practical Imperialist: Letters from a Danish Planter in German East Africa 1888–1906* (Leiden: Brill, 2006), 160.

27. Glassman, *Feasts and Riot*, 164.

28. Parpart and Rostgaard, *The Practical Imperialist*, 151.

29. "Nachrichten aus Myambani. Quartalbericht von Miss. Augustus (4. Quartal 1904)," *Evangelisch-Lutherisches Missionsblatt* 60, no. 7 (1 April 1905): 165–66.

30. For a similar example from the southern part of the colony (Songea), see also P. Joh. Haefliger, "Chronik von Kigonsera," October 12, 1901, Peramiho Abbey, Songea, Tanzania.

31. Albinus, "Dienstreise im Bezirk Ssongea," 15 November 1904, Bundesarchiv (BArch) R1001/234, pp. 15–16.

32. Albinus to Gouvernement, 15 November 1904, BArch, R 1001/234, pp. 17–18; Michels to *Gouverneur*, 20 July 1914, TNA, G 9/23, p. 148.

33. Lorne Larson, "A History of the Mahenge (Ulanga) District, ca. 1860–1957" (PhD diss., University of Dar es Salaam, 1976), 109.

34. Jan-Georg Deutsch, "Celebrating Power in Everyday Life: The Administration

of Law and the Public Sphere in Colonial Tanzania, 1890–1914," *Journal of African Cultural Studies* 14, no. 1 (2002), 96. For examples of cases heard in *shauris* in Tanga in 1906, see "Shaurihalle," *Usambara Post*, 14 April 1906. See also Pesek, *Koloniale Herrschaft*, 277–83.

35. Hans Poeschel, *Bwana Hakimu: Richterfahrten in Deutsch-Ostafrika* (Leipzig: Koehler und Voigtländer, 1940), 58. See also Hildebrandt, *Eine deutsche Militärstation*, 53; Pesek, "Cued Speeches: The Emergence of Shauri as Colonial Praxis in German East Africa, 1850–1903," *History in Africa* 33 (2006): 409; Prince, *Gegen Araber und Wahehe*, 115–16.

36. Prince, *Gegen Araber*, 115. See also Charisius to Rechenberg, 16 January 1907, BArch R 1001/227, p. 5; and Missionsinspektor Weishaupt, "Überblick über unsere Missionsstationen in Ostafrika. (Fortsetzung.) 4. Moschi," *Evangelisches-Lutherisches Missionsblatt* 67 (1912): 206.

37. Diary entries for 16–24 June 1898, Leipzig Institut für Länderkunde, Nachlass von Prittwitz und Gaffron, Box 248, Folder 6.

38. Pesek, "Cued Speeches," 409–10.

39. See, for example, Tabora Annual Report for 1908, TNA, G 1/6, pp. 29–32; and Reuss to parents, 19 May 1909, BArch, KlE 857/1.

40. Reuss to parents, 19 May 1909, BArch KlE 857/1.

41. Poeschel, *Bwana Hakimu*, 169.

42. Burkhard Vieweg, *Macho Porini—Die Augen im Busch: Kautschukpflanzer Karl Vieweg in Deutsch-Ostafrika: Authentische Berichte 1910–1919* (Weikersheim: Margraf Verlag, 1996), 144. See also Hildebrandt, *Eine deutsche Militärstation*, 3, 54–55.

43. Vieweg, *Macho Porini*, 144.

44. Lionel Declé, *Three Years in Savage Africa* (Bulawayo: Books of Rhodesia, 1974), 386–87; Prince, *Gegen Araber*, 115; Willmann to Schanz, 11 April 1905, TNA, G 9/31, p. 117.

45. Willmann to Schanz, 11 April 1905, TNA, G 9/31, pp. 115, 117.

Pioneers of Empire?

The Making of Sisal Plantations in German East Africa, 1890–1917

Hanan Sabea

In 1925, Richard Hindorf commented on the prospect of sisal production in East Africa:

> Nobody who would have visited German East Africa right before the war and had familiarized himself with its life, which visibly carries the imprints of sisal production, would have ever imagined that 22 years earlier no sisal agave, nor any other fibrous agave existed in German East Africa . . . It is my strong conviction that in no long a time East Africa will be the most important sisal producing area in the world.[1]

Hindorf's conviction came true, and sisal's rise to prominence, which had begun in German East Africa (GEA), continued unabated for almost three-quarters of a century, after the end of German colonial rule in the area. Sisal plantations rose from 1 in 1893 to 54 by 1913, and production jumped from a mere 0.6 tons in 1898 to 20,835 tons in 1913, comprising almost 30 percent of the total value of GEA exports.[2] Equally significant, sisal plantations became a key site carrying the imprints of modern colonial power relations. Sisal plantations epitomized the ideals of a colonial project whose agents were striving to establish visible signs of their power and values on a new terrain. But who were the agents who made this process possible?

Combining knowledge gained from ethnographic and archival research in London and Tanzania, and oral histories with sisal plantation workers, and supplementing these with secondary sources, I argue that African workers on nascent sisal plantations were key agents in shaping everyday life in GEA, particularly in this case the making of sisal plantations. A key node in this process was constituting life and work on sisal plantations as "a way of life," as their descendants insisted in their oral accounts. This "way of life" was premised on the workers' ability to negotiate and challenge the novel configurations of space and time and the disciplining of laboring bodies that were being instituted as markers of European plantations. Control over hours of day and night, rest and work, over mobility, sociality, and access to land were primary sites over which workers, managers, and colonial officials constantly struggled. Equally important was maneuvering the many layers of supervision and surveillance that structured the plantation as a universe on its own, distinct from surrounding village life by its orderliness and regularity. These everyday practices and negotiations of land and labor relationships on the plantations highlight first continuities and changes between pre-colonial and colonial contexts.

The new socio-economic and political order that ensued in German East Africa was not a replica of what prevailed earlier, nor was it a complete break from laboring practices African men and women devised prior to the imposition of colonial rule. In fact, as I demonstrate below, experience and encounters of porters along the caravan routes or on Arab plantations during the early to mid-nineteenth century constituted facades of "the cultural familiar" that informed how workers constituted life on sisal plantations. Second, the everyday lives of men and women on sisal plantations crystallize the limitations of colonial desires and rationalities. "Sisal as a way of life" was marked by the constant struggle to subvert structures of authority that undermined workers' ability to retain control over time, labor, land, and mobility. As a consequence the making of colonial life in GEA did not follow the script colonial agents imagined and desired. Yet what was established during these first two decades of the twentieth century would mark Tanzania's socio-economic and political history for more than a century to come.

After a brief note on sisal and the precarious nature of its production in GEA, I discuss the value of plantations as signs of the colonial order being established. There I argue that the racial paradigm that defined colonial visions of the new terrain and its inhabitants as well as the challenges that faced the plantation sector obstructed the ability of colonial agents to recognize the agency of Africans in shaping the worlds they inhabited and the terms of their engagement with European planters. The latter is most crystallized in the negotiations over land and labor that marked the making of plantation culture, a theme that I discuss in the following section. There I highlight the diverse points of contention in the making (and unmaking) of colonial governmentality, as well as the threads that connect the practices of plantation workers to the experiences of laboring men and women prior to the imposition of colonial governance.

Sisal: The "Tree of Wonder" on a World Trip to Tanga

Sisal is a hard fiber originating in Mexico. Although used for centuries, it was not until the early nineteenth century that *agave* fibers were "discovered." This discovery was triggered by a surge of European interest in the plant for industrial purposes, an interest that intensified with the invention of machine harvesters, automatic grain binders, and hay balers by the mid-nineteenth century. By the 1890s *agave* fibers diffused around the world, primarily moving within the orbits of colonial empires, namely, the British, Dutch, and German.[3]

The "romantic epic"[4] of sisal is captured in a trip around the world of 1,000 sisal plants from Yucatan to Tanga imported by Dr. Richard Hindorf, the German botanist employed by the Deutsch-Ostafrikanische Gesellschaft (DOAG) in 1890s, and of which only 62 survived. These 62 plants "founded the sisal industry in Tanganyika."[5] But who were the sisal planters and why did they decide to invest in sisal—then an unfamiliar commodity—on the shores of East Africa? Hindorf's story contains some of the answers that connect the story of a commodity to the colony and planters.

The Schöllers who founded Amboni, which is a leading company in sisal production since the 1890s, are a case in point. Hindorf's travels from the Far East to Africa, his position as a botanist at DOAG, the chartered company administering German territories in East Africa, and his reliance on science in experimenting with the flora of distant places to find the most suitable species for economic exploitation, were parts of a colonial process that started with exploration and discovery and ended with conquest. Hindorf (and his contemporaries, like Rudolph Schöller) became part and parcel of the official matrix of making empire through their respective realms of science and economic enterprise. They all shared the expansive desires, the want for control over land and its resources, and the curiosity about the unfamiliar, and were backed by the authority of science, the gun, and the Bible. Rudolph Schöller's actions, inexplicable sometimes along economic lines, can be understood as partaking in a similar project of expansion in distant lands that were to be mapped along reference points set in the metropolis.

Born in Düren in 1827, Rudolph Schöller joined an industrialist family with a tradition in spinning and weaving. In the wake of colonial conquest, he bought shares in the *Kommanditgesellschaft Karl Perrot & Co.* One of the company's initial activities was the acquisition of land, and by 1894 their holdings reached 21,779 ha of agricultural land in addition to numerous properties in towns. Due to conflicts among board members *Karl Perrot* was liquidated and the *Westdeutsche Handels und Plantagen Gesellschaft* incorporated, with Rudolph Schöller holding 33 percent of its shares. He added more land, invested in plantation infrastructure, and experimented with tropical commodities like coffee, gum, coconut, rubber, and vanilla. Given the success of sisal experiments by Dr. Hindorf and the relative increase in value of sisal, the *Westdeutsche* shifted to *Agave Sisalana* by 1900. However, at the turn of the century the market for East African sisal was limited, with almost all of it ending up on the Hamburg market.[6] Sisal ranked low on the hard fiber scene: the German navy declined to incorporate East African sisal into its rope needs, as the latter proved "unsatisfactory" compared with the long-standing position of abaca for marine purposes.[7] The alternative was agricultural twines, and that is where sisal started enlarging its market share. Germany's increasing, though limited, demand for hard fibers (from 8,000 tons in 1904 to 11,000 tons by 1910) motivated planters and settlers to invest in sisal despite oscillation in market prices, and in a few years, sisal rose to prominence in the political economy of GEA.[8]

Plantations and Visions of Colonial Order

From the 1890s and until the eve of World War I, plantations with sisal eventually becoming the leading commodity were major sites in the reconstruction of a colonial territory, a process that built on existing institutions and relationships, while European agents were attempting to transform them in the name of civilization and progress. Indeed as Rodney argued, "in the systematic colonization of German East Africa, the first major institution which was established was the plantation."[9] I suggest that plantations occupied an indispensable position in GEA despite competitions, tensions, and failures precisely because they could be imagined by colonial agents as ideal sites for the political, economic, and socio-cultural order desired.[10] Plantations were microcosms for the larger colonial society; and despite all their shortcomings, the presence and practices of plantations were fundamental to the extension of German social, cultural, and political influence as well as the economic exploitation of colonial appendages for the service of the fatherland. Indeed, "Just as Zanzibar's impact had radiated through the country during the nineteenth century, so the plantations' impact radiated outward in German times."[11] And though Arab and Swahili plantations were just in the vicinity, for German colonial agents these enterprises could not approximate the European plantation: the race and religion of the planters, their partial reliance on slave labor, the paternalistic relationship between planter and workers, and the presumed laxity of the organization of production, all placed them outside of the orbit of what Europeans constituted as normal standards of practice.

Ironically, these colonial racial ideologies of distinction, superiority, and prowess, or what Fabian termed the "grammar of oppositions . . . which characterized colonial discourse from its beginnings,"[12] were at odds with what actually was happening in the territories in terms of shifts in social and economic relations in villages, towns, and plantations. For instance, villagers were already heavily involved in the production of cash crops and food for the growing populations in towns, Arab and Swahili plantations, and along the caravan routes. The commercialization of agriculture and the commoditization of labor were well under way from the 1860s,[13] while labor migration shaped relations in different parts of the territories and "showed an African face to the modern world."[14] Yet, it was the "denial of recognition" as Fabian termed it[15] that enabled colonial agents to imagine European plantations as starkly different and thus symbolizing the epitome of colonial order.

As economic enterprises defining colonial policy, plantations competed with settlers and African cash crop production.[16] It was primarily after the Maji Maji Rebellion and the systematic failures facing plantations that a more concerted effort to promote African production materialized. However, this did not mean any less official backing for plantations. In fact, since 1907 the number of corporate plantations and settler farms tripled, their investments in the economy reached new peaks, and their share of exports rose from 4 percent in 1907 to 4/7th in 1914.[17] While in the beginning coffee, coconut, cocoa, vanilla, and cardamom were planted, the picture by 1909 was certainly in favor of sisal (14,316 ha), followed by rubber (12,853 ha), cotton (6,367 ha), coconut (6,275 ha), and coffee (3,822 ha). In terms of workers, in 1902 the number of "colored" workers (*farbige Arbeiter*) on each plantation ranged between 150 and 350, while "white staff" (*weiße Beamte*) averaged 3. By 1909, the numbers jumped to 36,423 "colored workers" (by 1913 tripling to 91,892) and 332 "whites."[18]

Though there is nothing inherent in sisal that dictates its production on plantation basis, GEA sisal was constructed as a plantation commodity, almost exclusive to big companies who had the financial and political capital deemed essential for sisal. Since its inception, sisal was thus synonymous with power, capital, and progress, all ideals of a colonial project that was seeking not only economic profit but also visible signs of dominating presence.

Land and Labor in the Making of Sisal Plantations

In the process of instituting plantations the quest for a particular type of access to land (private property) and labor (disciplined bodies performing regular time-marked tasks) were challenged by prevailing practices of land and labor use that were at odds with colonial agents' visions, rationalities, and desires. The emerging plantation culture among workers and villagers, which often translated into problems in administering "natives" and disciplining labor, attest to the challenges posed to colonial powers and the ability of workers to constitute their lives in alternative ways to those imagined by colonial agents.

Land: Legalizing the Foundation of Colonial Order

The 1895 Imperial Land Decree divested African land rights: all land was ownerless (*herrenlos*), and ownership was invested in Empire (crown land), except when proof of ownership could be shown.[19] Preserving "native" land rights was legally defined as "present rights," which were recognized on the basis of physical occupation, while future rights were four times the present area under occupation. The 1896 Imperial Circular further distinguished between ownership rights and rights of occupation. While the former were based on proof of documented titles, those without title were constituted as a collective entity (the tribe) whose presence was recognized by virtue of laboring on the land (cultivation and use). Additionally, *Eingeborene oder andere Farbige* (natives or other coloreds) were not allowed to register land and "were prohibited from encumbering their landed property with mortgages or other charges, because the colonial government regarded them as not fit for participation in a basically German legal system."[20]

The 1895 Decree sanctioned land alienation in favor of European plantations and settlers and ensured the dispossession of many communities, thus pushing them into wage labor on possibly the same lands they used to hold. Land near villages was reserved for Africans' personal use. However, indigenous communities "were even not allowed to sell or to lease land which was situated within the reserved area to other Africans who did not belong to the group for which the respective area was created."[21] Not only were flexible social relationships fixed, but also equally important blood and genealogical ties fixed Africans spatially over the colonial landscape.

In contrast, DOAG controlled large tracts of land along the coast, using some of it for the establishment of plantations. It also started parceling land among prospecting planters, especially big plantation companies. Most of this land, particularly in the densely populated northeast, became the hub of sisal plantations. Europeans' thirst for land, especially on the coast and the northeast, compounded an already complex nexus of property, religion, kinship, and authority relationships that evolved over years between different groups of Africans, Arabs, Swahili, and Indians. On the one hand, such complexity shaped relationships surrounding authority, land, and labor once land moved into European hands (for instance, demands for protection that villagers expected from Europeans in return for land purchases).[22] On the other hand, the complexity of property relations became a resource in litigating claims to land. Though legally confined to the category of *Eingeborenen* (native), people appealed to a range of property relations and identities to contest loss of land or its devaluation without title.

That many sought registered and documented titles to the land they had occupied for years bespeaks the power of the singular mode of value that came to define the territories. It also signals the new technologies of power (laws and writing) deployed by the colonial state, though accessed and manipulated by its subjects in attempts to fend off the encroachments by the state over their resources and in their everyday life. This especially became more of a necessity with the heightened demand for land by plantations and settlers. Further, the influx of migrant labor to work on the plantations placed more demands on limited land resources. Conflicts over land intensified, especially with the multitude of transactions (use, lease, purchase, mortgage, exchanges) that were taking place between Africans, Indians, Arabs, and Europeans. The alienation of land also increased the vulnerability of local communities, economically, socially, and morally. Those who lost their land also lost the dignity of being able to refuse working for others as wage laborers on plantations. That planters and settlers very soon recognized this safeguarding mechanism of land is evidenced in their systematic demands to challenge Africans' access and rights to land in order to ensure the flow of laboring bodies.[23] Land and labor were inseparable in shaping relationships surrounding plantations.

Quantity or Quality: Parameters of the Labor Calamity

The labor question was not one of labor availability, though the diverse colonial interests couched it as such. What was absent was a particular form of labor: regular, stable, and disciplined to work a specified number of hours per day and days per month, receiving some form of remuneration, and within an organization of production that was harnessed by supervision, science, and technology.[24] This form of organization was already inscribed in Hindorf's account, fixing the standards of sisal, which were passed on year after year as the "bible of sisal."[25] Hindorf prescribed that an average plantation of 1,000 ha required a stable, highly disciplined labor force at the rate of 300 labor-days per year for every hectare of sisal to perform the year-round operations of cutting leaves, cleaning fields, planting nurseries, decorticating, drying, brushing, and baling sisal fiber. A supervisory team was paramount to guarantee adherence to productivity standards.[26] Resistance to laboring along these parameters (and under abusive and poor conditions) reinforced the quantitative argument (lack of sufficient numbers).

At the inception, the use of force prevailed on GEA plantations. To make chiefs comply with the demands for labor, coercion was used directly and indirectly, mostly in unison with local state agents. In Tanga, for instance, the district officer divided the district into eight to fifteen huts, each having to provide one worker at prescribed intervals to work on the plantations.[27] When this failed, the district officer in West Usambara issued "each Shambaa with a card obliging him to work for a European for thirty days every four months at a fixed wage."[28] Collaboration with headmen of interior regions to send workers to the plantation areas earned local authorities the disgrace of having "sold their people for a rupee a head."[29]

Though rhetorically deploring the use of slaves by Arab and Swahili planters as "something repugnant to the European mind,"[30] "slaves remained part of the colonial plantation economy until the end of German rule, often working along side long-distance labor migrants and local wage laborers and receiving a share of plantation wages."[31] Legally Germans could not own slaves. However, European planters hired slaves from Arab and Swahili planters, or rented them from labor brokers. They ransomed slaves and obliged them to work on plantations until full payment of the price of purchase. The government also ransomed slaves and sent them to German plantations to work off what they owed the state.[32]

DOAG also resorted to importing labor. The first batch of Javanese and ethnic Chinese (462 men) appeared in Tanga in 1892, then again in 1894. Asian indentured workers had a ten-hour workday, with two rest-days per month, and their wages were almost twice those paid to Africans. The experiment soon collapsed due to its expensiveness, bad conditions on the plantations (which resulted in desertions), attacks on European managers, and attempted riots.[33] Using convict labor was another option, and by "the late 1890s penal policy became a means for the state to channel hundreds of African men and women onto plantations and public works."[34]

Recourse to force, slaves, convicts, and imported labor reflected a belief affirmed by experience that the labor power of coastal people was unattainable. Refusing to acknowledge the rejection of plantation work as resistance to particular forms of working and living conditions, the reasons forwarded by European employers were couched in the language of race. The inhabitants of the coast were projected as the epitome of the lazy indolent native. Further, access to land allowed coastal people a degree of independence that kept them away from plantation work.[35]

The alternative was tapping the labor power of people from the interior, relying on migrant labor. To recruit workers, plantations relied on Arab and Indian contractors and merchants, on headmen, as well as workers returning home.[36] In addition to recruited migrants, others moved to the coast on their own. Porters, mainly Nyamwezi of western parts of the territories, formed the genesis of migrant labor on European plantations.[37] In addition to porters, in early 1900 people from the south of the territories (especially the Ngoni) and Makonde migrants from neighboring Mozambique found their way to northern plantations.[38] From 1908 onward, the effects of the Maji Maji Rebellion, famine, ecological disasters, land alienation, the ease of transport and movement afforded by roads and railways, intensive recruiting, and the burden of tax payments expanded the groups involved in plantation labor. In short, despite all conflicts among employers of labor, the discourse of labor shortage, and workers' resistance to being converted into a stable, disciplined workforce, in actual numbers people moving into plantation work increased. While at the turn of the century the numbers were within the range of 10,000, by 1912–13 they reached 91,892.[39]

It is undeniable that the state adopted policies to narrow the alternatives available for people, thus forcing them into plantation labor. Even food relief distribution at times of famine was linked to plantation work.[40] Paying taxes, phrased as an obligation to the state, was key in pushing people into plantation wage labor. Shifts in economic structures and deskilling of the caravan workforce due to colonial restrictions meant that many former wage workers moved to plantation work.[41] Others joined plantation labor to meet temporary household needs for cash, satisfy their desires for wealth, and find new ways of life. Paying bride-wealth without falling into debt to elders and local patrons was a reason to seek temporary wage-work on European plantations.[42] The glamour associated with travel and adventure, with new commodities, and with coastal cosmopolitan culture as propagated by Indian and Arab merchants and contractors, drove many to coastal plantations.[43] Especially for those already involved in the caravan trade and on Arab plantations, migration to earn cash was not a novelty. Their experiences and practices informed the actions of those who followed.[44]

Many workers negotiated terms of work and leisure on plantations. This ability to set their own terms was countered by legislation that classified workers' choice of time, length, and place of work, standards of tasks, their mobility and sociality as breaches of contract, punishable by law. The 1896 law elaborated the concept of working contract.[45] These regulations, which tied workers to the plantation through a legally binding relationship, were instrumental in controlling and disciplining labor through the specification of space (particular plantation), time (length of contract), and punishable offenses. Corporal punishment underpinned labor management. Underlying the centrality of punishment is the assumption and fear of the criminality of the laboring lot and the primitivity of *The African*, who "is a born slave, who needs his despot like an opium addict needs his pipe"; hence the "sole task of the administration in a colony is to discipline natives for white enterprises."[46] Equally important, the primacy given to punishment bespeaks a daily reality confronted by planters: the ability of workers to challenge the structures of power and surveillance that were instituted to regulate every aspect of their lives.

The management of workers was premised on how labor was classified. The racial distinction between white staff and colored workers reflected the hierarchies of a colonial social order of which plantations were a part. Workers were further classified by their origin, that is, from the district, hence local and indigenous, or recruited, thus distant and alien.[47] Only in Tanga for the year 1902 do we find a more detailed classification of workers on the basis of gender and age: women and children were counted separately, though women and children were not allowed to sign contracts for work in distant areas until 1913.

It was mainly the distinction of "local" and "recruited" that prevailed in managing conditions of labor on plantation. "Labor was divided into day (or casual) labour and contract (or recruited) labour. The day labourers were not bound by any master, and worked on plantations near their homes. They were usually given piecework and paid for it the same day. Contract Labourers were recruited up-country, and were signed on for 180 or 240 working days."[48] The concern was how to manage the native and labor questions, namely, recruiting, the potentially unregulated movement of natives around the territories, and the effects of labor migration on both home and employment areas (in terms of payment of taxes in home areas, the absence of men from local food and cash crop production, the mixing of tribes and the immoralities associated with it). It was precisely this set of concerns that was articulated in the 1909 regulations, where the absence of migrant men from their home villages was limited to nine months, recruiting was brought under the supervision of the state, and the unregulated movement of men was addressed.[49] Yet whatever planters believed, decreed, or desired, in practice men, women, and children managed to constitute through their actions, aspirations, and the constraints they faced what came to be known as "sisal as a way of life."

The Texture of a "Way of Life"

"Sisal as way of life" and the specificity of sisal plantation culture were embodied in the spatial layout of the plantation. From descriptions and maps in Hindorf (1925) and Kisbert, the historian commissioned to write the annals of Amboni, and according to oral accounts of workers I interviewed in Tanga during fieldwork between 1994 and 1997, plantations were located in the midst of dense village settlements, appearing as a geometrical frame of same-sized blocks divided into identical rows carrying equally spaced sisal plants and surrounded by same-length field roads. In the center was the factory complex for sisal processing, along with the offices of the manager, his top supervisory team, and the clerks. Plantation rail ran through the fields, and leading to the factory. The labor camps housing workers were located at the edges of the plantation, blending into the villages nearby.[50] Workers and villagers crossed the village and the plantation in search of work, relations, goods, resources, services and places to hide in case of desertion. Land on the plantation was a potential resource for villagers, and workers could access plots in villages for farming purposes. Working for extra cash was a possibility both on the plantation as day labor and in villages. Shops, clinics, markets, *shauris* (negotiation or mediation meetings), and tax *barazas* (centers for tax collection) were held on plantations for villagers and workers. Many villagers were workers on the estates, and many estate workers were residents in the villages.[51] Layers of supervisors, watchers, reporters, and camp *askaris* moved around the fields and factory and labor camps day and night, thus placing property, people, and their places of work and sites of intimacy and sociability under constant surveillance.[52]

Different temporal routines marked plantation culture and its surroundings, in work and sociality. Thus while the life cycle of the sisal plant defined the spatio-temporal organization of plantation work, planting and harvesting seasons in nearby villages and distant ones from which migrant workers came shaped the pattern of labor movement in and out of plantation work and the number of days worked. Paydays and festive nights of wedding or initiation ceremonies fueled managers' discourse about lazy drunken Africans who lacked discipline and work rigor. These nights also epitomized the obsession and fear about African permissiveness, pleasures, sexuality, and emotions that in the minds of managers, administrators, and missionaries always had the potential of getting out of control.[53] To mitigate such dangers, administrators and managers placed camps under watch of *askaris* and stipulated that dancing and beer brewing be subjected to licensing and permits, while missionaries preached against the immorality of plantation life and the heathenness of African customs.

In the same way that order, discipline, and control typified life on sisal plantations, subversion and resistance comprised its other face. In fact, many of these practices carry the imprints of experiences of porters detailed by Rockel,[54] affirming his argument that many a practice that defined the culture of porters was reinvented in the encounter of workers on European plantations. The oral accounts of workers were replete with stories about going slow, not showing up for work, refusing to work in bad fields, not completing the task, rejecting plantations with bad managers, and deserting. Others forged names or traded tax receipts to avoid or seek plantation labor, or adopted other names to escape arrest in cases of desertion.[55] In the camps much like the safari camps of porters many workers and villagers danced without permits, and women brewed beer without license, or joined men in the camps and were labeled prostitutes. *Utani* (form of joking relationships), songs, and what Rockel termed "culture of honor" were also markers of the social networks and forms of sociality that defined workers' lives on the plantations.

These everyday practices constituted life on sisal plantations as a "way of life," in its most peculiar, most resilient, yet also most ordinary facets. Sisal as a way of life was and remains a culture of work and sociality that was as much about subverting authority as it was about farming the land, earning a living, acquiring wealth, marrying, having children, maintaining friends and kin, moving around, and carrying on with ordinary social life. The thickness of this way of life embodies the experiences and social worlds that the mix of slaves, porters, migrant and local workers, Europeans, Arab and Indian merchants, and villagers brought to the plantations. They also bespeak how the experiences of porters as the first group of migrant wage workers came to inform and constitute the familiar in the making of lives of workers on the plantations.

Conclusion

The outbreak of World War I brought about a sudden end to the official German colonial project in GEA. The nascent sisal plantation sector was thrown into abyss, only to be revived shortly after the war, reaching under the British Mandate the prominence that Hindorf prophesied in his 1925 account. Defining the contours of British policy in Tanganyika in 1927 Sir Donald Cameroon argued, "We believed that we had in that respect in Tanganyika what was very nearly, if not quite, a clean sheet, and that, having a clean sheet on which to write that chapter of the history of Tanganyika, it was all the more important that we should write correctly."[56] What the British presumed by writing a chapter in the history of a place and a people differed little from what the Germans assumed after their conquest in 1890. Both colonial projects were premised on the idea of reworking a place and a people that were a "clean sheet" and saw Europeans as the main agents in writing the script on the blankness. But both British and Germans refused to recognize the agency and experiences of thousands of Africans who participated equally in shaping that space and the very colonial project of which they were part. Sisal plantations were one domain that magnified this making of colonial governmentality. Ironically, while plantations were central institutions in the making of the colonial terrain, they were also "threats" to the racial, political, economic, and moral order desired by planters and the state. Young single men were feared for being free from tribal authority, and the high rate of desertion meant that they could be roaming around the districts disturbing law, order, and morality[57] and undermining economic productivity. The increase in alien migrant men in plantation areas alarmed administrators who warned that the "original population has been swamped."[58] Encroachments and squatting on European plantations in an attempt to secure rights to land intensified conflicts, while the blurred boundaries between village and plantation undermined further the attempts of the colonial state at creating the orderly racial landscape defined by two separate spheres of native and white European. If we consider plantations as forming a crucial node at the center of the German colonial project, they were populated by the very margins of that order, namely, native subjects who managed to strike back at the very heart of Empire.

NOTES

1. Richard Hindorf, *Der Sisalban in Deutsch-OstaAfrika* (Sisal Cultivation in German East Africa) (Berlin: Reimer, 1925), 1, my translation.

2. Adolfo C. Mascarenhas, "Resistance and Change in the Sisal Plantation System of Tanzania" (PhD diss., University of California, 1970), 72; Hindorf, *Sisalban in Deutsch-Ostafrica*, 2.

3. Michael S. Yoder, "The Latin American Plantation Economy and the World

Economy: The Case of the Yucatecan Henequen Industry," *Review* 16, no. 3 (1993): 322.

4. Eldred Hitchcock, *The Sisal Industry of East Africa* (London: Beauchamp Printing, 1957), 3.

5. Hitchcock, *The Sisal Industry of East Africa*, 4.

6. Public Record Office/Colonial Office/691/1/51293. Disposal of Sisal From GEA, 1916.

7. Public Record Office/Colonial Office/691/1/45106. *Enemy Produce from GEA. Disposal in UK, 1916*.

8. Public Record Office/Colonial Office/691/1/51293. *Disposal of Sisal From GEA, 1916*; Juhani Koponen, *Development for Exploitation: German Colonial Policies in Mainland Tanzania, 1884–1914* (Helsinki: Tiedekirja, 1994), 206; John Iliffe, *Tanganyika under German Rule, 1905–1912* (Cambridge: Cambridge University Press, 1969), 100.

9. Walter Rodney, "Migrant Labour and the Colonial Economy," in *Migrant Labour in Tanzania during the Colonial Period: Case Studies of Recruitment and Conditions of Labour in the Sisal Industry*, ed. Walter Rodney, Kapepwa Tambila, and Laurent Sago (Hamburg: Institut fur Afrika-Kunde, 1983), 7.

10. Hanan Sabea, "Mastering the Landscape? Sisal Plantations, Land and Labor in Tanga Region, 1893–1980s," *International Journal of African Historical Studies* 41, no. 3 (2008): 415.

11. John Iliffe, *A Modern History of Tanganyika* (Cambridge: Cambridge University Press, 1979), 151.

12. Johannes Fabian, *Out of Our Minds: Reason and Madness in the Exploration of Central Africa* (Berkeley: University of California Press, 2000), 233.

13. Stephen J. Rockel, *Carriers of Culture: Labor on the Road in Nineteenth Century East Africa* (Portsmouth, NH: Heinemann, 2006), 86–90; Jan-Georg Deutsch, *Emancipation without Abolition in German East Africa, c. 1884–1914* (Athens: Ohio University Press, 2006), 77–82.

14. Rockel, *Carriers of Culture*, 231.

15. Fabian, *Out of Our Minds*, 228.

16. Koponen, *Development for Exploitation*, 167–74.

17. Koponen, *Development for Exploitation*, 606; Thaddeus Sunseri, *Vilimani: Labor Migration and Rural Change in Early Colonial Tanzania* (Portsmouth, NH: Heinemann, 2002), 137; Chris Maina Peter, "Imperialism and Export Capital: A Survey of Foreign Private Investments in Tanzania during the German Colonial Period," *Journal of Asian and African Studies* 25, no. 3–4 (1990).

18. Tanganyika National Archives. G8/22. *Plantagenstatistik, 1902–1903*; Tanganyika National Archives. G8/24. *Plantagenstatistik, 1908–1909*; Tanganyika National Archives. G8/26. *Plantagenstatistik, 1910–1912*.

19. Ministry of Lands, Housing and Urban Development. The United Republic of Tanzania. *Report of the Presidential Commission of Inquiry into Land Matters. Volume I. Land Policy and Land Tenure Structure*. Dar-Es-Salaam, Tanzania, 1994.

20. Harold Sippel, "Aspects of Colonial Land Law in German East Africa," in *Land Law and Land Ownership in Africa: Case Studies from Colonial and Contemporary*

Cameroon and Tanzania, ed. Robert Debusmann and Stefan Arnold (Bayreuth: Bayreuth African Studies Breitinger, Bayreuth University, 1996), 24.

21. Sippel, "Aspects of Colonial Land Law in German East Africa," 30.

22. See James Giblin, "Land Tenure, Traditions of Thought about Land and Their Environmental Implications in Tanzania," *Tanzania Zamani* 4, no. 1/2 (1998): 17–18.

23. Sabea, "Mastering the Landscape," 417–18.

24. Koponen, *Development for Exploitation*, 322.

25. Personal interview with a former sisal plantation manager, Tanga, May 1995.

26. Hindorf, *Sisalban in Deutsch-Ostafrika*, 12–26.

27. Department of Labour, Tanganyika Territory, *Annual Labour Department Reports*, 1927, 7; Koponen, *Development for Exploitation*, 343.

28. Iliffe, *A Modern History of Tanganyika*, 153; Koponen, *Development for Exploitation*, 400.

29. Department of Labour, Tanganyika Territory, *Annual Labour Department Reports*, 1928, 9.

30. Public Record Office/Colonial Office/691/4/20885. *Slavery, 1917*.

31. Sunseri, *Vilimani*, 26.

32. Deutsch, *Emancipation without Abolition*, 181–93; Thaddeus Sunseri, "Slave Ransoming in German East Africa, 1885–1922," *International Journal of African Historical Studies* 26, no. 3 (1993).

33. Sunseri, *Vilimani*, 55; Koponen, *Development for Exploitation*, 336–38; Louis Mihalyi, "Characteristics and Problems of Labour in the Usambara Highlands of East Africa during the German Period, 1885–1914." *East Africa*, May 1970.

34. Sunseri, *Vilimani*, 55–56.

35. Koponen, *Development for Exploitation*, 323–26.

36. Sabea, "Mastering the Landscape," 420.

37. Rockel, *Carriers of Culture*, 4.

38. Edward A. Alpers, "'To Seek a Better Life': The Implications of Migration from Mozambique to Tanganyika for Class Formation and Political Behavior," *Canadian Journal of African Studies* 18, no. 2 (1984): 370; Iliffe, *A Modern History of Tanganyika*, 161; Sunseri, *Vilimani*, 56–60.

39. Tanganyika National Archives. G8/22. *Plantagenstatistik, 1902–1903*; Tanganyika National Archives. G8/24. *Plantagenstatistik, 1908–1909*.

40. Koponen, *Development for Exploitation*, 346.

41. Rockel, *Carriers of Culture*, 221.

42. Margot Lovett, "On Power and Powerlessness: Marriage and Metaphor in Colonial Western Tanzania," *International Journal of African Historical Studies* 27, no. 2 (1994).

43. James D. Graham, "A Case Study of Migrant Labor in Tanzania," *African Studies Review* (1970); Brad Weiss, "A Religion of the Rupee: Materialist Encounters in North-West Tanzania" *Africa* 72, no. 3 (2002); James Giblin, *A History of the Excluded* (Athens: Ohio University Press, 2005).

44. Rockel, *Carriers of Culture*, 75; Frederick Cooper, *Plantation Slavery on the East Coast of Africa* (New Haven: Yale University Press, 1977).

45. Sunseri, *Vilimani*, 62.

46. Carl Peters cited in John Iliffe, *Tanganyika under German Rule, 1905–1912* (Cambridge: Cambridge University Press, 1969), 64.

47. Tanganyika National Archives. G8/22. *Plantagenstatistik, 1902–1903*; Tanganyika National Archives. G8/26. *Plantagenstatistik, 1910–1912.*

48. Department of Labour, Tanganyika Territory, *Annual Labour Department Reports, 1926*, 5–6.

49. Iliffe, *Tanganyika under German Rule*, 103–7.

50. Hindorf, *Sisalban in Deutsch-Ostafrika*, 12–26; Wolf Kispert, *Pioniere in Ostafrika. Teil I.* (Amboni: Tanga, n.d.).

51. Sunseri, *Vilimani*, 150–52.

52. See also Sunseri, *Vilimani*, 152–53.

53. Sunseri, *Vilimani*, 154–56.

54. Rockel, *Carriers of Culture*, 181–95.

55. Sunseri, *Vilimani*, 143; Rockel, *Carriers of Culture*, 192–94.

56. Public Record Office/Colonial Office/691/89/18168. *Permanent Mandates Commission, 1927.*

57. Sunseri, *Vilimani*, 176–77.

58. Tanganyika National Archives. Early Series/1733/16. *Pangani District Annual Report, 1924.*

"Zake: The Papuan Chief"[1]

An Alliance with a German Missionary in Colonial Kaiser-Wilhelmsland (Oceania)

Gabriele Richter

The most renowned theoretician of Oceania, Epeli Hau'Ofa, was not content with discussions that focused on Oceania as a place of merely *colonial* exploitation and suppression. Although he taught his students to be aware of the devastating and persistent consequences of colonialism, to him the sole focus on colonialism ignored the fact that the people of Oceania had a history before imperialism. Moreover, to Hau'Ofa, discussing domination and subordination as the major theme obscures another important perspective—that the people of Oceania were always "major players" in shaping their own history.[2] In coining the phrase of Oceania as a "sea of islands" he emphasized that the people of this region were always thinking on a scale as large as the ocean. "We Are the Ocean," the title of one of Hau'Ofa's essay collections, suggests that Hau'Ofa specifically addressed the various relationships that the people of Oceania build and have built, either at home or by exploring other regions of the world.

Like Johannes Fabian, Epeli Hau'Ofa stressed the relational aspects of each encounter with the past.[3] Building relationships in Oceania has always involved exchange systems of all kinds, from those involving artifacts to others based on the exchange of "mentefacts."[4] A theoretical framework to describe encounters in Oceania, and thus the role of local actors, cannot afford to overlook the reciprocity of relationships. As Hau'Ofa reminds us, building relationships is an Oceanic strength, and thus one might require different non-continental categories to depict this process more adequately. In this regard, I suggest that the concept of the "ally" is more useful than the notion of the "mediator" to capture processes that took place between Germans and Oceanic people in the region. The idea of the "mediator" does not describe the shared experience of a relationship. This aspect needs to be addressed in a terminology that stresses the relationship and not only the performance of a single person or the circumstances of the encounter. A relationship both shapes "allies" and redefines what and who the allies are or will become. In Hau'Ofa's work the term "alliance" appears only in passing, but, to me, it captures what Hau'Ofa calls the "totality of relationships."[5] The term "alliance" highlights that the relationship had a particular shape defined by both sides. Additionally it is both a reference to earlier discussions of alliances and kinships as well as an implicit reminder that one is not only born with kin in this world, but that there are also kin that we make.[6] In analyzing an alliance between a New Guinean man and a German man, this essay highlights a certain kind of relationship— one based on manipulation, exchange, innovation, and masculinity.

Kaiser-Wilhelmsland

This essay focuses on Zake (d. 1923), a man from what is today Papua New Guinea (an independent state north of Australia), and the alliance he forged with a German missionary. Their encounter occurred at a time when the northern part was still a German colony ("Kaiser-Wilhelmsland" or "German New Guinea"). Among the Germans within a part of this region, the Huon Peninsula, the two main colonial forces were the German administrative personnel and Lutheran missionaries from Germany. Zake's ally became the German missionary Christian Keyßer (1877–1961). In reading anew Keyßer's published texts about Zake[7] and the studies on Keyßer with references to Zake and comparing them with select sources by and about members of Zake's language group, which a student of the Lutheran seminary collected in 1970, previously neglected aspects of the story come to the fore.[8] Seen from a Papua New Guinean perspective, the story of Zake and Keyßer differs from mission narratives. In my discussion Zake appears as an outstanding individual from New Guinea who acquired and used knowledge about the "foreign" Germans to his own advantage. To be more precise, he built the particular relationship with the missionary Keyßer to reach the traditional goal of becoming a Big Man, that is, to gain a position of power.[9] Zake's smart assessment of the situation and his courageous initiative indicate that he could pragmatically use the presence of the local German mission. He achieved, for his people, that the mission station would be in the neighborhood to provide goods and, for himself, that he was able to gain a leading role as an "ally" to a powerful man who in return became powerful within Zake's community. This exchange of powers for the sake of gaining power within their respective communities explains at least in part the title of Christian Keyßer's book *Zake: The Papuan Chief.* Zake, however, was never "the" chief of all the people in German New Guinea (and certainly not within the larger region of today's Papua New Guinea). It is hard to estimate how many different language groups were in German New Guinea by Keyßer's time, but in today's independent Papua New Guinea, combining in roughly two parts the former German as well as the former British part, there are 700 to 1,000 different language groups.[10] In other words, Zake's influence was far from being colony-wide. Power over his people was marginal within the scope of a far larger region. Thanks to Keyßer, however, Zake rose up to become the chief of not only one particular language group among many others. But Keyßer's goal was higher. In the 1930s, when Germany was left with only dreams of being a colonial power, Keyßer published a book on Zake that conveyed an image of Zake as the ingenious leader of a larger group—including the people of the by-then Australian colony, "the" Papuans.

The Lutheran missionary work in German New Guinea originated in Neuendettelsau (Franconia/Germany).[11] In 1886 the German missionary Johann Flierl (1858–1947) arrived, and with the help of six men from New Britain, affiliated with the Methodist Mission, Flierl built the first mission station called Simbang. When malaria threatened to kill all Germans in Finschhafen the then-dominant *Neuguinea-Compagnie* decided to move to another part of the country. Missionary Flierl, however, opted to stay.[12] As a result the missionaries were now the only Germans to do trade with. With mission schooling and the founding of new mission stations, and, luckily, the survival of the majority of missionaries, the Lutheran mission established itself on the Huon Peninsula of New Guinea also as the major local political force. The first baptisms took place in the year that missionary Christian Keyßer arrived, 1899. Yet not until Keyßer's arrival did many see a "decisive breakthrough" occurring.[13] In missiological studies up until today, Keyßer aligned himself with a certain ethnic population, Zake's people, in order to create a new entity, called in mission circles the "people of God."[14] What these studies interpret as the transcending of the ethnic divisions in a land of great diversity, however, could also be coined as a strategic and political expansion—both of Zake's people (Kâte people) as well as Keyßer's people (German Lutherans). An indication of the political relevance of this alliance is that, as historian Peter Hempenstall remarked, mostly due to this mission society's success, German colonial control was able to reach inland on the peninsula.[15]

Keyßer's Portrait of Zake

Keyßer's *Zake: The Papuan Chief* was published in 1934 and reissued in 1950. Earlier, in the 1920s, he had already published a few pages on Zake, but with the book Keyßer honored Zake as a man of courage and initiative while also demonstrating the mission's influence over local peoples' lives.[16] The publication is the only one to date in which Zake is portrayed extensively.

As Keyßer described in detail, he was aware that Zake's rise to becoming an important man in the region started long before his arrival.[17] Around 1884 Zake was a young man from the coastal village Bâre (Bare/Bale/Barec/Dobeo) when he and his friends glimpsed a large white boat further south, perhaps the "Samoa" under the command of German scientist Otto Finsch. Naturally curious, these men went to the landing spot later called Finschhafen. After finally making contact with the people on the boat the men appeared to them to be ghosts with no toes (because of their shoes) and with skin hanging from their bodies (a reference to their clothes).

Zake and others tried to exchange goods, but the local population of Finschhafen pushed them out. This place was the home of the Yabim people, and Zake belonged to the Kâte people. Zake's village Bâre was further north from the Yabim area. Seemingly successfully, the Finschhafen people soon monopolized the valuable trade with the newcomers. A year later Zake succeeded in breaking the monopoly and was employed by the company in Finschhafen. It can be expected that not only goods like steel axes laid the cornerstone of his career but also his increasing knowledge of the Germans. His dealings with the missionaries must be seen in this light.

When malaria turned Finschhafen into a death trap for Germans and the administration moved elsewhere, the Lutheran mission did not want to move. In a conversation with the company's medical doctor the missionaries were advised to at least move to a higher altitude.[18] In 1892 the leading German Lutheran missionary Johann Flierl and his colleague Georg Pfalzer (1866–1945) both came to the village of Bâre. According to Keyßer's account, they happened to meet Zake who was fishing and catching crabs.[19] Zake evidently led the missionaries up to Sattelberg where the Lutheran missionaries found a place high enough to be free of malaria and thus perfect for a retreat center.

All this happened before Keyßer came to German New Guinea. Within a year after his arrival in 1899, Keyßer visited Zake at Bâre. By that time Zake was competing with a man called Zumaiang for being a Big Man within their ethnic group Kâte.[20] Zumaiang was from the neighboring village Tâgi. According to Keyßer, when he arrived the two argued over the distribution of pig meat. Keyßer's New Guinean companion called Baluna acted in the manner of a local policeman and not only protected Keyßer with a rifle but stopped the dispute. Later Keyßer praised Zake for being cleverer than Zumaiang, but Keyßer's support for Zake is connected to Zake's support for the mission. Zumaiang, on the other hand, was considered courageous to call Keyßer's companion Baluna names like the "barking dog of whites."[21] Zake, in contrast, listened to Keyßer's biblical stories, such as an anti-Semitic version of the killing of Jesus. Still in the 1950s, Keyßer recalled that the story enraged Zake and that referring to "the" Jews he stated: "These vicious liars! These murderers! How can you nail a human being on a cross alive! Even your own people, [even; G.R.] the chief! And he only did good things to his people! We brown people are not so bad! Jesus should have come to us; we would have welcomed him."[22]

These details are recorded in Keyßer's publications. How are we to interpret Keyßer's account in general? Keyßer was interested in writing about his mission work and his successes. Stressing how he established himself as a powerful man in the region was part of ensuring the continuing influence of the mission society. Between the lines, however, the text also states that Keyßer gave Zake new food for thought and that Zake probed new ways of thinking. Zake asked what Keyßer thought and why he did things the way he did. His questions about God's power were also questions about the foreigners' powers, which was a real concern for the local communities. German punitive expeditions were common, and even today the Tok Pisin language of Papua New Guinea has a few German words—one of them "strafim" for punishing.[23] Zake tried to understand and above all conceptualize the power of the Germans also by theologizing the problem.[24] As quoted by Keyßer, Zake regretted that the "whites" did not come before and bring the message about God because "You whites own so many beautiful things. We browns, on the other hand, are poor people."[25]

The Other Perspective: An Oral Source on Zake

In the 1970s many educational institutions in Papua New Guinea encouraged students to collect oral sources. One such institution was the Martin Luther Seminary at Lae (Papua New Guinea), which was an English-speaking training seminary for prospective pastors. In 1973 a student of the seminary, Advent P. Melkisede, wrote his final thesis on the Sattelberg congregation and interviewed older men about the congregation, but he also consulted literature mostly by German missionaries in the local Kâte language. Melkisede gave his thesis the title "Christ Danced in Sattelberg between 1888–1914." In his fifty-page text he focused on the years of German colonialism. The original name for Sattelberg is Qeracharuc, that is, cassowary and crab, as Melkisede explains right at the beginning of his work.[26] Melkisede's text not only gives in part a different version of the events at Sattelberg/Qeracharuc but also offers an entirely new perspective on the larger developments.

Located in the Kâte area, Sattelberg became the center of the Lutheran mission in New Guinea for a number of reasons, among which Zake's influence was the most important one. With his thesis Melkisede intended to "show . . . how the Sattelberg circuit has played a most important role in the development of ELCONG [Evangelical Lutheran Church of New Guinea; G.R.] and the Lutheran Church as a whole."[27] In September 1973 Melkisede went to Finschhafen and spoke with Kâte elders there. The two men were Fuapo (born 1908) and Honeoc (born 1900).[28] They had not been able to witness the earliest encounters between Zake and Keyßer that took place around 1900 but they had both known Zake and Keyßer personally.

In the 1970s these men confirmed that during the earliest times of German colonial presence very few Kâte men were able to meet people from the mission and the companies.[29] They also remembered the Lutheran missionaries exploring the area around Finschhafen because Flierl's doctor recommended moving to a higher altitude. In the company of Georg Pfalzer, Flierl walked to the Kâte area together with Zake who "had had good contact with the companies, so the companies had told Flierl about this chief Zake."[30] Earlier, the company had asked Zake to accompany an exploration team to the Kâte area. When in 1886 and 1887 three German scientists went on an expedition for the German *Neuguinea-Compagnie* (Carl Schrade, Max Hollrung, and Carl Schneider) Zake was chosen as the guide to lead the men to his home area. In other words, Zake first led the scientists into the mountainous area, and only later did he guide the Lutheran missionaries to what became known as a center of Lutheran identity in New Guinea: Sattelberg. This is the first detail that is not mentioned in mission publications. Yet, it is not surprising that the missionaries didn't want to stress in their publications that they profited from and were influenced by the colonial network. It seems most unlikely that Flierl and Pfalzer simply ran into Zake while they were wandering around the Kâte area, as implied by Keyßer in the earlier referenced text. Zake then led them to the place called Qorafung, which was further north and no longer in the Kâte area, because Flierl had directed him to do so. Flierl did not want to stay in the region of Sattelberg but instead wanted to go further north into the Cromwell Ranges.[31] What happened then, however, shows that Zake and his men had no such interest in leading the missionaries further north into a region of non-Kâte peoples; for their own interests they wanted to keep the missionaries in their sphere of influence and have a settlement of missionaries in their community, as Melkisede wrote; they did not want to lose the opportunity to make use of the connection with "whites" and the prospect of gaining goods. The oral source stated that at night the men kept telling Flierl's porters stories about "bad people, cannibals, sorcerers and great fighters" who lived in the Cromwell Range region.[32] They scared Flierl's porters, and the next day, the porters fled as soon as possible. The German missionaries were left alone, and they could only hope for Zake's practical help. Generously, Zake led the group up to Sattelberg instead. When the group arrived in Sattelberg, Zake talked to his friend Raqac, a resident, to see if there was any ground where the missionaries could settle. A pig was slaughtered, and the agreement was sealed.[33] In Melkisede's account, it can be concluded, the local population was the actor shaping history—not the continental missionaries.

Of course the men from the other main mission area, the Yabim area, were not happy to lose any missionaries to the Kâte people, even if the Yabim mission station remained. Not surprisingly they refused to help Flierl with the construction of the new station: "The Yabems told him not to go to Sattelberg for the Kâtes would bring lots of trouble to him, but Flierl did not listen to them [. . .]."[34] In 1892, at the time when Flierl and his family moved to Sattelberg, Zake and his people were able to steal the cargo that Flierl brought, as the oral source recounted.[35] Nevertheless, a permanent house was established at Sattelberg. Whatever attracted Zake's people to allow a permanent station, it was surely not any great interest in hearing about Christianity. When another missionary, Johann Decker (1864–1958), became the first to learn the Kâte language and told the Kâte people biblical stories the people said: "What is the use of hearing the fairy story? We have lots of fairy stories from out forefathers so we don't want to hear your stories."[36]

Melkisede's account then introduces Keyßer, who is referred to as "Chief Zake's best friend" (which is similar to how Keyßer introduced Zake as his best friend) and describes the way in which Keyßer "followed Zake and mimicked" him: "Whatever Zake did he did it too."[37] I will discuss this dynamic between the two in detail in the next section; at this point, it is important to bear in mind the outcome of the earlier and later relationships between the missionaries and the Kâte people: Melkisede's account frankly implies that change happened because of local ingenuity and initiative to *make history*. Indeed, the new mission station united the Kâte people, and through Keyßer, who demonstrated the power of his rifle, Zake gained a form of power that was not so easy to understand and thus to challenge by any local at the time. According to Fuapo and Honeoc, Keyßer shot through some shields hitting the trees behind them, telling the men: "Have you seen it? [. . .] Okey [*sic*] don't you ever talk about fighting again. If you go to fight I am going to tear you up into pieces with my gun like those shields of Yours [*sic*]."[38] The mission work, here, appears to be more of muscles and arms than of words. It is a rather masculine way of missionizing.[39]

The Dancing Festival: Zake and Keyßer

The title of Melkisede's account of his interviews, "Christ Danced at Sattelberg," implies, among other things, that dancing was a part of the events surrounding the history of the Kâte people from Zake's earliest attempts to make contact with the German foreigners. The culmination point of his success in establishing contact was the so-called Bâre festival, a dancing festival. In the memories of Melkisede's interview partners this festival was all about accusing people openly of magic, which meant to break the taboo of keeping magic, and in particular magic aimed at killing someone, hidden at all times. Yet, Melkisede's text does not go into details over the public accusations including Zake's self-accusations that he also tried to kill someone with magic. Melkisede's account describes in detail the pre-Keyßer story of how smart and active Kâte people gained the mission station for their neighborhood. Why is Keyßer's story about the Kâte festival stressed so little? Melkisede mentions in passing that Keyßer "called a meeting" and "Zake helped him."[40] I suggest that Melkisede was interested to show how the Kâte people gained power as a group, rather than focusing on a single man, namely, Zake.

In Keyßer's account, Zake and Keyßer invited people to this festival. Bâre was Zake's home ground, and holding such a festival gave the organizers prestige and political power. In other words it was an important step toward becoming a Big Man. For Keyßer the festival was also a decisive moment in his relationship with Zake and his people. This festival laid the foundation for the future successes of the Lutheran mission enterprise—both in Keyßer's own thinking as well as in later mission chronicles and studies.[41]

Like any traditional dancing festival the event included the sharing of a meal, for which both Keyßer and Zake provided the means, as well as dancing from sunset. Keyßer's colleagues already considered dancing with suspicion,[42] but dancing at night seemed even more suspect. Keyßer justified his support for a dancing festival to his critics by saying that the songs would not be understood after conversion anyway.[43] This is, however, a perspective projected on the event in retrospective. Keyßer's colleagues would have called the event "heathen" and certainly would have fought it as evil. Keyßer downplayed the "heathen" element for the German readers in his account: They were (supposedly) just some songs. In other words, to ensure the success of the mission enterprise "heathen" practice was justified.

Zake gave the first long speech, then Keyßer spoke, then Zake, and finally Keyßer again.[44] During his second speech Zake admitted that he had ordered the death of some man, and then Keyßer named and exposed the most influential men suspected of being "magicians," many of whom were present at the festival. In doing so Keyßer undermined the authority of these men. Of course those were also the men with whom Zake competed for power, and the exposure weakened all these men—leaving only Zake with a new power source: Keyßer. The festival ended with Keyßer's German-Australian lay brother, Gottlieb Keppler (born 1871), firing two or three shots—a significant sign because the participants of the festival had to abandon their weapons before entering the festival ground.[45] The contrast was clear: Keyßer was not weakened and, moreover, demonstrated his rifle power. At the same time Zake was Keyßer's friend and thereby aligned with the now most powerful figure in the region. Keyßer later wrote that he and Zake had agreed on the shooting.

Who was the driving force? Whose initiative was the festival? Papua New Guinean missiologist Numuc Kemung argued that the festival had been Zake's idea, but it was "Keyßer's day,"[46] because Keyßer sent out the invitations, spoke first, and contributed large quantities of rice, which Melkisede's text does not mention.[47] In his publication, Keyßer presented himself more modestly, merely as the co-organizer of the event.[48] It was Zake who drew up the rule that nobody was permitted to bear any weapons. Zake welcomed the guests, and he talked most of the time.[49] Keyßer wrote that he himself spoke at the actual beginning of the festival, but this may be a matter of interpretation. Keyßer's published text states that he merely also (!) invited people.[50] As archival evidence also indicates, Zake and Keyßer both contributed pig meat, which made both at least co-organizers in the eyes of the public.[51]

Did Zake manipulate Keyßer? Or did Keyßer manipulate Zake? In light of the various accounts it is fair to suggest that Zake, rather than Keyßer, was the center person here. Zake's personal gain was great. As Keyßer indicated, Zake competed with another important man from the region over power—Zumaiang.[52] Zumaiang was Zake's brother-in-law, and both men were competing friends rather than enemies. Prior to the festival the balance of power between the two seemed to have been even.[53] However, when Zumaiang opposed Keyßer, Zake sided with Keyßer.[54] Possibly this incident settled the matter between them long before the festival. Perhaps the festival itself did not decide the matter as some think,[55] but the festival illustrated Zake's growing influence and power. When Zumaiang danced at the festival, he may have thereby reacted to Zake's and Keyßer's new roles.[56] The festival was the public announcement of an alliance between two powerful men and, implicitly, also the groups supporting them. Epeli Hau'Ofa mentions the importance of the alliance, and in certain ways Zake was a model for someone from Oceania who had, to paraphrase Hau'Ofa, the ocean within.[57] Zake's vision of a joint enterprise between his group and the mission group led to a unique collaboration.

The outcome proved to be successful for both allies. Despite the negative attitude of Keyßer's superior Johann Flierl, Keyßer did indeed gain power through the festival.[58] Later on he not only found supporters for his approach to missionary work within the mission society's hierarchy in Germany but also became one of the most prolific and prominent writers and spokesmen for the Lutheran New Guinea mission.[59] Kemung explains Keyßer's leading mission role with cultural and material aspects as mutual give-and-take, a specific and particular form of "nareng-gareng" (in the Kâte language).[60] Importantly, Keyßer knew how to give and take in order to gain influence. In later years it was the Kâte community that first sent out their own men to serve in different ethnic communities as missionaries and was bound to what the leading men and Keyßer had agreed upon as the Christian way and to enter catechism. Up to the present day the Neuendettelsau mission would call this above-mentioned so-called mission method the "Keyßer method,"[61] which meant to evangelize ethnic groups, instead of individuals, by using local mechanisms of alliances as well as the display of gun power or at least references to colonial gun power.

Conclusion

Keyßer writes that after the festival he was afraid of the Kâte men; many threatened Keyßer for exposing them as sorcerers. After the festival Zake tried to reassure Keyßer, telling him: "Let go! People are stupid and will not get smart immediately. I used to have very little understanding also; then suddenly I had an insight and from then on it all became clear to me—one by one. I have not yet understood everything, but probably that will come with time."[62]

Within the parameters of successful mission work this statement can be taken as reflecting Zake's insight into the knowledge of Christianity and civilization. Yet, the initial "insight" might be much more complex. Zake was a man of initiative, courage, and maybe even luck who conducted the festival in order to gain power as a local leader. He also demonstrated publicly his strong alliance with Keyßer. In 1926 Keyßer called Zake a "diplomat" that he felt "drawn to" because of their mutual curiosity and willingness to teach one another about themselves and their culture and religion.[63] Keyßer was Zake's ally in a social system that encouraged men to compete with each other for power and to expand their authority. Zake might have found many different ways of reaching this goal of gaining power, but, as it happened, even before Keyßer, he met German men of the *Neuguinea-Compagnie* at Finschhafen, later Bavarian missionary Flierl, and finally Keyßer. Keyßer was Zake's assurance that at least one rifle and the mission's connection to the colonial forces were always on his side. Moreover, Keyßer, more than Flierl, was the source of wealth and knowledge. Keyßer, however, also gained from Zake. At least in the eyes of people like his superior Steck, Keyßer's work was supposedly more authentic.[64] Zake surely contributed to this impression.

Part of this authenticity was that Keyßer and Zake embraced and mutually enhanced the construction and maintenance of their masculinity. Keyßer fostered a Christianity of masculinity, a "muscular Christianity."[65] Keyßer and Zake's alliance gave them both not only an attribute of becoming "bigger" but also more "masculine," and male friendship was a part of this alliance.[66] Values like strength and courage as well as the exclusion of women were the foundation of their relationship. Their gains were mutual, and the festival was one expression of this mutuality, because it served both men's respective agendas so well. Zake aimed to establish his own position as a leading man and used the foreigner's power to augment his own. Zake was not only able to use the missionary's presence as somehow beneficial to the Kâte people. Above all, and this is a fact not mentioned anywhere except in Melkisede's paper, it was due to Zake that Sattelberg and the Kâte people became so important to the Lutheran mission. If Zake had *not* used strategic information politics on Flierl, the Lutheran mission might have looked different. Moreover, Zake staged a festival that disempowered the visible and invisible powers of his local opponents. I would suggest that the account in Melkisede's text on the dancing festival is so brief because the festival was, so to say, the inauguration of Zake but also of Keyßer as Big Men. Zake's initial attempts to align with German colonial forces and then later missionaries foreshadowed the events that followed, in particular Zake's rise to power.

Zake responded to the shifts and changes instigated by the Germans. By talking to the new powers and certainly not avoiding them he took as many chances as possible and trusted that things would become clearer day by day. Perhaps he was thus even better equipped to deal with events as they unfolded than most German missionaries in New Guinea, who only in hindsight had thought of trying to understand the New Guinean side, and finally took it to heart that they knew quite little. From the beginning Zake's attitude was to take whatever truth he discovered in all the turmoil and to move on from there—step by step.

To date German missiologists, in hoping to understand the nature of the

German mission in New Guinea, focus on Keyßer and his contribution to the larger mission enterprise. At times they comment on Keyßer as a leading missionary who, from 1922 to 1939, was mission inspector and teacher at the mission seminary in Neuendettelsau/Germany and thus shaped generations of missionaries in New Guinea. Yet within New Guinea and due to Zake and others, the Lutheran mission was in fact no longer only molded by German "Neuendettelsau," but also significantly by the Kâte people, that is, "Sattelberg." They too put their stamp on the form and shape of the mission work: To support them and a model of centralized national power, Keyßer opted for Kâte as the language that all (!) Lutheran Christians in New Guinea ought to speak, which later caused many Australian officers to worry about their hold on the colony.[67] Whatever Zake's responses to German colonial and, later in the 1920s and 1930s, merely mission power meant within the multiple different contexts, he did not appear as someone who would miss on opportunity to improve his peoples' and certainly not his own situation. Looking through the lens of Keyßer's 1930s publication promoting Zake as a leader of "the" Papuans is evidence of Keyßer's high esteem for and even idealization of Zake, with which he places Zake as "big" and a "man" at the center of the events of Lutheran mission work in New Guinea. Perhaps the account also sheds a bit of this "glory" on Zake's friend and ally Keyßer. However, it does not tell today's readers how much Germans contributed to making Zake "big" as well as a "man." Zake's power and wealth, however, were rooted in Zake's manipulation and exploitation of, as well as exchange with, Germans. By entering into an alliance with the German newcomers, Zake redefined what power but also masculinity meant in his cultural and religious context.[68]

NOTES

1. Title taken from Christian Keyßer, *Zake: Der Papuahäuptling* (Neuendettelsau: Freimund Verlag, 1950 [1934]).
2. Epeli Hau'Ofa, *We Are the Ocean: Selected Works* (Honolulu: University of Hawai'i Press, 2008), 63.
3. Johannes Fabian, "You Meet and You Talk: Anthropological Reflections on Encounters and Discourses," in *The Fuzzy Logic of Encounter: New Perspectives on Cultural Contact*, ed. Sünne Juterczenka and Gesa Mackenthun (Münster: Waxmann, 2009), 23–34.
4. Roland Posner, "Kultur als Zeichensystem: Zur semiotischen Explikation kulturwissenschaftlicher Grundbegriffe," in *Kultur als Lebenswelt und Monument*, ed. Aleida Assmann and Dietrich Harth (Frankfurt am Main: Fischer Taschenbuch Verlag, 1991), 37–74.
5. Hau'Ofa, *We Are the Ocean*, 35, 31.
6. Cf. Louis Dumont, *Introduction to Two Theories of Social Anthropology: De-

scent Groups and Marriage Alliance, ed. and trans. Robert Parkin (New York: Berghahn Books, 2006); on the specific Papua New Guinean context, e.g., Brian du Toit, "Filiation and Affiliation among the Gadsup," *Oceania* 35, no. 2 (1964): 85–95.

7. Christian Keyßer, *Anutu im Papualand* (Nuremberg: Glocken-Verlag, 1926), 24–28 and picture between 16 and 17; cf. Keyßer, *Zake*.

8. There are two distinct discourses on the history of Papua New Guinea outside of Papua New Guinea. The internationally most well-known school is the so-called Canberra School, the Australian-led discussion that used to center around Canberra's Australian National University. But there are also many different mission and ethnology/ anthropology circles elsewhere for which this particular topic is of importance. On the Lutheran mission topic, most discussions take place in Franconia, Germany, because of the heritage of the Neuendettelsau mission. Cf. A. C. Frerichs, *Anutu Conquers in New Guinea: A Story of Seventy Years of Mission Work in New Guinea* (Columbus, OH: Wartburg Press, 1957), 39; D. Georg Pilhofer, *Die Geschichte der Neuendettelsauer Mission in Neuguinea*, vol. 1, *Von den ersten Anfängen bis zum Kriegsausbruch 1914* (Neuendettelsau: Evang.-Luth. Missionsanstalt Neuendettelsau, 1961), 133; Herwig Wagner, "Beginnings at Finschhafen: The Neuendettelsau Mission jointly with the Australian Lutheran Church," in *The Lutheran Church in Papua New Guinea: The First Hundred Years, 1886–1986*, Herwig Wagner and Hermann Reiner, eds. (Adelaide: Lutheran Publishing House, 1986), 31–83, here: 45; Theodor Ahrens, "Die Aktualität Christian Keyßers," *Zeitschrift für Mission* 14 (1988): 94–110; John Garrett, *Footsteps in the Sea: Christianity in Oceania to World War II* (Suva: Institute of Pacific Studies, University of the South Pacific, 1992), 6–9; Traugott Farnbacher, *Gemeinde verantworten: Anfänge, Entwicklungen und Perspektiven von Gemeinde und Ämtern der Evangelisch-Lutherischen Kirche in Papua-Neuguinea* (Hamburg: LIT, 1999), 177–78: Rufus Pech, "Deutsche evangelische Missionen in Deutsch-Neuguinea 1886–1921," in *Die deutsche Südsee 1884–1914: Ein Handbuch*, ed. Hermann Joseph Hiery (Paderborn: Schöningh, 2002), 384–415; Jürgen Stadler, *Die Missionspraxis Christian Keyßers in Neuguinea 1899–1920* (PhD diss., Erlangen-Nuremberg, 2004; Nuremberg: VTR, 2006), 107–16; Keyßer, *Anutu im Papualand*, 24–29.

9. Literature on "Big Man": cf. Paul Roscoe, "New Guinea Leadership as Ethnographic Analogy: A Critical Review," *Journal of Archaeological Method and Theory* 7, no. 2 (June 2000): 79–126.

10. Ron Asher and Christopher Moseley, *Atlas of World's Languages* (2nd, rev. ed.; London: Routledge, 2007).

11. Wagner, "Beginnings at Finschhafen," 31–37.

12. Finschhafen was the seat of the German colonial administration on the Huon Peninsula, and named after its German "discoverer" Otto Finsch (1839–1917).

13. Wagner, "Beginnings at Finschhafen," 44.

14. Farnbacher, *Gemeinde verantworten*, 169, trans. G.R.

15. Peter J. Hempenstall, *Pacific Islanders under German Rule: A Study in the Meaning of Colonial Resistance* (Canberra: Australian National University Press, 1978), 193.

16. Keyßer, *Anutu im Papualand*, 24–30.

17. Keyßer, *Zake*, 3–6.

18. Wagner, "Beginnings at Finschhafen," 39.

19. Keyßer, *Zake*, 7.

20. Keyßer, *Zake*, 14.

21. Keyßer, *Zake*, 15.

22. Keyßer, *Zake*, 36; trans. G.R.

23. Wolfgang Wendt and Fritz Blanz, *Tok Pisin Bilong Papua Niugini: Das Pidgin von Papua-Neuguinea; Wörterbuch zum Sprachkurs* (Neuendettelsau: Evang.-Luth. Kirche in Bayern, 1998), 21.

24. Cf. Bill Gammage, *The Sky Travellers: Journey in New Guinea: 1938–1939* (Melbourne: Miegunyah Press and Melbourne University Press, 1998), 1.

25. Keyßer, *Zake*, 47.

26. Advent P. Melkisede, "Christ Danced in Sattelberg between 1886–1914," Master's thesis, Martin Luther Seminary (Lae, Papua New Guinea, November 10, 1973), 2.

27. Melkisede, "Christ Danced in Sattelberg," 3.

28. According to Kâte linguist Edgar Suter (e-mail message to author, March 4, 2010), Fuapo means "I was born" and Honeoc means "he might see."

29. Melkisede, "Christ Danced in Sattelberg," 9–10.

30. Melkisede, "Christ Danced in Sattelberg," 11.

31. Different perspective provided by D. Georg Pilhofer, *Johann Flierl der Bahnbrecher des Evangeliums unter den Papua* (Neuendettelsau: Freimund-Verlag, 1962), 24; cf. D. Georg Pilhofer, *Die Geschichte der Neuendettelsauer Mission in Neuguinea*, vol. 1, *Von den ersten Anfängen bis zum Kriegsausbruch 1914* (Neuendettelsau: Evang.-Luth. Missionsanstalt Neuendettelsau, 1961), 93.

32. Melkisede, "Christ Danced in Sattelberg," 11.

33. Melkisede, "Christ Danced in Sattelberg," 12.

34. Melkisede, "Christ Danced in Sattelberg," 13.

35. Melkisede, "Christ Danced in Sattelberg," 14; cf. Pilhofer, *Die Geschichte der Neuendettelsauer Mission in Neuguinea*, vol. 1, 95.

36. Melkisede, "Christ Danced in Sattelberg," 15.

37. Melkisede, "Christ Danced in Sattelberg," 18.

38. Melkisede, "Christ Danced in Sattelberg," 24.

39. Charles Wilde, "Acts of Faith: Muscular Christianity and Masculinity among the Gogodala of Papua New Guinea," *Oceania* 75, no. 1 (Sept. 2004): 32–48.

40. Melkisede, "Christ Danced in Sattelberg," 23.

41. In Keyßer's work: Keyßer, *Anutu im Papualand*, 30–32, also 50–51; cf. Keyßer's 1903 letter about the festival in Stadler, *Die Missionspraxis Christian Keyßers*, 481–82; others: Fontius, 1975:55; Wagner, "Beginnings at Finschhafen," 44–46; Ahrens, "Die Aktualität Christian Keyßers," 99–100; Kemung, *Nareng-Gareng*, 112–15; Pech, "Deutsche evangelische Missionen in Deutsch-Neuguinea 1886–1921," 392–93; Stadler, *Die Missionspraxis Christian Keyßers*, 107–29.

42. D. Georg Pilhofer, *Die Geschichte der Neuendettelsauer Mission in Neuguinea*, vol. 2, *Die Mission zwischen den beiden Weltkriegen mit einem Überblick über die neue Zeit* (Neuendettelsau: Evang.-Luth. Missionsanstalt Neuendettelsau, 1963), 142.

43. Keyßer, *Zake*, 51; cf. Keyßer, *Anutu im Papualand*, 27–29.

44. Keyßer, *Zake*, 51.

45. Two in Keyßer, *Anutu im Papualand*, 29; three in Keyßer's letter quoted in Stadler, *Die Missionspraxis Christian Keyßers*, 482.

46. Kemung, *Nareng-Gareng*, 115.

47. Similar: Wagner, "Beginnings at Finschhafen," 45.

48. Cf. Ahrens, "Die Aktualität Christian Keyßers"; Stadler, *Die Missionspraxis Christian Keyßers*; Wagner, "Beginnings at Finschhafen"; Keyßer, *Anutu im Papualand*; Keyßer, *Zake*.

49. Keyßer, *Zake*, 50.

50. Keyßer, *Zake*, 51; cf. Wagner, "Beginnings at Finschhafen," 45.

51. Stadler and his findings on Keyßer contradict Keyßer's account of the events in 1926 in which Keyßer states that there was no pig slaughtered for the festival; Jürgen Stadler, *Die Missionspraxis Christian Keyßers*, 113n455,482; Keyßer, *Anutu im Papualand*, 27.

52. Theodor Ahrens, "Die Aktualität Christian Keyßers," *Zeitschrift für Mission* 14 (1988): 94–110; here: 100.

53. Keyßer, *Zake*, 13–14.

54. Keyßer, *Zake*, 15–17.

55. Stadler, *Die Missionspraxis Christian Keyßers*; cf. Ahrens, "Die Aktualität Christian Keyßers," 100.

56. Keyßer, *Zake*, 51.

57. Hau'Ofa, *We Are the Ocean*, 41–59.

58. Stadler, *Die Missionspraxis Christian Keyßers*, 113–14, 134–36.

59. Theodor Ahrens, "Lutherische Kreolität: Lutherische Mission und andere Kulturen," in *Luther zwischen den Kulturen: Zeitgenossenschaft–Weltwirkung*, ed. Hans Medick and Peer Schmidt, (Tübingen: Vandenhoeck & Ruprecht, 2004), 421–51.

60. Numuc Zirajukic Kemung, *Nareng-Gareng: A Principle for Mission in the Evangelical Lutheran Church of Papua New Guinea* (Erlangen: Erlanger Verlag für Mission und Ökumene, 1998), 112.

61. On the Keyßer method cf. for instance Frerichs, *Anutu Conquers in New Guinea*, 55, 142–43; E. A. Jericho, *Seedtime and Harvest in New Guinea* (Brisbane: New Guinea Mission Board/UELCA, 1961), 114; Pilhofer, *Die Geschichte der Neuendettelsauer Mission in Neuguinea, vol. 1*, 134–35; Wagner, "Beginnings at Finschhafen," 44–46; Kemung, *Nareng-Gareng*, 104–30; Farnbacher, *Gemeinde verantworten*, 34–38, 168–208; Pech, "Deutsche evangelische Missionen in Deutsch-Neuguinea 1886–1921," 392–95, 399–402; Stadler, *Die Missionspraxis Christian Keyßers*.

62. Keyßer, *Anutu im Papualand*, 30; trans. G.R.

63. Keyßer, *Anutu im Papualand*, 24, trans. G.R.

64. Karl Steck, "Gedanken zu Bibelworten als Morgen- und Abendandachten geboten bei der Heldsbach Hauptkonfrerez: 10.-20. Januar 1915," folder 50.1 Bavarian Mission Archives (today *Mission EineWelt*), Neuendettelsau/Germany.

65. Wilde, "Acts of Faith," 33.

66. Cf. Matthew C. Gutman, "Trafficking in Men: The Anthropology of Masculinity," *Annual Review of Anthropology* 26 (1997): 393–94.

67. Hank Nelson, "Loyalties at Sword-point. The Lutheran Missionaries in Wartime New Guinea: 1939–45," *Journal of Pacific History* 8 (1978): 203.

68. I would like to express my deep gratitude for the help I received from the late archivist Manfred Keitel of the Bavarian mission archive (today Mission EineWelt) who generously shared his broad knowledge with me.

Part 2

Resistance, Anti-colonial Activism, and the Rise of Nationalist Discourses

Germany and the Chinese Coolie

Labor, Resistance, and the Struggle for Equality, 1884–1914[1]

Andreas Steen

The Chinese coolie was a prominent figure in the three decades of German colonial history: as a commodity, as indentured laborer, and in discourse.[2] German shipping companies and agents had long been active in coolie transfer and transportation, but it was only after Bismarck agreed to the German Empire's colonial expansion in 1884 that plantation owners on the Pacific islands began to discuss systematic employment of Chinese workers. Already one year later, Dr. O. W. Stübel, consul in Apia, Western Samoa, pointed to the problem of labor shortage and predicted, "[o]ne will have to get used to the idea of acquiring Chinese workers. Indigenous labor will only be of subsidiary usefulness."[3] The coolie question was precarious, especially after the *Reich* took over direct administration of German New Guinea on April 1, 1899, and officially turned Western Samoa into a colony on March 1, 1900. Both colonies were administered separately and struggled over the most important aspect of their economic existence: access to cheap labor. This was not solely a German problem but became an issue in imperial rivalries because the Melanesian Islands also served as a labor reserve for British planters in Fiji and Queensland, and French planters in the New Hebrides and New Caledonia.[4]

By the time German plantation owners gained their first experience with Chinese workers in German New Guinea in the 1880s, the darkest years of the Chinese "coolie trade" belonged to the past—an estimated 1.6 million Chinese coolies (*huagong*) had left their country by 1875.[5] Due to political uncertainty and economic misery caused by over-population, unemployment, natural disasters, and local rebellions, emigration continued "voluntarily," but often ended in indentured labor under all sorts of binding contracts.[6] When anti-Asian immigration laws came into effect in the mid-1880s, Chinese migrants preferred to settle in Southeast Asia and lands around the Indian Ocean and the South Pacific.[7] Many of them continued to work in a violent and humiliating environment, often described as "slave-like."[8] The Qing Government, in the meantime, had become eager to protect Chinese emigrants abroad and pursued a policy that defied two prominent beliefs in Europe and Germany, namely, that of the superiority of the "white race," including its concept of civilizing the "lower races," and the negative discourse of the "yellow peril."[9]

The image of the Chinese coolie was complex and filled with ethnic prejudices; he was pitied and feared, but his cheap labor was needed, and high profits were to be made. The total number of Chinese workers recruited for the German colonies in the Pacific until 1914 was comparatively small, not exceeding 10,000.[10] Unsatisfied with the working conditions on German plantations, coolie resistance relied on different strategies, all of which underscored his agency, networking power, and governmental support. Quite to their advantage, the Pacific Islands were at the periphery of the German empire and of little strategic interest; Germany's main motive was economic exploitation. Administration depended on the appointed governor and his ability to successfully negotiate with the various interest groups. For several reasons, the two colonies followed different—if not contradictory—policies, including with regard to coolie employment. The coolie, however, managed to adapt to and even change the working conditions. Especially after Chinese authorities recognized that Germany was dependent on Chinese support for the economic survival of German Samoa, resistance against coolie and migrant exploitation, combined with rising nationalism, turned the coolie and his fate into a source of power struggles between China and Germany.

German New Guinea and the Failure to Attract Chinese Labor

In 1884, New Guinea was divided into three sections: with the Dutch in the west, the British in the southwest, and the Germans in the northeast ("Kaiser-Wilhelms-Land"). The latter was part of the Imperial German Pacific Protectorates in Melanesia, all of which were administered by the powerful New Guinea Company (Deutsche Neuguinea-Kompagnie), a private company founded in 1884 in Berlin and acting under Imperial Charters. The New Guinea Company mainly cultivated coconut palms and engaged in the copra business, but also grew coffee, cotton, kapok, tobacco, lemon grass, maize, and taro in small quantities. Conflicts, serious clashes, abuses, and armed fights between foreigners and various native groups were common and created a tense environment. In 1889, 79 coolies were imported from Singapore, because it had turned out that "the tobacco-growing industry cannot be conducted without employing Chinese coolies."[11] Laborers were needed in large numbers, but the colonial project was severely hampered by the region's climate and geographical conditions. Apart from various forms of sickness and disease, it was the more prevalent malaria of the mainland coast that "killed Melanesians, Chinese, Malays and Germans in numbers so great as to constantly disrupt the company's operations. . . . Out of 313 Chinese on one plantation in October 1891 only 110 were capable of working eight weeks later and by Christmas 83 were dead."[12] The colony was threatened by an annual death rate of 21 percent among its workforce, faced British and Dutch competition and opposition when it came to labor recruitment, and only managed occasionally to recruit Chinese coolies from Singapore or Shantou (Swatow).[13]

The situation changed after the *Reich* had taken over the colonial administration in 1899, mainly because of the initiatives of the new governor, Dr. Albert Hahl (1868–1945), who shared many of the racial prejudices of his generation and served from 1901 to 1914.[14] Due to the exploitation of the native workforce and the high mortality rate, Hahl feared a dramatic reduction of the native population. In 1901, at a time when planters began to regard the costs for import and employment of Chinese coolies as too high to make profits,[15] Hahl introduced a new scheme to attract skilled Asians to the territory, for example tailors, saddlers, mechanics, cooks, shoemakers, barbers, and carpenters. His dream evaporated after a scandal in the following year, when "ten Chinese tradesmen were publicly flogged for refusing to do road work on Sunday, and all but two were sent back to Singapore, where they complained to the British authorities."[16] The *Straits Times* published a long article in January 1903 that revealed and criticized the dangers for Chinese in a seemingly lawless colony.[17] As it turned out, the Chinese had been illegally recruited in order to circumvent British law. In order to prevent international criticism the colonial administration abolished flogging of Chinese in the same month.[18] The incident added to the already bad reputation of German New Guinea, and it did not help much that Hahl issued an ordinance in February 1904 that imposed no special restriction on Chinese immigrants apart from official registration.[19]

While Hahl continued to promote his policy of attracting Asians to the colony, the New Guinea Company and the plantation owners secured their rights to control labor recruitment and employment, including various forms of punishment and contract extension. At this point, the planters had no interest in importing "expensive" and privileged Chinese coolies but decided to concentrate their recruiting efforts on the "cheap" native population in the colony's territory, often by force. As a result, labor recruitment "was transformed from a labour trade into systematic labour mobilization."[20]

Chinese workers acted outside of this violent system and were successfully—though not without problems—recruited for the phosphate mines in Nauru in 1907.[21] The coolie's safety was guaranteed by the fact that Chinese authorities had begun to heavily observe Chinese emigration since 1903, as Hahl remarked in 1909. In the same letter he dismissed the request to introduce flogging of Chinese in Nauru, mainly because it would be a hindrance to the successful recruitment of Chinese workers and damage the colony's reputation. However, to him, "the low educational level of the Chinese coolie made severe forms of punishment indispensable," and his recommendation for the ongoing Sino-German negotiations (discussed below) was to generally exclude Chinese from corporal punishment, with a "special program" to be continued in German New Guinea.[22]

By 1910, the result of the new policy was obvious and also written into the *Annual Report*: "So far neither Chinese nor Malays are employed anywhere yet as plantation labourers."[23] Threatened by news about the climate and working conditions on German plantations, the Chinese never regarded this colony as a favorite destination for emigration. The fact that they were legally treated as "natives" but equipped with special rights, for instance no flogging, was not enough to attract large numbers. However, in 1912 the 926 Chinese in the whole Protectorate were said to constitute "the most numerous and economically the most important component of the non-indigenous coloured population."[24] A Chinese quarter had been established in Rabaul, and Chinese often worked as free laborers and traders. Two years later, "fewer than one in seven of 1377 Chinese in the Old Protectorate were labourers."[25]

"No Equality, No Coolies": Threatening the Economic Survival of German Samoa

The situation in Western Samoa was different because it was administered by Governor Wilhelm Solf (1862–1936) until 1911. Due to his conviction and the colony's local situation, Solf enforced strict control of Chinese employment and implemented a policy that was later continued by his successor Erich Schultz.[26] Basically because the "colonial government presented itself as a protector of Samoan rights and traditions," practicing what George Steinmetz called "salvage colonialism," tension and conflict with the plantation owners existed throughout this period.[27]

For Solf, Western settlers posed the greatest threat to Samoan people and culture, especially after 1900 when the number of plantations began to increase rapidly, from 41 to 124 in 1903.[28] The scarcity of labor put their economic survival in danger and had three main causes. First, according to the colonial administration, Samoan people could neither be forced to work nor flogged. Second, Samoan planters were denied access to the native labor force in German New Guinea. The only exception was the long-established and influential Deutsche Handels- und Plantagen-Gesellschaft (DHPG), which through agreements with the colonial administration had already managed to secure this privilege in 1888.[29] Third, Chinese settlement in Samoa was prohibited since the Samoan chief King Malietoa Laupepa (r. 1880–98) had issued a ban in 1880.[30]

Under these circumstances, Solf was asked in January 1901 if he would approve the import of 1,000 Chinese coolies from Honolulu.[31] The planters soon persuaded him to lift the ban on Chinese immigrants, but shared his fear that the colony might be overrun by Chinese, who would soon dominate local trade and threaten Samoan culture. Solf was quick to issue a new government ordinance that allowed him to control every aspect of Chinese immigration before the first 239 Chinese workers from Shantou arrived in Apia in April 1903.[32] The workers were immediately sold out (*ausverkauft*), though the costs were regarded as far too high.[33] The *Samoanische Zeitung* was full of praise for the transfer but felt inclined to tell the planters that they should handle the workers with care, "what some of the gentlemen seem not to understand. On this occasion we would also like to mention that Chinese are human beings who have feelings similar to our own."[34] This sentence came as a warning and already foretold future problems.

The general aim of Solf and the plantation owners was now to organize and guarantee annual recruitment on a regular basis. While the scheme was discussed and calculated, German endeavors were confronted with a new standard, if not model, when Great Britain and China signed a convention to regulate the employment of Chinese labor on May 13, 1904.[35] Shortly thereafter, German recruitment faced severe obstacles, and in 1906, several voices in Samoa and Berlin stressed the importance of a Sino-German convention regarding coolie employment. However, until an agreement was finally signed on March 19, 1913, each coolie transport had to be negotiated separately. In sum, altogether 3,846 coolies were shipped to Apia on seven shiploads (1903, 1905,

1906, 1908, 1909, 1911, 1913), the last one arriving with 1,039 coolies on board. The details of this protracted negotiation process have been analyzed by John A. Moses (1977). Here it is sufficient to characterize the points of contention and focus on forms of Chinese resistance.

Several issues developed into recurring topics of negotiation. Most important were the regulations of coolie import and employment, which were designed to control and discipline his activities in all possible ways. Protests about breaches of contract either by German planters or Chinese coolies were as common as struggles over wages, working hours, food rations, (advance) payment, gambling, health care, and forms of punishment. China's critique that German colonial law put coolies below the status of "natives," which allowed planters to insist on flogging as a legal means of punishment, raised the conflict to a higher and political level, combined with the resolute demand for legal equality with "non-natives" and the right of free settlement in Samoa. These points were debated in a repetitive pattern of negotiation and interaction that usually began with the planters' request for Chinese workers.[36]

By the end of 1905, Chinese workers began to complain about the terrible working conditions in letters they sent home; some appeared as posters, for example, in Hong Kong.[37] According to the German Consul in Shantou, Herbert von Borch, China's critical observation of German coolie business began in 1906, due to unusual recruitment methods. A trade that had been running smoothly for decades by accepting certain secret practices had suddenly become official and almost public because of middleman F. Wandres' lack of financial recourses and his direct involvement of the consular body: "The result is that this emigration, though not noteworthy in relation to the total number of external migration, has now taken the first place in the general discussion and critique."[38] Adding to this, about 400 Chinese workers from Samoa had managed to send a complaint to the Chinese embassy in Berlin via the consulate in Honolulu and the embassy in Washington about their working conditions. In late 1906, Yang Sheng, the Chinese Minister in Berlin, censoriously commented on the German coolie contract, which he thought was unclear and failed to protect the coolies. Two weeks later, he received explicit instructions from Beijing: this contract can not be changed, but one should be very careful with future contracts.[39] On January 8, 1907, the Chinese minister sent a note to the German Foreign Ministry, criticizing payment of wages, overwork, inedible food, caning as reaction to complaints, and forceful denial of home return after contract expiration.[40] While complaints from other consuls in Samoa urged Solf to execute a serious investigation, news about the working conditions also appeared in the Chinese press, "at a time when Chinese students in England, France, Belgium, and Germany were beginning to agitate about ill-treatment of coolies in Samoa."[41] Sun Baoqi, the new Chinese Minister in Berlin, then advised his government to open a consulate in Samoa.[42] Chinese officials sent the two commissars Lin Shufen and Lin Runzhao from Shantou and Canton, respectively, to Samoa to inspect the working conditions. In summer 1908, when the colony had just become self-supporting because of high profits in the cocoa trade, parts of their critical and ruinous reports began to circulate in local newspapers.[43] Lin Runzhao's report inspired Prince Qing Yikuang from the Foreign Bureau (*Waiwubu*) to send a long and unambiguous list of complaints to the German envoy in Beijing.[44] Probably Lin Shufen's practical advice to the governor-general in Canton had even more impact:

> Samoa has large plantations and if no more coolies are imported, a great number of these plantations will be ruined. We have to make use of this [situation], in order to press for an advantageous arrangement of the coolie contracts. Samoa needs coolies too desperately; therefore it has to listen to our demands. My advice for coolie contracts in the future would be to first and foremost stress the advantage of the coolie, and not to back down on this point. Thereby his Excellency would achieve great merits with regard to the coolie affair.[45]

China's officials were satisfied with the reports and the instructions they received. When Germany began to officially negotiate a Sino-German convention in 1909, Lin Shufen was appointed as the new Chinese deputy in Shantou; Lin Runzhao was formally accredited as the first Chinese consul in Apia in March 1910. With these two key positions occupied by experienced "Samoa critics," the serious confrontation between the Chinese government and the German Colonial Administration thus began.

The revolution that overthrew the Qing Dynasty and the founding of the new republican government in late 1911 at first had only little effect on the negotiations, mainly because Lin Shufen and Lin Runzhao were confirmed in their posts.[46] The latter's increasing insistence on legal equality and "non-native" status reflected the demands of the new government and dominated the harsh tone of the negotiations, encouraged by the fact that Japanese were not considered as belonging to the "coloured tribes" in German Protectorates since 1900.[47] However, it was not before the conditions in Samoa were criticized as "slave-like" and a serious affront to Chinese prestige that the colonial administration assented to prohibit flogging and to elevate the Chinese in Samoa on the basis of the German civil law code (*bürgerliches Recht*) to the status of "non-natives."[48] On January 6, 1912, the new ordinance with twenty-four paragraphs came into effect.

Meanwhile, Governor Solf was promoted head of the Colonial Office in Berlin in 1911, and, together with his successor Schultz, continued to strictly oppose "free Chinese settlement" in Samoa. The Planters' Association was more pragmatic, due to economic pressure and the immediate need for about 600 workers. It appealed to the Reichstag in November 1911 and agreed that the government should allow free settlement if this guaranteed constant supply.[49] Lin Runzhao, on the other hand, continued his critique and irritated Chinese officials who consequently denied German labor recruitment.

The situation improved only in 1913, after the German Foreign Office had again explained to the Chinese legation in Berlin the particular situation of Samoa and the danger of unrestricted Chinese settlement for the Samoan population. It guaranteed the coolies' safety, increased wages, food rations, and gardening plots. It also offered the possibility—or alternative—to settle elsewhere in the German dominion after contracts expired, preferably in German New Guinea. Another argument put forward was that Germany required very few coolies, compared to the numbers working in British and Dutch colonies.[50] This time, the new government gave its approval after both parties had agreed on a monthly wage of 20 marks. The sudden change was also attributed to the efforts of Elmershaus von Haxthausen, the German Minister in Beijing, who in a memorandum from January 20, 1913, had underscored once more that all demands were met and that Germany was ready to finalize a treaty. If China still refused permission, one could only consider this as an unfriendly act.[51] The government under Yuan Shikai had good reason to exert its pressure on Canton, because Yuan emphasized a good relationship with Germany, employed German military advisers, and planned to dispatch a group of officers to Germany for military training.[52] Since Yuan had not been elected president by then, and the new republic had not been recognized by the foreign powers, he might have feared that Germany would link the coolie question to diplomatic recognition—corresponding requests had already been sent to Berlin.[53]

On March 19, the contract was finally signed. In addition, von Haxthausen promised to inform the government in Apia that Chinese were allowed to lease land and engage in a variety of trades after their contracts expired; the Chinese authorities promised that coolie recruitment would not require special permissions in the future, provided the Samoan planters acted according to the contract.[54]

Samoa, a Paradise for Chinese Workers?

The comparison of German New Guinea and Western Samoa reveals entanglements as well as competition and contradictions of German colonial policy and practice in the Pacific. Employment of Chinese labor was an economic necessity, though much less for the planters in German New Guinea. However, since 1903, when Governor Hahl prohibited flogging of Chinese and thereby improved their status to "privileged natives," severe challenges of German reputation always enforced improvement of the coolies' working conditions. This was especially true for Western Samoa, where coolies had to be imported, irrespective of the costs, and where Governor Solf controlled every aspect of employment to protect the colony and its population from the "yellow peril." The status of Chinese was even below the natives, yet dependency on their labor undermined Solf's power, increased China's possibilities of resistance, and incited officials to successfully struggle for improvement and "non-native" equality.

The violent working condition, in some cases involving murder and death penalties, constant fights over profits, and a strong superiority thinking of Western plantation owners and employees, were commonplace during this period.[55] In Samoa, flogging of Chinese was only abolished in 1911, and one year later the Deutsche Samoa Gesellschaft complained about laziness, lack of respect, discipline, and control on the plantations. Planters hoped for the reintroduction of corporal punishment and in German New Guinea even called repeatedly for the introduction of universal forced labor in 1913.[56] Western Samoa, nevertheless, was a special case and, therefore, was easily picked out by Chinese authorities to teach the Germans—and by extension the foreign powers—a lesson. Consul Lin Runzhao seriously fulfilled his task, but were his reports always correct? Consul Rössler complained to the Director of the Foreign Bureau that Lin "had not visited the plantations for years" and "passed the complaints of the coolies over to the government without any proof."[57] The coolies surely had much to complain about, but despite all criticism, it might be useful to mention that, for instance, in 1908 out of 522 workers whose contracts had expired, 293 were said to have extended their contract for another one to three years.[58] There were other examples: In 1911, 25 coolies handed over 10,000 marks to the captain for safekeeping on their return voyage. In 1912, coolies from Samoa transferred 70,000 marks via the Deutsch-Asiatische Bank in Hong Kong to China.[59] Some coolies, it was reported, had already stayed in Samoa for ten years.[60] And in April 1913, nearly 1,500 workers had been signed on, but only 1,039 could sail to Apia.

Building on these facts, the *Tsingtauer Neueste Nachrichten* praised Samoa as the "Paradise of Chinese Workers."[61] The article mentioned the privileges and rights bestowed on Chinese coolies in Samoa, underscored that the
majority of them remained voluntarily in the colony, and painted a harmonious
picture of working life in the colony. It mentioned neither Chinese complaints
nor the fierce struggle behind each of the paragraphs in the contract, but intended to convey the message that Germany had granted equal status and favorable conditions out of sheer friendship. This rhetoric notwithstanding, the
southern "coolie question" had not damaged Germany's reputation, at least not
in the eyes of the new "northern" government, underscored by the fact that
Germany was China's strongest trading partner after Great Britain and Japan in
late 1913. However, the German dream, to combine Chinese immigration in
Samoa with "free settlement" in New Guinea, was not fulfilled. Moreover,
equality in Samoa was still negotiated. In March 1914, the Chinese Minister in
Berlin informed the Foreign Ministry that the prohibition of alcohol consumption for Chinese contradicts the promise of equality.[62] Five months later, New
Zealand troops occupied Western Samoa, and in August 1915, 900 out of 1,200
coolies were reported to have prolonged their expired contracts.[63] China did,
however, not succeed in negotiating "free settler" status with Colonel Logan,
then in charge of the New Zealand forces. He rejected the request and repatri-
ated over 1,200 Chinese between 1914 and 1920—without replacement.[64] After a decade of heated debates in Apia and along the south China coast, in
Berlin and Beijing, the struggle that finally defined the general conditions for
a "Paradise of Chinese workers" had come to an end, for both Germany and
China.

NOTES

1. The article grew out of the research project "Germany and China, 1848–1911:
Intercultural Modes of Interaction and International History," carried out at Free University Berlin (Sinology) and Beijing University (History), and funded by the German
Research Foundation (Deutsche Forschungsgemeinschaft). I gratefully acknowledge
this support.

2. The word "coolie" dates back to the mid-seventeenth century and is of Indian
(Urdu) origin, meaning "day-laborer." It is a derogatory term that referred to indentured
laborers and was later also widely used by the colonial powers in Asia and the Pacific
to denote unskilled workers, usually from India and China.

3. Quoted from John A. Moses, "The Coolie Labour Question and German Colonial Policy in Samoa, 1900–14," in John A. Moses and Paul M. Kennedy, *Germany in
the Pacific and Far East, 1870–1914* (St. Lucia: University of Queensland, 1977), 235.

By the end of the decade, first plans were discussed to recruit Chinese workers for the German colonies in German-East Africa. See Sebastian Conrad, *Globalisierung und Nation im deutschen Kaiserreich* (Munich: Beck, 2006), 213.

4. Doug Munro and Stewart Firth, "German Labour Policy and the Partition of the Western Pacific: The View from Samoa," *Journal of Pacific History* 25, no. 1 (June 1990): 86.

5. Zhang Xiaomin, "Wan Qing zhengfu dui haiwai huaqiaoren de baohu" [The Late Qing Government's Protection of Overseas Chinese], *Sheke Congheng* [Social Sciences Review], 23, no. 3 (2008): 216.

6. An overview of "indentured labor" is provided by David Northrup, *Indentured Labour in the Age of Imperialism, 1834–1922* (Cambridge University Press, 1995).

7. Until 1940, over 19 million Chinese settled in these areas. See Adam McKeown, "Global Migration 1846–1940," *Journal of World History* 15, no. 2 (2004): 157.

8. On the Dutch tobacco plantations in Sumatra see Jan Breman, *Taming the Coolie Beast: Plantation Society and the Colonial Order in Southeast Asia* (Delhi: Oxford University Press, 1989), and Frances Gouda, *Dutch Culture Overseas: Colonial Practice in the Netherlands Indies, 1900–1942* (Amsterdam University Press, 1995).

9. On China's protective policy see Ji Manhong, "Lun wan Qing zhengfu dui Dongnanya huaqiao de baohu zhengce" [The Late Qing Government's Protective Policy of Overseas Chinese in Southeast Asia], *Dongnanya yanjiu* [Southeast Asian Studies], No. 2 (2006): 52–56, and Luo Jincai, "Xiantan 1860 nian yihou wan Qing zhengfu waijiao huaqiao de biaoxian" [The Attitude of the Late Qing Government towards Protection of Overseas Chinese after 1860], *Fujian Luntan* [Fujian Tribune], No. 1 (2008): 38–39; on the fear of the "yellow peril" in the United States and Germany see Ute Mehnert, *Deutschland, Amerika und die "Gelbe Gefahr". Zur Karriere eines Schlagworts in der Großen Politik, 1905–1917* (Stuttgart: Franz Steiner Verlag, 1995); Stanford M. Lyman, "The 'Yellow Peril' Mystique: Origins and Vicissitudes of a Racist Discourse," *International Journal of Politics, Culture, and Society*, 13, no. 4 (2000); Klaus Mühlhahn, *Herrschaft und Widerstand in der "Musterkolonie" Kiautschou* (Munich: R. Oldenbourg Verlag, 2000); and Conrad, *Globalisierung und Nation*.

10. Between 1903 and 1914, about 4,000 Chinese coolies were recruited for the plantations in Samoa (Moses, "Coolie Labour Question," see also below); according to Wu Fengbin ("Yapian zhanzheng hou cong Shantou chukou de qijue huagong" [About the Indentured Overseas Chinese who left from Shantou after the Opium War], in *Nanyang wenti yanjiu*, no. 2 (1988): 78), more than 3,000 coolies worked in the phosphate mines of Nauru, 1907–1913; Jon Goss and Bruce Lindquist ("Placing Movers: An Overview of the Asian-Pacific Migration System," *Contemporary Pacific* 12, no. 2 (2000): 389) speak of 6,000 Chinese recruited by British agents for German New Guinea (1885–1914).

11. Peter Sack and Dymphna Clark, eds., *German New Guinea. The Annual Reports* (Canberra: Australian National University Press, 1979), 7, 51.

12. Stewart Firth, *New Guinea under the Germans* (Victoria: Melbourne University Press, 1982), 37, 35.

13. Stewart Firth,"The Transformation of the Labour Trade in German New Guinea, 1899–1914," *Journal of Pacific History* 11, no. 1 (1976): 51.

14. In 1896, at the age of twenty-eight, Hahl arrived at Herbertshöhe, where he

acted as imperial judge (1896–99) and deputy governor (1899–1901) and was "something of an authority on the Pacific" when he became governor. See Peter Biskup, "Dr. Albert Hahl—Sketch of a German Colonial Official," *Australian Journal of Politics and History* 14 (1968): 342.

15. Sack and Clark, *Annual Reports*, 233.

16. Firth, "Transformation of the Labour Trade," 62.

17. *The Straits Times,* article in two parts, 19./21.01.1903 (BArch R1004–8–14 (I), 99–100). See also Firth, *New Guinea under the Germans,*116.

18. Firth, *New Guinea under the Germans,* 116.

19. Firth, "Transformation of the Labour Trade," 62.

20. Firth, "Transformation of the Labour Trade," 52.

21. Report, incl. the contract, sent by Krause, German Consulate Swatow, to Imperial Chancellor, 31.01.1907 (BArch R1001–6286, 140–45).

22. In short, Hahl proposed money fines and long imprisonment. Since prisoners were judged differently from workers, they were not exempted from forced labor and corporal punishment as a means of deterrent. See Hahl, Herbertshöhe, to Imperial Colonial Office, 12.09.1909 (BArch R1001–2339, 47–49).

23. Sack and Clark, *Annual Reports*, 310.

24. Sack and Clark, *Annual Reports*, 340.

25. Firth, *New Guinea under the Germans*, 117.

26. See Paul M. Kennedy, *The Samoan Tangle: A Study in Anglo-German-American Relations, 1878–1900* (Dublin: Irish University Press, 1974), 272. Solf received a doctoral degree in Indian philology, and learned Urdu and Persian at the "Seminar für Orientalische Sprachen" in Berlin. In 1888, he gave up his position at Oxford, worked as a translator at the German Consulate in Calcutta (1889–91), studied law, and in 1896 worked at the Colonial Office. In April 1898, Solf arrived in German East-Africa, and few months later he was appointed to Samoa as German Consul. For his biography see Eberhard von Vietsch, *Wilhelm Solf: Botschafter zwischen den Zeiten* (Tübingen: Wunderlich, 1961), and Peter J. Hempenstall and Paul Tanaka Mochida, *The Lost Man: Wilhelm Solf in German History* (Wiesbaden: Harrassowitz, 2005).

27. George Steinmetz, *The Devil's Handwriting: Precoloniality, and the German Colonial State in Qingdao, Samoa, and Southwest Africa* (Chicago: University of Chicago Press, 2007), 317ff.

28. Moses, "Coolie Labour Question," 237.

29. Munro and Firth, "German Labour Policy," 100. Since 1878, the DHPG was the successor company of the influential and aggressive company John Cesar Godeffroy and Son (of Hamburg), which had set up its headquarters in Apia in 1857. The DHPG received German government support and became the country's "sole tangible claim to Samoa." See Munro and Firth, "German Labour Policy," 98, and A. E. Bollard, "The Financial Adventures of J. C. Godeffroy and Son in the Pacific," *Journal of Pacific History* 16, no. 1 (1981), and R. P. Gilson, *Samoa 1830 to 1900: The Politics of a Multi-Cultural Community* (London: Oxford University Press, 1970).

30. Ben Featuna'i Liua'ana, "Dragons in Little Paradise. Chinese (Mis-) Fortunes in Samoa, 1900–1950," *Journal of Pacific History* 32, no. 1 (1997): 29.

31. Voigt, Vailima, to Solf, Apia, 24.01.1901 (R1004- 8–13 (I), 94–95).

32. Published on March 7, 1903, in *Samoanisches Gouvernements-Blatt*, the decree contained seven articles. The governor's approval was needed for Chinese immigration, operating handicraft business, and land lease. Chinese were prohibited to buy land and to trade. Infringement would lead to a money fine, three months in prison or a fine of 500 marks for each Chinese (BArch R1004- 8–13 (II), 178).

33. See F. Wohltmann, *Pflanzung und Siedlung auf Samoa. Erkundungsbericht* (Berlin: Verlag des Kolonialwirtschaftlichen Komitees, 1904), who also provides a detailed list of all the costs.

34. *Samoanische Zeitung*, 02.05.1903.

35. The "Convention between the United Kingdom and China respecting the Employment of Chinese Labour in British Colonies and Protectorates" consisted of 15 paragraphs.

36. See, e.g., the 16-page report of F. Wandres about his third arrangement of coolie transfer to Samoa, written in Swatau, August 1, 1906 (BArch, R901–30657).

37. Liua'ana, "Dragons in Little Paradise," 32.

38. Borch, Swatow, to Imperial Chancellor, 08.02.1909 (BArch, R901–30660).

39. Yang Sheng, Berlin, to the Waiwubu, 02.11.1906; and the reply from the Waiwubu, 16.11.1906 (in *Huagong chuguo shiliao huibian*, Vol. 1).

40. On August 29, 1907, the Foreign Ministry, Berlin, sent a "Verbalnote" to the Chinese Embassy, which simply "washed away" all complaints by accepting misunderstandings, blaming the Chinese for all kinds of fraud, and underlining law and order in the German colony (BArch, R901–30658).

41. Moses, "Coolie Labour Question," 241, and Liua'ana, "Dragons in Little Paradise," 33.

42. Sun Baoqi, Berlin, to Waiwubu, 08.11.1907 (in *Huagong chuguo shiliao huibian*, No. 1).

43. See Kennedy, *Samoan Tangle*, 275. A collection of Chinese newspaper articles, 1908–1911, in German translation can be found in BArch R901–30658, 30659, 30656, 30665.

44. Prince Qing to Graf von Rex, November 16, 1908 (BArch, R901–30660). Also criticized was the fact that according to the contract the salary had to be paid in Mexican Dollars but was paid in Marks instead. The Colonial Office was asked to refund the financial deficit of $90,106.86 in salary for three previous transports.

45. See "Bericht Lin Shu Fen's an den Generalgouverneur der 2 Kuangprovinzen," German translation, 14 pages (BArch, R901–30658).

46. The situation in Shantou and Samoa is covered in the reports of Borch, Shantou, to Imperial Chancellor, 08.12.1911 (BArch R1001–2327, 63–69), and Schultz, Apia, to Secretary of State, Colonial Office, 09.01.1912 (BArch R1001–2327, 80–86).

47. See the Memorandum of the Chinese Legation, Berlin, "Memorandum—Treatment of Chinese Samoan Island," 23.12.1910, in English (BArch, R1001–5588).

48. Moses, "Coolie Labour Question," 246. See Yinchang, Berlin, to Secretary of State Kiderlen-Waechter, Foreign Ministry, 22.02.1911 (BArch R1001–5588, 11–19).

49. Moses, "Coolie Labour Question," 249.

50. See Moses, "Coolie Labour Question," 253. The argument referred to Great Britain's success in recruiting 63,296 men from north and south China only for the

South African mines between 1904 and 1906. See Peter Richardson, "The Recruiting of Chinese Indentured Labour for the South African Gold-Mines, 1903–1908," *Journal of African History* 18, no. 1 (1977): 85–108.

51. V. Haxthausen, Beijing, to Imperial Chancellor, Berlin, 06.02.1913 (BArch R1001–2328, 168–71).

52. Andreas Steen, *Deutsch-chinesische Beziehungen 1911–1927: Vom Kolonialismus zur "Gleichberechtigung"* (Berlin: Akademie-Verlag, 2006), 63–64.

53. See, e.g., Schultz, Gov. Samoa, to Solf, Reichs-Kolonialamt, 10.02.1913 (BArch R1901–30667); and "Deutsche Samoa Gesellschaft—Auszug aus den Briefen unserer Niederlassung vom 25. März und 5. April 1912" (BArch R1001–2327, 147–50).

54. Dr. Lo Pan Hui, Canton, to Consul Rössler, 08.04.1913 (BArch R1001–2328, 203–4).

55. On Chinese crimes, violence, and punishment, see "Zur Kuli-Frage," in *Samoanische Zeitung*, No. 27, 03.07.1909. On the Sino-Dutch disputes, see Ching-Hwang Yen, *Coolies and Mandarins: China's Protection of Overseas Chinese during the Late Ch'ing Period (1851–1911)* (Singapore: Singapore University Press, 1985), 194–203.

56. Deutsche Samoa Gesellschaft, letters, 25.03.–05.04.1912 (BArch R1001–2327, 147–50). See also Firth, "Transformation of the Labour Trade," 64.

57. Rössler, Canton, to Dr. Lo Pan Hui, Canton, 25.03.1913 (BArch R1001–2328, 202–3).

58. Schultz, Apia, to Imperial Colonial Office, June 16, 1908 (BArch R901–30659).

59. "Chinesische Arbeiter für Samoa," *Der Ostasiatische Lloyd*, No. 17, 25.04.1913.

60. "Rechtliche Gleichstellung der Chinesen mit den Weissen auf Samoa," in *Hamburger Nachrichten*, März 1912 (BArch R1001–2327, 130); "Koloniales," in *Kreuz-Zeitung*, 16.03.1912.

61. "Samoa, das Paradies chinesischer Arbeiter," in *Tsingtauer Neueste Nachrichten*, 05.03.1913.

62. Verbalnote, Chinese Legation, Berlin, to German Foreign Ministry, 16.03.1914 (BArch R1001–2329, 108).

63. Henniger, Pflanzervereinigung von Samoa, to German Consul, Swatow, 16.08.1915 (BArch R1001–2329, 145–46).

64. Liua'ana, "Dragons in Little Paradise," 34.

The Other German Colonialism

Power, Conflict, and Resistance in a German-speaking Mission in China, ca. 1850–1920

Thoralf Klein

Ever since research on mission history passed from the hands of the mission societies and theologians into those of historians, sociologists, anthropologists, and so on—that is, since about the 1960s—two major approaches have developed. The earlier of the two focused on the role of Christian missions within the political and cultural framework of imperialism and colonialism. Taking up anti-colonial impulses from 1920s China and 1960s Africa, its proponents pointed to the entanglement of missionaries with the expansion of imperialism, their functions within the colonial state, and their contribution to the "colonization of hearts and minds."[1] Since the 1990s, this approach has given way to a controversial debate on whether missions constituted a more independent force that was able to counterbalance the ill effects of colonialism.[2] The second, more recent approach deals with the cultural dynamics of encounters between missionaries and indigenous populations, pointing to the creative processes they set in motion.[3]

The two approaches that I have just outlined with somewhat broad strokes are, of course, not wholly irreconcilable. On the contrary, reflection on their relationship might lead to a fresh assessment of both mission and imperialism/colonialism. I suggest that both be treated as irreducible phenomena, making it impossible to make use of one to fully explain the other. Their relationship is best described as an "elective affinity."[4] Not only does this perspective shift attention to a comparison between the two, pointing to the intrinsic colonial qualities of the way mission societies managed their indigenous congregations. It also enables analysis of the colonial structures of Christian missions in contexts where no formal colonialism, but informal imperialism existed—as was the case in China, which is at the center of this essay. Like other states with a functioning bureaucratic apparatus (such as the Ottoman Empire, Persia and Japan), China was never formally colonized but was subjected to a system of "unequal" treaties that granted Europeans and Americans of different nationalities legal privileges and ensured their economic dominance. Only the British crown colony of Hong Kong and a number of leaseholds along the coast—usually acquired around 1898—such as German-occupied Jiaozhou 膠州, were ruled as full-fledged colonies.[5] With the exception of these territories, Christian missions thus operated in areas under Chinese jurisdiction, but at the same time were placed under the legal protection of the treaties, which was upheld with the backing of the consuls and occasionally military forces of their home countries.

The colonial character of Christian missions in the nineteenth and early twentieth centuries can be identified in different ways. According to the German historian Jürgen Osterhammel, what characterizes colonialism is that "fundamental decisions affecting the lives of the colonized people are made and implemented by the colonial rulers in pursuit of interests that are often defined in a distant metropolis. Rejecting cultural compromises with the colonized population, the colonizers are convinced of their own superiority and of their ordained mandate to rule."[6] Indeed it was the missionaries on the spot or even the headquarters of mission societies back in Europe or the United States who decided what was best for "their" Christians, and in doing so, displayed that same "beneficial ruthlessness" that Gayatri Spivak has ascribed to British colonialism in India.[7] It is especially important to note that the motives behind the mission enterprise were not entirely altruistic, as it was ultimately directed toward establishing the Kingdom of God, an end that would benefit not only the receivers of the missionary message but also the mission societies and all supporters of the mission movement.

One might even go further: By trying to mold the converts according to the norms and practices of the Christian milieu from which they themselves originated (mostly rural Catholicism or the Pietist/Evangelical strand of Protestantism), the missionaries pursued what Homi Bhabha has called the strategy of mimicry: a "desire for a reformed, recognizable Other, *as a subject of a difference that is almost the same but not quite.*"[8] In this attempt missionaries subjected the neophytes to power structures that, in many though not in all mission societies, ultimately grew out of those that governed the relationship between missionaries and the directories of the mission societies. As the American sociologist Jon Miller has shown, in centralized mission societies the authority of the home board was based on a combination of traditional, bureaucratic, and charismatic rule.[9] This Weberian perspective ought to be complemented by a Foucauldian one, as the directories often also relied on strategies of control described by one missionary as "superintendence and sub-ordination."[10] Missionaries, who had often internalized techniques of (mutual) surveillance, could in turn impose them on the indigenous Christians placed under their responsibility.[11] In this capacity, they were expected to enforce regulations exhibiting an uncompromising stance toward all beliefs and prac-tices considered incompatible with Christianity.

How did indigenous Christians react to this missionary policy? How did they stake out a place of their own within the colonial framework imposed upon them by the missionaries? In the remainder of this essay, I will provide an answer by taking a closer look at the Evangelical Mission Society of Basel (*Evangelische Missionsgesellschaft zu Basel*), generally known as the Basel Mission. Founded in 1815, it was both a local, national, transnational, and global enterprise. The members of its directory board, the so-called Commit-tee, were co-opted from among the urban bourgeoisie of the Swiss city of Basel. Its main reservoir of financial resources and manpower, however, lay in Southwestern Germany, with the state of Württemberg alone accounting for almost one-third of its income and for almost half of the missionaries sent to China between 1846 and 1914.[12] As early as the mid-nineteenth century, the Basel Mission began to emphasize its rootedness in German culture. And since it began to send missionaries to the German colony Cameroon in 1885, its leaders officially began to designate it as a German mission.[13] At the same time, however, the Basel Mission worked under different colonial regimes—Danish and later British on the Gold Coast (present-day Ghana, since 1828) and British in South India (since 1840)—as well as the transnational informal empire in China (since 1847).

As these varying political frameworks indicate, the power relations be-tween the Basel Mission and its indigenous congregations worked indepen-dently of the mission society's affiliation with a particular colonial power. Rather, the authority of the society and its missionaries rested on a number of legal, social, and cultural arrangements designed to inculcate in the Basel Mis-sion's Christians a "Christian way of life" (*christliche Lebensordnung*).[14] Fore-most among these were the Church Regulations (*Gemeindeordnung*), a codi-fied set of rules drawn up to establish a uniform global standard for the spiritual—and to some extent also mundane—life of the Basel Christians that established the Basel Mission as a colonial phenomenon in its own right.[15] In this essay, I analyze this phenomenon in three parts: Two case studies from China will be followed by a concluding section that places my findings in a broader context.

Establishing Missionary Power: Zhang Fuxing and the Early Congregations in Northeast Guangdong, 1852–67

Like all Protestant missions, the Basel Mission was a latecomer in China, which had been a target of Catholic missionary activity for several centuries. After the Vatican had forbidden crucial elements of the Jesuit strategy to accommodate Christianity to Chinese culture, the Yongzheng 雍正 emperor of the ruling Qing 清 dynasty (1644–1911) in 1724 declared Christianity illegal and expelled most foreign missionaries, forcing the existing congregations underground. Frustrated in their attempts to circumvent this ban, both Catholic missionaries and their Protestant counterparts—who arrived in China from 1807 onward—eventually threw in their lot with imperialism.

In this respect, the Basel Mission is quite a typical case. In sending its first missionaries to China in 1846, it responded to the favorable conditions for evangelization opened up after China had been forced to sign the first of the so-called unequal treaties in the wake of the disastrous Opium War (1839–42) against the British. In these treaties, China unilaterally granted foreigners a number of legal and economic privileges, extraterritoriality and consular jurisdiction being the ones from which mission work benefited the most. In addition, the Qing government also issued toleration edicts, allowing Catholics to openly practice their religion—a privilege that Protestants were quick to claim for themselves.

Like other German missions, the Basel missionaries strongly preferred the rural hinterland as a field of work to the treaty ports China had had to open to free trade and foreign residence. By concentrating on the southernmost province of Guangdong 廣東 and on one particular linguistic group—the Hakka (Mandarin: *Kejia* 客家)—the Basel Mission sought to lay the foundation for establishing formalized church structures. In the years prior to 1860, however, this strategy was hampered by a number of limitations. As foreigners had no right to travel in the interior, and the German consular representation lacked a legal basis, the first Basel missionaries had little opportunity to venture far inland; moreover, they lacked the necessary linguistic and cultural skills, as well as sufficient numbers. This is why they had to rely on Chinese catechists and evangelists who could make use of their local ties to gain a foothold in remote places.[16] On the other hand, the necessity of inculcating a "Christian way of life" in assistants and new believers required that they be placed under the control of the missionaries. The two elements of the Basel mission strategy were in conflict with each other and must of necessity lead to tensions. The best-documented controversy involved one of the Basel Mission's most prominent Chinese Christians, a man named Zhang Fuxing 張復興.

Born in 1811 or 1812 as the son of an itinerant merchant and laborer, Zhang had settled in Hong Kong in the mid-1840s. While working as a peddler, he converted to Christianity and made contact with the Basel missionaries, who appointed him as a preaching assistant (*Predigt-Gehilfe*).[17] In 1852 he returned to his ancestral village of Gaoqi 高磜 in Changle 長樂 district to evangelize there, making use of his local ties. Although his family background was rather modest, his position as a salaried preacher and his mediating skills seem to have earned him the recognition of the Zhang 張 lineage, culminating in his becoming an elder of that lineage in 1859.[18] Lineage ties, based on patrilineal descent from a common ancestor, were a structuring principle of local society in much of China, but especially in the south, and overlapped with village organization in a fluid relationship.[19]

In the early years, the emerging congregation in Changle district—more than 200 persons in 1859[20]—was pretty much left to its own devices, developing into a network of laypeople under the leadership of Zhang and his associates. Communication with the Basel missionaries depended on Christians occasionally traveling to Hong Kong, where the missionaries had retreated after the outbreak of the Second Opium War in 1856. The position of the Changle Christians was volatile, however, as they suffered greatly from feuding, which was a characteristic feature of social life in nineteenth-century South China. Lineages and villages fought with each other—and occasionally amongst themselves—over scarce resources as well as matters of honor. The small Christian congregations were caught amid these conflicts: Sometimes Christians were persecuted by their own kin or neighbors, sometimes (as in the village of Zhangcun 章村, which became the center of the new congregation) they were harassed by outsiders and defended by their own relations. In Changle, therefore, much depended on Zhang's leadership not only in spiritual but also in secular and financial matters, into which he was increasingly drawn.[21]

Zhang's entanglement with local society was probably also the reason for his taking a concubine sometime in the late 1850s. His first marriage was childless, and therefore Zhang became the object of much derision, which affected not only his own prestige as a lineage elder, but also—he reasoned later—that of the Christian congregation. However, Zhang's decision constituted a clear violation of the Church Regulations, which explicitly outlawed polygamy after conversion to Christianity.[22] Apparently, Zhang had no qualms about his action, since his own reading of the Bible provided a perfect justification. As he explained to the elders of the Changle congregation, polygamy was a practice condoned by the Old Testament, if not by the New.[23]

The situation of the de facto independent Changle congregation changed after the end of the Second Opium War in 1860. As a consequence of military defeat, the Qing government had to conclude new treaties, which allowed all foreigners to travel and missionaries to acquire real estate in the interior of China. After Prussia, acting on behalf of other German states, had become a treaty power in 1861, the Basel missionaries (explicitly Catholics but de facto also Protestants) enjoyed the full protection of Prussian (and since 1871 German) consuls, the Swiss among them becoming "protégés" (*Schutzgenossen*) of Prussia and later of the German Reich. It is no coincidence, then, that the first Basel missionaries ventured into Changle district in 1862 and 1863, taking the first steps to incorporate the congregation there into the organizational fabric and power structure of the Basel Mission. Apart from baptizing converts and thus formally admitting them to the church (a prerogative of the missionaries that allowed them to prevent uncontrolled growth of the congregations), the missionaries also began to enforce church discipline. This meant that they would have to deal with Zhang's bigamy. Because of Zhang's influence over the congregation and his importance as its protector, the missionaries proceeded cautiously, first excluding him from Holy Communion, then dismissing him from the service of the mission, and finally expelling him from the congregation.[24] In his communication with the missionaries, Zhang was rather submissive and seems to have accepted his excommunication, referring to himself in his Hakka vernacular as a "fui ngoi nyin" or "person outside the church" (*hui wai ren* 會外人 in Mandarin).[25] This may have been an example of what Bhabha has called "sly civility."[26] In his talks with fellow Christians, Zhang, whose "frank and determined language" the missionaries had remarked upon earlier,[27] adopted a more aggressive posture. He was also slow in changing his ways. Significantly, he seems never to have renounced his position as lineage elder.[28] In the case of Zhang's bigamy, however, the Basel Misson was uncompromising, insisting on his separating from his concubine and on a public confession of his sins, after which he was readmitted to Holy Communion in late 1863.[29] In the following year, two missionaries were permanently stationed in Zhangcun, in order to better control the congregation. As Zhang's first wife died the same year, he was permitted to officially marry his concubine.[30]

Having solved the case of Zhang's bigamy, the missionaries took a final step that symbolized their takeover of authority over the Changle congregation, turning the house that served both as chapel and as Zhang's private residence into a mission station. Zhang had purchased the impressive three-story building back in 1859 on behalf of the Changle congregation; he himself had contributed about one-quarter of the purchase price and made considerable investments in the renovation of the house.

Part of the story is contained in a number of legal documents in Chinese and German preserved in the Basel Mission Archives. What the missionaries were aiming at is best captured in a paragraph in one of the German drafts that was later included in the official Chinese land deed:

> It goes without saying that the congregation established by the Basel Mission [. . .] will accept the church regulations of the Basel Mission, entrust itself to the direction of its missionaries [. . .] and honor the [members of the] Committee in Basel as its spiritual tutors.[31]

This passage makes it clear that the missionaries wanted to establish some sort of legal authority that would ensure their control over the lives of the Chinese Christians. This aim was underscored by the changes made by the missionaries, who wanted to give the building a more "European" character after making it their home in 1864. These changes were partly motivated by concerns for the health of the missionaries,[32] but they were also the outgrowth of a deliberate policy on the part of the Committee to separate the lifestyles of missionaries, on the one hand, and Chinese catechists and Christians, on the other.[33]

Owing to these circumstances, there was a lot more at stake than the simple transfer of real estate. The missionaries' standpoint was that Zhang had never legally owned the building but ought to receive compensation for his investments.[34] However, Zhang proved reluctant to evacuate the house, partly because he felt his authority was being threatened, partly because the compensation offered fell short of his expectations. He even went out of his way to lose his temper in the presence not only of a number of leading parishioners but also of two missionaries before he could be prevailed upon to make way for the missionaries.[35] The final settlement symbolically underscored the racial hierarchy within the Basel Mission congregations, which separated Europeans from Chinese assistants and ordinary Christians.

In the Zhang Fuxing case, the Basel missionaries successfully asserted their authority over the Changle congregation and secured its incorporation in the power structures of the Basel Mission, forcing Zhang to make all concessions.[36] Paradoxically, their victory was far from complete. Although they had coercive measures at their disposal, these were never fully sufficient to mold Chinese Christians according to the Pietist ideals of the Basel missionaries. Despite many tensions and conflicts, lineage and village ties continued to connect Chinese Christians to local society. The problem was aggravated by the dynamics of mission work itself, which constantly brought new converts into the church. In some of the most controversial issues—continuation of certain "heathen" practices, polygamy, infant marriages, and consumption of sacrificial meat—the missionaries either glossed over transgressions or slowly but gradually began to work out compromises with local practices.[37] Thus the resilience of the Chinese Christians shaped the Basel Mission's Chinese church as much as did the input of the missionaries.

Challenging the Power of the Missionaries: The Independence Movement in Songtou, 1887–1913

Given the strong missionary bias in the archival record left by the Basel Mission, any materials of Chinese origin deserve particular attention. Among these are a few documents relating to the independence movement in the congregation of Songtou 嵩頭, a village in Guangdong Province. The most comprehensive among these is a booklet describing the history of that congregation.[38] Written in the early 1920s, it appeared not under the auspices of the Basel Mission, but in Shanghai 上海, illuminating the ways that Christians had become able to organize outside of their mission society.

The driving force behind the independence movement was one Zhong Qingyuan 鐘清源, a catechist and later a pastor in the Basel Mission. According to the Basel Mission's rule of avoidance, he was never stationed in his native village of Songtou, but he wielded considerable influence in the congregation owing to his lineage and village ties.

The Songtou independence movement manifested itself twice: first in the late 1880s and again in 1912. In 1887, Zhong Qingyuan launched an initiative to raise money in order to prepare the congregation for self-government, which was then the avowed policy of the Basel Mission.[39] Since about the 1840s and thus much earlier than administrators in the colonial bureaucracies, prominent leaders of the transnational Protestant missionary movement had advocated self-governing, self-financed, and self-propagating churches.[40] In China, the Basel Mission had embarked on a similar policy since about 1875, promising congregations self-administration if and when they were able to pay the salary of the local preacher. Until about 1910, however, the Committee in Basel as well as the missionaries in the field were focused on setting up structures for a future (Hakka) Chinese church and pressured the congregations for ever higher church taxes.[41] Their one-sided exactions made self-administration a rather unattractive option for catechists and congregations, the more so as the latter hardly had a say in the matter. Most congregations therefore remained passive and reluctant to comply with the missionaries' demands, and the move of the Songtou congregation was an unusual one.

By 1888, the congregation had collected a sum of more than 33,000 cash. In June of that year, five Songtou Christians went to see the local missionary, Otto Schultze, and offered to pay the salary for a pastor or catechist. The missionary would continue to oversee the latter's work, but the congregation would take financial administration into their own hands.[42] Schultze's reply is very typical for the attitude of the Basel missionaries toward "their" Chinese Christians and toward the self-government of congregations. He declared that although the congregation was able to attain self-sufficiency, it was not yet ready for self-government; he also suspected dubious motives behind the Christians' desire to control the church property. Although some missionaries saw their authority threatened,[43] the Christians did not seek an open conflict with the missionaries. Rather, tensions simmered down, only to resurface in the early 1910s.

By the time the self-government movement in Songtou reemerged, both the political framework and the Basel Mission's policy on indigenization had undergone profound changes. In the years after 1905, the mission had stepped up its attempts at introducing church self-government. By ordaining Chinese pastors from 1906, it had created an indigenous high-level clergy that performed the same functions as the missionaries, although it was placed under their supervision and hence still marginalized. For the Chinese Christians, however, the distinction between European missionaries and Chinese pastors was hardly obvious, as members of both groups were referred to as *mushi* 牧師 ("shepherd," the literal translation of "pastor"). At the political level, the Republican revolution of 1911 led to the first official recognition of Christianity in China, as the revolutionary government granted religious freedom in its provisional constitution of 1912. Moreover, the revolution fueled hopes for a speedy liquidation of imperialism that would help China to attain international equality within a new world order.[44] Although these hopes were later thwarted, many people shared them at the outset of the Republic. It is therefore hardly a coincidence that in late 1912, a movement for self-government emerged within the Basel Mission's Chinese churches.

In contrast to the 1887 initiative, which was purely local, the new movement encompassed a greater number of congregations. But again Songtou took the lead, as Zhong Qingyuan was the guiding spirit behind the movement and had mobilized his kinship and village ties. Half of the twenty-two signatories of the manifesto outlining the aims of the movement were from Songtou.[45] The text, issued in November 1912, criticized the "spirit of dependence" prevailing in the Basel Mission's congregations and declared "full Chinese responsibility for all matters of the church" as the goal of the movement. As in 1887/88, the most immediate objective goal consisted of raising money to pay a pastor's salary, with any surplus to be invested in a hospital or a business venture.[46] In January 1913, Zhong Qingyuan was elected pastor of the independent congregations and became one of eight directors of the independent church. Impatient with the sluggish progress toward self-government in the Basel Mission, Zhong and the other directors made it plain that their initiative was the first step toward complete independence of all its Chinese congregations.[47] Zhong himself was reported as saying that according to the policy of the Basel Mission, the Chinese Christians would have to wait for self-government "till Doomsday."[48] On the other hand, the manifesto had expressed a desire to collaborate with the European missionaries, and Zhong's activities were not intended to provoke them: He preached in the chapel of the independent church, went on some evangelization tours, and founded a girls' school.

Somewhat naively perhaps, the leaders of the independence movement seem to have counted on the support or at least acquiescence of the missionaries. But although some missionaries were indeed sympathetic, the majority, and especially those in leading positions, expressed their disapproval of the independent churches.[49] While suspecting xenophobia as the driving force behind the independence movement, they themselves employed sinophobic arguments, declaring it impossible to strike a compromise with Zhong and other leaders, who, being Chinese, would not honor an agreement.[50] Owing to the lack of support from the missionaries and probably also to the shortage of funds, the independence movement soon lost its impetus and dissolved in late 1913, about one year after its reemergence. Zhong Qingyuan was especially bitter at the hostility of the missionaries, who had even rejected his financial claims on the grounds that he had quit the mission on his own initiative.[51] Left with no alternative, Zhong, like most of his associates in the independence movement, eventually returned to serve the mission.

It would seem that the attempts of the Songtou congregation at achieving independence had been a failure. Both in 1887/88 and in 1912/13, the independence movement gave in at the least token of resistance on the part of the missionaries, testifying to the degree that the Chinese Christians, both laymen and clergy, had internalized the principle of obedience despite the many tensions and grievances between them and the missionaries. But this impression is somewhat misleading. In fact, the abortive initiatives at achieving self-government profoundly influenced subsequent developments in two ways: First, they brought together a group of people committed to the cause of an independent church, initially on the basis of lineage and villages, later on a churchwide basis. In terms of personnel (and to some extent also resources), the movement of 1887/88 paved the way for that of 1912/13, while the latter formed the nucleus of a future independent church. Second, they fundamentally altered the relationship between Basel missionaries and Chinese Christians. Again, the alarm with which some missionaries greeted the initiative of 1887 anticipated the shock wave that the independence movement of 1912/13 sent through their ranks. This shock convinced them that the mission could not unilaterally impose self-government on the church but needed the active participation of the clergy and church elders, who represented the congregations while the clergy were employees of the mission.[52] As early as September 1913, three synods that were held simultaneously and included Chinese delegates had elected mixed European-Chinese directorates and agreed on organizational guidelines for a self-governing church. It is impossible here to trace the tortuous and conflict-ridden process that led to the establishment of that church, the Chongzhenhui 崇真會, in 1924 and to its attaining full independence in 1932. What is of importance here is to note that the actions of Zhong Qingyuan and his fellows in 1912/13 had changed the course of the entire process, testifying to the agency of Chinese Christians even in failure.

Conclusion

In the preceding sections, I have presented, so to speak, case studies within a case study, selecting two specific moments in the development of one particular mission society. However, the findings of these case studies have implications for our understanding of power structures not only in other mission areas of the Basel Mission but in nineteenth- and twentieth-century Christian missions in general.

To begin with, it should have become clear that the hierarchy of power within the Basel Mission in China was in no way influenced by any of the imperialist powers on the spot, including the German Reich. There can be no doubt that imperialism, both as a transnational and a German national enterprise, backed the presence of the Basel and other missionaries in the Chinese hinterland, but it neither fostered nor interfered with the growth of the Chinese Christian congregations. This lends credibility to my argument that the power structures within Christian missions must be viewed not as an extension of secular colonialism but as a kind of colonialism in its own right.[53] This is why I refer to the power structures within the Basel Mission—a "German" mission by its own definition—as an "other" German colonialism. Without denying the multifaceted interactions between Christian missions and imperialism/colonialism, what I want to point out in this essay is the structural parallels between the two. They existed because both Christian missionaries and the agents of imperialism/colonialism met with the same local conditions and, in confronting them, exhibited a similar sense of superiority. To the extent that there was an ideological difference between the two, it lay in the source that this sense of superiority was derived from—a secular idea of progress on the one hand, the perceived necessity of spreading the Kingdom of God and the claim to a better understanding of the Christian doctrine on the other.

With this in mind, I go on to argue that as historians, we must understand the development of Christian missions in the nineteenth and twentieth centuries, like that of imperialism, as a long-term process stretching in a long arc from the gradual establishment of authority over indigenous people to the gradual dismantling of that authority and the establishment of independent indigenous institutions. Its specific temporal structure would vary from place to place and from one mission society to the next.

In the case of the Basel Mission, the two episodes related above were crucial stages of that process. As the Zhang Fuxing case shows, what I call the colonial strategy of the missionaries consisted in establishing themselves as the only source of authority and suppressing any competing claims within the mission congregations and sometimes even in society at large. There were other cases—less prominent, but similar—in the Basel Mission in China.[54] And the same pattern is discernible in the other fields of work of the Basel Mission as well as in other mission societies in China and other parts of the world, with the specifics varying according to local circumstances.[55] In the official discourse of Christian missions, missionary authority was spiritual and served the higher purpose of expanding the Kingdom of God. But there was a more worldly aspect to it, as the missionaries, most of whom originated from what has been called the "middling classes"—peasants, artisans, merchants, and the like—certainly climbed up the social ladder to wield power over a group of dependents—their congregations—in such a way as they would never have been able to at home.[56] On the other hand, indigenous catechists or Christians could derive authority from a number of sources. Combination of an official function in the mission with local and kinship ties as well as membership in a social elite, as in Zhang Fuxing's case, was not unusual and particularly threatening to the missionaries, which is why they sought to confine such persons to an inferior rank in the colonial and racially constructed hierarchy of the mission. In the majority of cases known to me, the missionaries were quite successful at this, as the outcome of the Zhang Fuxing case clearly shows.

However, although Christians usually found it difficult to question missionary authority, that authority was in fact rather circumscribed—a fact that I have not been able to examine in much detail, but that I want to draw attention to in passing. There were two reasons for this: The Christian congregations were often spread over a vast area, so the missionaries were unable to constantly monitor their conduct. Like the seats of colonial administration, mission stations constituted "islands of rule" (*Inseln von Herrschaft*), from which an understaffed administration tried in vain to control its social environment.[57] This problem was exacerbated by a second factor, the dynamics of the mission enterprise itself, which constantly added newly converted members to the Christian congregations. It reinforced local ties that knit together Christians and non-Christians and enhanced in the converts a willingness to accommodate their new belief to the pre-Christian concepts and practices in which they had been raised and that their conversion could not simply eclipse. However, the very fact that the colonial power structures created by the missionaries were not all-encompassing created tensions between them and the Chinese Christians, with missionaries convincing themselves that spiritually, the congregations were not fit for self-government.

The Songtou case, on the other hand, marks the beginning of a process that led to the decline of missionary authority and to the establishment of an independent church with a distinctly local flavor. This was a dynamic that unfolded elsewhere in China, in other fields of work of the Basel Mission, throughout the German colonies, in the colonial world in general, and in countries under the sway of informal imperialism—in other words, practically everywhere Christian missions were active. Of the different forms that process might take on,[58] the takeover of the mission churches by the indigenous clergy and Christians—as in the Basel Mission in China and elsewhere—is perhaps most similar to processes of decolonization because in both cases the advocates of independence had to take over the institutions that had governed them and use them to their own ends.

As an example in what might be called the decolonization of mission churches, the Songtou case points to the difficulties inherent in that process, especially in its initial phases. Although several decades had elapsed since the Zhang Fuxing case, the Songtou Christians exhibited the same difficulties to stand up to the missionaries to pursue their own interests. Several factors enhanced the ongoing colonial power structure of the Basel Mission: the almost total dependence of the congregations on financial assistance, the volatility of the Christians' position within local society, the credibility of the missionaries' claim to a better understanding of the Christian doctrine, and, last but not least, the spiritual bond created by a shared belief. On the other hand, the Songtou case shows once more how the kinship and village ties in which the Christians remained enmeshed provided them with an alternative source of power from which to challenge the authority of the missionaries. It is interesting to note, however, that as the indigenization of the Chongzhenhui gained momentum, these ties became increasingly irrelevant for the leadership of the new church. The professional clergy that took over from the missionaries had been trained by them and came to share their outlook on local institutions such as lineage and village. Like the postcolonial bureaucracies in the newly established states in Africa and Asia,[59] the clergy of the independent churches became a link between postcolonial developments and the colonial past, but it was but one factor in an independent Christianity that displays varying degrees of mixture between the legacy of colonial missions and the influence of local cultures.

NOTES

1. T. O. Beidelman, *Colonial Evangelism: A Socio-Historical Study of an East African Mission at the Grassroots* (Bloomington: Indiana University Press, 1982), 6. For the development of anti-missionary thinking, cf. Brian Stanley, *The Bible and the Flag: Protestant Missions and British Imperialism in the Nineteenth and Twentieth Centuries* (Leicester: Apollos, 1990), 15–29.

2. Dana L. Robert, "Introduction," in *Converting Colonialism: Visions and Realities in Mission History, 1706–1904*, ed. Dana L. Robert (Grand Rapids, MI: Eerdmans, 2008), 1–20; Ian Copland, "Christianity as an Arm of Empire: The Ambiguous Case of India under the Company, c. 1813–1858," *Historical Journal* 49 (2006): 1025–54; Andrew Porter, *Religion versus Empire? British Protestant Missionaries and Overseas Expansion, 1700–1914* (Manchester: Manchester University Press, 2004).

3. Paul Jenkins, "Sources of Unexpected Light: Experiences with Old Mission Photographs in Research of Overseas History," *Jahrbuch für Europäische Überseegeschichte* 1 (2001): 157–67; Peter van der Veer, *Imperial Encounters: Religion and Modernity in India and Britain* (Princeton: Princeton University Press, 2001).

4. For an elaborated version of this argument see Thoralf Klein, "Mission *und* Kolonialismus—Mission *als* Kolonialismus: Anmerkungen zu einer schwierigen Wahlverwandtschaft," in *Kolonialgeschichten: Regionale Perspektiven auf ein globales Problem*, ed. Claudia Kraft, Alf Lüdtke, and Jürgen Martschukat (Frankfurt am Main: Campus, 2010), 142–61; cf. Thoralf Klein, "The Basel Mission as a Transcultural Organization: Photographs of Chinese Christians and the Problem of Agency," in *Getting Pictures Right: Context and Interpretation*, ed. Michael Albrecht, Veit Arlt, Barbara Müller, and Jürg Schneider, (Cologne: Köppe, 2004), 41.

5. See, for example, John Carroll, *Edge of Empires: Chinese Elites and British Colonials in Hong Kong* (Cambridge: Harvard University Press, 2005); Christopher Munn, *Anglo-China: Chinese People and British Rule in Hong Kong, 1841–1880* (Richmond, Surrey: Curzon, 2001); Klaus Mühlhahn, *Herrschaft und Widerstand in der 'Musterkolonie' Kiautschou: Interaktionen zwischen China und Deutschland, 1897–1914* (Munich: Oldenbourg, 2000); Carol G. S. Tan, *British Rule in China: Law and Justice in Weihaiwei, 1898–1930* (London: Wildy, Simmons & Hill, 2008).

6. Jürgen Osterhammel, *Colonialism: A Theoretical Overview* (Princeton, NJ: Wiener, 1997), 15–16.

7. Gayatri Chakravorty Spivak, "Can the Subaltern Speak?," in *Marxism and the Interpretation of Culture*, ed. Cary Nelson (Urbana: University of Illinois Press, 1988), 305.

8. Homi K. Bhabha, *The Location of Culture*, new ed. (London: Routledge, 2004), 122.

9. Jon Miller, *Missionary Zeal and Institutional Control: Organizational Contradictions in the Basel Mission on the Gold Coast, 1828–1917* (Grand Rapids, MI: Eerdmans, 2003).

10. Otto Schultze, "The Policy of the Basel Mission among the Hakkas," *Chinese Recorder* 47 (1916): 722.

11. Tobias Eiselen, "'Zur Erziehung einer zuverlässigen, wohldisziplinierten Streiterschar für den Missionskrieg.' Basler Missionarsausbildung im 19. Jahrhundert," in *Mission im Kontext. Beiträge zur Sozialgeschichte der Norddeutschen Missionsgesellschaft im 19. Jahrhundert*, ed. Werner Ustorf (Bremen: Überseemuseum, 1986), 47–120.

12. Thoralf Klein, *Die Basler Mission in der Provinz Guangdong (Südchina), 1859–1931. Akkulturationsprozesse und kulturelle Grenzziehungen zwischen Missionaren, chinesischen Christen und lokaler Gesellschaft* (Munich: Iudicium, 2002), 111.

13. Karl Rennstich, "The Understanding of Mission, Civilisation and Colonialism in the Basel Mission," in *Missionary Ideologies in the Imperialist Era, 1880–1920*, ed. Torben Christensen and William R. Hutchison (Århus: Åros, 1982), 96–100.

14. The term is taken from the official history of the Basel Mission: Wilhelm Schlatter, *Geschichte der Basler Mission. Vol. 2: Die Geschichte der Basler Mission in Indien und China* (Basel: Verlag der Basler Missionsbuchhandlung, 1916), 400.

15. "Ordnung für die evangelischen Gemeinden der Basler Mission in Ostindien und Westafrika," 2nd ed., 1865, Preface, Mission 21, Basel Mission Archives (hereafter: BM/A) Q-9.21/20 b.

16. Jessie Gregory Lutz and Rolland Ray Lutz, "The Invisible China Missionaries: The Basel Mission's Chinese Evangelists, 1847–1866," *Mission Studies* 12 (1995): 204–27. The Basel Mission strictly distinguished between the two groups: Catechists were employees of the Basel Mission, received a salary and received instruction from the missionaries (since the 1860s in the Basel Mission schools), whereas evangelists worked without pay and lacked formal training. "Revidirte Katechisten-Ordnung vom Jahre 1863", § 3, BM/A A-9-1/II-1. In addition, there were other groups of assistants, such as the missionaries' language instructors, schoolteachers, and medical personnel.

17. There exist different versions of Zhang Fuxing's early biography in the Basel Mission Archives, some of which may have been tailored to fit his later status as one of

the founding fathers of the Basel congregations. The earliest account of Zhang's life is in a report by Theodor Hamberg, 1852, BM/A A-1,2 (1852)/23. It is far less elaborate than the later ones, especially Zhang's obituary: Heinrich Bender, "Lebensskizze des verstorbenen Tschong Fuk hin, in Verbindung mit der Gründung der Tschonglok Mission," 18 June 1880, A-1,14 (1880)/70. This text, in turn is based on an manuscript that was compiled anonymously around 1865 but is in the handwriting of Bender and his wife: "Aus der Chronik der Station Tschongtshun," A-10.1/9,5.

18. Report by Zhang Fuxing in Changle, trans. Philipp Winnes, 9 September 1859, Hong Kong, BM/A A-1,4 (1859)/8; Philipp Winnes, "Geschichte der Entstehung und Ausbreitung der Gemeinde in Tschong-lok," 1862, A-1,4 (1862)/19; Bender, "Lebensskizze des verstorbenen Tschong Fuk hin."

19. See, for example, David Faure, *The Structure of Chinese Rural Society: Lineage and Village in the Eastern New Territories, Hong Kong* (Hong Kong: Oxford University Press, 1986); Helen F. Siu, *Agents and Victims in South China: Accomplices in Rural Revolution* (New Haven: Yale University Press, 1989); John Lagerwey, "Preface," in *Meizhou diqu de miaohui yu zongzu* 梅州地區的廟會與宗族 (Temple Festival and Lineages in Meizhou), ed. Fang Xuejia 房學嘉 (N.p.: International Hakka Studies Association, Overseas Chinese Archives and Ecole Française d'Extrême-Orient, 1996), 1–14.

20. Report by Zhang Fuxing in Changle, trans. Winnes.

21. Winnes, "Geschichte der Entstehung und Ausbreitung der Gemeinde in Tschong-lok"; "Aus der Chronik der Station Tschongtshun"; Bender, "Lebensskizze des verstorbenen Tschong Fuk hin."

22. "Ordnung für die evangelischen Gemeinden der Basler Mission in Ostindien und Westafrika," § 97.

23. Philipp Winnes, "Sieben Sonntage in Tschong-lok. Predigt. Taufunterricht. Taufen," 1863, BM/A A-1,5 (1863)/17; Bender, "Lebensskizze des verstorbenen Tschong Fuk hin."

24. For an overview of the process cf. "Aus der Chronik der Station Tschongtshun." For the missionaries' justification and more details cf. Winnes to Joseph Josenhans, 10 July 1862, BM/A A-1,4(1862)/7; Winnes to Josenhans, 12 November 1862, A-1,4 (1862)/15; Rudolf Lechler to Josenhans, 23 December 1862, A-1,4 (1862)/16; Minutes of the Committee of the Basel Mission, 4 February 1863 (hereafter cited as Minutes of the Committee).

25. Lechler to Josenhans, 5 December 1863, BM/A A-1,5 (1863)/10. For Zhang's submissiveness cf. also Lechler to Josenhans, 23 December 1862, A-1,4 (1862)/16.

26. Bhabha, *The Location of Culture*, 141–42.

27. Winnes, "Geschichte der Entstehung und Ausbreitung der Gemeinde in Tschong-lok." Writing posthumously, the missionary Otto Schultze remarked upon Zhang's "irritable and quick-tempered character." Schultze, "Geschichte der Basler Missionsstation Tschong-tshun zum 25jährigen Bestehen am 27. October 1889," 15 April 1889, BMA A-1,23 (1889)/120. Some of Zhang's remarks to fellow Christians are repeated in a report by Lechler, 14 September 1863, A-1,5 (1863)/6.

28. Jessie Gregory Lutz and Rolland R. Lutz, *Hakka Chinese Confront Protestant Christianity: With the Autobiographies of Eight Hakka Christians, and Commentary* (Armonk, NY: Sharpe, 1998), 51.

29. Minutes of the Committee, 8 April 1863; Lechler to Josenhans, 5 December 1863, BMA A-1,5 (1863)/10.

30. Bender to Josenhans, 31 October 1864, BM/A A-1,5 (1864)/12.

31. Draft agreement between the Committee of the Basel Mission, and the congregation in Changle concerning the mortgage of the house acquired by the congregation, § 4, BM/A A-1,5 (1865)/17. The more elaborate Chinese version is in the deed of the transfer, dated 9 January 1866, is in A-31.7,1 d/2.

32. According to Schultze, "Geschichte der Basler Missionsstation Tschong-tshun," Bender was sick until he had had some of the rooms and one window enlarged.

33. "Revidirte Katechisten-Ordnung vom Jahre 1863," § 36; cf. Klein, *Die Basler Mission*, 187–88.

34. Annual Report by Bender, 9 January 1865, BM/A A-1,5 (1864)/13; Lechler to Josenhans, 27 November 1865, A-1,5 (1865)/16.

35. Bender, "Lebensskizze des verstorbenen Tschong Fuk hin"; Schultze, "Geschichte der Basler Missionsstation Tschong-tshun."

36. Lutz and Lutz, *Hakka Christians Confront Protestant Christianity*, 51.

37. For examples, see Thoralf Klein, "Wozu untersucht man Missionsgesellschaften? Eine Antwort am Beispiel der Basler Mission in China," *Jahrbuch für Europäische Überseegeschichte* 5 (2005): 90–97; Klein, "The Basel Mission as a Transcultural Organization," 42–46.

38. *Songtou jiaohui shi* 嵩頭教會史 (History of the Congregation of Songtou) (Shanghai: Budao Shushe, 1923).

39. *Songtou jiaohui shi*, 15–16. According to a report by Schultze, 4 July 1888, BM/A A-1,22/159, the reason for the call for donations was that the congregation was preparing for the expiring of the mortgage on their meeting room due in 1895.

40. C. Peter Williams, "The Church Missionary Society and the Indigenous Church in the Second Half of the Nineteenth Century: The Defense and Destruction of the Venn Ideals," in *Converting Colonialism: Visions and Realities in Mission History, 1706–1904*, ed. Dana L. Robert (Grand Rapids, MI: Eerdmans, 2008), 86–111; *The Ideal of the Self-Governing Church: A Study in Victorian Missionary Strategy* (Leiden: Brill, 1990).

41. Klein, *Die Basler Mission*, 335–47.

42. Report by Schultze, 4 July 1888. For the congregation's finances, cf. *Songtou jiaohui shi*, 20.

43. Report by Schultze, 4 July 1888.

44. Guoqi Xu, *China and the Great War: China's Pursuit of a New National Identity and Internationalization* (Cambridge: Cambridge University Press, 2005).

45. Georg Ziegler to Theodor Oehler, 30 November 1912, BM/A A-1,52/108; *Songtou jiaohui shi*, 22.

46. "*Tichang mou di zili Yesu jiaohui yuanqi. Fu jian zhang* 提倡某地自立耶穌教會緣起.附簡章," 1912, BM/A A-1,52/309; cf. *Songtou jiaohui shi*, 20.

47. The directory of the independent congregations to the Committee, German translation, 1913; Zhong Qingyuan to Ziegler and Heinrich Gieß, German translation, 1913, both in BM/A A-3.20,1/H.

48. Otto Schultze, Memorandum "Der Ausbau unserer Missionskirche in China," 1912, BM/A A-9-2/II-11a.

49. For a critical view of the movement see Gieß to Zhong Qingyuan (in Chinese), 27 April 1913 and 18 March 1914, BM/A A-20,46; Ziegler to Committee, 26 May 1913, A-3.20,1/H. For favorable comments cf. Karl Ramminger to Oehler, 19.11.1912, A-1,52/307; report by Karl Kiehlneker, 10 April 1913; Schultze, comments on a petition by Zhong Qingyuan, both in A-3.20,1/H.

50. Annual report by Heinrich Gieß, 15 February 1912, BM/A A-1,49/109; comments by Gieß on a petition by Zhong Qingyuan, 25 February 1913; Wilhelm Maisch, Comments on report by Kiehlneker, 5 July 1913, both in A-3.20,1/H.

51. Gieß, Chinese letter to Zhong Qingyuan, 18 March 1914, BM/A A-20,46.

52. Maisch, report on the East River Dongjiang Synod, 13 September 1913, BM/A A-3.21,6.

53. Jeffrey Cox, *The British Missionary Enterprise since 1700* (New York: Routledge, 2008), 156.

54. For a similar case cf. the report by Charles Piton, 1 June, 1873, BM/A A-1,8/122.

55. For the Basel Mission on the Gold Coast, cf. Sonia Abun-Nasr, *Afrikaner und Missionar: Die Lebensgeschichte von David Asante* (Basel: Schlettwein, 2003), 77 f., 206–9. For the experience of other mission societies cf. Cox, *The British Missionary Enterprise*, 152–60; Jean Comaroff and John L. Comaroff, *Of Revelation and Revolution: The Dialectics of Modernity on a South African Frontier*, vol. 2 (Chicago: University of Chicago Press, 1997), 78–85; Birgit Meyer, "Christianity and the Ewe Nation: German Pietist Missionaries, Ewe Converts and the Politics of Culture," in *Weltmission und religiöse Organisationen: Protestantische Missionsgesellschaften im 19. Jahrhundert*, ed. Artur Bogner, Bernd Holtwick, and Hartmann Tyrell (Würzburg: Ergon, 2004), 560–61.

56. C. Peter Williams, "'Not Quite Gentlemen': An Examination of 'Middling Class' Protestant Missionaries from Britain, c. 1850–1900," *Journal of Ecclesiastical History* 31 (1980): 301–15; cf. Thorsten Altena, *"Ein Häuflein Christen mitten in der Heidenwelt des dunklen Erdteils." Zum Selbst- und Fremdverständnis protestantischer Missionare im kolonialen Afrika 1884–1918* (Münster: Waxmann, 2003), 206–14; Mühlhahn, *Herrschaft und Widerstand*, 322–27.

57. Michael Pesek, *Koloniale Herrschaft in Deutsch-Ostafrika. Expedition, Militär und Verwaltung seit 1880* (Frankfurt am Main: Campus, 2005), 244–59.

58. Klein, "Mission *und* Kolonialismus—Mission *als* Kolonialismus," 153–56.

59. Cf. Andreas Eckert, *Herrschen und Verwalten: Afrikanische Bürokratie, staatliche Ordnung und Politik in Tanzania, 1920–1970* (Munich: Oldenbourg, 2007).

Nationalism and Pragmatism

The Revolutionists in German Qingdao (1897–1914)

Jianjun Zhu

German Qingdao (1897–1914) was the urban area of the German Kiautschou Leasehold (Jiao'ao Leasehold in Chinese), which was occupied by the Germans in 1897 and was leased under force from Shandong Province of China in 1898. Recent scholarship on German Qingdao has focused on the complexity of the colonial society in German Qingdao and highlighted various kinds of response, resistance, and negotiation of the Chinese against German colonial rule, which based analysis on different Chinese groups.[1] So far, varying degrees of academic interest in Chinese officials, businessmen, and coolies have brought more or less light to understanding Chinese responses to German colonialism. Nevertheless, there is one social group that has received disproportionately little attention, namely, the revolutionists in German Qingdao.

Clearly, the German colonial authority in Qingdao supported the Qing government before and during the Revolution of 1911 when the Han Chinese revolutionists strived to overthrow the government that was founded and ruled by Manchu emperors. However, German Qingdao was not beyond the reach of the revolutionists. From 1906 to 1908, some concealed revolutionists resided in German Qingdao and undertook revolutionary activities secretly. They were expelled in 1908 due to exposure of their identities. In the next three years, the German colonial administration did successfully keep Qingdao quiet in general from organized revolutionary actions against the Qing government, even during the 1911 Revolution that eventually resulted in the fall of the Qing Dynasty. But then in 1912, soon after the Republic of China was founded, German Qingdao was visited by the revolutionists' leader Sun Yat-sen, accompanied by several of the revolutionists who had been in Qingdao during 1905 through 1908. Those revolutionists' responses to German colonialism are to be examined in this essay.

German colonialism in Shandong could be summed up into two main types of activities. On one hand, German Qingdao was built to be an exhibition of German achievements and was characterized by German features and modern techniques, as the German colonial authority in Qingdao resolved to create a modern and effective "model colony" to showcase "the special German colonialism with scientific planning, professional implementation, and government supervision."[2] On the other hand, the Germans expanded from Qingdao into the interior of Shandong, seeking railway-building and mining privileges. The two types mingled together, making the German image among the Chinese very complicated. Furthermore, the degree of the German colonial power's involvement in each type of activity was not balanced and fixed during Germany's seventeen years of presence in Qingdao. In fact, the previously vigorously forced German colonial expansion policy began to move toward a cultural policy since 1906 in view of the Qing government's abolition of the imperial examination system and Chinese intellectuals' enthusiasm for Western learning. It showed clear changes since 1909, when Qingdao began to be planned and developed more as a cultural center and became more significant for demonstrative and educational purposes.[3] This essay gives attention to the revolutionists' response to both types of German colonial activities and the change of German colonialism in Qingdao and Shandong.

The revolutionists' responses to German colonialism were more complicated than those of other groups, given that the revolutionists entered German Qingdao not to make a living or make a profit, but to prepare for their ambitious national agenda. Therefore any examination of the interactions between the revolutionists in German Qingdao and the Germans shouldn't be conducted only in light of factors within German Qingdao; instead the revolutionists' overall agenda outside the leasehold should also be taken into consideration. This essay tries to do so from the perspective of nationalism.

The rise of Chinese nationalism is generally regarded as a significant response of China to imperialistic aggression at the end of the nineteenth and the beginning of the twentieth centuries, and nationalism is considered "an undercurrent during troubled times."[4] Nevertheless, nationalism is not a single, unified force and "is rarely the nationalism of the nation, but rather marks the site where different representations of the nation contest and negotiate with each other."[5] Furthermore, the nationalistic view of the same force also negotiates with its past and future and evolves along with changes in time and space. Clearly, the Chinese revolutionists at the turn of the twentieth century formulated "nationalism" on an ethnic base that "called for a specifically Han Chinese revolution against the Manchu Qing"[6] so as to establish a new nation-state with new civilization, which was different from the "nationalism" overarching all the people of Qing including Manchu, as advocated then by intellectuals such as Liang Qichao[7] and revealed to some degree in the actions taken by the Qing officials in Shandong against the expansion of German colonial power.[8] However, shortly following the 1911 Revolution, the revolutionists announced the new principle of "wuzu gonghe" (harmonious cohabitation of five ethnicities). What remained unchanged was the revolutionists' enthusiastic pursuit of a new Westernized civilization. It is against this broad background that this essay explores and analyzes the nationalistic responses of the revolutionists who were in direct contact with German Qingdao—once the so-called showcase of German civilization.

The essay consists of three sections, each of which examines the revolutionists' responses through analyzing one of the three important German Qingdao-relevant cases involved by them, namely, the establishment of the Zhendan Public School, the establishment and closure of the Mining Protection Society, and Sun Yat-sen's visit to German Qingdao in 1912. With the examination illustrating the revolutionists' complicated attitudes and the difference between the response of the revolutionists in Qingdao in 1905–1908 and in 1912, the essay argues that the revolutionists in Qingdao adopted a nationalism distinguished by pragmatism toward German colonialism.

The Establishment of the Zhendan Public School

From 1906 onward, German Qingdao began to see revolutionists who came back from Japan where they, as students from Shandong, had joined the Tongmenghui, the Revolutionary Alliance founded in 1905, whose slogan was to "expel the Manchus, restore China, found a republic and equally divide the land ownership." Before that time the revolutionists in Shandong were concentrated in two other major cities of the province—the capital city Jinan and the open port city Yantai. In 1906, Tongmenghui member Luan Zhijie secretly established a publishing house in Qingdao to publish revolutionary books.[9] Another revolutionist, Luan Xinghe, set up the Qingdao branch office of the revolutionary periodical *Morning Bell* (published in Japan) for its distribution in China.[10] Luan Xinghe left Qingdao in 1907 to go to the south to take part in an uprising.

More revolutionists came into Qingdao at the end of 1907 and in 1908. Among the earliest well-known revolutionists was Chen Gan (Styled Chen Minghou), a Tongmenghui member who already had strong national feelings.[11] He was followed by Zhou Jingfu, Li Yueqiu, Liu Guansan, and others. Chen

Gan made acquaintance with local people and admitted a local construction contractor by the name of Lu Ziren as a member of the Tongmenghui.[12] They worked together to establish a school in German Qingdao, with Lu Ziren offering the financial support and acting as a handler.[13] In the spring of 1908 a public school was set up with the name of Zhendan, which literally means "a rising sun on the horizon" and is also a name referring to China in Sanskrit.

Why did the revolutionists choose to establish a public school in German Qingdao? Certainly initially because establishing a school to educate the young and train revolutionary personnel was one of the main tasks and activities for the revolutionists all over China at the time. Second, currently available materials show the reason might mainly lie in the fact that German education was ranked very highly by them and German Qingdao was regarded as a base of German achievements; their exact and specific considerations remain not quite clear owing to a shortage of relevant materials, though. In an article introducing Zhendan Public School in the Shanghai-based *Shenzhou ribao* (*National Herald*), the first revolutionary newspaper in China, on May 13, 1908, the author stated the reason as this: China was backward in education, so numerous students went abroad to study in Japan. However, Japan's science, technology, and education were learned from Europe where Germany excelled over the other countries in those aspects. Chinese students should learn authentic knowledge from Germany instead of Japan. As Germany brought its achievements to German Qingdao where nineteen schools had been set up, the Zhendan Public School would benefit students with new and advanced knowledge from its location in German Qingdao.[14]

A similar opinion was expressed in their call for contributions and donations in the same article. They complained that China was disdained because most Chinese were uneducated, and the shortage of proper education resulted from the obscurantist policy of the dictatorial system. It was this huge humiliation that prompted them to establish schools. And the advantage of establishing a school in German Qingdao was twofold. One was that Shandong boasted a long education history, one immersed in the heritage of traditional education. More important, in German Qingdao "the school could be nurtured by the newest education achievements of Germany." Therefore the revolutionists stated that the Zhendan Public School would play an important role in creating students with a global vision and citizen spirit, and herewith bring to China a bright future.[15] It could be seen that German Qingdao was claimed by the revolutionists as representing a new civilization that could be emulated, which reveals the practical consideration in their concern for shaping China as an equal nation. Whether they say this from the heart or just as an excuse, it does reveal that German Qingdao's construction and cultural policy exerted an effect.

Because the revolutionists in German Qingdao didn't openly trumpet revolution, Zhendan Public School caught no immediate attention from the German Kiautschou government regarding its revolutionary purpose. In fact, however, the school was run with an emphasis on revolution. Many Tongmenghui members came to Zhendan Public School to work as teachers, such as Tao Chengzhang, Yan Chengzhang, Jing Dingjiu, Shang Zhen, Chen Hanyuan, and Han Weizhai.[16] They developed courses according to perceived revolutionary needs. For example, alongside courses like Sinology that were taught by Tao Chengzhang, Jing Dingcheng, and Han Weiqi, the school offered the subject of military affairs, emphasizing both military theories and training.[17] Lu Xiuwen, Shang Zhen, and Wang Ming were in charge of military education, and Lu Ziren, Li Peilan, Zhao Xijiu, and Wang Hutao gave the students military training.[18] Tao Chengzhang lectured on the waning and waxing of the Chinese as a nation in history,[19] and Zhang Ji purposely came back from Japan to lecture on socialism.[20]

The revolutionists at Zhendan Public School also actively liaised with the local people outside the school for the cause of overthrowing the Qing government. In order to raise money, the revolutionist Zhao Guang set up the Liyong Dyeing and Weaving Company.[21] In 1908 there appeared one newspaper in German Qingdao, the *Qingdao Times*, which exposed the corruption of the Qing government and advocated to overthrow the Qing dynasty.[22] It is believed to be published by the same group of revolutionists.[23] Thus soon after its opening Zhendan Public School presented a scenario of vitality.[24] However, their comparatively calm relationship with the German colonial authority was to change with the mining rights issue in the autumn of 1908, which was related to Shandong's interests.

The Mining Protection Society

Mining rights were an important issue between the Chinese and the Germans in Shandong. The *Kiaochow Lease Treaty* of 1897 gave Germany the privilege of building two railways in Shandong and mining rights within 30 li on each side of the railways. One railway ran from Qingdao to Jinan via Weixian, Qingzhou, Boshan, Zichuan, and Zouping, the other from Qingdao to Jinan via Yizhou and Laiwu County.[25] The former, termed the Jiaoji Railway, was finished in 1904, and the latter, the Jiaoyiji Railway, was never built. Nevertheless, in 1908 the Germans began to explore five mining areas, in Yizhou, Yishui, Zhucheng, Weixian, and Maoshan in Yantai. They insisted that the five areas were along the previously proposed Jiaojiyi Railway and that they had tried in 1907 to obtain the consent from the Shandong government on an agreement that the five mining areas would be operated jointly. This aroused great concern among those Chinese who had become more and more conscious of national rights.

The revolutionists in Qingdao as well as those in Jinan and Yantai played an important role in objecting to this issue. Chen Gan, Liu Guanshan, and Yu Hongqi, a Tongmenghui member at the Jinan Normal College, initiated and formed the Mining Protection Society in the provincial education circle in May 1908. They sent out an *Elementary Introduction to Shandong Business Circle, Education Circle and Those Shandongnese Sojourning outside Shandong*, revealing the dangers that the German seizure of mining rights would cause to Shandong people and calling for the protection of sovereignty. They argued that the so-called joint operation of the five mining areas was just a name instead of a reality. The Chinese students in Japan also held meetings to discuss how to resist. They wrote to the officials in Beijing who were Shandong natives, the Foreign Affairs Ministry, and the Shandong Governor Yuan Shuxun to seek their support. What the Shandong education circle proposed was first to demand that the government negotiate with the Germans. If the Germans gave up the five mining areas upon negotiation, China would manage the mining independently. If the Germans refused to abandon it, they suggested carrying out such boycotts as (1) to stop working for the Germans; (2) to stop buying German goods; (3) to stop taking German trains; (4) the shopkeepers in Qingdao to go on strike; (5) the students in any school with German teachers to go on strike.[26]

The Mining Protection Society caught the attention of both the German colonial authority and the Shandong government. The German consulate in Jinan sent a note to the Shandong governor, arguing that, in reality, the five mining areas had not been operated jointly just because the Chinese did not hold enough stocks to establish an officer. Thus, he argued, it was the Chinese who discarded the rights themselves, and it was the Chinese's duty to collect more capital to make the joint operation a reality.[27] Shandong Governor Yuan Shuxun considered the Mining Protection Society to be just making trouble out of nothing after he failed to persuade them at the outset. He then announced the dissolution of the Mining Protection Society in November.

At the end of 1908 the German colonial authority also took action, asking

Chen Gan to leave Qingdao. Moreover the Zhendan Public School was asked to shut down. According to Chen Gan's account, in the afternoon on 22 November (according to the Chinese calendar), Chen Gan went to the German Kiautschou Governor's Office to have a talk on the request sent to him the day before. The interpreter said they knew from the German envoy in Beijing that Chen Gan was the leader of the Mining Protection Society and Zhendan Public School was established by him. He told Chen Gan the Kiautschou Governor had decided to ask him to leave Qingdao in one month and that the Zhendan Public School must be closed. Chen Gan said he was indeed a member of the Mining Protection Society because he felt duty-bound as a Shandongnese. He indicated that he was agreeable to leaving Qingdao, but it was not proper to close Zhendan Public School, as the school was established by many people, not just himself. Since the school was not against the German law, Chen Gan argued, there was no reason to shut it down. Certainly Chen Gan's argument did not succeed. On 4 December in the Chinese calendar, the Zhendan Public School was officially closed.[28]

The revolutionists of the Zhendan Public School indignantly publicized this news through the *Statement on the Germans' Destruction of the Zhendan Public School*. In addition to describing how Chen Gan was given the expulsion order, the statement expounded once again the original intention of establishing the Zhendan Public School as follows:

> Qingdao Zhendan Public School was initiated from the Shandong education circle and was supported by the enthusiastic gentlemen all over the country. The aim of setting up the school just lied in that the Germans had showed wilder and wilder ambitions since they occupied Jiao'ao. They had seized the railway rights and the mining rights, and would control the education rights. China's future would be full of crisis. Thinking of this, everyone with hot blood would feel indignant and consider resisting. So that was the reason to establish the school. We wanted to make high talents for future restoration, a hidden way to check the Germans' cruel power.[29]

Clearly, after the Mining Protection Society was dissolved and the Zhendan School was closed, there was a discourse change regarding the reasons for setting up Zhendan Public School. The new statement emphasized the purpose of resisting the German colonial expansion, no longer that "the school could be nurtured by the newest education achievements of Germany," as indicated before.

Angered at both the German colonial authority's closure of the Zhendan Public School and the Germans' expansion of its railway and mining rights, the revolutionist viewed them as the beginning of Germany's occupation of the whole Shandong Province in the future. Thus the new statement called on the "Chinese compatriots" and "Shandongnese compatriots" to pay attention to the seriousness of Germany's seizure of Shandong rights.[30]

The new Shandong governor Sun Baoqi advocated redeeming the mining areas, and his way of dealing with the mining issue was also strongly questioned and opposed by the revolutionists. Chen Gan organized an association of Shandongnese natives, under which the Institute for Shandong Railway and Mining Studies was set up and affiliated.[31] One of his official letters to the Shandong officials in Beijing clearly revealed the revolutionists' opinion on mining rights. Chen Gan introduced in the letter the background of the mining issue, stating that the Shandong governors always acted against the will of the people to extend the exploration contract of the five mining areas with the Germans since 1898, even though there had been several moments and chances for them to retrieve the mining rights. He denounced the Shandong governors as placing greater emphasis on maintaining a harmonious relationship with the Germans than protecting the rights of the Chinese. In his view, more than 60 percent of Shandong had been lost to the Germans whose existence in Shandong was "like maggots on bones," and the Shandong governors were just "gathering the wealth of the people for the German devourer."[32] The letter indicated the revolutionists' claim that the Qing government was selling the rights of China to Germany.

In reviewing the sufferings of the Zhendan Public School and the Mining Protection Society, an article in the *Northern Times*, a newspaper published in Yantai by the revolutionists, also alleged in March 1909 that the Chinese were tragically living under the dual oppression from both the Germans and the Qing officials. The article said that the German Kiautschou government's closure of the Zhendan Public School, mainly because of resenting one person, was first and foremost a display of power. The act showed that disagreement was not allowed, even though Chinese officials gave away rights with both hands and the Germans' encroachment reached an intolerable extent. Otherwise one would be regarded by the Chinese officials as having ulterior motives and would be banished from the leasehold by the German colonial authority.[33]

As this case demonstrates, revolutionists such as Chen Gan developed greater disappointment and resentment toward the Qing government, and their attitude toward the German Kiautschou government grew increasingly critical as well. In articles from the *Northern Times*, whose issues from February to

July 1909 are still accessible, disclosure of the German expansion and the Qing officials' betrayal of China became a keystone. For instance, on 12 March the newspaper published "Only Shandong Has No Territorial Sea Rights?" reporting that the Germans were trying to control the sea water outside the leasehold. On 4 April the newspaper published an article titled "Expansion of the German Financial Interests," on 24 April "Expansion of the German Military Force," on 8 May "Management of the Germans," and on 7 May the "Defense of the Germans." The Northern Times also showed concern about education. There was a report on Germany's plan to set up a university in Qingdao in the 27 April issue and the "Recent News on the Qingdao University" in the 3 May issue. The newspaper raised the question regarding the Future of Education Rights[34] and lamented foreign influence in an article entitled "Too Many Foreigners Establishing Universities."[35] Some articles on the harmony between the Shandong governor Sun Baoqi and the German Kiautschou government tacitly suggested that he was acting in conjunction with the German expansion.[36] The *Northern Times* also targeted the so-called civilized administration of the German Kiautschou government. The article "Administration of the Civilized Country" on 30 April revealed the partiality of the administration toward the Germans and the injustice done to the Chinese, illustrating that the so-called civilized administration was only an empty reputation.[37]

Therefore, the closure of the Mining Protection Society and the Zhendan Public School under the joint suppression of the Qing government and the German Kiautschou government caused the revolutionists to express more acute criticism of both the Qing government and the German colonial authority. Their criticism of the Qing government had focused on corruption and dictatorship prior to the two events, but changed to stress the betrayal of China's interest afterward. The initially good impression of the German civilization in Qingdao from a pragmatic point of view that had been publicly expressed prior to the two events became hardly heard; rather, revolutionists lashed out at the German expansion and the unjust administration. Such criticism of the Qing government selling China's interest to German expansion became a powerful discourse in arousing and mobilizing people to support the uprising during the revolutionists' pursuit of their agenda.

Sun Yat-sen's Impression of the German Qingdao

From 1908 to 1912, German Qingdao witnessed big changes in the city. In addition to further building of good railroads, ports, buildings, forestry and other municipal construction development under the German administration,[38] the new cultural policy began to reveal more effects. The annual report of Kiautschou Leasehold from October 1908 to October 1909 recorded in detail the number and high quality of more schools, hospitals, libraries, an observatory, and so on set up in Qingdao, among which the Qingdao Special High School (commonly referred to as Sino-German College) was viewed as the most significant, as the college offering German knowledge and spirit in four schools (engineering and manufacturing, medicine, politics and law, and agriculture and forestry) to young Chinese also received Qing government support as a joint venture and could enroll new students China-wide,[39] which means in the German colonial authority's eyes that the influence of German culture and education would reached beyond the limited area of the leasehold. According to *dagong bao* no. 2626 on 10 November 1909, there were 69 Chinese students enrolled at the time of the school's opening in October 1909. But a German newspaper article in *Tsingtauer Neueste Nachrichten* on 5 October 1907 reported that the Shandong Education Commissioner selected 85 students through an entrance examination attended by over 200 applicants, including 36 from Shandong, 8 from Zhili, 7 from Jiangsu, 7 from Zhejiang, 6 from Jiangxi, 5 from Guangdong, 4 from Fujian, 4 from Sichuan, 3 from Anhui, 3 from Hubei, 1 from Hunan, and 1 from Manchuria. Of the 85 students, 31 would attend the advanced class. In the next several years following its opening, the college offered highly qualified teachers and enjoyed a good reputation in the neighborhood, and thus the number of its students kept increasing.[40]

During this period, there were still some revolutionists who lived quietly in German Qingdao. The previous revolutionists' group broke up with the shutdown of Zhendan Public School. While some leaders such as Chen Gan, Liu Guansan, and Xu Jingxin were forced to leave Qingdao to go to other cities, others stayed and took factory jobs to live through the hard times and raise funds in the meantime.[41] During the 1911 Revolution period, there were some more revolutionists coming into Qingdao in hope of finding a sheltering harbor, but most felt it was not that easy. Not a few revolutionists were arrested by the German colonial authority; for example, a revolutionist named Zhen Shidao was arrested for trying to organize a celebration meeting for Sun Yat-Sen being elected provisional president, as well as an uprising. Even an uprising organized in the suburb country town Jimo also failed under the joint repression of the German colonial authority and the Qing government.[42] Therefore not many revolutionists stayed for a comparatively longer time in German Qingdao. Though less is known about their remarks about German Qingdao, available historical materials show that the fast-changing city did leave Sun Yat-sen with a deep impression..

Sun Yat-sen's visit to German Qingdao took place in September 1912. At the time the establishment of the Republic of China had been declared, and the 1911 revolution had brought the Qing emperor to abdicate. Yet the new republic faced an array of construction problems. Sun Yat-sen resigned his post as the provisional first president of the Republic of China in April 1912 and took a position as the director of *railway* development due to his construction concern. In that autumn Sun Yat-sen made inspections around China for railway building and publicized his plan to build a 200,000 li railway over the course of ten years. It was against this background that Sun Yat-sen visited the German Qingdao.

Sun Yat-sen arrived in Qingdao on 28 September, accompanied by Liu Guanshan and other revolutionists. They received a warm welcome from the Chinese.[43] Sun Yat-Sen spent three days in Qingdao, leaving on 1 October. Qingdao impressed him with its beauty and order. He expressed his admiration for the city on several occasions. During his short meeting with the German governor Meyer Waldeck on 29 September, Sun Yat-sen said the forestation, harbor, and road works in Qingdao were not only admirable but also worthy of modeling to the Chinese.[44] At the meeting at Guangdong Huiguan on 30 September, Sun Yat-sen gave a speech, emphasizing once again that the Republican construction needed to learn from Western civilization. In his eyes Qingdao had been changed into an unmatched splendid city after being exposed to German culture for fourteen years. Its valuable construction achievements displayed exemplary virtue.[45] On the same day Sun Yat-sen visited the Sino-German Special College and gave a lecture, which has caught wide academic attention so far. Impressed by the successful management of German Qingdao, he asked the students to learn from the Qingdao model and advance the model to other parts of China.[46]

Sun Yat-sen's speeches and lectures are very impressing, especially in contrast with the previous remarks from the revolutionists around 1908 and 1909. Sun Yat-sen uttered no words of anti-colonialism in his 1912 visit, nor did he mention restoring rights. His speeches regarding to German Qingdao indicated only expression of amiability and willingness to learn from German Qingdao and co-operate with the Germans. Even today people may be surprised at Sun Yat-sen's attitudes.

In fact Sun Yat-sen's attitude was not surprising, given his speech at the welcome meeting in Jinan on 27 September just before his visit to Qingdao. In the speech, he called on all parties and groups to unite as the "destruction has ended and construction just began." In terms of railway building, Sun thought it would take China a hundred years if the 200,000 li of railway were to be built by the Chinese themselves. So he proposed three ways to help finish it in ten years: first, to build on loans; second, to build jointly with foreigners; third, to put it out to contract with the foreigners and to take back the railway without compensation when the contract expired. Among the three ways, the last one was considered by Sun Yat-sen as the best choice, because "China was in shortage of capital, talents and means and having the foreigners build railways on contract would solve the problem." This must have been an awakening to the revolutionists and gentries who had been striving to retrieve railway rights and mining rights for China for a decade. As to this, Sun Yat-sen gave a practical explanation: A country couldn't have its big plan succeed unless it joins with the strength of other countries. Chinese people had to take an open policy if they wanted development.[47] This speech actually set a keynote for his Qingdao trip. It was with these ideas in mind that Sun Yat-sen uttered his praise of German Qingdao.

Several days after he left Qingdao, Sun Yat-sen talked about Qingdao when interviewed by the German reporter Erich von Salzmann. He said again he was very satisfied with Qingdao and stressed Qingdao could serve as a model for Chinese city development. "If every county send [sic] ten people to visit Qingdao and learn its administrative management, town, streets, wharves, harbours, university, forestation, public works, and government management, China would benefit greatly." When Erich von Salzmann asked his opinion on the question of taking over Qingdao after the Kiautschou Lease Treaty would expire in 99 years time, Sun Yat-sen stated that China would pay for Germany's cost for building such a model city upon its return to Chinese administrational sovereignty, and he would send officials and students to learn from Qingdao. He viewed Germany as a country that was not that short-sighted, mercenary, and exploitive. As he said, different from Britain and other countries, Germany based everything upon science and created things systemically, orderly, and correctly, and Germany possessed special achievements in all scientific and technological systems, which was what China needed in order to break with tradition.[48] It could be seen that he found in German Qingdao useful and practical methods for China's construction.

Sun Yat-sen's remarks were sincere rather than opportunistic. Later, although he had no opportunity to put his ideas mentioned above into practice, as Germany was soon driven out of Qingdao by Japan in 1914, Sun Yat-sen followed the previous German Qingdao's example on land management. He hired William Schrameier, who developed the land policy for the German Qingdao, as his adviser on land administration matters.[49] Clearly, what counted as important to revolutionists like Sun Yat-sen in 1912 were methods to promote China's development as a state. So it comes as no surprise that German Qingdao earned high marks from Sun Yat-sen.

As examined above, the revolutionists' response to German colonialism in Qingdao was not at all simple but rather complicated, varying with specific situations and against changes both within the leasehold and in China nationwide, particularly the revolutionists' own agenda. During the years when they prepared to overthrow the Qing government, they were both interested in the German civilization as showcased by German Qingdao and alert to German expansion into further inland. Therefore they advocated preserving railway and mining rights for the Chinese while admiring the German achievements on the other hand. Nevertheless their specific experience of the closure of the Mining Protection Society and the Zhendan Public School created bitterness toward both the Qing government and the German Kiautschou government, which came to be criticized as jointly harming China, with the former blamed for betraying China's interest to the latter. Such discourse became popular in the revolutionists' media and was useful in that period when they were fighting the Qing government.

However, when Sun Yat-Sen paid his visit soon after the founding of the Republic of China to German Qingdao, the showcase had been in full display for around five years under the cultural policy, and the revolutionists had just overthrown the Qing dynasty and hoped to put their long-conceived notion of new civilization into the task of national construction. Thus beautiful and orderly German Qingdao could overwhelmingly impress them with its "scientific" German administration and modern civilization, which they were eager to advocate and promote.

The responses of the revolutionists in Qingdao indicates that German Qingdao coming as a showcase of German civilization did have a long-lasting impact, causing the revolutionists' nationalism to become more pragmatic. Moreover the contrast between the responses around 1908 and 1912 further reveals that the revolutionists' pragmatic nationalism was also a result of the revolutionists' purposeful choices during colonial contacts and interactions. From the then semi-colonialized vast China, those revolutionists with their own subjectivities arrived in German Qingdao to see, to learn, and to use, according to their own agenda there and elsewhere.

NOTES

Author's Note: I thank Klaus Mühlhahn, Nina Berman, and Patrice Nganang for their comments on the earlier draft of this article.

1. Klaus Mühlhahn, *Zai mofan zhimindi Jiaozhouwan de tongzhi yu dikang— 1897–1914 nian Zhongguo yu Deguo de xianghu zuoyong* [*Power and Resistance in the "Model Colony" of Kiautschou—interaction between China and Germans 1897– 1914*], trans. Sun Lixin (Jinan: Shandong University Press, 2005); Hermann J. Hiery and Hans-Martin Hinz, eds., *Alltagsleben und Kulturaustausch: Duetsche und Chinesen in Tsingtau 1897–1914* [*Everyday Life and Cultural Exchange: Germans and Chinese in Tsingtau, 1897–1914*] (Wolfratshausen: Ed. Minerva, 1999); Fu-the Huang, *Qingdao: Chinesen unter deutscher Herrschaft 1897–1914* [*Qingdao: Chinese Under the German Rule, 1897–1914*] (Bochum: Projekt-Vel, 1999).

2. Klaus Mühlhahn, *Zai mofan zhimindi Jiaozhouwan de tongzhi yu dikang— 1897–1914 nian Zhongguo yu Deguo de xianghu zuoyong* [*Power and Resistance in the "Model Colony" of Kiautschou—interaction between China and Germans 1897– 1914*], 1.

3. Li Gongzhen, "Deguo dui Hua wenhua zhengce de kaiduan [The Beginning of the German Cultural Policy towards China]," in *Zhong De guanxishi wencong* [*Selected Works on the History of Sino-German Relations*], ed. Liu Shanzhang and Zhou Quan (Qingdao: Qingdao Press, 1991), 212–28.

4. Luo Zhitian, *Luanshi qianliu: minzu zhuyi yu zhengzhi* [*Undercurrent in Troubled Times: Nationalism and Politic*] (Shanghai: Shanghai Ancient Books Publishing House, 2001), 1.

5. Prasenjit Duara, *Rescuing History from the Nation: Questioning Narratives of Modern China* (Chicago: University of Chicago Press, 1995), 8.

6. Rebecca E. Karl, *Staging the World: Chinese Nationalism at the Turn of the Twentieth Century* (Durham: Duke University Press, 2002), 26.

7. Joseph R. Levenson, *Lian Ch'i-ch'ao and the Mind of Modern China* (Berkeley: University of California Press, 1953).

8. John E. Schrecker, *Imperialism and Chinese Nationalism: Germany in Shantung* (Cambridge: Harvard University Press, 1971).

9. Ding Weifen, "Shandong Gemingdang shigao [History of Shandong Revolutionists]," *Shandong wenxian* [*Shandong Literature*] 3 of vol. 1 (1975): 17.

10. Ding Weifen, "Shandong Gemingdang shigao [History of Shandong Revolutionists] -continued," *Shandong wenxian* [*Shandong Literature*] 4 of vol. 1 (1975): 35.

11. Chen Jun and Tong Lirong, "Chengong minghou xiansheng zhuan [Biography of Honorable Mr. Chen Minghou]," in *Chenminghou jiangjun: Shishi qishi zhounian jinian ji* [*General Chen Minghou: Festschrift of 70 Yahrzei*], ed. Chen Jun and Tong Lirong (Beijing: China Literature and History Publishing House, 1997), 3–13.

12. Ding Weifen, "Shandong Gemingdang shigao [History of Shandong Revolutionists] -continued," 30.

13. Chen Jun and Tong Lirong, "Chengong minghou xiansheng zhuan [Biography of Honorable Mr. Chen Minghou]," 13; Ding Weifen, "Shandong Gemingdang shigao [History of Shandong Revolutionists] -continued," 31.

14. "Zhendan gongxue zhi yuanqi [Origin of Qingdao Zhendan Public School],"

shenzhou ribao (*National Herald*), May 13, 1908, 1; Shandong guanbao (Shandong Gazette) 78:37.

15. "Zhendan gongxue zhi yuanqi [Origin of Qingdao Zhendan Public School]," 1.

16. Ding Weifen, "Shandong Gemingdang shigao [History of Shandong Revolutionists] -continued," 31.

17. Wei Lan, "Tao Huanqing xiansheng xingshu [Brief Biography of Mr. Tao Huanqing]," *Xinhai geming shi congkan* [*Collected Articles on the History of the 1911 Revolution*] 6 (1986): 78; Ding Weifen, "Shandong Gemingdang shigao [History of Shandong Revolutionists]," 17.

18. Chen Jun and Tong Lirong, "Chengong minghou xiansheng zhuan [Biography of Honorable Mr. Chen Minghou]," 13.

19. Ding Weifen, "Shandong Gemingdang shigao [History of Shandong Revolutionists] -continued," 31.

20. Li Hongsheng, "Chen Gan yu Shandong geming yundong [Chen Gan and Shandong Revolutionary Movement]," in *Chen Gan jinian wenji* [*A Collection of Articles in Memory of Chen Gan*], ed. Chen Jun and Tong Lirong (Hong Kong: Tian Ma Publishing, 2001), 12.

21. Ding Weifen, "Shandong Gemingdang shigao [History of Shandong Revolutionists] -continued," 35.

22. Qu Qi, "Xinhai geming qian Shandong baozhi jianshu 1894–1911 [A Brief Description of Shandong Newspapers Prior to Xinhai Revolution, 1894–1911], "*Shandong shizhi ziliao* [*Historical and Biographical Materials of Shandong*], 1 (1982): 176–77; Liu Xiaohuan and Xu Zhongli, "Chen Gan yu zhongguo jindai baokan xinwen shiye [Chen Gan and Modern Chinese Journalism and Press]," in *Chen Gan jinian wenji* [*A Collection of Articles in Memory of Chan Gan*], ed. Chen Jun and Tong Lirong (Hong Kong: Tian Ma Publishing, 2001), 255–56.

23. Ma Gengcun, *Tongmenghui zai Shandong* [*Tongmenghui in Shandong*] (Jinan: Shandong Renmin Publishing House, 1991), 57.

24. Ding Weifen, "Shandong Gemingdang shigao [History of Shandong Revolutionists] -continued," 32.

25. Yuan Rongsou, *Jiao'ao zhi* [*Jiao'ao Chronicle*] (Taipei: Wenhai Publishing House, 1969), 30–32.

26. "Shandong liuxue jie zhi baokuang banfa [Ways of Mining Protection Put Forward by the Overseas-Educated Students Circle]," *Shuntian shibao* [*Shuntian Times*], Aug. 28, 1908, 7.

27. "Jinan deling ze huaren fangqi quanli [The German Consulate in Jinan Blamed Chinese for Discarding Rights]," *Shuntian shibao* [*ShuntianTimes*], Sept. 25, 1908, 7.

28. "Jiaodu guanbi zhendan gongxue xiangqing [Details of the Kiautschou Governor's Closure of Zhendan Public School], " *Shuntian shibao* [*ShuntianTimes*], Jan. 7, 1909, 2.

29. "Zhendan gongxue bei deren pohuai gonggaoshu (Statement on the German's Destruction to the Zhendan Public School)," *Shuntian shibao* [*ShuntianTimes*], Feb. 27, 1909, 5.

30. "Zhendan gongxue bei deren pohuai gonggaoshu (Statement on the German's Destruction to the Zhendan Public School)," *Shuntian shibao* [*ShuntianTimes*], Feb. 27, 1909, 5.

31. Li Hongsheng, "Chen Gan yu Shandong geming yundong [Chen Gan and Shandong Revolutionary Movement]," 13.

32. Chen Gan, "Zhi Beijing tongxiang guan de gonghan [Official Letter to the Shandong Officials in Beijing]," in *Chenminghou jiangjun: Shishi qishi zhounian jinian ji* [*General Chen Minghou: Festschrift of 70 Yahrzeit*], ed. Chen Jun and Tong Lirong (Beijing: China Literature and History Publishing House, 1997), 103–4.

33. *Bohai ribao* [*Northern Times*], Mar. 21, 1909, 5.

34. *Bohai ribao* [*Northern Times*], May 3, 1909, 4.

35. *Bohai ribao* [*Northern Times*], June 8, 1909, 3.

36. *Bohai ribao* [*Northern Times*], July 14, 1909, 4.; July 15, 1909, 4.

37. *Bohai ribao* [*Northern Times*], Apr. 30, 1909, 4.

38. Dirk Alexander Seelemann, "Social and Economic Development of the Kiaochao Leasehold (Shantung, China) under German Administration, 1897–1914" (PhD diss., University of Toronto, 1982).

39. *Xuebu guanbao* [*Official Publications by the Ministry of Education*] (Taipei: Forbidden City Museum, 1970), 97 of vol. 3, 538–39; Mo Er (Mohre), ed., *Qingdao quanshu* [*The Complete Book of Qingdao*] (Qingdao, 1912), 210–14; *Shuntian Shibao* [*Shuntian Times*], Aug. 27, 1909, 5.

40. Zhe Chengzhi, "Qingdao tebie gaodeng zhuanmen xuetang [Qingdao Special High School], *Shandong wenxian* [*Shandong Literature*], 4 of vol. 6 (1980): 37–65.

41. Ma Gengcun, *Tongmenghui zai Shandong* [*Tongmenghui in Shandong*], 155–56.

42. Ma Gengcun, *Tongmenghui zai Shandong* [*Tongmenghui in Shandong*], 157–62.

43. "Sun Zhongshan youli Qingdao ji [Sun Yat-sen Travelling around Qingdao]," *xiehe bao* [*Xiehe News*], Oct. 5, 1912, 5.

44. "Sun Zhongshan youli Qingdao ji [Sun Yat-sen Travelling around Qingdao]," 6.

45. "Sun Zhongshan youli Qingdao ji [Sun Yat-sen Travelling around Qingdao]," 6.

46. *Kiautschou-Post*, compiled and published in 1912, 828–29.

47. Sun Yat-sen, *Complete Works of Sun Yat-sen*, vol. 2 (Beijing: Zhonghua Book Company, 1982), 480–81.

48. William Matzat, *Shan Weilian yu Qingdao tudi fagui* [*Wilhelm Schrameier and Land Legislation in Qingdao*], trans. Jiang Hong (Taibei: Research Institute of Chinese Land Policy, 1986), 49–50.

49. William Matzat, *Shan Weilian yu Qingdao tudi fagui* [*Wilhelm Schrameier and Land Legislation in Qingdao*], 27–36.

Anti-colonial Nationalism and Cosmopolitan "Standard Time"

Lala Har Dayal's *Forty Four Months in Germany and Turkey* (1920)

B. Venkat Mani

Cosmopolitanism—as a philosophical ideal, political value, subject of epistemological inquiry, principle of conceptual organization of communities and collectives, and above all, an empowering phenomenon that helps overcome and/or transcend the material and symbolic confines of allegiance to the nation-state—has undergone significant resurgence in the first half of the twenty-first century.[1] In the light of mass migration of peoples around the world in the second half of the twentieth century, in a socio-political text complicated by decolonization and political autonomy on the one hand and global capital expansion and multinational techno-economic corporatism on the other, cosmopolitanism has acquired new dimensions and gained new ground. The positioning of cosmopolitanism as a desired antidote for a separatist multiculturalism or fanatic nationalism frequently occurs in the privileged context of already established nation-states.[2] Cosmopolitanism as a communitarian affiliation that transcends immediate identitarian markers of class, creed, religion, language, and so on, relies largely on the presence of the nation-state as an evaluative principle. This very fact accords discussions of cosmopolitanism either a presentist or a curiously de-historicized dimension. Consequently, the role of a pre-emergent nation-state within the politico-theoretical ambition that energizes cosmopolitanism gets a short shrift. In addition, in the consistently "antagonal" positioning of nationalism and cosmopolitanism, the "diagonal" repositioning of anti-colonial nationalism and cosmopolitanism often remains under-discussed.

In this essay I wish to identify some of the above-mentioned gaps and schisms in contemporary discussions of cosmopolitanism by way of turning to a historical moment from India in the early twentieth century, during which anti-colonial nationalism formed and informed cosmopolitan affiliations on a global scale.[3] I propose that cosmopolitanism does not insinuate an absolute transcendence of the category of the nation. In fact, it enriches from the exacerbating energy of the nation-state. In a colonial context, anti-colonial nationalism does not stand in a mutually exclusive relationship to cosmopolitanism—in fact the two can be understood in an asymmetrical symbiosis.

The second half of this essay discusses Lala Har Dayal[4] (1884–1939), a man of many careers: political commentator in English, Hindi, Urdu, and Punjabi; Orientalist and short-term professor of Indian Philosophy at Stanford University; revolutionary activist and pro-violent anarchist who later became a scholar of Buddhism; anti-colonial ideologue and cosmopolitan nationalist. Through his political activism, revolutionary work, and his writings, he made "East" his career, albeit largely in the geo-cultural centers of the United Kingdom, United States, and continental Europe. Throughout his life, he was marked by, and derived energy from, a peculiar sense of historical predicament that surfaces in innumerable moments of his self-positioning as representative of multiple political collectivities. Har Dayal makes an apt case for challenging any simplistic conceptualization of anti-colonialism as theory and/or praxis. Indeed it is the triangulation of Har Dayal's anti-colonialism with his nationalism and cosmopolitanism that is at the core of *Forty Four Months in Germany and Turkey. February 1915 to October 1918: A Record of Personal Impressions* (1920).[5] This trajectory will hopefully assist in making a case for the examination of a unique intellectual position against German imperialism, colonialism, and expansionism through military power and diplomacy at the beginning of the twentieth century.

Pheng Cheah and Bruce Robbins use the word *cosmopolitics* to lay emphasis on a restructuring and rethinking of the term *cosmopolitanism*. They defined *cosmopolitics* as "less than kin or friendship but a good deal more than polite or innocent nonrelation"[6] and "as an apposite term for the global force field of the political."[7] The German term *kosmopolitisch*—in alignment with Wieland and Kant's use of the adjective *cosmopolitan*—regains currency in discussions of Europe through its use by Jürgen Habermas in his influential and much-discussed essay "Die postnationale Konstellation und die Zukunft der Demokratie." Habermas stresses in his essay the need for reevaluation of national sovereignty and state-structure vis-à-vis the reorganization of Europe as a confederation of nation-states. Arguing forcefully for an attenuation of real and metaphorical national boundaries, Habermas concentrated on the question of the European civil society's mutual affiliation, parallel to the affiliation to the nation inhabited by the populace, and the state, which the populace legitimizes as democratic subjects of polity.[8]

These two epistemological moments enable a demonstration of how the terms *cosmopolitical* and *cosmopolitan* are deeply embedded in the discursive imaginations of the nation and the state in the larger history of European modernity. An examination of these lexical entities at the beginning of the twenty-first century thus prompts one to conceptualize the tension between the ontogeny and the phylogeny of Europe when the colonial subject is dislodged and purloined from the genealogy of European cosmopolitics.

Cosmopolitanism, simply stating, draws our attention to the human self's propensity to engage with others through affiliative processes. These processes could be conditioned by a particular kind of education/formation (*Bildung*) of the Self, yearning (*Sehnsucht*) for the Other, and/or these processes could bring into relief the necessarily equitable nature of self-realization and self-assertion (*Selbsteinwirkung und Selbstbestimmung*) of both the Self and the Other based on humanitarian principles, on a purportedly universal terrain. *Cosmopolitics*—in the global force-field of the political—highlights precisely the obstructions, distractions, and pre-conditions that complicate the text and texture of affiliations between Self and Other. The cosmopolitical explains affiliation by recounting, and accounting for, moments of disaffiliation and disjuncture that arise due to the inherent inequitability of human subjects that exists despite principles of Humanitarianism and Universalism. If cosmopolitanism—through access to education, yearning, and possibilities of self-assertion—might insinuate a sense of privilege, cosmopolitics accounts for the inaccessibility, turning the acquired or inherited privilege into a willingly, and sometimes vulnerably inhabited claim. Both the terms converge as they convey stepping across several lines of race, religion, language, and nationality—as a responsibility and/or an obligation. As I have argued elsewhere in great detail, it is this understanding that assists in conceiving cosmopolitanism *not* as a perpetual privilege but as an occasion-specific claim.[9]

While certain forms of nineteenth- and early twentieth-century cosmopolitanism evoke rootlessness and/or grand presumptions of belonging to the entire world, "new cosmopolitanisms"—plural, results of the rethinking—highlight the situationality and locatability of cosmopolitical affiliations.[10] These affiliations have been presented in registers of multiplicity and plurality—as attachments, detachments, and re-attachments—with those who inhabit spaces beyond familiar and familial ties of kith and kin. A brief disciplinary differentiation might be useful here, even if to jettison later. Socio-political thinkers formulate questions of affiliation by considering ethics, rights, equity, and law, both national and international—in the context of political citizenship. Literary and cultural critics translate these concerns in extra-juridical contexts by examining the materiality and symbolism of everyday practices and artistic expressions that assert and/or upset questions of home and belonging in the context of cultural citizenship.[11]

From Jacques Derrida's seminars "Of Hospitality" and the "Question of the Foreigner" to Ulrich Beck and Edgar Grande's collaborative work *Das kosmopolitische Europa*; from Martha Nussbaum's much debated essay "For the Love of Country?" to Kwame Anthony Appiah's *Cosmopolitanism: Ethics in the World of Strangers*—much has been asserted, affirmed, and confirmed about the need to consider the changing nature of the human subject's sense of political, cultural, and social affiliations.[12] Such assertions, affirmations, and confirmations have invited a rich set of critical positions as well: David Hollinger's sharp critique of Martha Nussbaum in *Postethnic America*, Craig Calhoun's cautionary account of cosmopolitanism as a privilege of "Frequent Flyers," and Timothy Brennan's passionate polemic against the homogeneity of cosmopolitan literary writings in his book *At Home in the World*, to list just a few.[13] From Europe to North America, there seems to be expressed a dire need for the creation of a cosmopolitan society, one that would utilize internal and external differences rather than suppressing them, and work toward a what Ulrich Beck calls a "differential integration" of its subjects in order to optimally fulfill its transnational obligations and connections.[14]

At the risk of sounding tendentious, let me spell out three overlapping affinities shared by laudatory *and* denunciative discursive evaluations of cosmopolitanism. First, most theories of "new" cosmopolitanisms set up binary opposites in order to identify and explore dialectical tension between forms of human affiliation. Second, in the course of such explorations, the task of reflecting on the manner of human affiliations becomes central to conceptualizing a cosmopolitan space. Third, such specialized arrangements of the manner of human affiliations demonstrate a peculiar "recursive" treatment of the nation-state through an unreflective mobilization of "time." This, I am later going to argue, leads to the construction, in theoretical discussions, of an illusory "cosmopolitan standard time" from which the "colonial moment"—one that is distinctly marked by anti-colonial nationalism and cosmopolitanism—is purloined.

Cosmopolitanism itself is analyzed in terms of its internal conceptual dialectics, expressed through various sets of binary opposites: concept vs. phenomenon, feeling vs. thought, ideology vs. sentiment, consciousness vs. practice, disposition vs. acquisition, privilege vs. claim, abstract idea vs. a set of decipherable and legible script, and so forth. Theories of cosmopolitanism focus largely on the manner of human affiliations—how and why can or should human subjects affiliate with each other. Such affiliations are distinguished through the following sets of binaries: native vs. foreign, familiar vs. strange, citizen vs. non-citizen, resident vs. alien, individual vs. communitarian, local vs. extra-local, ethnic vs. post-ethnic, national vs. transnational and so forth. Recent discussions of cosmopolitanism imply and endorse overcoming of "older affiliations" to nation, language, ethnicity, and so forth, such as those that are caused by accidents of birth or those that are inherited—to the "newer" ones, such as those that are acquired and willfully inhabited—best illustrated by Seyla Benhabib as a distinction between communities of fate and belonging (Ethnos) and communities of affiliation through residence (Demos).[15]

While these observations pertain to the manner of cosmopolitan affiliations—their spatial imaginations carry marks of binaries as well: intra-communitarian vs. inter-communitarian, intra-cultural and inter-cultural, para-national vs. transnational, to list just few. In other words, there is a marked space, an interiority that a cosmopolitan subject seeks to escape. By this logic, the distance between that interiority and exteriority becomes the measuring unit of a subject's cosmopolitanism or cosmopolitics. In other spatial imaginations, specters of base and superstructure continue to make their presence conspicuous through binaries of above and below. Cosmopolitanism as a privilege of the above is displaced by a specific subaltern cosmopolitanism from the below.[16]

From the long list of binaries I have listed, it might be noticeable that most are associable with spatial and mannerist imaginations of cosmopolitanism. Temporality is often glossed over as a difference between the old and the new. The best illustration of this observation can be found in the essay "Four Cosmopolitan Moments," co-authored by sociologists Robert Fine and Robin Cohen. The authors categorically state that "there is no particular theoretical weight attached to the word 'moment': rather, it serves as a convenient device to anchor some key debates and antinomies." They confess that their "choice is much less than comprehensive, but rather more than arbitrary."[17] With statements and confessions in place, they go on to identify the following four moments of cosmopolitanism: "the ancient world (Zeno's moment), the Enlightenment (Kant's moment), post-totalitarian thought (Arendt's moment) and late North American thought (Nussbaum's moment)."[18] If this were to be accepted as the chronology of cosmopolitanism in the history of Western thought, then the cosmopolitan time zone lies somewhere between Cyprus and Massachusetts. The cosmopolitan standard time, by this logic, can be calculated as the average of the mean of the time zones in which contemporary Cyprus, Kaliningrad, New York City, and Boston lie. Easy!

I am being partially facetious here. But more seriously, instead of rejecting this timeline altogether just because it is primarily Western, or merely indulging in polemics in the name of some vague non-Western nativism, it is necessary to draw our attention to serious epistemological flaws in this time line and its consequent establishment of a cosmopolitan European present. Three observations might be pertinent here: first, if Immanuel Kant's essay on Perpetual Peace is to be considered the first systematic articulation of cosmopolitanism in the project of European modernity, cosmopolitanism in itself (*an sich*) is a political project, one that reflects organization of power and maintenance of peace within national boundaries. Second, while it is correct—as Ulrich Beck and Edgar Grande have argued—that Kantian cosmopolitanism predates the systematic and aggressive nation-building in Europe in the nineteenth century, the leap to Arendt's moment in the 1950s (Fine and Cohen) will remain problematic unless Arendt's moment is contextualized as a response to high-stakes nationalist politics in Europe in the first half of the twentieth century. Third, Nussbaum's moment from the beginning of the twenty-first century cannot be detached from post-9/11 concerns of religion-based terrorism and its problematic retort through US nationalism.

In sum, it seems like any attempt to define, redefine, and restructure an understanding of "new" cosmopolitanisms through cosmopolitics accrues ineluctable significance to the nation, national political space defined by geographical boundaries, and national cultural space that arranges its wares and goods (*Kulturgut*)—languages, ethnicities, religions, and so forth—between the boundaries of that national space. The predicament of cosmopolitanism, as noted earlier, lies then in a creative unsettling of affiliation to all things national—boundaries, wares, history, and memory. No matter how loose the hyphen between the nation and the state, the compound noun *nation-state* acquires a specific "recursive" dimension—in mathematical terms—as a unit and as a value. The nation-state repeats itself, either indefinitely or until the point is reached when nationalism and patriotism can be distinguished vis-à-vis cosmopolitanism; or the nation-state itself involves the repeated application of the function of the cosmopolitanism to its own value.

The most vivid illustrations of such recursive articulations of the nation-state can be found in Nussbaum's essay "Cosmopolitan and Patriotism" and Appiah's fairly sympathetic reading of Nussbaum in his piece "Cosmopolitan Patriots." Nussbaum evaluates cosmopolitanism by trying to measure the distance between "politics of nationalism and politics of difference," proposing that "nationalism and ethnocentric particularism are not alien to each other, but akin [. . .]."[19] (Appiah stresses the symbiotic—as opposed to parasitic—relationship between the nation and the cosmos outside the nation by invoking the idea of homeland, indicating, "In a world of cosmopolitan patriots, people would accept the citizens' responsibility to nurture the culture and politics of their home.")[20] Both these thinkers mobilize examples from the colonial contexts to think through the complicated relationship between patriotism/nationalism and cosmopolitanism. Nussbaum deploys Rabindranath Tagore's novel *Ghare Bahire* (1915–16; *The Home and the World*, 1919); Appiah recounts his father's commitment to Ghana. As Nussbaum and Appiah evaluate cosmopolitanism in tandem with patriotism, the significance of the colonial contexts and the special dimensions such contexts might accrue to the imagination of cosmopolitanism get short shrift. In other words, as cosmopolitanism acquires primacy vis-à-vis the national space, the colonial context itself becomes tertiary: a weirdly empty canvass that is nonetheless perfect for abstract representations of amorphous patriotism.

If these observations hold currency, then an argument that results in a time zone that conveniently places Europe or the United States outside of the larger organization of the world into nation-states is anything but cosmopolitan. An account of European cosmopolitics therefore cannot afford to surpass the inherent connections between European nation-building and the project of colonialism that occurred parallel to, coincided with, and had tremendous reciprocal impact on the very formation of modern Europe and its former colonies. That said, even an allusion or acknowledgment thereof shall not be sufficient; this timeline will remain flawed if it is bracketed between the foundational moment of a post-colonial nation-state, somewhere in the early to mid-twentieth century and its immediate present in the twenty-first. In other words, the examination of nationalism and nation-states as organizational principles of a society / a community (*Gesellschaft/Gemeinschaft*) and alluded emancipation from them through filters of cosmopolitanism cannot merely privilege the moment of decolonization and the advent of postcoloniality. For this, it will have to take into consideration a different kind of nationalism, one that does not easily allow denunciation, for it was posed and posited as emancipation from foreign affiliation; indeed in terms of national territorial sovereignty.

In brief, the peculiar articulation of cosmopolitanism as patriotism bereft of nationalism reveals its inadequacy in contexts where socio-political affiliations to the colonizing power filter any anticipation of decolonization and formation of the nation-state. If "Europe is postcolonial"—as Etienne Balibar asserts in *We the People of Europe?*—many more questions can make the space before the question-mark even more meaningful. What kind of connections and disconnects exist between colonialism and cosmopolitanism? Does colonization necessarily create the kind of allegiances to the empire that might be locally situated, but not nationally defined? If for a moment cosmopolitanism were to be considered as a willful overcoming of merely local and national allegiances, does it make all cosmopolitans imperial and colonial? Or are there structures of cosmopolitan thought that in effect de-structure the governance of the very empire that initiated them?

To illustrate the significance of these questions, let us pursue them through a discussion of Har Dayal and his *Forty Four Months in Germany and Turkey*—a text that elaborately articulates the question of cosmopolitanism prior to the foundation of a decolonized nation-state of India.

In the fall of 1905, Lala Har Dayal, an Indian student in his early twenties, arrived in England on a state scholarship and began his education at the Honors School of Modern History in St. John's College, Oxford. Born and raised in a family of upper-middle-class businessmen in Delhi, Har Dayal had studied English literature at St. Stephen's College, Delhi, and Government College at Punjab University, Lahore (now in Pakistan). In England he became associated with Shyamaji Krishnavarma, a leader of the Indian revolutionary movement and the editor of the journal *The Indian Sociologist*. After four successful academic terms, in early 1907 Har Dayal suddenly resigned from his scholarship, because, as Krishnavarma explained, "he [held] that no Indian who really leaves his country ought to compromise his principles and barter his rectitude of conduct for any favour whatever at the hands of the alien oppressive rulers of India" (Preface). For love of country, Har Dayal briefly went back to India. He began his revolutionary work, which ranged from giving passionate speeches to writing political articles as well as nationalist songs in Hindi, Urdu, and Punjabi, and plotting violent conspiracies against the British Empire. In 1908 he joined Shyamji Krishnavarma in Paris; but their irresolvable disagreements—some allegedly involving the editorial direction of *Vande Mataram*, a new journal started by Har Dayal—led to Har Dayal's move, by way of Algeria and Martinique, to San Francisco in 1911. His revolutionary work in India continued in San Francisco through a range of activities, which involved formation of secret societies, promotion of arguments in favor of use of violence, and, most famously, publication of the newspaper *Ghadar* (Mutiny), which gave voice to a number of Indian revolutionaries and their sympathizers in the first two decades of the twentieth century. Har Dayal's political engagements cost him his short time (unpaid) lectureship at Stanford University and eventually led to his arrest by the US government in 1914. He was declared an "undesirable alien." Released briefly on bail, he escaped to Switzerland, and in January 1915 he arrived in Berlin.

Here, along with Virendranath Chattopadhyaya (1880–1937) and Champakraman Pillai (1891–1934), Har Dayal gained recognition as one of the prominent Indian nationalists who made Berlin a major organizational center for anti-colonial activism outside of India. These activists took advantage of the tense relationship between Great Britain and Imperial Germany that surfaced clearly in German foreign policy toward British colonies. Har Dayal became the architect and self-appointed executor of what came to be known as the "Hindu-German Conspiracy."[21] Despite the use of "Hindu" in its name, the Conspiracy actually involved a mobilization of Indian Muslims against the British through the Ottoman Caliphate—a highly influential political and spiritual center for Indian Muslims in the first two decades of the twentieth century. Disguised as a Kenyan businessman, Har Dayal went to Istanbul in 1915 to plot a military attack on British India through Afghanistan.

Har Dayal's "missions" in Berlin and Istanbul were catastrophically unsuccessful, and he returned to Berlin in 1918. In 1920 he was able to move to Sweden, where he wrote *Forty Four Months in Germany and Turkey*, a bitter and passionate account of his years in Berlin and Istanbul, and, as I will shortly explain, an about-turn of his ideological convictions regarding an independent Indian nation-state. Har Dayal's strongest defense of British colonialism through a critique of German nationalism and imperialism won him favors from the British government again. The slim volume was instantly translated into Hindi and distributed widely in India by the British government. The publication also paved the way for his return to London in order for him to pursue a doctoral degree at the School of Oriental and African Studies, and eventually turned him into a "desirable alien" in the United States. Har Dayal visited the United States in 1939 to lecture on the topic "Hints of Self-Culture" and died in Philadelphia, reportedly from a heart attack.

Except for the two short sentences on *Forty Four Months*, what I have presented so far are just a few of the most consistent facts about Har Dayal that I have been able to assemble. My sources include Nirode K. Barooah's histories of Indian-German political relationships in the nineteenth and early twentieth centuries (1977, 2004) and two important biographies of Har Dayal published in the 1970s—one authored in Hindi (Dharmavir, 1970) and the other in English by an American journalist (Brown, 1975). For Barooah, Har Dayal becomes the disgruntled political strategist whose dreams of grandeur obstruct the success of the "Hindu-German" conspiracy. Dharmavir portrays Har Dayal as a world-class political thinker and a revolutionary who privileges British colonialism against German imperial ambitions; Brown's account of Har Dayal establishes him as a revolutionary social reformer and a political rationalist. Despite differences, all three commentators discuss Har Dayal as an internationally traveled, polyglot "world-citizen," who never lost touch with the interests of his motherland, whose "love of country" became central to his life and his work against colonialism and imperialism.[22] Curious claims indeed, when considered against the conclusion of *Forty Four Months*:

> English and French will serve to unite the Orient and Occident in indissoluble bonds of comradeship. For us, Indians and Egyptians, English literature should be a treasure of worth untold. English history should be a mine of the noblest wisdom for us and our children. England has much to give us besides protection and organisation. We are now heirs to all that the Englishman holds in fee as his birthright. England is free and great and we can share in this freedom and greatness as worthy citizens of the greatest State that the world has yet seen. England will achieve what Alexander dreamed of, and Rome partially accomplished. We, too, are called to this work.[23]

The brief remarks that Barooah, Dharmavir, and Brown make about *Forty Four Months* indicate that they never actually read beyond the first two sections of the text. One could speculate about the reasons for such negligence. The anecdotal nature of the text could be the primary reason. Har Dayal begins the book by stating, "I shall speak from direct personal experience. I shall not quote from books and newspapers" (1). A related comment could be made about the egregious commentaries on German and Turkish national mentalities and individual citizens' psychological propensities that Har Dayal presents with great fervor. The following two examples illustrate this observation: "The most noticeable feature of German society as a whole is the spirit of excessive megalomania that pervades it. The Germans believe that they are the greatest, wisest, bravest, ablest, noblest, and best people on earth" (3); or "[. . .] the Turks, as a nation, are utterly unfit to assume the leadership of the Muslim world. They have been, and are, only a predatory tribe, without culture and political capacity [. . .] they have no great or noble national literature" (31). And third, even though the text compromises its own political ambition through a complete submission to England and Englishmen, it stages a particular tension between the sanguine "filiative" and the socio-historical "affiliative." To express along with R. Radhakrishnan, "It is this undecidability of blood as it straddles the filiative and affiliative orders that has rendered all nationalisms a scandal."[24] Har Dayal moves from the decided subscription to a nationalized thinking to perform its undecidable nature in *Forty Four Months*, making it a statement of a crucial turning point in his biography.

While it is beyond the scope of this essay to provide or speculate a psychological reasoning for Har Dayal's ideological shifts, or to rectify purportedly erroneous details of his multiple careers,[25] there is one moment in the text that might serve as an apt point of departure to think through the complicated narrative of cosmopolitanism vis-à-vis anti-colonial nationalism that Har Dayal creates in his text: "I am a cosmopolitan in spirit, and can judge and criticize with an unbiased mind." At the very beginning of his book, Har Dayal identifies its target readership as "educated classes of India Egypt, and other Oriental countries" (2). The questionability of an "unbiased mind" notwithstanding, Har Dayal leaves several traces that assist in reconstructing an imagination of cosmopolitan affiliations in tandem with nationalist predicament of an educated colonial subject. His acerbic remarks on Germans and Germany, his critique of German expansionist and military ambitions in Asia, and his vociferous dismissal of Germany as a potential colonial power attest to these observations.

Har Dayal's criticism of Germany—spread across the four sections, the preface, and the conclusion that constitute *Forty Four Months*—appears in the most concentrated form in Sections I and IV, entitled "General Impressions" (1–28) and "Germans in Asia" (78–96) respectively. Sections II and III, "In Constantinople" (29–54) and "'Asia Minor' in Berlin" (55–77), focus largely on observations on Turks and Turkish political officials, and Indian and other Asian intellectuals in Berlin respectively. In his critique of Germany, "megalomania" (3), militancy (7–9), arrogance (8–9), barbarism (2, 16), hostility (21), deception (80), betrayal (94–95), and the feeling of racial superiority (90) emerge as keywords. Har Dayal considers Germans in the Kaiserreich as people who have forgotten the idealism of Kant and Goethe (9–10) and have moved to a "cult of force" (10) to promote a "Weltreich" (10). At the very beginning of his discussion of Germany, he declares the entire country "a political bedlam" with "no trace of wisdom" (12). His vicious remarks could be connected with the feeling of racial superiority he experiences among his German colleagues: he equates "German attitude towards Orientals" with "[some Americans'] defense of slavery" (15). He sees Germany as a country that frequently indulges in the disavowal of International Law to compromise the sovereignty of other nations, even within Europe (14–15). He declares Germans incapable of understanding compassion for human suffering beyond national boundaries (17) and considers Germany in power in Europe and the world as a "diabolical ogre" (19). He deems the "much advertised 'Kultur'" (85) besotted with reactionary medievalism and despotism in the garb of modern-day bureaucracy (23–24). Foreshadowing his thoughts are also observations on German authoritarianism and power hierarchies, expressed, according to him, through the strangely medieval practice of using titles, such as "Herr Kommissar," as forms of address (22–23).

These lines of critique continue in Section IV where Har Dayal discusses Germany's role in Asia, specifically in Turkey and Persia. He declares Germans "morally bankrupt" and states that they have "failed miserably." By drawing on accounts of "unnamed" Turkish and Persian officials and politicians (and sometimes Muslim scholars), Har Dayal considers Germans as incapacitated to comprehend "Oriental courtesy and morality" (83), declaring that "Germans will live in the Oriental tradition as liars and swindlers for a long time" (88). Once again, he draws attention to the German "nigger-politik" [sic], which makes them think of themselves as belonging to another, higher human species than Asians or Africans (90). Section IV ends with the assertion, "German inroad in Asia will remain a troubled dream" (96).

These emotional, anecdotal, and admittedly sensational remarks on Germany cannot be dismissed as the rant of a madman. They must be understood against the context of what Har Dayal conceives of as colonialism at this particular point of time in his life of ideas, and his sense of cosmopolitanism that constitutes his self—which collides with the nationalism he sees in Germany. While it can be safely, and rather easily, stated that Har Dayal's volume could have been a strategic piece of writing to win British favors again, his critique of German imperialism cannot be merely read as leverage. The following two passages in particular reveal a forceful critique of German racialist thinking, which Har Dayal confronts with a strong political argument in favor of the equitable nature of human subjects:

[. . .] I am opposed to German colonisation in Africa and Asia even on a small scale. The Germans are morally unfit to administer colonies, because they do not recognise our common human nature at all. In the colonies the Europeans are absolute masters of the native population. They have weapons, organisation, and scientific knowledge, and their will is law. [. . .] The weak and helpless Africans can only say "We, too, are men, brothers, and Christians." This appeal is their only refuge. [. . .] The moral standards of the colonising nation determine the fate of the inferior race.

For this reason the Germans must not be allowed to use rule over the primitive tribes of Africa or Asia, for they can manage a colony only as a meat-packing company manages its cattle farms. (17–18)

In the passages following immediately, Har Dayal goes overboard against potential German colonies: "In all English, French, American and Italian colonies the civil rights of the population and the elementary laws of morality are scrupulously respected by the white rulers" (19). This statement is particularly hard to digest in the light of the almost contemporary Jallianwala Bagh Massacre (1919) in Amritsar, India, when an unarmed civic assembly was "dispersed" with gunshots by General Dyer and his platoons. Nonetheless, the preceding and the following references to German sense of superiority as a race and the Germans' consideration of all other human beings as "sub-human" (17) provide a rather dismal view of Har Dayal's short-term engagement with Germans. This severe disgust and desperation, which is identifiable throughout the text, further fortifies Har Dayal's own struggle with colonialism as a ruling strategy. Anti-colonial nationalism—expressed selectively through vocabularies of human rights and embedded consistently in the syntax of cosmopolitan conjecture—finally softens, in that it becomes a set of negotiations between the colonizer and the colonized. Toward the end of *Forty Four Months*, Har Dayal repeatedly promotes "mixed" administration of British and French colonies in Asia and Africa. This idea receives extreme exaggeration in the "Conclusion," in which England is declared to have "a moral and historical mission in India" (97) and is projected as "the trustee of the future of Asia and Africa" (99–100). Har Dayal's anti-colonial nationalism, which supported even militant forms of struggle for independence from 1905 to 1918, underwent a change after the war and succumbed to the victory of the British and French; whether informed by Realpolitik, a sense of defeat, or sheer personal and political pragmatism, Har Dayal assigns to "weak oriental nations" the position of "protégés of the great European powers," admitting along the way that these nations "cannot maintain independent nation states" (99–100). Refuting "Irish nationalism," "Jihad," or even "Pan-Islamism" (98), Har Dayal proceeds to propose a "Federation of the World" (103), where colonialism remains a political reality.

There is no doubt that in the period following World War I, Har Dayal's anti-colonial nationalism turned on itself. Without justifying it, or providing a blemish-resistant account of his cosmopolitanism, it is important to present the two as part of his conflicting ideology, which, nonetheless, asserts the inclusion of the colonial subject in the larger discourse of European cosmopolitics.

Throughout his stringent critique of Germany's military expansion, Har Dayal remains attentive to loss of the *Weltgeist* (world spirit) in the wake of the *Weltreich* (world empire) and *Weltmacht* (world power) that marks German political aspiration. The heightened spirit of German nationalism, the militarization of political subjects in the time of war, and the intensification of a particular German socio-cultural identity, all seem to be detrimental to a cosmopolitan spirit that for Har Dayal is embodied in German thought and literature proposed in the nineteenth century. His characterization of military nationalism as provincial and narrow-minded further appends this idea. Thus expansionist military nationalism defeats any peaceful affiliation with those not tied through blood and soil; however, to think that religion might successfully acquire the position of such an agency is quickly debunked by him. Admittedly, his critique of Turkey is often rendered delirious due to his conflation of Ottomans with Turks. However, his message to Muslim colonial subjects in India and Egypt is simple—Pan Islamism is an affiliative decoy placed by the Ottoman Empire to assure political dominance over Muslim subjects that reside outside of the boundaries of the Ottoman Empire. Out of the plethora of complex and complicated problematization of organizing and uniting communities of the world around military power or religion, Har Dayal draws attention to colonialism itself as a viable organizational principle for affiliations of world communities.

Toward the beginning of this essay I referred to cosmopolitics as an "occasion-specific claim" in the global force-field of the political. In conclusion, three points are worth articulating. First, Asian and African reactions to German imperialism or colonialism cannot be evaluated merely as attestations of a "pure" and uncompromised political will or ideology, but rather, as a set of socio-political relations that impact the very global force-field of the political. Second, as Har Dayal's *Forty Four Months* attests, cosmopolitics is not a simplified form of rootless cosmopolitanism, rather a mode of thinking about dominance and subjugation, equitable claims and inequitable political realities. And last, but not the least, the discomfiture between anti-colonial nationalism and cosmopolitanism sheds light on circumstances where communitarian affiliations through the paradigmatic nation-state are largely imaginary and ideological. Despite patriotic sentiment and nationalist ideology, the moment of decolonization and consequently the formation of the nation-state are anticipated, longed for, but not guaranteed, in the political future. In light of the "Conclusion" of *Forty Four Months*, this is a very discomfiting fact indeed, but must be spelled out, precisely because it assists in imagining the asymmetrical geometries of cosmopolitanism, colonialism, nationalism, and patriotism, whereby the "love of country" can only be evaluated against the established affiliation with the colonizer, and an emergent relationship with other colonial subjects—a decidedly cosmopolitan strategy. The discomfiture of the fact is by no means a point of arrival. It serves as an apt point of departure to explore anti-colonial nationalism that belongs to a post-national constellation even when it is pre-national. The purloined colonial subject, when reinstated in stature, reveals the chaotic reality of the colonial space outside the standard time of European cosmopolitics.

NOTES

1. See Pheng Cheah and Bruce Robbins, *Cosmopolitics: Thinking and Feeling Beyond the Nation* (Minneapolis: University of Minnesota Press, 1998); Amanda Anderson, *The Powers of Distance: Cosmopolitanism and the Cultivation of Detachment* (Princeton: Princeton University Press, 2001); Vinay Dharwadker, *Cosmopolitan Geographies: New Locations in Literature and Culture* (New York: Routledge, 2001); Steven Vertovec and Robin Cohen, *Conceiving Cosmopolitanism: Theory, Context and Practice* (New York: Oxford University Press, 2002); Seyla Benhabib, *The Rights of Others: Aliens, Residents, and Citizens* (Cambridge: Cambridge University Press, 2004); Anthony Appiah, *Cosmopolitanism: Ethics in a World of Strangers* (New York: W. W. Norton, 2006); Rebecca L. Walkowitz, *Cosmopolitan Style: Modernism Beyond the Nation* (New York: Columbia University Press, 2006); B. Venkat Mani, *Cosmopolitical Claims: Turkish-German Literatures from Nadolny to Pamuk* (Iowa City: University of Iowa Press, 2007). This is by no means an exhaustive list, just a (selective) representation of major trends in philosophy, sociology, political theory, and literary/cultural criticism.

2. For an exception see Walter Mignolo, "The Many Faces of Cosmo-polis: Border Thinking and Critical Cosmopolitanism," *Cosmopolitanism*, ed. Carol A. Breckenridge et al. (Durham: Duke University Press, 2002), 157–88.

3. A clarification is essential here: nation building is always an exclusionary process, as has been argued in the large body of scholarship in the past quarter of a century. Hegemonic nation-states create their own colonial subjects, often within the boundaries of the nation-states. This is relevant even in the case of a postcolonial nation such as India. The intention here is not to paint in broad strokes a mural that renders nation building in colonial, anti-colonial, or even postcolonial situations undifferentiated. That these processes are still complicated by specific historical conditions of Asia, Africa, and Latin America cannot be denied. Within the scope of this essay, I am drawing on a specific example from India that serves as a response to British and German colonialist agendas, energized by the tension between nationalist and cosmopolitan aspirations. For a detailed study of a distinct set of examples from the Indian context see Leela Gandhi, *Affective Communities: Anticolonial Thought, Fin-de-Siècle Radicalism, and the Politics of Friendship* (Durham: Duke University Press, 2006).

4. The Hindi word *Lala* is an honorific title. It refers to a businessman, so it obvi-

ously insinuates social class and power hierarchies; it can however be used as a term of endearment, which is perhaps why Har Dayal's colleagues starting referring to him as Lala Har Dayal. Har Dayal's major biographer in English, Emily C. Brown, refers to him as Har Dayal. His Hindi biographer Professor Dharmavir refers to him as Har Day-alji ("ji" is an honorific suffix). Har Dayal published his works without the title "Lala." See Emily Clara Brown, *Har Dayal: Hindu Revolutionary and Rationalist* (Tucson: University of Arizona Press, 1975); Dharmavir, *Lala Hardayal. Prasiddha Deshbkahta Lala Hardayal ka Jeevan tatha unke Samaya ke Krantikari Andolana* (Delhi: Rajpal and Sons, 1970). All citations from Brown and Dharmavir are from these editions. Note that in the Hindi title *Hardayal* is one word. Har Dayal himself perhaps split his name into two to conform to the Western practice of name/surname, as he spent most of his time abroad.

5. Henceforth referred to as *Forty Four Months*. All citations and page numbers are from this edition.

6. Bruce Robbins, "Introduction, Part 1: Actually Existing Cosmopolitanism," in Cheah and Robbins, *Cosmopolitics*, 12.

7. Phengh Cheah, "Introduction, Part 2: The Cosmopolitical Today," in Cheah and Robbins, *Cosmopolitics*, 31.

8. Jürgen Habermas, "Die postnationale Konstellation und die Zukunft der Demokratie," in Jürgen Habermas, *Die postnationale Konstellation. Politische Essays* (Frankfurt am Main: Suhrkamp, 1998), 91–169.

9. Mani, *Cosmopolitical Claims*. See also Mani, "Kosmopolitismus und Weltliteratur: Thesen gegen die Herrschaft der Ego," in *Das Argument: Zeitschrift für Philosophie und Sozialwissenschaften*, 54.4 (2012): 501–9; Gerhard Bauer and Julia Schöll (eds.), special issue on "Kosmopolitismus in der Weltliteratur."

10. Walkowitz, *Cosmopolitan Style*.

11. These observations are pertinent to disciplinary evaluations of cosmopolitanism and not meant to dilute the symbiotic relations between legal and literary texts.

12. Jacques Derrida, *Of Hospitality* (Stanford: Stanford University Press, 2000), 45; Ulrich Beck and Edgar Grande, *Das kosmopolitische Europa: Gesellschaft und Politik in der zweiten Moderne* (Frankfurt am Main: Suhrkamp, 2004); Martha Craven Nussbaum, *For Love of Country?* (Boston: Beacon Press, 2002); Appiah, *Cosmopolitanism*.

13. David Hollinger, *Postethnic America: Beyond Multiculturalism* (New York: Basic Books, 1995); Craig Calhoun, "The Class Consciousness of Frequent Travelers: Towards a Critique of Actually Existing Cosmopolitanism," in Vertovec and Cohen, *Conceiving Cosmopolitanism*, 86–109; Timothy Brennan, *At Home in the World: Cosmopolitanism Now* (Cambridge: Harvard University Press, 1997).

14. Ulrich Beck, *Der kosmopolitische Blick, oder, Krieg ist Frieden* (Frankfurt am Main: Suhrkamp, 2004), 7–20.

15. Benhabib, *The Rights of Others*, 207–16.

16. Breckenridge et al., *Cosmopolitanism*.

17. Robert Fine and Robin Cohen, "Four Cosmopolitan Moments"; Vertovec and Cohen, *Conceiving Cosmopolitanism*, 137.

18. Ibid. I am thankful to Patrice Nganang for the following insight in his editorial comments, which further illustrates the problem in Robin and Cohen's selective enumeration of cosmopolitanism: "[T]here is a distinction in Arendt's writing between

three moments: first the Kantian cosmopolitanism, which is expressed in a lifelong admiration for the American Revolution, albeit its effective acceptance of slavery; second, her presentation of a world of rights to have rights, and third, a return of the repressed first moment during her confrontation with the Civil Rights movement in the US. All three, I would say are arguments with cosmopolitanism."

19. Nussbaum, *For Love of Country*, 5.

20. Appiah, *Cosmopolitanism*, 22.

21. In the past five years, Har Dayal has garnered attention of several scholars, evidenced by publications in the discipline of History, more specifically the sub-branch of History of Ideas. See Kris Manjapra, "The Illusions of Encounter: Muslim 'Minds' and Hindu Revolutionaries in First World War Germany and After," *Journal of Global History* 1, no. 3 (Nov. 2006): 363–82; Shruti Kapila, "Self, Spencer and Swaraj: Nationalist Thought and Critiques of Liberalism, 1890–1920," *Modern Intellectual History* 4, no. 1 (April 2007): 109–27; Harald Fischer-Tiné, "Indian Nationalism and the 'World Forces': Transnational and Diasporic Dimensions of the Indian Freedom Movement on the Eve of the First World War," *Journal of Global History* 2, no. 3 (Nov. 2007): 325–44. These three scholars mention *Forty Four Months* briefly, mostly to reference Har Dayal's experiences in Germany and Turkey, rather than in a theoretical framework of nationalism/cosmopolitanism as attempted in the current essay. For in-depth discussions of German-(British) Indian diplomatic relations and military histories see Nirode K. Barooah, *India and the Official Germany, 1886–1914* (Frankfurt am Main: Peter Lang, 1977). Brown and Dharmavir also discuss the conspiracy in their biographies of Har Dayal. A detailed account of the Indian independence movement conducted outside of India can be found in Visvamitra Upadhyaya, *Videson mein Bharatiya Krantikari Andolana* (New Delhi: Pragatishila Jana Prakashana, 1986).

22. In an interview given to the major Indian English daily *The Hindu* in 2005, the noted literary and cultural critic Homi K. Bhabha called Har Dayal (along with Lala Lajpat Rai and Madame Bhikaji Cama) "interesting precursors to the global discourse." See Sacchindananda Mohanty, "Face to Face: Towards a Global Citizenship. *The Hindu*," http://www.hinduonnet.com/lr/2005/07/03/stories/2005070300020100.htm.

23. Har Dayal, *Forty Four Months in Germany and Turkey. February 1915 to October 1918: A Record of Personal Impressions* (London: P. S. King and Son, 1920), 102–3.

24. R. Radhakrishnan, *Theory in an Uneven World* (Oxford: Blackwell, 2003), 102.

25. Brown and Dharmavir could not be more different in their treatments of the ideological, political, and intellectual shifts that Har Dayal went through during his lifetime. A comparative study of these two biographies provides a rich set of materials worthy of a separate investigation. Unfortunately, to adhere to the permissible word-limit this note had to be massively truncated.

Acting Cannibal

Intersecting Strategies, Conflicting Interests, and the Ambiguities of Cultural Resistance in Iringa, German East Africa

Eva Bischoff

On 17 August 1909 Karl Axenfeld, a representative of the *Berliner Missionsgesellschaft*, addressed Max Berner at the *Reichskolonialamt* (German Colonial Office) to complain about the execution of a group of African men and women in the German colony *Deutsch-Ostafrika* (German East Africa). He wrote:

> A few months ago, the *Deutsche Kolonialblatt* published a detailed report on a case of cannibalism in Ubena (district Iringa) and noted that the cannibals, who all had confessed to the crime, had been sentenced to death and executed. I was concerned about this incident because to my knowledge man-eating does not occur among the Bena. [. . .] Alas, the death sentence already has been pronounced by a European administration on the basis of a mistake in law.[1]

About eight months earlier, on 28 December 1908, ten indigenous persons had been put to trial. They were found guilty not only of murdering a number of women, men, and children but also of consuming the flesh of their victims. Captain Ernst Nigmann, who had conducted the trial and served as the official representative of the German colonial administration at the military outpost in Iringa, was convinced that the accused were members of a cannibalistic cult that had to be destroyed before it could spread any further. For the same reason, he sentenced another six people to death for allegedly practicing cannibalism on 28 February and 29 March 1909. As Axenfeld's letter demonstrates above, the local missionary society and its members criticized Nigmann's decision. The *Missionsgesellschaft* filed a complaint, arguing that Nigmann had been deliberately misled by the African chiefs and that he had been instrumentalized in their prosecution of witchcraft, thus encouraging "uncivilized" superstitions instead of eradicating them. An investigation ensued.

It is my aim to locate possible motivations and probable political tactics of the African men and women involved in the Iringa trials. I argue that denouncing members of their own community as cannibals to the German officials, an act that might be considered a form of collaboration, was instead an effort to maintain outlawed cultural practices as well as political control within the indigenous community itself. As such, it can be seen as an act of cultural and social resistance. My case study engages with recent scholarship on the role of African dignitaries and clerks as mediators, collaborators, and facilitators of German colonial rule[2] and demonstrates that in German East Africa colonial rule was established within a network of indigenous policies and strategies.

My analysis maps the lines of conflict between various German colonial actors, in particular the *Berliner Missionsgesellschaft* and the local representative of the colonial government, Ernst Nigmann, by drawing on archival records of both the Colonial Office and the missionary society. This historical material gives insight into the intersecting strategies, conflicting interests, and policies pursued by the various social actors in colonial German East Africa at the beginning of the twentieth century. Although no testimony or other document written by those Africans who were involved in the events has survived, a careful *reading against the grain* of the official records and the missionary society's documents discloses competing interpretations of the events. This, in turn, allows us to glimpse into the cracks and folds of German colonial rule, in which the room for movement and maneuver available to African dignitaries unfolded. These patterns of agency that are pursued by the colonized will be outlined in the second part of this essay, followed by concluding remarks on indigenous agency, as exemplified here by the Iringa trials. In this way, my analysis connects to David Kim's recently published deliberations on the role *Askari* translators played in the proceedings.[3] In contrast to Kim, however, I will focus on social practices instead of problems of translation and will interpret the soldiers' role within a larger network of intersecting agendas and intentions pursued by Europeans and Africans alike.

Before delving into the Iringa cases more deeply, it is important to note that anxieties about cannibals were not restricted to the European imaginary. For instance, cannibalism was rumored among African communities to be the motivation behind the transatlantic slave trade. Colonial administrators, missionaries, and priests were often suspected of partaking of human flesh or blood, especially in light of the rituals of the Catholic Mass. Other allegations were directed toward physicians and medical personnel, whose frequent inter-

est in blood samples seemed dubious to the African population who was subjected to medical exams and treatments.[4] Moreover, the production of European scientific knowledge about cannibalism relied heavily on statements of
African mercenaries, bearers, and servants concerning the alleged cannibalistic
practices of ethnic groups that an expedition might encounter en route. As a
consequence, European knowledge about the "savage cannibal" must be regarded neither solely as European phantasm nor as mere African superstitious
imagination, but as the result of conflicting strategies and mutual interactions
between Africans and Europeans.[5]

German East Africa: Who Is the Shepherd of African Souls?

In 1908, the year of the first of the Iringa trials, German East Africa was recu-
perating from the violent suppression of the Maji-Maji Rebellion, which en-
tailed a twofold legacy of devastation and political change. Between 1905 and
1907, German troops had killed approximately 75,000 people and systematically destroyed the agrarian basis of the population's livelihood by burning
crops and fields alike. As a result, an even greater number of Africans died of
starvation or from one of the many epidemic diseases that broke out. About 25
percent of all African women living on the territory of the German colony at
the time of the uprising became permanently sterile as a long-term consequence of the pervasive hunger and trauma induced by the war.[6] The use of
extreme violence during the Maji-Maji War was no exception, but rather a
common practice to crush anti-colonial insurgencies. Among these were the
uprisings of the Hehe (1891–98), whose major settlements were located in the
Iringa district.[7]

Simultaneously, the Maji-Maji War accelerated an already ongoing
change in colonial policy in general and in German East Africa in particular,
connected to the policy adopted by Bernhard Dernburg, State Secretary and
head of the newly created Imperial Colonial Office.[8] He and his followers no
longer wanted to rule by superior force (*"Zerstörungsmittel"*), but by methods
of sustainable government (*"Erhaltungsmittel"*).[9] Or, to put it in Foucauldian
terms, instead of ruling by the sword, German colonial officials aimed to control, regulate, and optimize the lives of the indigenous population of its colonies: They wanted to govern by means of biopower.

Part of this new "colonial governmentality"[10] was to acknowledge indigenous systems of values or beliefs. As a consequence, juridical decisions concerning Africans had to suit both German legal standards and African tradi-

tions.[11] The aim was to maximize the exploitation of the African workforce and natural resources with a minimum of (military) intervention. The colonial administration was understood as the "good shepherd" of a colonial society, which was hierarchically structured along the fault lines of race, class, and gender.[12]

However, the colonial administration's ambition to exercise a benevolent "pastoral power," to use another Foucauldian term,[13] over colonial subjects, conceptualized as the wards of the state, challenged a more traditional and already established claim on Africans' souls: namely, that of the missionary. This strained the already tense relationship between Christian missionary societies, the Imperial Colonial Office, and the colonial administrations and its representatives.[14] There were multiple reasons for these conflicts, which were waged despite the fact that Christian ethics and values supported the European colonial project on a general, ideological level.[15]

With regard to the Iringa cases, there are two general points of contestation between the colonial administration and the missionary societies that must be taken into account: first, the use of African languages in missionary schools, and second, the tolerance of Islam as a monotheistic religion by the colony's administration. Designed as a calculated concession to the African elites to foster future cooperation, the latter undermined the missionaries' claim to represent the "superior" belief system. Meanwhile, the use of African languages in school was opposed by the German colonial administration, although it was an important didactic tool for the missionaries and significantly eased Christianization.[16]

The documents of the Hehe synod, located in the Iringa district, demonstrate that the political difficulties posed to its work in German East Africa in general were reflected in conflicts at a local level. According to the synod's report to the society's central committee in Berlin, 1909, the year of the second and third Iringa trials, was a year of conflict between the mission and the colonial administration. According to the missionaries, the situation was aggravated by the conduct of a particular colonial civil servant in Iringa itself. This man, the aforementioned Captain Ernst Nigmann, neglected the necessary administrative neutrality in religious matters and undermined the missionaries' efforts by forcing African laborers to work on Sundays and keeping their children from attending school.[17] The report of the synodical meeting in 1908 gave an account of accusations against African or "colored teachers," who supposedly had illegally forced indigenous children to attend the missionary school, as well as disputes about the missionaries' plans to expand their work by founding a settlement in Usangu.[18] Although not all reports explicitly mentioned Nigmann's name, none left any doubt that he was at the center of the missionaries' critique. Thus, the missionaries' complaints against the death sentences he pronounced in the case of the supposed cannibals were part of a long-standing and ongoing conflict between the local representatives of the military and administrative aspect of German colonialism, on the one hand, and the missionary facet, on the other.

However, the missionaries themselves took different positions according to their location in the organization's hierarchy. Whereas the missionaries in German East Africa articulated a harsh critique, the *Komite* [*sic*], the central board of the *Berliner Missionsgesellschaft*, urged them to exercise caution: In case the representative of the colonial administration did not share the organization's religious beliefs, it was the missionaries' task to come to terms with him and establish a "good relationship."[19]

The man who inspired these controversies, Ernst Nigmann, was an ambiguous figure. On the one hand, he had participated in crushing the Hehe Uprisings between 1891 and 1898 and was subsequently promoted to captain in 1902. One year later he became head of the military district of Kilimatinde. From 1903 to 1910, he was administrative and military leader of the district of Iringa, which encompassed the residential area of his former adversaries, the Hehe. He had also fought in the Maji-Maji War.[20] On all levels of his military career, Nigmann was an active proponent of the first phase of German colonialism in East Africa, which had ruled by force and fear. On the other hand, he simultaneously represented the new governmental colonial policy advocated by Dernburg's Colonial Office. During his home leaves, he studied economics, anthropology, and law at the University of Berlin with special emphasis on colonial politics, the study of ethnic groups of German East Africa, and colonial law.[21]

Nigmann described his time as head of the Iringa station as a success. He claimed to have acquired a "detailed knowledge of the land, its inhabitants, [their] customs and traditions," and to have learned not only Kiswahili but also the mother tongue of the Hehe, Kihehe.[22] According to him, the Wahehe needed to be ruled firmly and justly. Governing them was comparable to the education of a "healthy boy," preferring the company of an "uncle," who would teach him how to "swim and row but, if necessary, would also pull his ears," to that of an "aunt, who would give him sweets and merely scold him with mild words."[23]

Nigmann's choice of metaphors, combining the hygienic discourse with the familial sphere, demonstrates that he conceived of his duties as part of the governmental strategies outlined by Dernburg's new colonial administration. He legitimized the colonist's role as a patriarchal-familial one and promoted a biopolitical colonial policy that aimed at the "healthy development" of the indigenous population. In this respect, his views differed considerably from the notions of most officers serving in the German colonial *Schutztruppe*: as members of the Prussian landed elite, these *Junker* perceived their role and that of the indigenous population in reference to traditional categories of serfdom and Prussian militarist discipline. Moreover, their behavior was informed by Orientalist racism.[24]

Witchcraft or Cannibalism? Competing Interpretations

The alleged cannibals were tried in a so-called *schauri*, a legal institution that served as a central tool of colonial rule in German East Africa. Each *schauri* was a performative spectacle: Its course and the spatial arrangement of its participants were orchestrated to demonstrate the power of the German colonial masters.[25] In terms of function, it oscillated between a public hearing of the local chiefs or community leaders and a criminal or private court of law. In criminal cases, such as the trials against the alleged Iringa cannibals, its participants included not only two white assessors but also at least one translator and two respectable representatives (*Jumben*) of the African population living in the district in question. The head of the local administrative district acted as the presiding judge.[26] In places where no such district had been established yet, he was replaced by the head of the local military station, which was the case in Iringa.[27] Simultaneously, the *schauri* was a montage combining elements from German bureaucratic procedure and African diplomatic and legal practices. It was created in the early days of the *situation coloniale* to conduct negotiations between the leaders of military or research expeditions and the local population, and integrated the representatives of the German colonial power into the indigenous diplomatic systems.[28]

From the perspective of the colonizers, the *schauri* was also embedded in the German legal system and an essential tool for colonial jurisdiction, especially in its dealings with the population of African descent under the so-called *Eingeborenenrecht*. This body of law, far from being a homogeneous and codified set of rules, combined indigenous norms with edicts of the German colonial administration and defined what was to be considered as an *Eingeborenen-delikt* (native offense), such as false testimony without being under oath or "certain practices, relying on the natives' superstitions, for example poison tests, manipulations of sorcerers, etc."[29]

As a result, judges presiding over a *schauri* drew upon the German criminal code, the *Reichsstrafgesetzbuch* (RStGB), and exercising this judiciary power was considered part of the civilizing mission.[30] On the other hand, in deference to Dernburg's governmental principles, white judges also had to take into account African customs and traditions.[31] However, the colonizer's knowledge of indigenous legal customs was limited, as traditions were diverse and most often passed on orally.[32] To properly consider African legal practices, white men presiding over a *schauri* often had to rely on the knowledge of indigenous representatives and the linguistic expertise of their translators.[33] This dependence gave African dignitaries and clerks the opportunity to influence the white men's decisions.

As presiding judge in the trials against the alleged cannibals in Iringa, Nigmann relied on the knowledge he had acquired during his anthropological and legal studies at the University of Berlin. This is most visible in his choice of words and line of argument in his report on the *schauri*, which followed the model of a written opinion of the court, summarizing the findings of a German criminal lawsuit. Nigmann formally stated that all of the Africans in question were guilty of murder according to section 211 of the German criminal code (RStGB), as all of them had administered a deadly poison "without exception intentionally, with deliberation" to kill the victims, to consume their flesh or to use their remains in occult practices, a form of sorcery.[34]

According to his findings, most of the cult's members were women who had been trained by a man named "Malukansi," the head of the cannibalistic secret society. To join the cult, a woman had to murder a child and bring its corpse to one of the society's clandestine nocturnal meetings where its raw flesh would be consumed collectively. Often, the women killed their own children, and the ringleader handed back the skulls to be used as a bowl for future poison-making.[35] Thus, Nigmann summarized, the accused displayed an "almost unbelievably low level of ethical concepts [. . .] One can say they stand far below [the level of] an animal."[36] Their deeds were a typical example of so-called native offenses, resulting from superstitious delusions. As such, their cannibalistic crimes were not covered by the German criminal code. Each judge had to find an appropriate form of punishment on his own accord by weighing European legal standards against indigenous traditions. Nigmann found this to be an easy task because cannibalism was "a crime so severe, not only according to European but also to the notions of the natives, that its atonement can be only death."[37] He legitimized the death sentences against the alleged cannibals by referring to both the colonial *mission civilisatrice* and biopolitical considerations: "One can see from the trial how these people gradually developed a taste for human flesh. If this society is not eradicated, it is to be feared that this cannibalism will spread further."[38]

From this point of view, administering the death sentence was a preventive, hygienic measure to protect the African population from future infection by cannibalistic practices. Cannibalism was considered a governmental problem: German colonial rule aimed not only at uplifting their colonial subjects but also at establishing new (European) standards of moral hygiene. The Colonial Office shared Nigmann's assessment: right beside the list of death sentences in Nigmann's report from 28 December 1908 we find a handwritten comment "bravo!" dated 22 January.[39]

There was, however, a competing interpretation of the events and testimonies given during the *schauri* in Iringa in 1908/09. Reconstructed by the local missionary Carl Nauhaus, this version relied on his personal knowledge of the Bena language and interviews he conducted with neighbors of the alleged cannibals and, arguing from his own perception of local politics, emphasized the agency of the African chief.

As Nauhaus stipulated, Nigmann's judgment had been misled by a simple but significant mistranslation: the exact word used by the prosecuting party, the witnesses, and the accused alike, translated to mean cannibalism, referred not to the material intake of nourishment but to a form of spiritual consumption. This particular verb, *vuhavi*, designated the transfer of property or payment, for instance to describe the incorporation of property into the holdings of the local chief or the withholding of salary by an employer. More important, it was used in the contexts of witchcraft.[40]

According to Bena folklore, Nauhaus reported, witches, or *vahavi*, sent their souls to a spiritual journey to inflict pain and suffering among their fellow men. They could "stab or strangle" their victims "internally," causing them to die suddenly or to waste away from a painful disease.[41] Rumors about witchcraft usually arose if people died of unknown diseases or if a series of inexplicable deaths occurred. In pre-colonial time, it had been the chiefs' task to identify the witches and put an end to their misdeeds. To discover the perpetrators, who often traveled unconsciously during their sleep, they relied on the professional help of a sorcerer, who identified the witches by means of a ritualistic probe.[42] The sorcerer's assessment was considered accurate and final, even by the suspects who had no memory of their spiritual cannibalism but were absolutely convinced of their guilt. And this, according to Nauhaus' reconstructions, was exactly what had happened before the official *schauri* in Iringa began.[43] All Bena were aware of the spiritual implication of the notion *vuhavi*. As a result, they often neglected to mention it but spoke instead simply of cannibalism, which in this context never meant anthropophagy but witchcraft.[44]

Those who truly understood Bena language and culture, Nauhaus argued, were aware of this. Nigmann, however, assumed that a form of corporeal cannibalism had occurred, displaying a severe lack of knowledge of the traditions and customs of the population living in his district. Even worse, because of his ignorance, he had been manipulated by the indigenous population. Relying on his linguistic skills and the interviews he had conducted, Nauhaus theorized that the local chief, in cooperation with the witch-hunting sorcerer, had staged the trials. With the transfer of penal jurisdiction to the German colonial administration, the chief faced a situation in which he would be unable to fulfill his protective role and dreaded the loss of power and influence resulting from this insufficiency. To uphold his authority, he publicly accused those women who were seemingly proven to be witches of cannibalism. Moreover, being "a true expert of the German legal system," knowing that a form of material evidence would be required, he equipped them with bones and skulls which were easy to find amid the devastation left by the Maji-Maji War.[45] Thus, while carefully circumventing the reference to witchcraft that was prohibited by both the missionaries and the colonial administration, the chief, from his point of view, managed to protect the members of his community from further attacks by soul-eating witches, thereby fulfilling his protective duties and securing his position among his people. To achieve this goal, however, he lied, deliberately spread misinformation, and used the German colonial jurisdiction for his own purposes.

Nauhaus' report contained two points of critique, both directed against Nigmann. First, in his ignorance of local African traditions, Nigmann had misjudged the charges before him. Second, Nigmann's lack of knowledge made him vulnerable to indigenous influence and manipulation. As a consequence, he issued unjustified death sentences, unwittingly supported superstitious beliefs, and undermined the civilizing mission of German colonialism. As we have seen above, Nauhaus' superiors and fellow missionaries did not always act in unison. With regard to Nigmann's failure to shoulder the white man's burden, however, they all agreed. In his letter to the Colonial Office, Karl Axenfeld, wrote: "The most regretful part of this whole affair is not, however, that [. . .] 16 innocents have been put to death, but that the German legal system has passed a sentence which affirmed the people's disastrous belief in witchcraft and its opinion that the supposed witches have to be killed by law."[46]

Movement and Maneuver: Conclusion

As Andreas Eckert and Albert Wirz have argued, studies on German colonialism have unduly overlooked the agency of the colonized, especially of the local elites and intermediaries, in the *situation coloniale*.[47] However, it is difficult to determine whether or not the actions of the marginalized demonstrate more than the mere shadow of (inter)dependencies in asymmetrical relationships of power, a problem also considered by historians of microhistory.[48] From the perspective of postcolonial theory, which is closely intertwined with Foucauldian concepts of power, the question of how individual subjects, themselves an effect of power relationships and discourses, can in turn actively intervene and shape discursive structures, is an even more complex issue. Homi K. Bhabha, whose analyses of the ambivalences of colonial discourse and relationships of power have been instrumental in this context, emphasizes that "agency requires a grounding, but it does not require a totalization of those grounds; it requires movement and manoeuvre, but it does not require a temporality of continuity or accumulation."[49]

Sadly, no testimonies or other written sources of the Africans involved in the Iringa trials have survived. However, by counterbalancing Nigmann's official reports with missionary documents and the reconstruction of events by the missionary Carl Nauhaus, the complexity of the local political situation unfolds: It was characterized not only by an antagonism between colonizers and colonized but also by a long-standing conflict between different factions of the German colonial project, namely, the *Berliner Missionsgesellschaft* and the military head of the colonial administration in Iringa, Captain Ernst Nigmann.

Moreover, in reviewing the missionary's reconstruction of events, the motivations and interests of the African dignitaries involved in the *schauri* against the alleged cannibal cult in 1908/09 become apparent. Although, regarding the rivalry between Nigmann and the missionaries, we have to take Nauhaus' interpretation with a grain of salt, his reconstruction indicates significant room for movement and maneuver, in other words for *agency,* on the part of the local African leaders. His interpretations are supported by the findings of recent scholarship, which has demonstrated that colonial subjects manipulated and exploited the European colonial system to their own ends. In Africa, for example, the accusation of cannibalism was often employed as a "political weapon" to oust political rivals;[50] in German Papua New Guinea, enemy clans and tribes strategically directed German expeditions by accusing their adversaries of anthropophagy, effectively waging a war by proxy.[51]

Thus, Carl Nauhaus' considerations indicate a significant influence and room for maneuver that African notables exploited to uphold cultural and spiritual practices as well as their own political status, all of which were threatened by the imposition of German colonial rule and colonial governmentality. Making their fellow men and women act as cannibals in the eyes of the German judiciary can be seen not as collaboration but as an act of cultural and social resistance.

NOTES

1. "Brief Karl Axenfeld an [Max] Berner," 17 August 1909, BArch R 1001/827, 18–19, here 18 and 19. All translations from German sources are mine (if not indicated otherwise). I would like to thank Nicole Kvale, Heideking-Fellow at the Anglo-American Department of the School of History at the University of Cologne in 2009/10, for kindly reading through and commenting on a first draft of this essay, which derived from my doctoral thesis, published as *Kannibale-Werden: Eine postkoloniale Geschichte deutscher Männlichkeit um 1900* (Bielefeld: transcript, 2011).

2. Albert Wirz, "Einleitung: Körper, Raum und Zeit der Herrschaft," in *Alles unter Kontrolle: Disziplinierungsprozesse im kolonialen Tanzania (1850–1960)*, ed. Albert Wirz et al. (Cologne: Rüdiger Köppe, 2003), 5–34; Andreas Eckert, "Konflikte, Netzwerke, Interaktionen. Kolonialismus in Afrika: Zum Gedenken von Ulrich Haarmann (1942–1999)," *Neue Politische Literatur* 44, no. 3 (1999): 446–80, and Andreas Eckert, *Herrschen und Verwalten: Afrikanische Bürokraten, staatliche Ordnung und Politik in Tanzania, 1920–1970* (Munich: Oldenbourg, 2007).

3. David Kim, "The Scandals of Translation: Cannibalism and the Limits of Colonial Authority in the Trial of Iringa, December 1908," *German Studies Review* 34, no. 1 (2011): 130–31.

4. Heike Behrend, "Kannibalischer Terror," in *Africa Screams: Das Böse in Kino, Kunst und Kult*, ed. Tobias Wendl (Wuppertal: Peter Hammer, 2004), 168–70; Richard C. King, "The (Mis)uses of Cannibalism in Contemporary Cultural Critique," *Diacritics* 30, no. 1 (2000): 110–12.

5. Behrend, "Kannibalischer Terror," 165.

6. Horst Gründer, *Geschichte der deutschen Kolonien* (Paderborn: Schöningh, 2004), 157–64; John Iliffe, *A Modern History of Tanganyika* (Cambridge: Cambridge University Press, 1979), 199–202; Jigal Beez, *Geschosse zu Wassertropfen: Sozioreligiöse Aspekte des Maji-Maji-Krieges in Deutsch-Ostafrika (1905–1907)* (Cologne: Rüdiger Köppe, 2003), 102–7.

7. Michael Pesek, *Koloniale Herrschaft in Deutsch-Ostafrika: Expeditionen, Militär und Verwaltung seit 1880* (Frankfurt: Campus, 2005), 191–204; Thomas Morlang, "'Die Wahehe haben ihre Vernichtung gewollt.' Der Krieg der 'Kaiserlichen Schutztruppe' gegen die Hehe in Deutsch-Ostafrika (1890–1898)," in *Kolonialkriege: Militärische Gewalt im Zeichen des Imperialismus*, ed. Thoralf Klein et al. (Hamburg: Hamburger Edition, 2006), 80–108.

8. Detlef Bald, *Deutsch-Ostafrika, 1900–1914: Eine Studie über Verwaltung, In-*

teressengruppen und wirtschaftliche Erschließung (Munich: Weltforum, 1970), 75–105; Pesek, *Koloniale Herrschaft*, 202–3.

9. Bernhard Dernburg, *Zielpunkte des Deutschen Kolonialwesens: Zwei Vorträge* (Berlin: Mittler & Sohn, 1907), 9.

10. David Scott, "Colonial Governmentality," in *Anthropologies of Modernity: Foucault, Governmentality, and Life Politics*, ed. Jonathan X. Inda (Oxford: Blackwell, 2005), 25.

11. Dernburg, *Zielpunkte*, 8.

12. Michel Foucault, *Geschichte der Gouvernementalität I: Sicherheit, Territorium, Bevölkerung: Vorlesung am Collège de France (1977–1978)*, trans. Claudia Brede-Konersmann and Jürgen Schröder (Frankfurt: Suhrkamp, 2004), 185–93.

13. Foucault, *Geschichte der Gouvernementalität I*, 187–91, 192–93.

14. Michael Weidert, "Zur Geneaologie missionarischer Macht. Das Beispiel der katholischen Kolonialmission in Deutsch-Ostafrika," in *Ethnizität und Geschlecht: Postkoloniale Verhandlungen in Geschichte, Kunst und Medien*, ed. Graduiertenkolleg Identität und Differenz (Cologne: Böhlau, 2005), 39–40; Hans-Werner Gensichen, "Mission und Kolonialismus: Überlegungen zur Morphologie einer Beziehung," *Zeitschrift für Missionswissenschaft und Religionswissenschaft* 77 (1993): 25–34; Jürgen Becher, "Die deutsche evangelische Mission. Eine Erziehungs- und Disziplinierungsinstanz in Deutsch-Ostafrika," in *Alles unter Kontrolle: Disziplinierungsprozesse im kolonialen Tanzania (1850–1960)*, ed. Albert Wirz et al. (Cologne: Rüdiger Köppe, 2003), 141–69.

15. Horst Gründer, "Mission und Kolonialismus—Historische Beziehungen und strukturelle Zusammenhänge," in *Christliche Heilsbotschaft und weltliche Macht: Studien zum Verhältnis von Mission und Kolonialismus. Gesammelte Aufsätze von Horst Gründer*, ed. Franz-Joseph Post et al. (Münster: Lit, 2004), 9–10; Gerhard Besier, "Mission und Kolonialismus im Preußen der Wilhelminischen Ära," *Kirchliche Zeitgeschichte* 5, no. 2 (1992): 249–53; Wolfgang Reinhard, "Christliche Mission und Dialektik des Kolonialismus," *Historisches Jahrbuch* 109 (1989): 358.

16. Horst Gründer, *Christliche Mission und deutscher Imperialismus: Eine politische Geschichte ihrer Beziehungen während der deutschen Kolonialzeit (1884–1914). Unter besonderer Berücksichtigung Afrikas und Chinas* (Paderborn: Schöningh, 1982), 96–97.

17. "Niederschrift der auf Kidugala vom 17.-25. Oktober [1909] tagenden Synode," Archiv des Berliner Missionswerkes im ELAB, bmw-1/6501, 32–60, here 47, 48–50.

18. "Niederschrift der Tagung der Synode (6.-13. September 1908) auf Lupembe mit Anlagen," Archiv des Berliner Missionswerkes im ELAB, bmw-1/6500, 94–128, here 118–19, 123, 124.

19. "Schreiben des Komite der Berliner Missionsgesellschaft, an die Herren Superintendenten und Missionare der Hehe-Synode," 18 January 1910, Archiv des Berliner Missionswerkes im ELAB, bmw-1/6501, 72–88, here 72–73.

20. Ernst Nigmann, *Geschichte der kaiserlichen Schutztruppe für Deutsch-Ostafrika* (Berlin: Mittler & Sohn, 1911), 31–59, 102–7.

21. He continued his studies after transferring to the military headquarters in Berlin during 1913 and 1914, and received his doctorate after the end of the First World War

in 1919. See his study records for the years 1904, 1907, 1910, 1913, 1914, and 1919 (GStAPK, VI. HA Nl Nigmann/24, 29, 31, 32, 37–38, 54) and the invitation to the public defense of his doctoral thesis on 30 October 1919 (GStAPK, VI. HA Nl Nigmann/55).

22. "Lebenslauf des Oberstleutnants Nigmann," 5 May 1918, GStAPK, VI. HA Nl Nigmann/48, 2.

23. Ernst Nigmann, *Die Wahehe: Ihre Geschichte, Kult-, Rechts-, Kriegs- und Jagd-Gebräuche* (Berlin: Mittler & Sohn, 1908), 5. The term "Tante" (aunt) was used to refer to feminized male homosexuals during Imperial and Weimar Germany (Stefan Micheler, *Selbstbilder und Fremdbilder der "Anderen:" Männer begehrende Männer in der Weimarer Republik und der NS-Zeit* (Constance: UVK, 2005), 181–94). Its corrupted form "Tunte" is still used in Germany today for the same purpose. Nigmann's choice of words demonstrates how debates on German colonialism drew on sexual and gender norms (Susanne Zantop, *Colonial Fantasies: Conquest, Family, and Nation in Precolonial Germany, 1770–1870* (Durham: Duke University Press, 1997), 99–101).

24. Pesek, *Koloniale Herrschaft*, 194.

25. Pesek, *Koloniale Herrschaft*, 277, 279–80.

26. Johannes Gerstmeyer, "Eingeborenenrecht," in *Deutsches Kolonial-Lexikon.* 3 Vols., ed. Heinrich Schnee (Leipzig: Quelle & Meyer, 1920), Vol. 1: 510; Hans-Jörg Fischer, *Die deutschen Kolonien: Die koloniale Rechtsordnung und ihre Entwicklung nach dem Ersten Weltkrieg* (Berlin: Duncker und Humblot, 2001), 95–98, 167–70.

27. Until 1910, this also included the stations of Mahenge and Kilimatinde (Fischer, *Die deutschen Kolonien*, 123).

28. Pesek, *Koloniale Herrschaft*, 277–83. Hence, the Iringa trials were not, as Kim assumes, a military tribunal (Kim, "Scandals of Translation," 129). As a *schauri*, the trial relied not only on the translators but also on the collaboration and the knowledge of local dignitaries and community leaders, who in turn were able to exert their power and pursue individual or communal interests.

29. Gerstmeyer, "Eingeborenenrecht," 508–9, 511 (quote). See also Fischer, *Die deutschen Kolonien*, 66–73, 95–98. The German colonial administration applied a one-drop rule to determine the status of the African population. Parsi, subjects of the Japanese Emperor, and Christians from Goa or Syria, however, were exempted from the "native law" (Fatima El-Tayeb, *Schwarze Deutsche: Der Diskurs um 'Rasse' und nationale Identität 1890–1933* (Frankfurt: Campus, 2001), 131–39).

30. Gerstmeyer, "Eingeborenenrecht," 511.

31. Straehler, "Strafrecht," in *Deutsches Kolonial-Lexikon.* 3 Vols., ed. Heinrich Schnee (Leipzig: Quelle & Meyer, 1920), Vol. 3: 418.

32. On 3 May 1907, the German *Reichstag* gave an order to systematically record and codify the traditional African legal codes. The results of the survey, however, were not published until 1919 (Erich Schultz-Ewerth and Leonhard Adam, *Das Eingeborenenrecht: Sitten und Gewohnheitsrechte der Eingeborenen der ehemaligen deutschen Kolonien in Afrika und in der Südsee. Vol. 1: Ostafrika* (Stuttgart: Strecker & Schröder, 1929)).

33. Kim, "Scandals of Translation," 130–31.

34. "Öffentliches Schauri: In der Strafsache gegen das Mbena=Weib Mgalla u.

Sendepera wegen Mordes, Beihülfe [*sic*] zum Morde und Kannibalismus," 28 December 1908, BArch R 1001/827, 5–15, here 14.

35. Ibid., 13–14.

36. Ibid., 14.

37. Ibid.

38. Ibid.

39. Ibid., 12.

40. "Brief von Missionar Nauhaus-Kidugula an Missionsinspektor Lic. Axenfeld [Auszüge]," 2 July 1909, BArch, R 1001/827, 20–26, here 21–22.

41. Ibid., 20. Nauhaus' spelling of the term is heterogeneous: he also uses *vuhavi* (ibid., 22, 25).

42. Ibid., 23, 26.

43. Ibid., 22–25.

44. Ibid., 22.

45. Ibid., 26.

46. "Brief Karl Axenfeld an [Max] Berner," 17 August 1909, BArch R 1001/827, 18–19, here 19. This is a deliberate pique against Nigmann, which Kim misses in his analysis of the Iringa trials as he does not question the administration's conflation of cannibalism and witchcraft (Kim, "Scandals of Translation," 134).

47. Eckert, "Konflikte, Netzwerke, Interaktionen," 448; Wirz, "Einleitung," 10–19; Eckert, *Herrschen und Verwalten*, 19–22.

48. Alf Lüdtke, "Geschichte und Eigensinn," in *Alltagskultur, Subjektivität und Geschichte: Zur Theorie und Praxis von Alltagsgeschichte*, ed. Berliner Geschichtswerkstatt (Münster: Westfälisches Dampfboot, 1994), 141.

49. Homi K. Bhabha, *The Location of Culture* (London: Routledge, 2001), 185.

50. Carol P. MacCormack, "Human Leopards and Crocodils. Political Meanings of Categorical Anomalies," in *The Ethnography of Cannibalism*, ed. Paula Brown et al. (Washington, DC: Society for Psychological Anthropology, 1983), 51–52.

51. Bernd Leicht, "Kannibalen in Deutsch-Neuguinea: Der 'Andere' im kolonialzeitlichen Diskurs" (PhD diss., Universität Heidelberg, 2000), 74–75, 82.

The "Truppenspieler Show"

Herero Masculinity and the German Colonial Military Aesthetic

Molly McCullers

Introduction

Following the defeat of German troops in South West Africa (SWA, Namibia since 1990) by South Africa in 1915, rumors emerged of African men trained as German soldiers. These Herero men paraded in German uniforms and assumed the names and ranks of prominent German soldiers and officials in the territory.[1] South African administrators derisively referred to them as *Truppenspieler*, play soldiers. This derogatory term allowed Europeans to cognitively prevent Africans from transgressing well-established and long-cherished boundaries of white manhood. Hereros, in contrast, claimed such military masculinity by referring to themselves as *Otruppa*, appropriating the German *Truppen* and/or English *troops*. This essay examines how different Herero experiences of German colonialism—dispossession, genocide, and German military service—precipitated and influenced generational struggles to re-negotiate Herero masculinity. Further, this chapter explores the integral role of these debates to the broader reconstruction of Herero society in the aftermath of German rule.

The 1904 Herero genocide and the *Truppenspieler*, or *Otruppa*, have been popular topics in Namibianist scholarship.[2] This scholarship is focused in two main directions: German military history and Herero nationalism. Analyses of the German colonial military, the *Schutztruppe*, generally examine the culmination of German colonialism and ideals of military manliness into a particular culture of masculinity that condoned and encouraged violence.[3] This chapter goes further, exploring how exposure to German military masculinity and "Male Fantasies" enacted through atrocities in the proverbial colonial laboratory impacted colonized peoples.

Studies attentive to Herero history illuminate the *Otruppa*'s role in the re-coalescing of Herero society in the aftermath of genocide and the formulation of Herero nationalism and anti-colonial resistance.[4] While this scholarship is largely, as historian Jan-Bart Gewald admits, "unashamedly a history of the male elite," it neglects questions of gender identity and masculinity, and their relation to nationalist resistance.[5] A nationalist focus tends to paper-over internal generational power struggles among Herero men following the genocide rather than illustrating how nationalism and masculinity mutually constituted one another. *Otruppa* attempts to reconfigure Herero masculinity were central to processes of Herero societal regeneration.[6] Consequently, Herero nationalism was strongly inflected by "masculinized memory, masculinized humiliation, and masculinized hope."[7]

The troops were integral to the creation of a strong Herero national identity, but this process and identity were tightly bound to individual men's attempts to establish their place in society by recovering their manhood. Herero youths actively refashioned society and shaped the future by retooling German colonial experiences. The performative nature of the troops' parades, uniforms, insignia, and titles staked very public claims for a newly modified Herero masculine identity. Youths drew on German military aesthetics and manliness to rival older men whose power resided in precolonial notions of Herero masculinity based on patriarchy and patronage. The *Otruppa* provided younger Herero men an avenue to cope with the emasculating experiences of German colonialism and to reclaim and renovate Herero manhood in its wake. Reexamining the *Otruppa* by attending to masculinity reveals highly gendered generational struggles for social recuperation among Herero men.

Masculinities are culturally and historically specific, constantly rearticulated by forces of race, class, and generation. When examined in colonial contexts, dominant concepts, such as R. W. Connell's influential "hegemonic masculinity," in which one form of masculinity becomes socially and politically dominant, have come under fire.[8] In colonial encounters, institutional power rarely converged with the dominant culture. This incongruence often led to showdowns between indigenous and colonialist men and prevented the emergence of a masculinity combining colonial institutions with dominant indigenous culture. In South West Africa, German masculinity never usurped, but indelibly marked, Herero ideas of manhood, which were in turn entangled with Herero nationalism and anti-colonial resistance. Through the *Otruppa*, Herero youths devised an alternate masculinity that blended German military aesthetics with aspects of pre-German Herero manhood. The troops allowed youths to contest Herero elders' power and European colonialism, cope with genocide, and claim a place in a swiftly changing world. Exploring *Otruppa* masculinity provides further insight into the lasting effects of German colonialism and the dynamics of Herero society in the early twentieth century.

Imperial German Masculinities and Colonial Endeavors

Wilhelmine German society considered a regimented military establishment essential to recovering national pride and manliness in the wake of past defeats.[9] For middle-class youths, the military allowed them to partake in the nation. Sinha describes imperial militaries as a "realm into which they were welcomed, and where [the] authoritative fantasies of masculinity cultivated, [were] of the nation."[10] Military power and colonial expansion were vital to German national cohesion.

German boys were exposed to a heroic "Cult of Death for the Fatherland" from an early age through adventure books and popular culture in which "war was presented to them over and over again as the true test of manliness."[11] Religious ceremonies, funerals, processions, and other commemorations of national heroes, such as the Iron Cross, reinforced this cult of death. By portraying military glory as the path to true manhood, this heroic culture supported the national project of imperial expansion.[12] Bismarck's initial reluctance for colonial expansion created tension between a highly militarized state and few opportunities to gloriously defend it.

Consequently, youths began to form fraternal *Männerbünde*. Fraternities and/or secret societies had long been a part of central European culture. For German military youths, these groups "centered around an ostensibly virile masculinity [with] a near magical power to restore order and to reinvigorate society" and continued their military socialization.[13] They fostered aspirations of martial glory and manhood promised to members as boys. German colonial expansion in South West Africa in 1884 provided *Schutztruppe* members an opportunity to defend and possibly die for Germany, proving their manhood as worthy sons of the fatherland.

The *Schutztruppe* shared a masculine ideology derived from particular historical, political, and socio-economic circumstances. When combined with the freedom from moral sanctions and restraint so noted in the colonies, this ideology resulted in atrocity. Many *Schutztruppe* members in South West Africa later went on to join the notorious *Freikorps* and later still Hitler's SS.[14] Klaus Theweleit's controversial analysis of *Freikorps*' writings is highly revealing about their masculine culture and illuminates *Schutztruppe* history. A pillar of this masculinity was a commitment to eliminate anyone construed as falling into the category of dangerous femininity that threatened to consume or defile their manhood and/or the fatherland: loose women, communists, Jews, Gypsies, homosexuals, and indigenous peoples, especially Africans.[15] This misogynistic masculinity, encompassing racism and xenophobia, was essential to the fraternal cohesion supporting the *Schutztruppe* masculinity unleashed in the deserts of South West Africa. It encouraged unspeakable violence in the name of the trinity of fatherland, heroism, and manhood.

Encountering Herero Men

German soldiers expected a tropical paradise of women in South West Africa, but only an inhospitable and sparsely populated desert greeted them.[16] Herero pastoralists occupied the relatively well-watered highlands in central South West Africa. Although politically decentralized, five related but competing clans dominated the Herero political landscape in the 1880s.[17] Herero masculinity was then based on a man's control over people and cattle (the main measures of wealth), his clan lineage, and his age.[18] In this patriarchal society, senior men and chiefs were older and possessed large herds and ruled the household, the family, and in the case of chiefs, the clan.

Herero men aspired to be chiefs by establishing strong patronage networks by accumulating large herds of cattle to attract dependent followers. In exchange for protection and a share of the wealth, patrons could demand tribute, military service, and labor from their clients. Chiefs could either be born, that is, inherit considerable herds and therefore influence, or be made, in which youths managed to amass cattle, often by attaching themselves to a powerful patron, and consequently attracting large numbers of followers. Thus, patron-client relationships were often characterized by strife as ambitious youths challenged their patrons' authority.[19] Gaining wealth and prestige through cattle and clients allowed men to extend their connections across clans and further increase their status and influence. Patriarchy and patronage mutually constituted one another in Herero society, as in many African cultures in which "wealth in people" is essential to social standing.[20]

Germany intended South West Africa for a settler colony to relieve a perceived metropolitan population surplus and fulfill popular wishes for an empire.[21] German authorities convinced one of the most powerful Herero clan chiefs, Maherero, to sign a protection treaty in which the Hereros would come under German authority in exchange for aid against Herero enemies to the south. Maherero passed away shortly thereafter, and various claimants vied to inherit the chieftaincy. Maherero's son, Samuel, not a legitimate pretender to his father's wealth or title according to Herero custom, cunningly acquired the German government's support against his rivals by appealing to European notions of primogeniture. The Germans, seeking to divide the Hereros in order to facilitate colonial rule, obligingly named Samuel as Paramount Chief of the Herero in 1891.[22]

The paramountcy was a colonial invention that illegitimately placed Samuel Maherero above other Herero chiefs. By conspiring with the Germans, Samuel exhibited blatant disregard for the Herero customs that governed society, masculinity, and chieftaincy in order to accrue previously unheard-of power. A symbiotic relationship developed between Samuel and the Governor, each using the other to extend their personal power.[23] Samuel sold Herero cattle and lands to the Germans in exchange for alcohol, clothes, and other luxury items to extend his patronage network. He possessed a penchant for the German military aesthetic and was frequently photographed in a German-style uniform and stance. He further arranged his followers into European-style military divisions and frequently sent his men out with the German troops.[24]

The outbreak of a disastrous cattle epidemic left Hereros impoverished, their misfortune exacerbated by Samuel having sold their land to the Germans. Amid crushing poverty and settler rumors of a Herero revolt, a series of misunderstandings sparked a war between the Germans and Hereros in 1904.[25] Despite initial Herero successes, the arrival of General von Trotha and reinforcements caused a reversal of fortunes. Von Trotha, known for his ruthlessness, intentionally forced the Hereros east into the waterless Kalahari Desert to eradicate them. Although some Hereros fled to Bechuanaland, approximately 80 percent of the Herero population perished in the desert as a result of von Trotha's *Vernichtungsbefehl*, or extermination order.[26]

The combination of Samuel's actions, the bovine epidemic, and a war concluding in genocide led to a collective emasculation of Herero men who lost their land, their livestock and followers, and consequently their authority. Gewald argues that following these catastrophes, established chiefs "anxious to maintain their position . . . were forced to change the manner in which they maintained power, and new elites, capable of making use of the changed circumstances, came to the fore."[27]

Generational Frictions and *Otruppa* Masculinity

Survivors' experiences of the genocide and its aftermath differed along gendered and generational lines. Generally, women were interned in concentration camps, adult men were killed when captured, and youths were impressed into the German army as *Truppenbambusen*, valets and batmen.[28] The genocide destroyed resources upholding Herero patriarchal masculinity, putting all Herero men on equal footing. Herero elders were emasculated by the loss of cattle, land, and followers that sustained their prior dominance. For youths exposed to *Schutztruppe* ideals of manliness and military aesthetics as *Truppenbambusen*, new opportunities opened to redefine the parameters of masculinity.

Following the genocide, Hereros latched onto dominant European institutions in order to rebuild their world, particularly Christianity and the military, but made them distinctly Herero.[29] Hereros in the concentration camps, mainly women, children, and the elderly, were exposed to missionaries and converted in large numbers. Young men and boys who grew up as *Truppenbambusen* became soldiers. These European institutions were accompanied by a resurgence of older Herero practices, such as tooth extraction and circumcision.[30] These customs and institutions marked people as Herero, serving as ethnic boundary markers in the absence of land and cattle and promoted societal recovery.[31] Young men clung to the military structure to face rapidly changing circumstances and capitalize on new opportunities created amid such a moment of chaos. The *Otruppa* became a highly politicized and powerful organization as they vied with elders to control the direction of Herero society's reinvigoration. Redefining Herero masculinity became the language of conflict.

From Truppenbambusen to Otruppa

African servants in German households were commonly referred to as *Bambusen* in South West Africa. The word was extended to youths involved with the German military. Herero men had been part of the colonial military since the dawn of German occupation. Following the war, which ended in 1908, and the press-ganging of youths into service, Gewald estimates that there were approximately 1,000 *Truppenbambusen*.[32] Their experiences varied from abuse to intensely personal, sometimes sexual, relationships with German soldiers.[33] The *Otruppa* formed among *Truppenbambusen* around 1908 and was characterized by members wearing German-style military uniforms, parading, and taking on such names as "His Excellency Governor von Diemeling" or "Lieutenant Colonel von Estorff."[34] Although their precise origins are unclear, the *Otruppa* were undoubtedly influenced by experiences as *Truppenbambusen*.

When South African authorities gained control of South West Africa in 1915, they immediately learned of the *Otruppa* and speculated on their beginnings. One South African theory was that "the troops were the outcome of an original experiment of the Germans," or "a troop of Herero soldiers raised by the Germans."[35] While unsubstantiated, these theories illuminate the exercise and experience of German colonial power. Scholars argue that "colonial rule [focused on] the physical being of the colonized . . . as a site for the construction of its own authority, legitimacy, and control."[36] *Otruppa* masculinity was highly influenced by facets of military culture such as ranks, uniforms, drilling, and the more intangible aspects of homosociality, loyalty, and mutual aid. Through their military service, youths transformed themselves into men. Troop membership came to replace bygone initiation ceremonies controlled by elders that made boys into men. Consequently elders' masculinity came into conflict with that of the *Otruppa*. The chaos following the genocide provided young men opportunities to claim manhood independently of their elders. The German military aesthetic offered them a way of publically signifying that manhood.

The *Otruppa* performed functions similar to veterans' associations in which former soldiers attempt to recapture certain aspects of military masculinity.[37] It recreated the security of military orderliness in a chaotic time through uniforms, ranks, and drilling. The organization provided Herero youths with a social network and mutual aid, essential qualities of military masculinity.[38] Members claimed the troops were "designed to foster good fellowship and amusement," and to assist members financially.[39] This assistance was critical for Herero youths who had become detached from families during the genocide and faced social and financial uncertainty through transitions to a new colonial state, proletarianization, and a cash economy.

Otruppa masculinity challenged Herero elders' and colonial rulers' authority. Assuming German military ranks gave Herero youths an alternative hierarchy in which they could advance outside of elders' or colonial administrators' sanctions.[40] An *Otruppa* Colonel stated in 1927 that semi-autonomous troops existed in "all the larger towns in the territory" and that "membership is confined strictly to adult male Hereros. All are fairly young and none of the older men [are members]."[41] These young men were predominantly Herero, although some men of other ethnicities joined, and troops were common in both urban and rural areas.

While *Otruppa* masculinity conflicted with pre-colonial Herero masculinity, it possessed similarities to the latter. By advancing in rank, Herero men could exert influence over lower-ranking men, mirroring traditional Herero patriarchal patronage relationships. The *Otruppa* translated experiences of German colonialism and military masculinity into a new cultural idiom that demanded their political and cultural recognition as men within the colonial state and Herero society. As one member succinctly explained, "We do it so that we will be men."[42]

Deprived of the means of their former power and threatened by *Otruppa* masculinity, elders quickly cooperated with the South Africans to regain power. Despite elders' frequent resistance to the colonial state, the *Otruppa* viewed them as illegitimate leaders in collusion with the South African administration for personal aggrandizement.[43] For the *Otruppa*, Samuel Maherero, living in South Africa, was the legitimate chief. Although many elders were appointed as chiefs by the South Africans, many also possessed legitimate authority. Hosea Kutako was named Paramount Chief by the South Africans, but Samuel had also appointed him as his deputy. Hardly puppets, elders also took advantage of new colonial opportunities afforded them, using their connections to thwart *Otruppa* activities and reassert their masculinity and authority.[44]

Both elders' and South African administrators' masculinities rested on public respect and authority and were threatened by the *Otruppa*'s alternative hierarchy. Elders and officials used disparaging remarks regarding the troops' manhood in order to downplay fears of *Otruppa* masculinity, which evoked their common German enemy. Even the term *Truppenspieler* renders the organization as childish and utterly unmanly. One South African official described the organization as "really rather pathetic—the collection of funds to bury deceased members and, on such occasions, the childish dressing up and strutting around in imitation of the departed glories of an army whose pomp they admired."[45] Such statements were invariably followed by veiled comments warning of but trivializing the troops' potential danger. The Assistant Native Commissioner cautioned, "A thing that has been promoted in all innocence may develop into something more dangerous if it is not carefully controlled," and concluded, "the government is not very much in favor of it, not that they think the troops do harm."[46]

Herero elders likewise described the *Otruppa* as childish when trying to stamp out the movement using colonial power, stating, "We do not like our grown men to play in this way."[47] Other angles included appeals to tradition and the corruption of the youth. Senior Location Assistant Stephanus Hoveka metaphorically described the troops' ill effects on Herero society by sagely and vividly warning: "One putrefied spot in a piece of meat spoils the whole meat."[48] Elders further complained that *Otruppa* activities were "not according to our tribal customs."[49] Paramount Chief Kutako despaired of the organization as

bad for our young people, it is foolish, they give themselves titles of which they do not know the meaning. We have tried to see what good is to come out of the movement and we can find none. Young men neglect school to attend these drills in hope of getting a military title. . . . [I]t is useless and has a bad influence.[50]

Elders' true reasons for seeking the organization's destruction quickly surfaced. Aaron Mugunda, a member of the Windhoek Location Advisory board, complained, "The organization does not recognize the authority of the advisory boards; they are hostile to the properly constituted authority," and "The young men obey the orders of an officer in preference to the Boardman."[51]

Lines between the troops and the elders were often blurry, ambiguous, and shifting. Not all elders were threatened by the troops; some saw it merely as a social club.[52] Some *Otruppa* members defected to the elders' side as they aged and their political opinions and positions changed, for example, former troop member Boardman Aaron Mugunda. Generally, Herero men were divided along generational lines with youths belonging to the troops and elders cooperating with the South African government.

The *Otruppa*'s alternate masculinity gained them considerable popularity because they called elders' authority into question and, by extension, that of the South African state. The troops' powerful politicization caused Chief Kutako to declare in frustration that the organization was "undermining the nation," equating traditional Herero patriarchal masculinity with the nation.[53] Similarly to European revolutionary movements at the turn of the twentieth century, the *Otruppa* gained popular support by projecting a potent masculinity.[54] The troops generated popular support by offering Hereros seemingly new options for the future by evoking aspects of the past. Comparable European movements often followed wars and "generated abnormal, charismatic forms of authority . . . based on the miraculous aura of a leader who promised a religious type of transcendence . . . in terms of radically accentuated masculinity."[55] For the *Otruppa*, this was the figure of Samuel Maherero and his iconic German military uniform.

While in exile, Samuel Maherero became an *Otruppa* hero. His transformation from the individual largely responsible for Herero oppression, impoverishment, and emasculation under German rule, as well as a genocidal war, into a hero appears contradictory. However, for the *Otruppa*, Samuel symbolized new possibilities for social advancement and Herero masculinity. Though he should not have been a chief according to Herero customs, Samuel had become *the* leader at a very young age by taking advantage of new colonial opportunities. Through his own initiative, Samuel transformed himself into a chief both born and made. He represented a new kind of Herero man, and his

German-style uniform symbolized this corresponding masculinity. His funeral in 1923 brought generational tensions over Herero masculinity and the German military motif to a boiling point.

When Samuel died in Bechuanaland, Chief Hosea Kutako petitioned the government to transport his body to South West Africa for burial next to his father. The funeral lasted four days, and over 1,500 *Otruppa* paraded in full regalia. Samuel's funeral was the iconic public debut of the troops. Henrichsen and Krüger have argued that the mass showing of the *Otruppa* in uniform "signaled a symbolic resurrection of the Herero army," distilling public desire for an appropriate sense of Herero unity.[56] By parading at the funeral, the *Otruppa* commemorated the glorious, if disastrous, Herero past and paid homage to the icon of the new Herero man. It was a political coup for the *Otruppa*. Their new masculinity became synonymous with Herero culture, essential to the memorialization of the past and symbolic of new future possibilities. However, the funeral and its annual commemoration, continuing to the present, became a battleground between elders and the *Otruppa* over Herero masculinity.

While this funeral has become the epitome of Herero tradition, it was an amalgamation of Herero customs and German customs. Traditionally, Hereros were buried under a tree on which cattle horns were stacked, and graves were typically not visited on a regular basis.[57] Aspects of Samuel's funeral were closely reminiscent of German military funerals in the late nineteenth century, which *Truppenbambusen* may have witnessed.[58] According to the Chief Native Commissioner, the funeral "began early in the morning for a religious service which was held in the old German churchyard where the troops who had fallen in the Herero rebellion were buried."[59] The Lutheran service was performed by a German missionary. The *Otruppa* brass band played German military marches and "the chiefs [and] older descendants of Maherero knelt down some distance from the grave; somebody held an emotional speech, and then they all filed past the grave laying small stones, twigs, and leaves on the gravestone."[60]

The funeral's annual commemorations during the 1920s and 1930s served as the main political platform for the *Otruppa* to stake claims to manhood, seize elders' authority, and shape Herero social reconstruction. It was an opportunity to perform their masculinity and commemorate their iconic leader. *Otruppa* parades, like other military displays, served to project a powerful masculinity that defined its members as formidable and indomitable—in short, as men. They evoked past Herero bravery and united onlookers through a collective nostalgia. Simultaneously, the German military aesthetic re-emasculated elders by publically recalling their loss of authority.

Herero elders hotly contested *Otruppa* performances, masculinity, and versions of the past. Chief Kutako, the organizer of the funeral, viewed the *Otruppa* performances as a betrayal. He bitterly complained, "It is not our true custom to hold ceremonies at the graves of chiefs. It was not done in the old days."[61] As much as *Otruppa* performances unified Herero people, they were also highly divisive as they did not allow for alternative memories or masculinities. One South African official noted in 1937 that "many . . . Hereros, and they are of the loyal section (loyal to the elders and government), are not now going to the annual celebration at Okahandja because they say it is becoming increasingly a 'Truppenspieler' show."[62]

Colonial authorities outlawed *Otruppa* activities at commemorations in 1935 due to pressures from Herero elders and fears that the Nazis were training the *Otruppa* for insurgency by promising land and better wages. Each year thereafter the *Otruppa* "asked that as a special concession they be allowed to indulge in drilling on the days the Herero congregate at Okahandja for the pilgrimage to the graves of their departed chiefs," promising that "immediately [when] they leave Okahandja they will doff their uniforms."[63] They were almost always denied. This prohibition undermined their ability to publically challenge elders' authority and exhibit their masculinity.

The outbreak of World War II, in which many *Otruppa* members gladly fought for South Africa rather than Germany, eased generational tensions over Herero masculinity and authority. Following the war, more congenial relations between the elders and the troops began to develop for a variety of reasons. Natural aging made a significant difference in generational tensions over the troops. Men who had been elders at the time of the genocide began to pass on. The contentiousness of the German military aesthetic, and the troops' political use thereof, consequently declined. Original troop members in turn found themselves becoming elders, and their interests, particularly relations with the state and land policies, began to converge with the men they previously opposed.

Another reason for this increased cooperation was that the troops had proved themselves as Herero men through their sustained refusal to accede to the authority of elders and the colonial state. As political disputes surrounding the German military aesthetic receded, it came to symbolize Herero manhood and the Herero nation as persevering and independent. The troops became Herero cultural icons. Finally, the election of the apartheid government shortly after World War II encouraged a certain amount of solidarity across generations of Herero men. Although significant rifts developed in other areas of Herero society as a result of this administrative change, by and large, Herero men united politically across generations in opposition to the South African regime.

Conclusion

Otruppa conflicts with Herero elders in the period between the genocide and World War II reveal divisions and tensions rife within Herero society during its difficult reconstruction. These conflicts demonstrate the centrality of debates over gender identities and ideologies to processes of remaking society and creating a national Herero identity. Herero men's differing generational experiences of German colonialism played a crucial role in how they envisioned their own masculinities, what it meant to be a Herero following the genocide, and how one became a Herero man. Both elders and the youthful *Otruppa* used these experiences to regroup in the aftermath of colonial violence and take advantage of new opportunities where past possibilities had become untenable.

Herero elders coped with their emasculation resulting from German colonial policies and Samuel Maherero's actions by taking advantage of the transition to South African control in 1915. By cooperating with this new colonial government, elders were able to access state power to reinforce their own waning authority. In contrast, the *Otruppa* relied heavily on German military aesthetics and ideals of masculinity to redefine Herero manhood in order to enhance their status in colonial Herero society and escape elders' authority. They used their experiences within that organization to their advantage to recreate stability in uncertain times, and created a hierarchy that reflected older patriarchal and patronage structures, but was more permeable and beyond elders' and South African control. The troops found confirmation for their non-traditional masculinity and its accompanying aesthetics in the charismatic figure of Samuel Maherero, his initiative, and his wardrobe.

By 1950, *Otruppa* masculinity became normalized as Herero masculinity as a consequence of endurance, natural lifespan limitations, and changing political constraints. *Otruppa* performances and the annual commemoration of Samuel Maherero's funeral have continued to thrive into the present but serve an altered set of functions. On the one hand, the troops and their history have been appropriated by independent Namibia's Ovambo-dominated government and incorporated into the grand narrative of Namibia's Liberation Struggle. On the other, these performances are essential to Herero cultural survival in the face of what many Hereros see as a potentially overwhelming Ovambo onslaught in Namibian society and politics.[64] Further, these commemorations have been important sites for Hereros and Germans to continue to negotiate their pasts. Public apologies from the German government in 2004 and the Von Trotha family in 2007 to the Herero nation were made at such commemorations.[65] Many of the parameters of what it meant to be a Herero man altered significantly over the course of the first half of the twentieth century. However, certain aspects of precolonial Herero masculinity were carried over and melded with the German military aesthetic. The troops' new definition of manhood proved more durable and better suited to new colonial imperatives than its predecessor. While the emergence of this new masculinity was not without serious friction and contention, the *Otruppa* in their German-style military uniforms became the quintessential emblems of Herero men and the Herero nation.

NOTES

1. National Archives of Namibia (NAN) South West Africa Administration (SWAA) 432 A50/59, "Military Movement amongst Natives," 19 May 1917. See also Dag Henrichsen and Gesine Krüger, "'We Have Been Captives Long Enough. We Want to be Free': Land, Uniforms, and Politics in the History of the Herero in the Interwar Period," in *Mobility and Containment: Namibia under South African Rule, 1915–46*, ed. Hayes et al. (Athens: Ohio University Press, 1999), 149–74; Wolfgang Werner, "Playing Soldiers: The Truppenspieler Movement among the Herero of Namibia, 1915 to ca. 1945," *Journal of Southern African Studies* 16, no. 3 (1990): 485–502; Philipp Prein, "Guns and Top Hats: African Resistance in German South West Africa, 1907–1915," *Journal of Southern African Studies* 20, no. 1 (1994): 99–121.

2. See David Olusoga and Casper Erichsen, *The Kaiser's Holocaust: Germany's Forgotten Genocide and the Colonial Roots of Nazism* (London: Faber and Faber, 2010); Jan-Bart Gewald, *Herero Heroes: A Socio-Political History of the Herero of Namibia, 1890–1923* (Athens: Ohio University Press, 1999); Helmut Bley, *Namibia under German Rule* (Hamburg: Lit Verlag, 1996); Isabel Hull, *Absolute Destruction: Military Culture and the Practices of War in Imperial Germany* (Ithaca: Cornell University Press, 2005); George Steinmetz, *The Devil's Handwriting: Precoloniality and the German Colonial State in Quingdao, Samoa, and Southwest Africa* (Chicago: University of Chicago Press, 2007). Although the term *genocide* is contentious with reference to these events and only became commonly and retrospectively applied in the late 1970s, I contend that it appropriately describes German policies implemented between 1904 and 1907. For debates surrounding the use of the term *genocide*, see Brigitte Lau, "Uncertain Certainties," *Mibagus* 2 (1989): 4–5; Tilman Dedering, "The German-Herero War of 1904: Revisionism of Genocide or Imaginary Historiography?" *Journal of Southern African Studies* 19, no. 1 (1993): 80–88.

3. Klaus Theweleit, *Male Fantasies,* trans. Stephen Conway (Minneapolis: University of Minnesota Press, 1988), 50–51. See also Hull, *Absolute Destruction,* 91–181;

Susanne Zantop, *Colonial Fantasies: Conquest, Family, and Nation in Precolonial Germany, 1770–1870* (Durham: Duke University Press, 1997), 49–58.

4. Gewald, *Herero Heroes*. See also Henrichsen and Krüger, "Captives," and Werner, "Playing Soldiers"; Wolfgang Werner, *No One Will Become Rich: Economy and Society in Herero Reserves in Namibia, 1915–1946* (Basel: P. Schlettwein, 1998); Tony Emmett, *Popular Resistance and the Roots of Nationalism in Namibia, 1915–1966* (Basel: P. Schlettwein, 1999), 213–50.

5. Gewald, *Herero Heroes*, 289.

6. For an examination of *Otruppa* masculinity under South Africa rule, see Molly McCullers, "'We do it so that we will be Men': Masculinity Politics in Colonial Namibia, 1915–49," *Journal of African History* 52 (2011): 43–62.

7. Cynthia Enloe, *Bananas, Beaches, and Bases: Making Feminist Sense of International Politics* (Berkeley: University of California Press, 1990), 44. Anne McClintock, *Imperial Leather: Race, Gender, and Sexuality in the Colonial Conquest* (New York: Routledge, 1995), 232–34.

8. R. W. Connell, *Masculinities* (Berkeley: University of California Press, 1995); Lisa Lindsay and Stephan Miescher, eds., *Men and Masculinities in Modern Africa* (Portsmouth: Heinemann, 2003), 6.

9. Stefan Dudink and Karen Hagermann, "Masculinity in Politics and War in the Age of Democratic Revolutions, 1750–1850," in *Gender in History: Masculinities in Politics and War: Gendering Modern History*, ed. Stefan Dudink et al. (Manchester: Manchester University Press, 2004), 3–12. See also Mrinalini Sinha, "Giving Masculinity a History: Some Contributions from the Historiography of Colonial India," *Gender and History* 11 (1999): 445–60.

10. Mrinalini Sinha, "Giving Masculinity a History," 455. See also Dudink and Hagermann, "Masculinity in Politics," 14.

11. Karen Hagermann, "German Heroes: The Cult of Death for the Fatherland in Nineteenth Century Germany," in *Gender in History: Masculinities in Politics and War; Gendering Modern History*, ed. Stefan Dudink, Karen Hagermann, and John Tosh. (Manchester: Manchester University Press, 2004), 128.

12. Ibid.

13. Dudink and Hagermann, "Masculinity in Politics," 17. See also John Horne, "Masculinities in Politics and War in the Age of Nation-States and World Wars, 1850–1950," in *Gender in History: Masculinities in Politics and War; Gendering Modern History*, ed. Stefan Dudink, Karen Hagermann, and John Tosh (Manchester: Manchester University Press, 2004), 22–40.

14. Theweleit, *Male Fantasies*, 50–51.

15. Ibid. See also Horne, "Masculinities in Politics," 27–32.

16. Gesine Krüger, *Kriegsbewältigung und Geschichtsbewußtsein: Realität, Deutung, und Verarbeitung des deutschen Kolonialkriegs in Namibia, 1904 bis 1907* (Göttingen: Vandenhoeck & Ruprecht, 1999).

17. Heinrich Vedder, "The Herero," in *The Native Tribes of South West Africa*, ed. C. H. L. Hahn et al. (London: Frank Cass, 1966), 157–64. See also Gewald, *Herero Heroes*, 10–28.

18. Vedder, "The Herero," 164–75.

19. Prein, "Guns and Top Hats," 99–121. See also Meredith McKittrick, "Forsaking Their Fathers? Colonialism, Christianity, and Coming of Age in Ovamboland, Northern Namibia," in *Men and Masculinities in Modern Africa*, ed. Lisa Lindsay and Stephan Miescher (Portsmouth: Heinemann, 2003), 33–51.

20. Emmett, *Popular Resistance*, 42–47.

21. Zantop, *Colonial Fantasies*, 43–45. See also Lora Wildenthal, *German Women for Empire, 1884–1945* (Durham: Duke University Press, 2001), 1–13.

22. Gewald, *Herero Heroes*, 47.

23. Ibid., 61–73.

24. Ibid.

25. Ibid., 168–92.

26. Werner, "Playing Soldiers," 477–78. For disputes over precise figures, see also Lau, "Uncertain Certainties," and Dedering, "The German-Herero War of 1904."

27. Gewald, *Herero Heroes*, 8.

28. Werner, "Playing Soldiers," 481.

29. Gewald, *Herero Heroes*.

30. Emmett, *Popular Resistance*, 215–17.

31. Ernest Renan, "What Is a Nation?" in *Nation and Narration*, ed. Homi Bhabha (New York: Routledge, 1990), 8–22. See also Emmett, *Popular Resistance*, 215–22.

32. When the estimated 900 women and girls attached to the military as washer-women and prostitutes are added to this figure, approximately 13 percent of Hereros were involved with the German military. See Gewald, *Herero Heroes*, 206.

33. Krüger, *Kriegsbewältigung*. See also Werner, "Playing Soldiers," 481.

34. National Archives of Namibia (NAN) South West Africa Administration (SWAA) 432 A50/59, "Military Movement amongst Natives," 19 May 1917.

35. Ibid.

36. David Arnold, *Colonizing the Body: State Medicine and Epidemic Disease in Nineteenth Century India* (Berkeley: University of California Press, 1993), 8. Tony Ballantyne and Antoinette Burton, "Bodies, Empires, and World," *Bodies in Contact: Rethinking Colonial Encounters in World History* (Durham: Duke University Press, 2005), 1–18.

37. Paul Higate, "'Soft Clerks' and 'Hard Civvies': Pluralizing Military Masculinities," in *Military Masculinities: Identities and the State*, ed. Paul Higate (Westport, CT: Praeger, 2003), 33. John Hockey, "No More Heroes: Masculinity in the Infantry," in *Military Masculinities*, 18.

38. Hockey, "No More Heroes," 18.

39. NAN SWAA 432 A 50/59, "Minutes of the Herero Advisory Board," 25 November 1935; NAN SWAA 432 A50/59, "Report of Interview with Fritz Kasutu," 29 July 1938.

40. NAN SWAA 432 A50/59, "Interview with Truppenspielers: Statement Alphaeus Watsho," 4 October 1927.

41. Ibid.

42. NAN SWAA 432 A50/59, "Statement: Manuel Kanjua," 29 June 1940.

43. NAN SWAA 432 A50/59, "Extracts from the Minutes of a Meeting between the Assistant Native Commissioner, Windhoek, and Headmen Hosea Kutako and Nikanor Hoveka," 9 May 1938.

44. Werner, "Playing Soldiers," 488–89. Emmett, *Popular Resistance*, 238–42.

45. NAN SWAA 432 A50/59, "Truppenspielers," Memo from the Asst. Native Commissioner, Trollope, to the Chief Native Commissioner, 13 December 1935, p. 2.

46. NAN SWAA 432 A50/59, "Advisory Board Minutes of the Meeting of the 25th of November, 1935—Annexure."

47. NAN SWAA 432 A50/59, "Advisory Board Minutes—Windhoek: 26 November, 1935," p. 4.

48. NAN SWAA 432 A50/59, "Untitled Statement by Senior Location Assistant Stephanus Hoveka to Superintendent of Locations, Windhoek," 26 November 1935.

49. NAN SWAA 432 A50/59, "Advisory Board Minutes—Windhoek: 26 November, 1935."

50. Ibid.

51. Ibid.

52. Ibid. Boardman Mogatle described the movement as "merely play."

53. NAN SWAA 432 A50/59, "Notes on Interview With Hosea Kutako," 9 May 1938.

54. Horne, "Masculinities in Politics," 30.

55. Ibid.

56. Henrichsen and Kruger, 156.

57. Vedder, "The Herero," 164–75.

58. Hagermann, "German Heroes," 117.

59. NAN SWAA 432 A50/59, "A Herero Letter Describing the 1939 Herero Day," ca. August 1939.

60. Ibid.

61. NAN SWAA 432 A50/59, "Notes of Interview," 9 May 1938.

62. NAN SWAA 432 A50/59, "Herero Ceremonies—Omaruru," 24 November 1937.

63. NAN SWAA 432 A50/59, "Herero Royal Ancestral Graves: Okahandja," 29 May 1936.

64. This was a common and recurring theme brought up in interviews with Hereros during my fieldwork in Namibia in 2009 and 2010.

65. Reinhard Kössler, "Genocide, Apologies, and Reparation—The Linkage Between Images of the Past in Namibia and Germany," paper presented at AEGIS European Conference in European Studies; July 11–14, 2007; Leiden. Jürgen Zimmerer and Joachim Zeller, *Genocide in German Southwest Africa: The Colonial War (1907–1908) in Namibia and Its Aftermath* (Monmouth: Merlin Press, 2008).

PART 3

Remembering and Rethinking

Recollection and Intervention

Memory of German Colonialism in Contemporary African Migrants' Writing

Dirk Göttsche

The literature of African migrants writing in German for both German and African diasporic readers is arguably one of the few strands of German postcolonial literature, even if not many of the authors originate from Germany's former colonies.[1] Typically reflecting the authors' experience of Africa, migration to Germany, and life in the European diaspora, this mostly autobiographical literature emerged during the 1980s in the context of West German multiculturalism and the left-wing anti-colonialism promoted by the cultural revolution of the later 1960s. German literature of the African migration is a form of transnational literature, which has seen significant development since German unification and gives Africans a voice in contemporary Germany. At the same time, it also serves as a timely reminder of Germany's implication in European colonial history and in the postcolonial world of global migration. Critical engagement with colonialism and its continuing legacies both in Africa and in Germany is a central theme particularly in texts from the 1980s and 1990s, where personal and transgenerational memory of colonialism tends to play a defining role in representations of cross-cultural experience and emerging diasporic cultural politics. Contributing to the postcolonial project of "decolonising the mind"[2] in both hemispheres, authors such as El Loko, Aly Diallo, Chima Oji, Jean Paul Lissock, and Daniel Mepin[3] effectively intervene in Germany's politics of memory and promote, together with Black German writing of the period,[4] the rediscovery of German colonialism, which has since emerged as a prominent theme in German mainstream literature.[5]

Since the later 1990s, generational transitions combined with shifts in the background and context of migration, as well as changing postcolonial identity politics, have given rise to new types of postcolonial memory, in which the legacies of increasingly distant colonialism now intersect with other collective memory themes. German texts by younger African authors, such as Miriam

Kwalanda, Senait Mehari, Jones Kwesi Evans, Lucia Engombe, Stefanie-Lahya Aukongo, and Luc Degla,[6] recontextualize the transgenerational "post-memory" of colonialism, which is distinct from both personal memory and contested historical memory, in the light of transcultural experience in global migration, traumatizing violence in Africa, and diasporic achievement.[7] In addition, some texts also interlink postcolonial memory with prominent German memory discourses, such as memory of the German Democratic Republic and the *Wende*. Developing the "multidirectionality" of collective memory,[8] they thus participate actively in shaping contemporary Germany's polycentric culture of memory.[9] They also illustrate the crucial role of literature in cultural memory, understood broadly as "the interplay of present and past in sociocultural contexts," "ranging from individual acts of remembering [. . .] to group memory [. . .] to national memory with its 'invented traditions,' and finally to the host of transnational *lieux de mémoire* such as the Holocaust and 9/11."[10] Colonialism can be seen as such a transnational *lieu de mémoire*, explored in African migrants' writing from the perspective of transcultural migration with reference to African identity and memory as well as German cultural debate.

Within this wider context, this essay focuses on two case studies of how African literature in German remembers the African experience of German colonialism in Togo and Cameroon respectively, El Loko's *Der Blues in mir* (The Blues Inside Myself, 1986) and Daniel Mepin's *Die Weissagung der Ahnen* (The Ancestors' Prophecy, 1997). It should be noted that such African intervention in Germany's politics of memory is part of wider critical engagement with European colonialism and the continuing legacies of colonial history and racism in German society in African migrants' writing in German. After all, the British, French, Belgian, and South African administration of Germany's former African colonies after the end of World War I means that African memory of German colonialism is inflected with the experience of subsequent colonial rule by these powers, and increasingly also with the histories of decolonization, post-independence development and conflict within individual African states, and the overarching history of North-South relations.

Despite earlier precursors, such as Emily Ruete or Kum'a Ndumbe III,[11] a consistent tradition of German literature by African migrants and immigrants, both autobiographical and fictional, did arguably not emerge until the 1980s, when West German multiculturalism, the growing presence of African students and refugees, and post-1960s German engagement with anti-colonial theory from the period of decolonization, combined with the cultural impact of the

Green and One World movements, created the context both for African intervention in German critical debate and for openness to the African voice in
German publishers and readers.[12] Early African migrants' writing in German
from the 1980s and 1990s was largely, although not exclusively, by male African authors with academic backgrounds who grew up in their African countries
of origin during the age of decolonization and came to Germany for university
study. For them, memory of colonialism and critique of colonial legacies were
therefore defining aspects of diasporic self-assertion in literature that reflects a
time of highly politicized debate about social and cultural decolonization in
post-independence Africa, and about continuing racism and growing postcolonial immigration in Germany. Drawing on anti-colonial theorists such as Aimé
Césaire, Albert Memmi, and Frantz Fanon as well as European critical theory,
texts from this earlier period tend to operate with stark contrasts between Europe and Africa, and feature narratives of existential identity conflict between
African tradition and European modernity.[13] From the perspective of such
postcolonial identity crisis, they cast the colonial period, whose final years the
writers still remember from their youth, as an ambivalent space combining
colonial transformation of African societies with surviving "authentic" African
traditions from precolonial times, which some narratives try to reclaim despite
growing awareness of irreversible historical change. Within the discursive
framework that predominates during the 1980s and 1990s, memory of colonialism therefore forms part of a fundamental reassessment of African history
and culture in the face of neo- and postcolonial conditions and continuing im-
balances in the global distribution of power and wealth.

One of the earliest examples, and a highly literary text, is the "autobiographical story" *Der Blues in mir* by El Loko, an acclaimed artist from Togo,
who came to West Germany in 1971 with a German studentship enabling him
to study with Joseph Beuys at the Academy of Arts in Düsseldorf, until in
1978, facing deportation for outstaying his visa, he was forced to return. Since
1980 El Loko has been living in dual residence in Cologne and Togo.[14] *Der
Blues in mir* combines a concise autobiographical account of his youth, his
study at Düsseldorf, and his cultural identity crisis on his first return to Togo
with poetic prose and poetry, prints of the author's wood engravings, and fac-
simile reproductions of legal documents and media coverage relating to the
court case in which he fought deportation. While the latter theme intervenes in
the West German debate during the later 1970s and 1980s about German immigration and citizenship laws and the treatment of "foreigners," the autobiographical narrative also includes a stylized personal memory of El Loko's
youth during the period of decolonization, and explicitly historical memory of

German colonialism in Togo as a political and moral reminder of Germany's implication in the history of Africa.

The autobiographical narrative opens with a chapter in evocative poetic prose, which gives a highly condensed symbolic account of a day in El Loko's home village of Pédakondji, represented as a community at peace with itself and in harmony with nature, followed by an equally mythical summary of the village's weekly social calendar.[15] Zooming in on his own childhood, the narrator then clearly marks this idyll as a retrospective vision of paradise lost (13), moving from such idealization of traditional African culture, cast as essentially precolonial, to the boy's departure for secondary school in the capital Lomé at the age of twelve, which marks his final entry into the world of modernity and conflict. In the symbolic map of the story the road from the boy's home village to the more "progressive" neighboring village, which features a German-built church and a primary school, represents the transition from childhood paradise to adolescence as well as the "arterial connection [*Verbindungsader*] to foreign philosophies, foreign nations, foreign religions and traditions," and such exposure to the world of colonial "civilization" and its legacies is perceived as a threat to original cultural integrity (14). Indeed, Togo's independence in 1960, when El Loko was ten years old, is not even mentioned in the narrative, which suggests that in this assessment, continuing colonial influence far outweighed political liberation.

El Loko echoes other African writers in identifying the school and the church as primary sites of colonial power and influence. They are made responsible for an education that transforms the emergence of critical awareness in adolescence—"I began to question the world around me"—into a process of painful alienation from tradition and nature, resulting in a problematic "new identity" (17–18). Rather than enriching the adolescent, colonial and postcolonial schooling generates a violent "battle within [his] soul against the psychological transplantation" and forces the boy on the irreversible road of colonialism's "new ideology," which destroys "the old one in [him]" and obscures his original "memory" (17–18). Teaching in French, based on an exclusively European syllabus, only touches on African concerns from a firmly colonial perspective: "What I know about my country, however, was linked to Kaiser Wilhelm II; I only knew the Niger and its historical sites, Timbuktu, Djenne and Gao, from the reports of European explorers" (23). As the adolescent memorizes European colonial knowledge he is effectively forced to over-write the cultural memory of his own people. This neo-colonial attack on African "memory" (*Gedächtnis*) is clearly marked as brainwashing: "I felt like dirty washing [*schmutzige Wäsche*], which is on its way to the cleaner's" (23).

This early alienation from traditional African religion and culture is seen as the origin of a split identity ("a second self [*Ich*]"), metaphorically cast as infection with European thought (17–18). The metaphor of colonialism as disease also provides the framing motif of the entire narrative, the epigraph and conclusion of El Loko's autobiographical account and the book's title: "The poisonous serum, which Africa may once have taken deliberately, will continue to take its effect for centuries. And this precisely is *the Blues inside myself*" (5, 98). In reflecting his own experience of (neo-) colonial education and culture with reference to the African-American blues, El Loko places his literary discourse about postcolonial African identity and migration in the wider context of African diasporic history. Such oblique engagement with African-American cultural politics links his treatment of African identity problems to related identity discourses in Black German literature of the 1980s and 1990s.[16] Metaphors of disease in *Der Blues in mir* are not meant to cast Africans simply as victims of European colonialism. The epigraph's hint at African complicity in the development of colonial violence and transformation is supported throughout the text by a critique of African consent and agency in the promotion of colonial "progress": "Everyone agreed with civilization" (17).

Such African participation in colonial rule and development is a central theme in chapter seven, which combines a brief summary of German colonial rule in Togo with a radical rereading of the opening chapters and their idealized retrospective vision of traditional Africa as paradise lost. Far from being a precolonial idyll, El Loko's home village of Pédakondji now turns out to have played a crucial role at the forefront of German colonization as a river port, where the Germans contracted African workers to build a canal that facilitated transport to and from trade centers in Eastern Togo. The village was thus not only located close to the traditional political center Togoville, the residency of King Mlapa, with whom Gustav Nachtigal negotiated the so-called German protection treaty in 1884, the basis of subsequent colonial occupation; but it was also radically transformed by German colonial rule, and members of the author's family were deeply involved in this process. His grandfather witnessed and approved the colonial improvements to the country's infrastructure; other family members worked for the Germans, such as an uncle who acted as translator; the narrator's father belonged to the first generation educated in German schools, becoming familiar with German language and history; and even the more critical narrator commends the Germans' colonial achievements, "which eclipse contemporary developmental aid policy [*Entwicklungspolitik*]" (33). Rather than being cast as victims or opponents of German colonial rule, the local African population is presented as embracing the opportunities offered by colonial development, and they later remember their involvement with pride, keeping colonial awards and emblems of German culture, such as portraits of "Kaiser Wilhelm II" and "well-known German citizens" (33). At the same time, the narrator passes critical commentary on such naive memory of German colonialism in his father's and grandfather's generation, noting for example the imperial objectives of the village's colonial transformation, where his grandfather appears to have simply admired the Germans' hands-on approach to colonial development as opposed to the perceived aloofness of the French (33).

Germany's colonial involvement in Togo is thus presented in terms of the African memory of German colonialism and as a reminder to German readers that German colonialism became "part of history" there despite the transition to French colonial rule in World War I (34). El Loko only touches on the repercussions of the experience of later French colonialism for Togolese memory of German colonial rule, but he highlights very clearly the significance of oral history for the shaping of the African memory of German colonialism: "People continued to tell stories, adding new emphases every day. And they enjoyed listening and developing their own images and dreams" (34).[17] There is thus no transition from communicative to cultural memory, as critics would expect in a European context of nation-states and public media;[18] instead oral tradition invests collective memory with a particular dynamic that informs the memory of German colonialism with individual aspirations and shifting socio-political concerns. The narrator's own intellectual history is his case in point. He represents the transgenerational postmemory of German colonialism during the era of liberation from French colonial rule, and it is his early fascination with German language, art, and literature as well as with the values associated with German culture—"diligence and intellect [*Fleiß und Geist*]" (34)—that inspire his "dream" of Germany as the pathway to personal development and success.

Postmemory of German colonialism thus plays a defining role in the shaping of African postcolonial identity in *Der Blues in mir* and also in El Loko's development as an artist. The autobiographical narrative is organized around a series of identity crises that reflect the artist's ongoing "existential struggle for survival" between African tradition and European modernity, represented by German culture (34, 20). A first crisis during Francophone secondary schooling in Lomé is reflected with metaphorical reference to Fanon's anticolonial critique in *The Wretched of the Earth* (1961; German translation: *Die Verdammten dieser Erde*): "I knew I was cursed [*verdammt*]" (20). Abandoning his neo-colonial "thirst for power and wealth," El Loko turns to the arts and German culture, moves to Accra and makes full use of the Goethe Institute there, dreaming of Germany as paradise, as "the blessed country [. . .] of science and art" (20, 22). After his arrival in Düsseldorf in 1971, necessary disappointment with this stereotypical projection and initial artistic failure lead to a first re-appreciation of African values and African art, as suggested by his teacher Beuys: "You have to take your culture into account!" (28). Forced return to Lomé in 1978 in the wake of the deportation crisis and further disillusionment with the reality of living in Germany as an African then lead to one of the recurring tropes of migrant experience, the shock of returning to one's country of origin as a different person who finds that his society of origin has also changed beyond recognition. In the case of African migrants such as El Loko, heightened awareness of cultural difference and the continuing asymmetry in power and wealth between the North and the South inflect this general human experience with particular poignancy and with the problematic of cultural hybridization, which anti-colonial discourse, unlike more recent postcolonial theory, construes as *Zerrissenheit*[19] rather than as a site of "empowerment."[20] Quite a few recent African autobiographies, such as those by Kwalanda, Evans, Korn, and Mehari, conceive of German diaspora along similar lines as Bhabha's notion of a "Third Space" in a world of global migration and transcultural experience, while earlier texts, such as El Loko, tend to retain the idea of conflicting cultures, which leave the migrant stuck "in between" and renders hybridization a threat to personal identity.[21]

El Loko feels like "a stranger in his native country [*Heimat*]" on his return and notes "with horror" "that some European thought had seeped into [his] mind" (52). A return to his home village as part of his attempt to reclaim his African "roots" (94) turns into a traumatic turning point, when the returnee finds the village in desperate decay and decline, and the river and canal, the foundation of its former prosperity, overgrown with reeds. However, the experience of the impossibility of returning to the past, of having to cope with being "der Fremdkehrende" (88)—a neologism conflating the stranger with homecoming—also takes the narrator to the level of critical self-awareness and postcolonial critique that informs the narrative throughout. Both the poetic vision of supposedly precolonial African life in the opening chapters and the critical reassessment of German colonialism and its transformation in Togolese collective memory, discussed above, are written from the perspective of postcolonial self-assertion in the face of transcultural colonial and neo-colonial experience. Critical memory of German colonial rule and its African memorialization play a crucial role in eventually transforming renewed identity crisis into "a new mode of seeing [*ein anderes Sehen*]" (94), new perception, understanding, and appreciation of African culture and identity in the postcolonial age, and hence a new framework for modern African art, reflected in the volume's wood engravings and poems. *Der Blues in mir* thus oscillates between the melancholy vision of reclaiming African origins, supposedly untainted by colonial influence, and a multi-stage process of cultural reinvention that offers the hope of overcoming the deep-rooted legacies of colonialism identified in the course of critical cross-cultural self-assertion. It is significant therefore that the text ends in a moment of renewed transition and with the symbolic question "But where to [*wohin*]?" (98) rather than following the author back to Germany in 1980.

Similar cross-mapping of anti-colonial identity politics and postcolonial memory, albeit with reference to French and British colonialism, can be found, for example, in Aly Diallo's novel *Die Täuschung* (The Deception, 1987), originally written in French but published in German translation, and Chima Oji's autobiographical account *Unter die Deutschen gefallen: Erfahrungen eines Afrikaners* (Fallen Amongst the Germans: Experiences of an African, 1992), the most prominent African intervention in German cultural politics during the 1990s.[22] Based on Diallo's own experience of PhD study at the University of Hamburg during the 1980s, before he returned to Mali to become director of Mali's National Museum, *Die Täuschung* tells the story of a Malian student of ethnology in Hamburg, whose radical anti-imperialism and Pan-Africanism leave him increasingly disillusioned with Western thought and German multiculturalism as well as diasporic African politics, until he turns to writing as a means of transforming his "failed revolt" against the cultural and political legacies of colonialism into a more sustained process of intellectual decolonization.[23] In the context of the protagonist's postcolonial identity crisis, memory flashbacks into his earlier life in traditional Fulbe society again shift from initial idealization of a supposedly authentic precolonial culture to the acknowledgment of African implication in French colonial rule and painful awareness of the irreversible separation from traditional Fulbe thought. Echoing El Loko, both Diallo and Oji identify European colonial schooling as the primary site of colonial influence and cultural hybridization in twentieth-century Africa. Oji, who later returned to Nigeria as director of the School of Dentistry at the University of Nigeria in his native city of Enugu, focuses deliberately on a powerful critique of racism and discrimination in late 1960s to 1980s West Germany, reminding post-unification Germany of colonial legacies in the face of resurgent "hostility against foreigners and Neonazi activities [*Ausländerfeindlichkeit und neonazistische Umtriebe*]."[24] Memory of his childhood and youth in Nigeria again cast the age of (British) colonial rule and decolonization as an ambivalent space of "colonial brainwashing" and cultural "uprooting" (31–32), epitomized by European-style schooling, but also of surviving African culture and wisdom, which defy colonial racism and violence. As in *Der Blues in mir*, such personal memory of the period of decolonization includes post-memory of the onset of (British) colonial rule in the late nineteenth century, recollected in oral history. Recording the "tradition of handing down history orally" (18) in his native city of Enugu, which was a small village at the time of European "discovery," Oji retells the African experience of the first colonial encounter, as memorialized in Ibo collective memory. Echoing El Loko's reflection about the particular dynamic of such oral history, which inflects memory with later experience, this Ibo memory narrative also records the ambivalent response by the village "magician," who is said to keep the villagers from killing the unearthly white strangers, since they mean no harm, but also anticipates colonial occupation by warning them that this is only "the vanguard of large crowds of white men, who will enter our country in due course and will be superior in power" (17). This classic instance of "the Empire writing back" thus challenges European accounts of colonial history and confronts German readers with the African perspective.[25] The fact that the postmemory in question concerns British colonization is of far less importance than the reversal of the colonial gaze and the survival of African memory.

In El Loko's, Diallo's, and Oji's engagement with the memory of colonialism, Germany is largely synonymous with pre-unification West Germany. A partially different pattern emerges in Daniel Mepin's complex novel *Die Weissagung der Ahnen*, which combines similar consideration of the diasporic condition with a critique of East German anti-imperialism and memory of the *Wende*. The novel's main part tells the story of Taga Sinö, son of the "medicine man" and influential "keeper of tradition" in the village of Dengkkuop in the part of Cameroon that came under French administration after the end of German rule.[26] Sent to the German Democratic Republic for school and university education by the Socialist liberation movement fighting first French colonialism and then the government of independent Cameroon, Taga later finds himself persecuted as "resistance fighter" in post-independence Cameroon (177), while the demise of the GDR, post-unification crisis and the failure of his marriage to a German take him to the point of suicide: "No Cameroon, no Germany. I have reached the end [*Ich bin am Ende*]!" (188) Whereas this tragic construction of postcolonial diasporic identity eclipses the trope of *Zerrissenheit* in El Loko and Diallo, the novel's opening poem and its narrative framework, written in a style reminiscent of Latin American Magical Realism, opens up additional dimensions. The poem intervenes in German cultural politics by emphatically maintaining "Germany is my home [*Heimat*], Whether the Germans like it or not," casting the African immigrant as a participant in German history—"I helped celebrate the *Wende*"—and embracing the postcolonial concept of cultural hybridization: "I was reborn here" (5). The framing prologue and epilogue see the protagonist summoned to the "Court of Justice in the realm of the dead" and sentenced to "a revision of his first life" (193–94); the brief account of his second life in Cameroon, where he now succeeds as a prominent politician, who later becomes "the most famous writer of his country" (197), includes his short-lived marriage with an African-American of German descent, who turns out to be his granddaughter from his first life. This quasi-incest acts as a symbolic reference to a postcolonial world of global migration, which links Africa, Europe, and America in one overarching world history of transnational movement and exchange, but it also implies the mythical idea of the return of the past and the ongoing significance of (neo-) colonial legacies.

It is in this context of conceptualizing (post-) colonial history that the memory of German colonial rule in Cameroon, set against the violence of the anti-colonial liberation war against French rule during the protagonist's youth, becomes a significant theme in Mepin's novel. The key passage memorializes German colonialism through the personal memory of Taga's father Tafe (77–82), who admits that the French abolished forced labor when they replaced the Germans (24) but continues to be impressed by German colonial governance. As a member of the Cameroonian elite, Tafe appreciates Germany's colonial policy of minimal interference and Wilhelmine fascination with "men of power [*mächtige Menschen*]" (77). The centerpiece in this vignette of African colonial memory is an episode in which the German governor resolves a power struggle between Dengkkuop and a neighboring village by striking a deal between the village leaders that compels each of them to secure the support of his people so as to avoid the "wise governor" (80) handing over power to his rival. The view that this political feat is in the best interest of local Africans is endorsed symbolically by a kola nut oracle, which also underlines the German's knowledge of and respect for African tradition (81). While this memory portrays German colonial rule in Cameroon in a surprisingly positive light (despite some criticism), it also rejects a discourse of victimization and implies insistence on African equality and agency. This is particularly obvious when the narrative uses the term "Basic Law [*Grundgesetz*]" with reference to traditional African law (79), which implies that the precolonial legal system of this African society had the same authority and dignity as the *Grundgesetz* of the

Federal Republic of Germany today. It is therefore not only GDR support for Socialist liberation movements that takes Taga to East Germany but also his father's hope that his son will be able to blend German "wisdom with our own" for the benefit of African development (76). Despite the focus on the traditional African elite, Cameroonian memory of German colonialism is thus cast as part of African cultural and political self-assertion amid colonial and neo-colonial conditions. Other relevant passages discuss the influence of colonial language on African culture and neo-colonial French influence in formally independent Cameroon, where power politics continue "just like in the good old days of colonialism," providing an example of "failed decolonisation" (156, 170, 158).

German colonialism in Cameroon also plays a crucial role in Jean Paul Lissock's autobiography *Mein Freund, der weiße Mann* (My Friend, the White Man, 1997), a narrative of diasporic achievement in West Germany that casts postmemory of German rule as inspiration for the "dream of one day being a respected business man in Germany."[27] As far as I am aware, the only text devoted entirely to the critique of German colonialism in Africa is Kum'a Ndumbe III's Brechtian play *Ach Kamerun! Unsere alte deutsche Kolonie . . .* (Oh, Cameroon! Our Old German Colony, 1970/2005), which signals its intervention in German historical awareness in its very title. Contemporary African literature in German that engages with German colonial rule in East Africa or Namibia appears to be extremely rare (although fuller assessment will have to include publications in other languages). Lucia Engombe's and Stefanie-Lahya Aukongo's recent autobiographies, which originate from GDR support of the SWAPO's fight for Namibian independence, only include very limited memory of German colonialism in their narratives of youth in East Germany and diasporic identity crisis at the point of the *Wende* and Namibian independence in 1990.[28] However, they both work toward German postcolonial awareness by including appendices on Namibia's history and German colonial involvement, and Engombe underlines the cross-cultural objective in such historical contextualization with the heading "How the lines of destiny of the German and Namibian people intersect."[29] Both Engombe and Aukongo also develop the link between the memory of colonialism and memory of the *Wende*, already found in Mepin's *Die Weissagung der Ahnen*. Such cross-stitching of memory discourses in a transcultural context is a significant development in itself, which draws on the multidirectional potential of memory to introduce postcolonial perspectives into German cultural debates.

African memory of German colonialism, as reflected in the literature of Africans writing in German, thus underwent a process of gradual change from the generation represented by El Loko and Mepin, born in 1950 and 1948 respectively, to those authors born in the 1960s to 1980s. While none of them have personal memories of German colonial rule, the former draw on their own memory of decolonization during the 1950s and 1960s and transgenerational postmemory of German colonialism, which their parents or grandparents had witnessed. In both the autobiographies and novels by authors such as El Loko, Mepin, Diallo, Lissock, and Oji, memory of German (and French or British) colonialism plays a defining role in the often painful negotiation of postcolonial African identity, a struggle exacerbated by the unsettling experience of German diaspora. This personal link to the colonial past has arguably become more tenuous in the younger generations, putting German colonialism in perspective in the context of often arduous experiences of migration and the pressing problems facing postcolonial Africa. At the same time, the multicultural diversification of German society and the "rediscovery" of Germany's implication in colonial history have transformed the context of such African memory of German colonialism, giving it greater public resonance and facilitating the concept of "shared history," which informs, for example, Engombe's historical appendix. In both generations, however, such African memory of German colonialism acts as a poignant intervention in German cultural debate. Contributing to the emergence of postcolonial memory in Germany during the 1980s and 1990s, memory of colonialism in African migrants' writing today works alongside Black German writing in challenging established Eurocentric narratives of colonial history, and it reminds readers of the complexity and connectivity of colonial histories and legacies.

NOTES

1. See János Riesz, "Autor/innen aus dem schwarzafrikanischen Kulturraum," in *Interkulturelle Literatur in Deutschland: Ein Handbuch*, ed. Carmine Chiellino (Stuttgart, Weimar: Metzler, 2000), 248–62; Dirk Göttsche, "Der neue historische Afrika-Roman: Kolonialismus aus postkolonialer Sicht," *German Life and Letters* 56 (2003): 261–80; "Colonial Legacies and Cross-Cultural Experience: The African Voice in Contemporary German Literature," *Edinburgh German Yearbook* 1 (2007): 159–75; "Cross-Cultural Self-Assertion and Cultural Politics: African Migrants' Writing in German since the Late 1990s," *German Life and Letters* 63 (2010): 54–70; Sara Lennox, "Postcolonial Writing in Germany," *The Cambridge History of Postcolonial Literature*, ed. Ato Quayson, vol. 1 (Cambridge: Cambridge University Press, 2012), 620–48.

2. Ngugi wa Thiong'o, *Decolonising the Mind: The Politics of Language in African Literature* (London: James Currey, 1994).

3. El Loko, *Der Blues in mir: Eine autobiographische Erzählung*. Mit Holzschnitten des Autors; Nachwort von Al Imfeld (Oberhausen: Graphium Press, 1986); Aly Diallo, *Die Täuschung*, trans. Gabriele Henschke (Frankfurt am Main: Nexus, 1987);

Chima Oji, *Unter die Deutschen gefallen: Erfahrungen eines Afrikaners* (Wuppertal: Peter Hammer, 1992); Jean Paul Lissock, *Mein Freund, der weiße Mann: Von Kamerun nach Deutschland* (Berlin: Frieling, 1997); Daniel Mepin, *Die Weissagung der Ahnen: Roman. Kamerun* (Unkel/Rhein, Bad Honnef: Horlemann, 1997).

4. See Stefanie Kron, "Afrikanische Diaspora und Literatur Schwarzer Frauen in Deutschland," *Dossier Migrationsliteratur—eine neue deutsche Literatur?*, ed. Sibel Kara (Heinrich Böll-Stiftung February 2009; http://www.migration-boell.de/web/integration/47_2026.asp#6, accessed August 27, 2012); Dirk Göttsche, "Self-Assertion, Intervention and Achievement: Black German Writing in Postcolonial Perspective," *Orbis Litterarum* 67 (2012): 83–135.

5. See Dirk Göttsche, "Rekonstruktion und Remythisierung der kolonialen Welt: Neue historische Romane über den deutschen Kolonialismus in Afrika," *Deutsch-afrikanische Diskurse in Geschichte und Gegenwart: Literatur- und kulturwissenschaftliche Perspektiven*, ed. Michael Hofmann and Rita Morrien (Amsterdam: Rodopi, 2012), 171–95; *Remembering Africa: The Rediscovery of Colonialism in Contemporary German Literature* (Rochester, NY: Camden House, 2013).

6. Miriam Kwalanda, with Birgit Theresa Koch, *Die Farbe meines Gesichts: Lebensreise einer kenianischen Frau* (Frankfurt am Main: Eichborn, 1999); Senait Mehari, *Feuerherz* (Munich: Droemer, 2004); *Heart of Fire: From Child Soldier to Soul Singer*, trans. Christine Lo (London: Profile Books, 2006); Jones Kwesi Evans, with Kai Schubert and Robin Schmaler, *Ich bin ein Black Berliner: Die ungewöhnliche Lebensgeschichte eines Afrikaners in Deutschland* (Freiburg im Breisgau: Herder, 2006); Lucia Engombe, with Peter Hilliges, *Kind Nr. 95: Meine deutsch-afrikanische Odyssee* (Berlin: Ullstein, 2004); Stefanie-Lahya Aukongo, *Kalungas Kind: Wie die DDR mein Leben rettete* (Reinbek bei Hamburg: Rowohlt, 2009); Luc Degla, *Das afrikanische Auge* (Schwülper: Cargo, 2007).

7. Marianne Hirsch, *Family Frames: Photography, Narrative and Postmemory* (Cambridge: Harvard University Press, 1997).

8. Michael Rothberg, *Multidirectional Memory: Remembering the Holocaust in the Age of Decolonization* (Stanford: Stanford University Press, 2009), 4.

9. See Dirk Göttsche, "Deutsche Literatur afrikanischer Diaspora und die Frage postkolonialer Kanonrevision," *Postkolonialismus und Kanon*, ed. Herbert Uerlings and Iulia-Karin Patrut (Bielefeld: Aisthesis, 2012), 327–60.

10. Astrid Erll, "Cultural Memory Studies: An Introduction," *Cultural Memory Studies: An International and Interdisciplinary Handbook*, ed. Astrid Erll and Ansgar Nünning in collaboration with Sara B. Young (Berlin: de Gruyter, 2008), 2.

11. Sayyida Salme / Emily Ruete, *An Arabian Princess Between Two Worlds: Memoirs, Letters Home, Sequels to the Memoirs, Syrian Customs and Usages*, ed. with an introduction by E. van Donzel (Leiden: Brill, 1993; Arab History and Civilization. Studies and Texts, vol. 3); Kum'a Ndumbe III, *Ach Kamerun! Unsere alte deutsche Kolonie . . . : Ein Dokumentarstück in zehn Szenen* (Douala: AfricAvenir; Berlin: Exchange & Dialogue, 2005).

12. Julius Waldschmidt, "Salima bint Said & Emily Ruete: Ein Frauenleben zwischen Orient und Okzident," *Unbekannte Biographien: Afrikaner im deutschsprachigen Europa vom 18. Jahrhundert bis zum Ende des Zweiten Weltkrieges*, ed. Ulrich van der Heyden (Werder: Kai Homilius, 2008), 238–45; Sara Lennox, "Das afrikanische

Gesicht, das in deinem Raum spricht: Postkoloniale Autoren in Deutschland: Kum'a Numbe III und Uche Nduka," *Text+Kritik*, special edition, *Literatur und Migration*, ed. Heinz Ludwig Arnold (Munich: text + kritik, 2006), 167–76.

13. Frantz Fanon, *The Wretched of the Earth*, preface by Jean-Paul Sartre, trans. Constance Farrington (London: Penguin, 2001).

14. See El Loko, "Biografie," http://www.el-loko.de (accessed August 23, 2012).

15. El Loko, *Der Blues in mir*, 7–13. References to this text in parentheses; all English translations from the German are my own.

16. For illustration, see the pioneering volume *Farbe bekennen: Afro-deutsche Frauen auf den Spuren ihrer Geschichte*, ed. Katharina Oguntoye, May Opitz, and Dagmar Schultz (Berlin: Orlanda Frauenverlag, 1986), and May Ayim's poem "blues in schwarz weiss" in May Ayim, *Grenzenlos und unverschämt* (Berlin: Fischer, 2002), 188–89; for an introduction see two online dossiers: "Afrikanische Diaspora," by the Bundeszentrale für Politische Bildung, 30 July 2004 (http://www.bpb.de/gesellschaft/migration/afrikanische-diaspora, accessed August 23, 2012); "Schwarze Community in Deutschland," ed. Maureen Maisha Eggers, Heinrich Böll Stiftung, May 2006 (http://www.migration-boell.de/web/diversity/48_583.asp, accessed August 23, 2012).

17. "Man erzählte weiter, jeden Tag mit neuen Akzenten. Und gern hörte man zu und bildete sich dabei die eigenen Bilder und Träume."

18. Aleida Assmann, *Der lange Schatten der Vergangenheit: Erinnerungskultur und Geschichtspolitik* (Munich: Beck, 2006).

19. See, for example, Diallo, *Die Täuschung*, 161.

20. Homi K. Bhabha, *The Location of Culture* (London: Routledge, 1994), 2.

21. Bhabha, *The Location of Culture*, 37. Fadumo Korn, with Sabine Eichhorst, *Geboren im Großen Regen: Mein Leben zwischen Afrika und Deutschland* (Reinbek bei Hamburg: Rowohlt, 2004); *Born in the Big Rains: A Memoir of Somalia and Survival*, trans. by Tobe Levin (New York: Feminist Press and the City University of New York, 2006).

22. János Riesz, "'Angst überschattet unser Leben': Afrikaner in Frankreich und Deutschland," *Interkulturelle Texturen: Afrika und Deutschland im Reflexionsmedium der Literatur*, ed. M. Moustapha Diallo and Dirk Göttsche (Bielefeld: Aisthesis, 2003), 19–43; Dirk Göttsche, "Colonial Legacies and Cross-Cultural Experience," 165–66.

23. Diallo, *Die Täuschung*, 133, 171. See also Sonja Lehner, *Schwarz-weiße Verständigung: Interkulturelle Kommunikationsprozesse in europäisch-deutschsprachigen und englisch- und französischsprachigen afrikanischen Romanen (1970–1990)* (Frankfurt am Main: IKO, 1994), 123–45; Göttsche, "Colonial Legacies and Cross-Cultural Experience," 162–64.

24. Oji, *Unter die Deutschen gefallen*, 10. References to this text in parentheses.

25. Bill Ashcroft, Gareth Griffiths, and Helen Tiffin, *The Empire Writes Back: Theory and Practice in Post-Colonial Literatures* (London: Routledge, 2nd ed., 2002).

26. Mepin, *Die Weissagung der Ahnen*, 56, 41. References to this text in parentheses.

27. Lissock, *Mein Freund, der weiße Mann*, 9.

28. Engombe, *Kind Nr. 95: Meine deutsch-afrikanische Odyssee*; Aukongo, *Kalungas Kind*.

29. Engombe, *Kind Nr. 95*, 375.

The Shadows of History

Photography and Colonialism in William Kentridge's *Black Box/Chambre Noire*

Andrew J. Hennlich

An unsettled melancholia is at work in the South African artist and filmmaker William Kentridge's *Black Box/Chambre Noire* (2005, referred to here as *Black Box*). Kentridge's work interrogates South Africa's apartheid history, narrated through memory and witness, emphasizing what is forgotten in the formation of these narratives. "10 Drawings for Projection," the animations Kentridge is most known for, are formed through the process of erasure, photographing, and drawing again on a single sheet of paper, leaving a palimpsest on the page. Kentridge's work also reinterprets European theater, considering its relationship to Africa. *Ubu and the Truth Commission*, for example, inserts Alfred Jarry's absurdist King Ubu into South Africa's Truth Commissions. *Black Box*, commissioned by the Guggenheim Foundation and Deutsche Bank, specifically requesting a project on Germany, engages in these two strands of Kentridge's work. Kentridge pairs *Black Box* with his contemporaneous production of Mozart's opera *Magic Flute*, considering the relationship of *Magic Flute*'s Enlightenment rhetoric to its colonial other.

Black Box is comprised of a small stage-like space with five wooden curtains collaged with newspaper clippings. Behind each curtain runs a horizontal track for "automata," Kentridge's term for his mechanical puppets that are *Black Box*'s actors. At the back of the tableaux is a screen where Kentridge's animations, archival photos, and documentary film of German colonialism in Africa are projected. *Black Box*'s multimedia approach depicts a fragmentary history of German colonialism in South-West Africa focusing on the Herero massacre. *Black Box*'s central automaton, Megaphone Man, a megaphone-headed robot who wears a sandwich board bearing the word *Trauerarbeit* (Freud's term for the work of mourning), announces both a history and a future; it looks backward to history but signals to the audience that this melancholia still persists. Kentridge has stated the violence of the Herero massacre is

Fig. 9. William Kentridge, Miniature theater model for *Black Box/ Chambre Noire,* **installed at artist's studio, 2004. (Image courtesy of William Kentridge.)**

"not so far from us still."[1] While *Black Box* engages the Herero massacre, it also tells, through its pairing with *Magic Flute*, a history between the Enlightenment and colonial narratives lost in the purifying light thematized in *Magic Flute.*

Kristina Hagström-Ståhl, following Walter Benjamin, argues that *Black Box* creates a constellation of "negative" images (evoking photographic negatives), documenting histories outside of official European narratives of colonialism.[2] In doing so, Kentridge does not seek to denigrate the Enlightenment or *Magic Flute,* which he finds joy in, but rather by juxtaposing colonialism, Fascist violence, and the Enlightenment, *Black Box* necessarily complicates these historical narratives.

Black Box uses the Herero massacre as an example of colonialism's relationship to Enlightenment discourses. Christian missionaries and traders settled in South-West Africa in 1884. Reluctantly, Germany set up administrative controls. In January 1904, a Herero ambush of settlers and railway workers in an attempt to secure cattle and farmland brought them into conflict with the colonial administration.[3] To manage the war, Germany appointed General Lothar Von Trotha who undertook a ruthless pursuit of the Herero, with their complete destruction as his goal.[4] On August 11, 1904, the war reached its climax in Waterburg, where the German army encircled the Herero, expelling them into the desert, capturing survivors, and interning them in concentration camps.[5] These camps included Shark Island, referred to by German officials as *Todesinsel*, or Death Island, where death, not forced labor, was the objective of the camp's function.[6] Germany's execution policies and the prison camps left only 16,000 Herero (about 20 percent of the original population) alive after the war.[7] Furthermore, the Herero "victims' skulls were sent back to Germany to be measured, to prove the superiority of the 'Aryan' skull physical anthropology was established in Germany long before the Nazis," enjoining a constellation including other colonial discourses on racial hierarchies, Nazi eugenic studies, and racial pass laws under apartheid.[8]

Using the shadow as metaphor, Kentridge finds a closely bound dyad between the Enlightenment, shown in *Magic Flute*, and the enlightened dictator, which is in turn bound to the violence of colonial attempts, such as the Berlin Conference's aim of carving up Africa, to bring light to the "dark continent."[9] Kentridge sees Sarastro, the sorcerer and ruler of the Temple of the Sun in *Magic Flute*, as an example of this enlightened ruler. Sarastro professes a message of benevolence often undermined by his actions, holding the princess Pamina prisoner, keeping slaves, and violently punishing his servant.[10] His message of fraternity is met with images of brutality; the beating of the servant recalls postcards of lynched Herero sent back to Germany, which Kentridge references in his drawings for *Black Box*.

While historical debate circulates about the relations between German colonialism and Nazism, what is important here is the constellation they invoke.[11] The camp, for example, evokes the internment used in South-West Africa, by the United States in the Philippines, in South Africa during the Anglo-Boer War, and in the Nazi camps.[12] Another theme considered within *Black Box* is the eugenic science of Germany's colonial and Fascist histories. Kentridge represents the pleasure of the Enlightenment in *Magic Flute*, but he also narrates the brutality that represents the other side of Sarastro's fraternity. In their pairing, Kentridge also evokes the Nazi regime. He uses a score performed by the Berlin State Opera in 1937. For Kentridge, it creates an irony in Sarastro's proclamation: "Within these sacred halls, no vengeance is taken" (a passage also played in *Black Box*); applauded by Nazi officials, it undermines the fraternity of these words. It is the resonances between these histories, not necessarily a causal relationship between South-West Africa and the Holocaust, that is important for my reading.[13]

Black Box illuminates three aspects of the form: a black box theater, the camera's interior chamber (a *chambre noire*), and an airplane's flight data recorder.[14] Engaging with metaphors of the camera and theater, this essay argues that *Black Box*'s toy automata narrate history in the mode of Freudian melancholy, as lost objects within the history of the Enlightenment. The Megaphone Man invokes Freud's famous phrase *Trauerarbeit*. In his 1917 essay "Mourning and Melancholia," Freud outlines how the individual negotiates the loss of a cathected object. When such a loss occurs (Freud argues that this can happen to a nation too), the subject performs "work" to test the loss, thereby freeing the ego from its libidinal attachment to the lost object.[15] However, a neurosis occurs when the individual is not able to identify exactly what has been lost with the loss of the object. Mourning subsequently turns toward the ego, filling the subject with feelings of worthlessness and self-reproach.[16] Using toy automata as metaphors to explore this loss, *Black Box* shows the innocent joy expressed in *Magic Flute*, but it historicizes a darker side in the carving up of Africa, linking the two through the illuminated/dark dyad. In the opera, the prince Tamino waits in darkness to emerge into light, satisfying the gods and entering their fraternal kingdom. This movement from a darkened cave into the light, Kentridge argues, is functionally Plato's metaphor of the cave, where the slave is brought to the blinding light of truth by force.[17] An enlightened dictator, such as Sarastro, evokes a particular model of Enlightenment universalism that highlights its relationship to colonialism. In doing so, Kentridge does not condemn the Enlightenment, but rather the benevolent dictator that brings people to truth via force. In this system, *Trauerarbeit* becomes a useful historical tool; in it, the lost object remains intact, giving it a sense of what Freud terms "critical agency."[18] Following from Ranjana Khanna's study of psychoanalysis as a colonial "ethnography of nation-statehood," this essay engages psychoanalysis as a tool to read colonial violence, which reveals the specter of justice that haunts history.[19]

Shadows make the Enlightenment's dark side present (Kentridge makes shadow puppets and silhouettes throughout *Black Box*), a dialectic also made visible through the photographic interplay of light and shadow on the negative. Because the toy signifies *Trauerarbeit*, its play works through this pairing. The rhinoceros (a symbol of Africanness present throughout Kentridge's work, appearing in "10 Drawings for Projection" and his play *Faustus in Africa*) will, by the performance's end, reverse the metropole/colony polarity; and finally, the shadows cast across the projection's light become a crucial component of the *Black Box* qua camera by metaphorically fixing the historical meaning of their mourning on the photographic negative.

Connecting these historical fragments is a process of geographical *Trauer-arbeit* suturing Africa to Europe's Enlightenment. Kentridge prefers this fragmented history, feeling that its imperfections resist the singularity and violence represented by Plato's cave and the enlightened dictator.[20] Pairing *Black Box* and *Magic Flute* complicates representations of the Enlightenment: *Magic Flute* symbolizes its utopian end, and *Black Box* narrates its opposite in the shadow, documenting the force of bringing people to light by the force inherent in colonialism.[21] Through melancholia, the themes treated here—the Enlightenment, Africa, Europe, genocide, the Holocaust—cannot be divided; it is *Trauerarbeit*, always in process, that connects these tragic links of violence and history.

Black Box begins with the sound of mechanical drumming, as the Megaphone Man appears setting *Black Box*'s mournful tone. The sound heard is Phillip Miller's, a frequent collaborator of Kentridge's, reworking of *Magic Flute*'s overture.[22] Traditional Namibian music, pieces of a 1937 Berlin State Opera recording of *Magic Flute*, and Miller's compositions accompany the work. Kentridge's materials for *Black Box* are diverse: animations, documentary film, and puppets, including the Megaphone Man, a mechanical soldier formed from a compass, two Herero women—one formed from a spring with a piece of gauze and the other from a German postal scale, a running man formed from torn paper, and an exploding skull.[23]

The scenes form a procession of playful references clustering around images of the rhinoceros, the hunt, and signs of military discipline. Following the overture, intertitles overlaid upon maps move from Berlin to Houghton (the Johannesburg district where Kentridge lives) to Triomf and finally to Windhuk (Windhoek), Namibia's capital.[24] The robotic compass begins to march across the stage with a pointing arm, mimicking both an army march and a fascist salute that demarcates lines upon a globe in an act of mapping. The projection then morphs into a camera's shutter that captures images of the lynched men and Namibian landscapes as the running man sprints by. As "In diesen heil'gen Hallen" ("within these sacred halls," so named for Sarastro's aria in *Magic Flute*) is played, two filmed torn-paper puppets metamorphose into mechanical diagrams, striking a man with clubs. An intertitle shifts to Waterburg, as film footage of African grassland is projected, and the Namibian woman in headdress enters, bows, and retreats again. Kentridge then animates a shooting gallery: targets, animals, advertisements, and Herero men are shot at, as the running man sprints past archival images of Namibia including shackled men. Kentridge's shadow puppets follow this form of play. Through cast shadow and animation on the screen, Kentridge forms a rhinoceros, a cannon, and a German helmet whose horn resonates with the rhino.

Kentridge shows the compass measuring the skulls of German soldiers and Herero evoking eugenic research. In the final portions of the work, the rhino becomes a symbol of loss through Robert Schumann's *Rhinoceros Hunting in German East Africa* (1910–11) depicting hunters shooting a rhinoceros, congratulating each other on a successful hunt.[25] This scene reminds the viewer of the wider colonial practices in Africa. A robotic shattering skull performs a "dance macabre" on the stage, whose deathly referent pairs it with the rhinoceros's death in the hunting footage. A "Lament from the March of the Priests" follows, featuring the bowing woman set against a *Totenliste* (death register), mourning, it appears, for the Herero and for Pamina (reflecting the automata's dual status as Namibian and Queen of the Night). *Black Box* culminates with "Elegy for a Rhino," as the Megaphone Man gets an animated rhino to perform tricks, including a somersault over his head.

Black Box I: Play and the Theater

Play, invoked through the black box theater and an interaction between Kentridge's projections and the "automata," gives this complex project one of its most resonant layers of historical meaning. The use of the toy as a figure of play connects and binds the series of historical events Kentridge selects. It is also a topos that reveals the deep-seated violence in this history. To play with them in *Black Box* is to write history.[26] As Kentridge writes a melancholic history in this project, investigating the ruins of Namibian and German history, he also writes of the world of his childhood. Kentridge's parents shared their love of opera with him in a time when South Africa exerted administrative control over South-West Africa. His parents, as anti-apartheid lawyers in Johannesburg, also exposed Kentridge to the politics of racial violence at an early age. In dedicating his production of Mozart's *Magic Flute* to his parents, this first encounter of this complicated pairing of the Enlightenment and its violent dark side reveals itself in and as a children's play.

Perhaps the most crucially important toys in *Black Box* are the caliper and compass, both tools of measurement. Initially, we encounter the soldier figure formed from a compass inscribing arcs and mapping with a robotic arm that extends forward and back again as he makes his way across the stage. Rulers bind the stage as he marks lines upon a projection of a report. This compass soldier extends his arm to inscribe lines both on maps and along the boundaries of individual faces as they are measured for racial types. The compass's gesture becomes useful in colonial mapping and colonial race practices; an overlap of

Nazism and colonialism emerges as both discourses are tied to territorial expansionist projects and a race-based supremacist ideology, conditions also at work in apartheid narratives.

In a second act of measuring, a skull replaces a globe on its mountings, suggesting that the measurements taken on the skulls, infinitely extended, encompass a global worldview. This global view is undertaken with precision, showing a belief in the scientific component of ideologies of racial superiority and colonial control. And the precision of this dominance is matched through the photographic documentation of the curious other.

Black Box II: Photography

The photograph places *Black Box* in a colonial discourse. As a white opening is drawn on the outer curtains, the black box becomes a camera. "Zeiss" is scrawled atop the image, referencing the famous lens-makers. On the interior projection, newspaper clippings in negative, white-on-black format make up the shutter's pieces. The camera captures landscape images (a key theme in Kentridge's animations) and the postcard image of the lynched men.[27]

Later, an armadillo in white chalk is set against the black night sky, curling into a ball in its protective shell, fragmenting into the pieces of a shutter as it opens. In metaphorizing the camera's aperture as an animal, Kentridge renders the animal as active in the image's production, whereas earlier in *Black Box*, the animal was made a subject through the *Rhinoceros Hunting* film. In Schumann's footage, the viewer sees a rhinoceros in the bush, as a man dressed in khakis comes forward and shoots the animal at near point-blank range. The scene ends as a group of African men assists the hunters with the animal's corpse; it appears as though they were preparing to remove the foot as a trophy. The hunt is brutal and shocking: it is not the guns alone that shoot; the violence is also coded in the photograph, which attempts to be transparent and yet becomes complicit in the image's production. Susan Sontag's narrative of the photographic safari indicates how the camera replaced the gun: "One situation where people are switching from bullets to film is the photographic safari that is replacing the gun safari in East Africa. The hunters have Hasselblads instead of Winchesters; instead of looking through a telescopic sight to aim a rifle. . . . Guns have metamorphosed into cameras."[28] To take the trophy of the animal, a documentation of power and control, echoes the taking of skulls in South-West Africa. Each exists as a trophy of the power exerted over the empire.

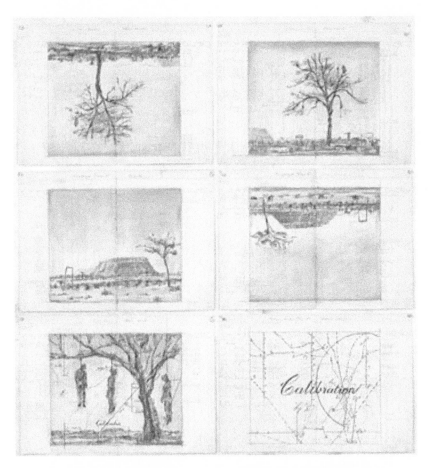

Fig. 10. William Kentridge, 6 drawings for *Black Box/Chambre Noire*, 2005. Charcoal, colored pencil, and collage on ledger pages (Mine Shares Account), each 47 x 67.4 cm. (Images courtesy of William Kentridge.)

Conclusion: Melancholic Rhinoceroses

The Megaphone Man's work takes its form in the conclusion by training the rhinoceros. Sadly, it cannot be completed; the ringleader announces a history and a loss, yet the fragments of *Black Box* are not resolved. This final playful dirge represents the majority of Kentridge's work, tying together two strands of his own life: European culture and the history of Africa. The connections be-

Fig. 11. William Kentridge, Miniature theater model for *Black Box/ Chambre Noire,* **installed at artist's studio, 2004. (Image courtesy of William Kentridge.)**

tween these two themes do not merge smoothly; the trauma of the object's loss never dissipates. As the joy of seeing the rhinoceros within Europe dissolves, we cannot but think of the somber woman (both Queen of the Night and Namibian) bowing in the brush, the brutal image of the animal being shot, and the skulls, measured and shattered.

The rhino is a central topos in Kentridge's work, making appearances in his animations and his theater work, whose elegance and absurdity convey the influence of Eugène Ionesco's play *Rhinoceros.* The image of the rhino in Kentridge's oeuvre symbolizes a loss within Africa, both literally, as we see the hunting of a species extinguished while Kentridge produced *Black Box,* and figuratively; the rhino becomes an ironic symbol of safety: it is safer to sleep in the game preserves than in Johannesburg due to the increasing violence and tensions resulting from immigration and class strife in post-apartheid South Africa.[29]

Within a larger historical context, the rhinoceros's ancient qualities suggest that the rhinoceros, like Africa in the "dark continent" view that is construed as being much like being in Plato's cave, is without culture. Yet its armor-like skin also suggests it is an image of violence and militaristic expansion. The animal signifies both aspects of Namibia's tragic history. The rhino appears in *Black Box* both as a drawing and in appropriated film footage, which leads the viewer between the optical dualisms of the shadow and its image. It is something at once alien to Europe and rooted at its core; the rhinoceros represents the wild animal of Africa and Asia, something of which awakens a sense of mystique and curiosity, but Kentridge takes it as being a key image of Europe. These rhinos, brought from the imaginary peripheries of European knowledge as a source of amazement and wonderment, become a double of the skull in *Black Box*. As the skull travels back to Europe having been a witness to the Herero massacre, the rhinoceros too becomes a part of European culture, communicating back with Europe and integrating itself into Europe's core. This transmission carries out the photographic fixing alluded to by the black box's camera metaphors: the rhinoceros becomes a beam or a trajectory from Africa within European consciousness. This is poignantly reflected not only in the images of the animal being hunted, but also in the closing sequences of *Black Box*. The rhinoceros performs a series of tricks under the direction of the *Trauerarbeit* cone, suggesting that the African other has been brought under the control of Europe.

Undertaking research for *Black Box* in Namibia, Kentridge visited a national park where the graves of German soldiers are kept and found a visitor's book containing messages such as "'thank you for taking such good care of the graves' and 'please can there be no more war in our times and you do such honor to these people.'"[30] Yet, there is no mention of the Herero massacre. *Black Box*'s *Trauerarbeit* works against the forgetting and erasure represented at the park, narrating through erasure both its history and its loss. Kentridge, considering the legacies of nationalism in South African landscape painting, argues that the landscape holds something "other than pure nature," invoking the violence that occurred on the South African landscape during apartheid and in Auschwitz.[31] Rendering a sense of history that cannot be fully erased, that haunts the present, allows their history to be documented, and as Khanna argues, creates a terrain for the demand of justice. It is from this force that *Black Box* draws its critical agency. It is not simply a causal relationship between Windhoek and Auschwitz, but also the demands for remembrance in South-West Africa made in *Black Box*, that create a terrain where these historical injustices become linked through a politicization of melancholia.

Such melancholic loss is symbolized through the deathly skull and the forgotten rhino. The rhino has become the symbol of loss and grief: the image of the rhino as a sign of the destruction of Africa (the species of rhino in the

Schumann film became extinct during Kentridge's work on *Black Box*, high-lighting the persistence of this destruction) in the name of European colonialism calls for remembrance. To turn inward is to locate the fragments of these histories, to transform and make a new image that undercuts the status quo of ideologies that would separate histories of colonialism and the Enlightenment. This work brings together concerns over loss that tightly bind historical narratives in Germany, South Africa, and Namibia while insisting on a stronger presence for the history of the "dark continent" globally, which like *Trauerarbeit*, must continually be worked through. This making is at the core of *Black Box*, revealed through his shadow puppets and toy automata, which metamorphose while engaging in this history. The toy can be that device most able to reconstruct and radically change the contexts of the images they are given. To be able to play, and to preserve some joy in the representation, allows one to go forward; this realization is at the core of the analyst's work, and of Kentridge's production.

NOTES

1. Cheryl Kaplan, "Inside the Black Box: William Kentridge in an Interview," *Db artmag* 31 (2005): accessed July 15, 2012, http://db-artmag.de/archiv/2005/e/7/1/383. html. This article also includes a number of additional images of *Black Box/Chambre Noire*.

2. Kristina Hagström-Ståhl, "Mourning as Method: William Kentridge's *Black Box/Chambre Noire*," *Arcadia* 45, no. 2 (2011): 350–51.

3. Helmut Bley, *Namibia under German Rule* (New Brunswick: Transaction, 1996), 149.

4. Ibid., 159, 164.

5. Ibid., 162.

6. Benjamin Madley, "From Africa to Auschwitz," *European History Quarterly* 35, no. 3 (2005): 446–47.

7. Bley, *Namibia under German Rule*, 150–51.

8. William Kentridge and Maria-Christina Villaseñor, *Black Box/Chambre Noire* (New York: Guggenheim Museum Publications, 2005), 51.

9. Ibid., 47, 49.

10. Hagström-Ståhl, "Mourning as Method," 341.

11. Jürgen Zimmerer argues that the Herero massacre was genocide, and Benjamin Madley believes it directly influenced Nazi theories on race. Robert Gerwarth and Stephan Malinowski, responding to Madley and Hannah Arendt's linking colonialism and totalitarianism, understand the German actions in South-West Africa as a part of a wider legacy of American and European colonial practices. See Robert Gerwarth and Stephan Malinowski, "Hannah Arendt's Ghosts: Reflections on the Disputable Path from Windhoek to Auschwitz," *Central European History* 42 (2009): 279–300; Madley,

"From Africa to Auschwitz"; and Jürgen Zimmerer and Joachim Zeller, eds., *Genocide in German South-West Africa*, trans. Edward Neather (Monmouth, Wales: Merlin Press, 2008).

12. Samuel Weber, "Bare Life and Life in General," *Grey Room* 46 (Winter 2012): 12–14.

13. Kaplan.

14. Kentridge and Villaseñor, *Black Box/Chambre Noire*, 51.

15. Sigmund Freud, *Murder, Mourning and Melancholia*, ed. Adam Phillips, trans. Shaun Whiteside (London: Penguin Books, 2005), 203–5.

16. Ibid., 205–6.

17. Kentridge and Villaseñor, *Black Box/Chambre Noire*, 45–47.

18. Ranjana Khanna, *Dark Continents: Psychoanalysis and Colonialism* (Durham: Duke University Press, 2003), 23.

19. Ibid., 6–7.

20. Angela Breidbach and William Kentridge, *William Kentridge: Thinking Aloud* (Cologne: Walther König, 2006), 97.

21. Kentridge and Villaseñor, *Black Box/Chambre Noire*, 51.

22. Hagström-Ståhl, 343.

23. Kaplan.

24. Triomf is a Johannesburg suburb where the apartheid government forcibly relocated black and coloured (a South African term for mixed race) residents to make way for working-class Afrikaner families. Johannesburg's city council has restored its original name of Sophiatown.

25. Kentridge and Villaseñor, *Black Box/Chambre Noire*, 95.

26. Ibid., 85.

27. See William Kentridge, *William Kentridge* (London: Phaidon, 1999), 122–27, for a discussion of his approach to landscape.

28. Susan Sontag, *On Photography* (New York: Picador, 1973), 15.

29. William Kentridge, "Learning from the Absurd" (Avenali Lecture, University of California at Berkeley, March 15, 2009), accessed January 29, 2010, http://townsend-center.berkeley.edu/webcast_Kentridge.shtml.

30. Kaplan.

31. Kentridge, *William Kentridge*, 110–11.

Germans and the Death-Throes of the Qing

Mo Yan's *The Sandalwood Torture*

Yixu Lü

Orientation

In 2001, a century after the final suppression of the Boxer Uprising, Mo Yan, a writer of considerable standing in the People's Republic and winner of the Nobel Prize for Literature in 2012, published a novel that has the German co-lonial presence in Shandong play a prominent role. The plot centers on the suppression of militant Boxers, who had attacked the German railway con-struction sites in the district of Gaomi, by the provincial governor Yuan Shikai in concert with German forces. Historical records show that German troops had been involved from March 1899 till late November 1900 in bloody clashes with both peasants and Boxers, occasioned by local resistance to the building of the railway from Qingdao to Jinan. The district of Gaomi, Mo Yan's birth-place, was occupied by these German forces in late 1900. Yuan Shikai then forced the populace to pay compensation to the Germans in early 1901. A particularly bloody conflict on 1 November 1900, in which the Germans be-sieged and demolished the fortified town of Shawo, resulted in an estimated 450 civilian casualties.[1]

In an afterword to his *The Sandalwood Torture*, Mo Yan recalls a visit to his home village in Gaomi in 1986, ten years before he began work on the novel. Hearing a melody from a popular art form, the "cat opera," reminds him of other such songs he had heard and sung in his youth, celebrating legendary and heroic local resistance to the German military in 1900, and this is offered by the author as the genesis of the novel he began to write in 1996.[2] It thus promises to be a Chinese response to the impact of German colonialism on a place and people with whom the author openly and strongly identifies. Its ap-parent affinities to the "nativist" school in contemporary Chinese fiction, whose best-known representative, the older writer Jia Pingwa, is also acknowledged in Mo Yan's afterword, lead to the further question as to how the colonial era in China is presented to a readership facing the more urgent issues of globalization. A French translation, *Le Supplice du santal*, appeared in 2006, followed by a paperback edition in 2009. A German translation also appeared in 2009 to coincide with the Frankfurt Book Fair's focus on China and was subsidized by the government of the People's Republic. An English version followed in 2012.[3]

This raises the question, to which I shall return at the end of this analysis, of the extent to which Mo Yan's novel adheres to or departs from an officially approved view of China's more recent history. Wang Ning's essay *The Mapping of Chinese Postmodernity* places him in that group of "avant-gardist" writers who "are seeking to compromise with the current trend of commercialization and to find a comfortable intermediate zone between writing for literature and writing for the market."[4] The question of compromise in the political sphere as well arises with Mo Yan's work more generally, since it has obviously provocative aspects but yet seems to set off no alarms with the censor and, indeed, can attract government subsidies to be translated. Reviewing a translation of short stories by Mo Yan written in the years 1985–87, Kam Louie describes their usually violent contents as "blood-thirsty" and "gut-wrenching," and concludes: "Personally, my stomach is not strong enough for me to say that I enjoy these stories, but they do represent a major trend in Chinese fiction of the 1980s."[5] Much the same comment might be made of the provocative subject-matter of large tracts of *The Sandalwood Torture*, but here the additional question arises of how the breaking of taboos relates to the treatment of China's past as a colonized nation. Mo Yan's earlier novels of the 1990s do combine an assault on the sensibilities of the average reader with an undercurrent of political commentary, and we must enquire of *The Sandalwood Torture* whether it also contains a subversive political sub-text.

Thus *The Republic of Wine*, first published in Chinese in 1992 and in English in 2000, is a social satire that revels in the transgressive theme of cannibalism. This was followed in 1995 by *Fengru feitun*, with the English translation *Big Breasts and Wide Hips* appearing in 2005. Here the obsessive transgression that carries the plot is evident from the title. Just as cannibalism in *The Republic of Wine* may be read in the words of its English translator Howard Goldblatt as an allegory meant "to portray the oppression of the common people by representatives of the 'people's government,'"[6] so sexuality in this novel has been given a plausible allegorical reading in terms of the history of China in the twentieth century by Rong Cai.[7] Such allegories are, of course, reductionist and can do no justice to the loving care with which Mo Yan, in *The Sandalwood Torture*, creates an epic out of the recent history of his native Gaomi. They also of necessity bypass the sophistication of Mo Yan's narrative techniques. In *The Sandalwood Torture* these include the apportioning of the narrative among the "voices" of the main characters, which sometimes overlap in time, thus giving different perspectives on the same events, sometimes advance the narrative in a conventional manner, but at others move back into the past in a way that may disconcert the reader. In addition, there is the factor that these "voices" are sometimes tied very closely to the fictional characters, while at others they permit the emergence of an omniscient narrator, but without such transitions being clearly marked.

Throughout the novel there also is the puzzling effect of narrative mirroring, since the voices always begin by purporting to sing arias from a "cat opera" that has, in fact, the same plot as the novel itself. In this sense, narrative episodes that begin in a realistic mode are often visibly transformed into posed theatrical tableaux, and this, in turn, creates a meta-fictional dimension of the novel that may leave many readers puzzled. For the question arises: where is the locus of the novel's dominant reality? Is it in the efforts of those characters that are sympathetically drawn to make a life for themselves in the face of adverse historical circumstances, or are these merely a pretext for extended game-playing with an operatic fiction? The novel gives no obvious answer. By way of compensation, Mo Yan offers the conventionally minded reader many passages of vividly realistic and evocative narration, which are especially effective when the life of the common people is in the foreground.

Indeed, his literary trademark could be seen as the ability to combine such evocations with a self-conscious virtuosity in the deployment of narrative modes that has left the linear narratives of socialist realism far behind. The intricacy of his plotting in each work does not permit, within the scope of this brief essay, an extensive comparison of his technique in *The Sandalwood Torture* with the narrative modes of his two preceding novels. Suffice it to say that he employs comparable techniques in each, although these are more likely to mystify the reader in *The Sandalwood Torture* for reasons I shall later enlarge on.

In terms of his reception in contemporary China, it seems that his obsessive transgressions are acceptable as long as they are situated within an ideological framework that observes certain Revolutionist political proprieties. *The Sandalwood Torture* abounds in transgressions of various kinds, but these are effectively kept under control by a plot that casts a cold and remorseless eye on the final decadence of the Qing Dynasty, demonizes Yuan Shikai as the embodiment of an inhumane drive for self-aggrandizement, and turns the common people of Shandong into the collective, heroic protagonist of the work. It, like the two novels before it, seems to rely on an aesthetic of excess in the foreground, while apparently remaining quite docile in the deeper, political dimension, but this conjecture remains to be tested.

Torture and the Colonial Intrusion

Mo Yan's transgressions in this work revolve most spectacularly and, indeed, repugnantly around the person of Zhao Jia, former Chief Executioner and Master of Torture at the Qing Court who, in the summer of the year 1900, lives in retirement in his birthplace Gaomi. Zhao Jia is a virtuoso of his craft and sees it, in an audience with the Dowager Empress, in positive moral terms: "Your servant is of the view that the executioner is indeed a reprehensible person, but the work he does is not. The executioner embodies the dignity of the state. Even if the state has a thousand laws, it all comes down to the fact that the executioner puts them into practice" (Ch 408; G 477).

This is, of course, *not* the dominant perspective offered by the whole novel. The narrative is carried by a plurality of voices, and the majority of them remind the reader incessantly that the Qing Dynasty is hopelessly corrupt, is on the point of collapse, and has lost all contact with traditional Chinese values, a process exemplified here by Zhao Jia's grandiose self-portrayal. In his youth Zhao Jia became an executioner in order purely to survive, but the years in whose course he puts 987 victims to death have left him with no identity but his craft, and it is Yuan Shikai who then orders the old man to carry out elaborate tortures that are described in such detail as to require a strong stomach on the reader's part. The victims in the longest torture-scenes are, first, Qian Xiongfei, a young officer who attempted to assassinate Yuan Shikai in 1898, and, second, Sun Bing, a former actor, tea-house proprietor and leader of the Boxers, who is the father of the Prefect of Gaomi's lover, the beautiful Meiniang, and a central figure in the novel. Qian Xiongfei is quite peripheral to the main plot, and the only effect of describing Zhao Jia's live dismemberment of him for twenty-five pages in the original text is to mark Yuan Shikai once and for all as a sadistic monster—a full two years before the main events in Gaomi. One should note the strategic positioning of this episode in the novel, since its appalling savagery precedes any atrocities committed by the foreign intruders. The message thus appears to be that the worst aspects of Qing misrule, as embodied in Yuan Shikai, can only be reinforced, not surpassed, by the German military.

The second elaborate torture, from which the work takes its title, is the culmination of the central plot and the final episode in the novel. The German military has had no part in the death of Qian Xiongfei or the earlier scenes depicting tortures carried out by Zhao Jia, but the devising of the sandalwood torture is a joint effort on the part of Yuan Shikai, the German commander in Shandong, and the former Chief Executioner. It is—significantly—the only scene in the novel in which any German character has anything at all to say.

Thus the thematics of torture raise the question of the impact of the "foreign Other" on the events of this fictional world. For the Germans may seem effectively relegated to the role of offering Yuan Shikai just a further pretext for yet another public exhibition of torture. Mo Yan follows history in having Yuan Shikai command massacres of Boxers in Shandong.[8] The novel ignores, however, the fact that his troops massacred only those Boxers who remained in Shandong, defying his order to leave the province and go to the region between Tianjin and Beijing. Rather, Mo Yan conflates historical German reprisals against attacks on the railway they were building near Gaomi with Yuan Shikai's overall and quite Machiavellian strategy.[9] In the novel, Yuan Shikai displays not the slightest interest in what the Boxers do or do not do outside the district of Shangdong. In contrast to the historical record, Mo Yan insists that troops sent by Yuan Shikai join with German soldiers in the destruction of a village near Gaomi, whereas in fact the Germans rejected such joint deployments, although in all other respects they saw in Yuan Shikai a model of collaboration.[10]

This is a perfectly legitimate strategy in a fictional version of history, but it does have a surprising effect on how the novel represents the "foreign Other," for it effectively turns the Germans into less interesting alter egos of Yuan Shikai. If one reconstructs the chronology of the novel—blurred, as one reads it, by the narrative "voices" leaping backward and forward in time—then Yuan Shikai has ordered the most gruesome and stomach-turning torture long before the Germans enter the plot at all. When they do so, only their commander is permitted a brief dialogue with Yuan Shikai. Even this individualization is toned down in a way that leaves him a barely sketched minor character. Mo Yan deliberately gave the German Commander a name that bears no phonetic resemblance to the name of the German commander who actually led the German punitive expedition in Gaomi in 1900.

This is not to minimize the effect of the German colonial *presence*. Mo Yan has so constructed his plot as to make the German colonial undertaking the single most important factor that destabilizes all the efforts of the Prefect of Gaomi, Qian Ding, to maintain a precarious balance between his Confucian values and the demands of his office. His failure and consequent humiliation plunges the district into turmoil and thus precipitates the catastrophe. The consistent depersonalization of the Germans leaves them as a force that will bring out the worst in those aspects of the late Qing that the author sees as incarnate in Yuan Shikai: without the Germans, his sadism would remain confined to the torture of the young officer Qian Xiongfei; as a catalyst, the German presence extends his destructive powers to encompass the death of characters and the negation of values that attract the reader's sympathies.

Sun Bing, while not yet a Boxer, has gravely wounded a German railway technician who was publicly molesting his wife. When he is finally captured and brought before Yuan Shikai and the German Commander, the latter's role is limited to suggesting a possible way in which an excessively cruel torture might be applied to the condemned man. It is left to Zhao Jia to propose the solution that Yuan Shikai enthusiastically adopts of keeping Sun Bing alive for several days while impaled on a shaft of sandalwood. Torture thus becomes a hyperbole that subsumes and obscures all specific aspects of German colonialism, which were surely different in historical terms from Yuan Shikai's cunning accretion of personal power, and lets them merge into a dull commonality with the latter's savoring of pain for its own sake.

For the rest, the Germans are like extras on a film set, present only in violent crowd scenes and distinguished from Yuan Shikai's troops purely by their physical characteristics ("green eyes"), efficiency, and readiness to massacre any Chinese in sight without asking questions. Yuan Shikai's bloodthirsty placating of the Germans is presented partly as cynical *Realpolitik*, partly as evidence of the sadism he has already displayed in abundance in the execution of Qian Xiongfei, so that the function in the plot of the "foreign Other" is kept to very narrow parameters and confined within the most banal clichés of "foreign devils." In the plot of this novel, it is as if a century has not passed since the events of summer 1900, while the literary techniques are, in direct contrast, evidence of Mo Yan's assimilation of Western influences, some of which Wang Ning has listed, although none is consistently active in the narrative.[11]

That the Qing Dynasty is moribund is spelled out in great detail in the monologues of Qian Ding, Prefect of Gaomi, one of the mixed characters in the novel, who is adrift between the humane doctrines of Confucian China; his passion for Meiniang, a vendor of dog's meat but Gaomi's greatest beauty; and what is demanded of him by his overlord Yuan Shikai. Aspiring to be a "father to his people," he is crushed by Yuan Shikai and becomes increasingly estranged from his role as part of the state machinery until, in the concluding pages of the novel, he finally breaks the mold of his office and puts an end to Sun Bing's torment with a merciful coup de grâce, frustrating the intention of Yuan Shikai and the Germans to make a spectacle of the Boxer's last moments as part of the ceremony to mark the opening of the railway.

Thus the interest of the novel in the "foreign Other" remains—in contrast to *Big Breasts and Wide Hips*—merely token. The Western reader may well regard this as a missed opportunity, since depiction of the Germans never breaks the mold of cliché. The portrayal of the German presence, however, gives rise to the following paradox: the Germans are essential to the plot but do not appear to merit any but the most perfunctory characterization. In this sense, one might describe their metaphoric function as that of an instrument the moribund Qing Dynasty uses to encompass and intensify its own self-humiliation. To be more accurate: it is the dynastic *idea* that is degraded in the wake of the colonialist intrusion. This is evidenced by the destruction of Qian Ding, the magistrate who still adheres to the old Confucian values. What the dynasty has become in reality is represented by Yuan Shikai, who rides the colonialist wave and is free at the end to wreak further havoc. However that may be, it is the author's choice to keep the central focus of the novel determinedly on the sympathetic Chinese characters, for it is in their portrayal that his real interest lies.

A Dysfunctional Family

During the demise of the Qing Dynasty, Mo Yan sees good as residing principally in the oppressed common people. However, his determination to avoid the simplistic templates of socialist realism results in an absence of idealization in the creation of his main characters. Rather, he assembles a totally improbable family constellation as a means of fleshing out the detail of a society on the verge of collapse. Meiniang, whose first "aria" and monologue open the novel, is the daughter of Sun Bing and the lover of Qian Ding. She is also the wife of Xiao Jia, the mentally retarded son of Zhao Jia, the retired Chief Executioner. In the novel's conclusion, she kills her father-in-law, while her lover kills her husband, by accident, and finally her father—so as to end his suffering and defy Yuan Shikai. She is pregnant with Qian Ding's child, but the novel is silent as to her future. It is implied that Qian Ding will commit suicide, as his final act leaves him no other resort. Thus the happy ending the reader is encouraged to expect toward the end of the novel, namely, that Qian Ding will strip off his robes of office, disappear into the masses with Meiniang and found a new family, is firmly ruled out.

While Mo Yan has created a family nexus whose final chaotic phase may remind us of the end of Shakespeare's *Hamlet*, but without the sane survivor Horatio, it is easy to see how individual characters contribute to the structural elaboration of the fictional world into which the reader enters. Repelling as the figure of Zhao Jia may be, his monologues offer vignettes of the Qing Court, notably of the historical execution of the six reformist "heroes" in 1898.[12] The mandarin Qian Ding's passion for Meiniang allows an exposition of the class barriers in Qing society, and the lamentable end of a love that has survived three whole years as a transgression of prevailing social norms is illustrative of a society that does not permit such liberties to go unpunished. A cameo role is even included for Qian Ding's aristocratic wife, who so far overcomes her background and her jealousy of Meiniang that she saves her rival's life when Meiniang and the local beggars make an unsuccessful assault on the *yamen* to free Sun Bing. Thus goodness may be found everywhere but in the overriding power structures.

The whole populace of Gaomi kneeling before the *yamen* and pleading exonerating circumstances for the rebel Sun Bing makes one of the most moving scenes of the novel, and—with an eye to the future—locates the sole center of hope in the unity of a people freed from class distinctions. Sun Bing, the actor turned rebel, opens the novel into the world of the "cat opera," which will occupy us in the final section. If Qian Ding becomes a mixed character through his over-long vacillation between his official role and what he feels to be right, Sun Bing is also made to fail as a hero through his arrogance, impulsiveness, and a subordination of humane values to theatrical effects. In this sense, he and Qian Ding have much in common across the social divide. Both are a congeries of human frailty, but both emerge from the final scene with their humanity restored. Neither seems equal to the love Meiniang bears them, and yet even she is not idealized, although she does emerge as the most interesting character in the novel.

She is full of an earthy vitality, but in the phase when she believes her love for Qian Ding is unrequited, her suffering elevates her to a heroine of the "cat opera"—as Mo Yan has chosen to represent it, for much of what is related of the origins and ultimate sophistication of this art form seems to be fictional. Her language is at times that of the gutter, at others highly stylized, indeed, so much so that it seems quite implausible that a people's art form such as the "cat opera" could produce such flights of elevated prose. Here more than elsewhere, the reader is led to the conclusion that the cat opera—while it may have its roots in a genuine popular tradition—is transformed by Mo Yan into whatever suits the purposes of his work.

Forcing such disparate characters into the one family constellation has the obvious further aim of demonstrating how the death-throes of the Qing Dynasty import chaos into the traditional Chinese family, irrespective of status. The bloody end of all the main characters except Meiniang foreshadows the collapse of a dynasty that is beyond salvation. Yuan Shikai survives, indeed will secure advancement, but this is because he is less than human, incarnating the worst of what is and what is to come.

Mirroring the Cat Opera

Mo Yan is an inveterate literary game-player. In a somewhat disingenuous afterword to the novel, he describes it as a nostalgic tribute to the popular art form that he came to love in his childhood and that still survives—albeit precariously—in the district of Gaomi. This is putting it very mildly, since the cat opera, in its fanciful elaboration, becomes the dominant meta-fiction that structures the whole novel. All the main characters—even Zhao Jia—sing "arias" from a work with the same title as the novel, and reminders of the plot's underlying theatricality come thick and fast. Yuan Shikai and the Germans do not have "arias" or inner monologues, but this is because they are never accorded the status of whole characters. The Boxer Uprising is evoked in strongly theatrical terms, so that, when German soldiers massacre a troupe performing cat operas to honor Sun Bing as he is close to death, it is open to the reader to decide whether they simply mistake the players for Boxer insurgents or else just automatically shoot anyone disturbing the order of the execution. The words with which the dying Sun Bing concludes the novel—"The performance is . . . over" (Ch 558, G 638)—remind the reader one last time that so many of the events and speeches in this monumental work are essentially theater.

I have termed Mo Yan's comments on his own work disingenuous, since nothing whatsoever in them refers to the scenes of torture that have no antecedents in the cat opera but throw the aesthetic unity of the work out of kilter. Moreover, his description of his own work seems deliberately inaccurate. He states that, "when I took up the work again, I was forced to recognize that it was full of magical realism." He then claims to have pruned all this out of the text "in favor of a stronger emphasis on popular appeal and a genuinely Chinese style" (Ch 566, G 651). In point of fact, a great deal of "magical realism" remains, especially in the evocations of the Boxer rituals, the "arias" of Meiniang, and the final tableau. It is, indeed, hard to imagine a version of this novel that could sustain more "magical realism" and more meta-fictionality without these dimensions splitting off from those passages of sustained realistic evocation that give readers some ground beneath their feet. Thus, with the exception of what he says about the novel's being set in the town where he grew up and his remarks on the centrality of the cat opera as he chooses to depict it, the afterword might seem to be about another version of the novel than the one to which it is attached. This means that, for want of other documentation, the reader is obliged to take a great deal of what is said about the cat opera on trust, both within the novel and in the afterword. The discrepancies between the afterword and the novel itself have the further effect of creating an aura of doubt as to whether this people's art form, in historical terms, came anywhere near the elaborate sophistication that the novel assigns it—yet more game-playing.

For the problem is that the torture scenes are also presented as highly theatrical tableaux, but, like contemporary May Day parades, they amount to official pageants of intimidation. The cat opera—so the novel tells us—arises spontaneously from the suffering of the oppressed; the torture scenes reinforce a point that is made so often about power in this disintegrating state that it is hard to see why Mo Yan did not simply omit the description of Zhao Jia slicing 500 pieces of live flesh off the body of Quian Xiongfei, for it may well result in some readers preferring not to persevere with the book. A further difficulty with the extended descriptions of torture is the apparent gusto with which Mo Yan narrates them.

When it comes to questions of literary evaluation, it is hard not to find long stretches of the novel self-indulgent on the author's part, since the narrative is simply too repetitious to sustain the interest of most readers. Even aficionados of torture have to wait a long while between orgies of cruelty. The run-up to the climax of Sun Bing's immolation in the concluding episode does indeed show brilliant literary craftsmanship, for Mo Yan finally stops ringing the changes on the plot's chronology and allows the narrative to gather pace. But the question remains: did this well-wrought finale require such a long drawn-out preparation? Answers will differ. Taken separately, the vignettes of Chinese life have their own fascination; it is their sheer quantity and repetitiveness that may tax a reader's patience. This bears on the questionable grouping of Mo Yan, mentioned earlier, with those "avant-gardists" who "compromise with the current trend of commercialization."[13] This may well apply to *The Republic of Wine*, but with *The Sandalwood Torture* the opposite seems to be the case. Rather, Mo Yan seems here to capitalize on his standing as a successful novelist to pay scant regard to market expectations: the novel will be bought anyway, especially if the torture scenes become notorious.

As a Chinese response to German colonialism, the novel is curiously uninformative and undifferentiated: any foreign colonial presence could have served as a catalyst for the former actor Sun Bing's transformation from a teahouse proprietor with a wife and two children into a fanatical leader of a Boxer offensive. For the Germans are made to be little more than symptoms of the sickness unto death that afflicts the Qing Dynasty, and all the virulence of this disease is concentrated in Yuan Shikai. No censor is ever likely to have trouble with that, though Western readers may wish the author had used the distance afforded by a century of Chinese history to allow some of his technical sophistication to flow on to his depictions of the specifically German colonial presence in Gaomi.

To return to the question I posed at the outset of whether, as in other novels, Mo Yan has built a subversive sub-text into this narrative of China's colonial past, one must recognize in the novel's background the increasing presence, in official Chinese publications, of the discourse of "national humiliation" in the 1990s as part of the state's "patriotic education" initiative in the wake of the Tiananmen Square massacre.[14] In the course of this, "policy was formulated [. . .] to *redirect* protest towards the external Other."[15] It is in this context that the depiction of foreign intruders in the novel should be assessed. My conclusion is that, at first glance, what Mo Yan gives with one hand he takes with the other. Readers are left in no doubt that the foreign intrusion is a prime factor in unleashing violence on the common people, that it brings no good to China, and that the foreign military has no compunction in massacring Chinese civilians. In these respects, it reinforces the discourse of "patriotic education."

Against this, the world of the Qing Court and Yuan Shikai, as portrayed in the "arias" and inner monologues of the executioner Zhao Jia in advance of any conflicts involving foreigners, is already so bereft of humane values and concern for the people's welfare that the foreign presence cannot make it worse. The depiction of the Boxer Uprising shows it as having its roots in the peasantry, yet the excess of "magical realism" in the depiction of Boxer rituals, especially the obtrusive intertextuality of these episodes with Wu Cheng'en's *Journey to the West*, threatens to transpose history into the realm of aesthetic play, as does the presence of the cat opera troupe in the final scene.

To return, by way of conclusion, to Mo Yan's enigmatic afterword to the novel, it is from here that we may derive some further insight into the status he accords the German colonial presence. There he dates the beginning of work on the novel to 1996, so that the negative portrayal of the Germans seems to accord in every way with the xenophobic official line promulgated in these years, as set out by Willy Wo-lap Nam.[16] Yet here he also speaks of an earlier version of the novel in which the "railway," emblematic of the colonial presence, had a much stronger "voice." But this version was allegedly discarded in favor of the novel as it appears: "Finally I decided to weaken the voice of the railway to let the voice of the cat opera come through more strongly" (Ch 566, G 651). Earlier in the afterword he has said that the essence of the novel is its "voices," and it is not going too far to say that the gift of a "voice" to a character within the fiction is a mark of the narrator's sympathy or approval. I have pointed out earlier, for example, that Meiniang is endowed with a "voice" in her arias whose elevated style and eloquence breaks the mold of her character as a seller of dog's meat. Not only are individual Germans denied a "voice" in this sense, but they are also depersonalized here as "the voice of the railway." The cat opera has a multitude of vital and lovingly crafted human voices, whereas the colonial voice is reduced to a mere function. One might therefore say the Germans are instrumentalized in the final version of the novel, and that this is the supreme insult.

The colonialists intrude on the plot as the railway intrudes on the rural landscape, disrupting its *feng shui* and destroying graves. Thus the dissolution of the precarious happiness of the main characters is set in train by the nameless German who happens to molest Sun Bing's wife at the marketplace. But colonial power is limited to the function of a chance disruption—the novel has already spelt out in abundance that the prime evil is vested in Yuan Shikai. It is as if the novel were saying: "By all means resent the foreign intrusion, but realize there is a far greater danger for the people in the decadence of the Chinese state." In this sense the novel does more than merely echo the official line of the late 1990s. It may also indicate Mo Yan's response to the impact of globalization on China: worse than any external threat is the betrayal of Chinese core values. For there is no ignoring the nostalgic perspective of the whole work. It is manifest in the apotheosis of the cat opera and also in the narrator's sympathy for the dilemmas of Qian Ding who vainly tries to uphold the best values of the Old China, anachronistic as this may appear. Mo Yan may thus be seen as creating a "historical" past that mirrors the official line of the era of Jiang Zemin, but also as blurring its contours in a way that is unobtrusively but effectively subversive—provided readers are able and willing to decipher the message.

NOTES

1. See Klaus Mühlhahn, *Herrschaft und Widerstand in der "Musterkolonie" Kiautschou* (Munich: Oldenbourg, 2000), 122–34; Annette S. Biener, *Das deutsche Pachtgebiet Tsingtau in Schantung 1897–1914. Institutioneller Wandel durch Kolonisierung* (Bonn: Selbstverlag Matzat, 2001), 42–47.

2. Mo Yan, *Tanxiang xing* (Beijing: Writers' Publishing House, 2nd ed., 2005); Karin Betz, trans., *Die Sandelholzstrafe* (Frankfurt am Main: Insel Verlag, 2009). An English translation by Howard Goldblatt with the title *Sandalwood Death* (University of Oklahoma Press) appeared in November 2012. My translation of the title, *The Sandalwood Torture*, is closer to the original, and will be used throughout this essay; references in the body of the text will be to the second Chinese edition of 2005 (Ch) and to the German translation (G). All translations from the Chinese text are by the author.

3. An enquiry to Professor Howard Goldblatt of the University of Notre Dame, the most frequent translator of Mo Yan into English, yielded the information that sales of Mo Yan's other novels in English were such that a subsidy was required to undertake the task of translating this one. With the awarding of the Nobel Prize, this situation is likely to change for future works by Mo Yan.

4. Ning Wang, "The Mapping of Chinese Postmodernity," *boundary* 2 24, no. 3 (Autumn 1997): 30.

5. Kam Louie, review of *Explosions and Other Stories*, by Mo Yan, *Australian Journal of Chinese Affairs* 29 (January 1993): 196.

6. Howard Goldblatt, "'The Saturnicon.' Forbidden Food of Mo Yan," *World Literature Today* 74, no. 3 (Summer 2000): 483.

7. See Rong Cai, "Problematizing the Foreign Other: Mother, Father and the Bastard in Mo Yan's *Large Breasts and Full Hips*," *Modern China* 29, no. 1 (2003): 122 f.: "Through the death of the foreign father and the rape of the woman, the native patriarch reclaims his right over the symbolic female body. Mother is punished for adultery, which takes on added offense because it involves an alien man and therefore insults the masculinist nationalist sensibility. [. . .] But undeniably the foreign Other has produced a stubborn presence."

8. Joseph W. Esherick, *The Origins of the Boxer Uprising* (Berkeley: University of California Press, 1987), 312: "The man who gained more than anyone as a result of the Boxer Uprising was Yuan Shikai. His bloody suppression of the Boxers in Shandong had saved that province from further interference and gained him important foreign admirers as well. In December 1901, he was appointed governor-general of Zhili and Commissioner of Northern Ports, taking charge of military and foreign affairs in North China."

9. Paul A. Cohen, *History in Three Keys: The Boxers as Event, Experience and Myth* (New York: Columbia University Press, 1997), 51: "In Shandong also [. . .] the staunchly anti-Boxer governor Yuan Shikai took effective measures to prevent loss of foreign life. Although more than 300 Chinese Christians were killed in the province, by far the largest number of casualties were Boxers who ignored Yuan Shikai's orders to proceed to the Tianjin-Beijing area to assist in fighting against the foreigners."

10. Biener, *Das deutsche Pachtgebiet Tsingtau*, 46: "Im Sommer [1900] hatte man den Bahnbau von Tsingtau bis Kiaotschou durch deutsche Truppen schützen lassen, nun wollte man bei der Verlängerung der Strecke bis Kaumi ebenso verfahren. Zunächst mussten die dort stationierten 600 chinesischen Soldaten von Yüan Schih-kai aus der 50-Kilometer-Zone zurückgezogen werden, was unverzüglich geschah."

11. Ning Wang, "The Mapping of Chinese Postmodernity," 26.

12. Wolfgang Bauer, *China und die Fremden. 3000 Jahre Auseinandersetzung in Krieg und Frieden* (Munich: Verlag C. H. Beck, 1980), 227.

13. Ning Wang, "The Mapping of Chinese Postmodernity," 30.

14. William A. Callahan, *China: The Pessoptimist Nation* (Oxford: Oxford University Press, 2010), 31–60.

15. William A. Callahan, "Historical Legacies and Non/Traditional Society: Commemorating National Humiliation Day in China," https://www.dur.ac.uk/resources/china.studies/Commemorating%20National%20Humiliation%20Day%20in%20China.pdf. Accessed May 28, 2013.

16. Willy Wo-lap Lam, *The Era of Jiang Zemin* (Singapore: Prentice-Hall, 1999), 265–76.

The Origins of German Minority
Cinema in Colonial Film

Patrice Nganang

How can one account for the changing definition of both *minority* and *Germany* while writing a history of Germany's minority cinema? This essay is an attempt to answer this very simple question. Any reflection on minority artifacts today has to confront Deleuze and Guattari who in *Kafka: Toward a Minor Literature*, as an answer to the question "What is minor literature?" suggest to understand minority in literature as being characterized by three things: first, the deterritorialization of language; second, the fact that everything in minority literature is political; and third, the fact that in such a literature "everything takes on a collective value."[1] But most important is that their three categories transform minority into *the condition of possibility* of a certain type of artistic (literary) expression that they call "minor." Although it sets my preliminaries, their theoretical disposition alone cannot solve the problems at hand, for it is indeed impossible to discuss the concept of minority in German cinema without also confronting the difficulty of clearly defining what a minority exactly is *in Germany*. The concept has undergone dramatic redefinitions, since its introduction into the German public language via the Minority treaties in 1919. That Germany has been since then the ground of the most murderous experiment on minorities, the Holocaust, also makes it problematic to only use "migration" as the theoretical stepping-stone around which minority would be understood, to analyze the German case. And furthermore, relating minorities to colonialism has to take into account the fact that colonialism in effect, and German colonialism for sure, was the rule of a minority. Thus, to limit myself to one German colony, Cameroon, it was the factual rule of the "*Kameruner Deutsche*," or of the "*Kameruner*," as the colonists are called in the films *Deutsche Pflanzer am Kamerunberg* (1936) and *Unser Kamerun* (1937) of Paul Lieberenz, over the so-called "*Eingeborene*" who outnumbered them.

If German colonial cinema was therefore a cinema made about a minority and its imagining of "natives," what then is minority cinema? More important: How is minority cinema then related to colonial cinema? The problem becomes rather complicated when considering the post–World War II constellation; one attempts to explore the increasing presence of "Turkish" characters in German films, for example, by giving them a genealogy that begins with the "Greek" Jorgos and the "Moroccan" Ali in Fassbinder's early films *Katzelmacher* (1969) and *Angst essen Seele auf* (1974) to conclude with the "Turk" Iskender in the award-winning film *Lola und Bilidikid* (1999) of German-Turkish director Kutlug Ataman. Such genealogy is questionable, most notably because it overlooks the unexpected figures of minority that install these three films into an underground teleology of masking and unmasking sexuality.[2] Yet it is not all: for how can one account for the fetishization of Sibel Kekilli, the German-Turkish shooting star of Fatih Akin's masterpiece *Head On* (2004), while at the same time forgetting the sheer sublimation of the foreign-born stars of German films of the silent era, Asta Nielsen or Pola Negri? Are racial categories that are being challenged in the public sphere in Germany today going to find their last entrenchment in the critical discourse on minorities, and this at the expense of the complex texture of the cultural artifacts that address them? Or to put it differently: can one be satisfied by tracing the history of Fatih Akin's *Solino* (2002) back to Fassbinder's *Katzelmacher* (1969), and forget that unlike the Turks, the Italians and Greeks are already as equally Europeans today as are the Germans? Yet such questions do not even address the equally important challenges that the rapidly changing notion of *cinema* create, at a time when film is being recomposed around the most intimate instruments, technologies, and screens of picture making and viewing (home video, cell-phone, iPod, video games, etc.), which are also increasingly appropriated by minority groups in their daily activities.

Since the appearance of minorities in German cinema coincides with the formal end of German colonialism, 1919, the date of signature of the first Minority treaties will serve as a historical marker in my analysis. I will restrict myself to a classical definition of cinema, by which I mean films that use celluloid as their preferred technology. Three notions will therefore inform my understanding of the concept of minority: first, Homi Bhabha's *negative definition*[3] of minority, which draws on Frantz Fanon and Julia Kristeva, to assert a concept of minority as "metonymy" of a performative zone of signification.[4] Interestingly, Bhabha's main examples for his definition of "minority" are "woman" and "migrants"—the Turkish *Gastarbeiter*. Thus, he writes: "It is from those who have suffered the sentence of history—subjugation, domination, diaspora, displacement—that we learn our most enduring lessons for living and thinking."[5] Needless to say, this is a vision of "minority" with which it is truly difficult for me to be satisfied with, even though it informs most of the literature on "minority discourse" in postcolonial studies. It is therefore in Carl Schmitt that I will find the terms to express my theoretical disagreement, to construct a *positive definition* of minority, and therefore formulate the second concept of minority that informs my analysis: minority, understood as a "borderline concept," as an "exception."[6] But it is essential to preliminarily rescue Schmitt's "exception" from its exegesis by the philosopher Giorgio Agamben, by simply repeating the precaution with which he introduces it in *Political Theology*: "The exception is to be understood to refer to a general concept in the theory of the state," he writes and insists: "*and not merely to a construct applied to an emergency decree or state of siege*."[7] I emphasize the last segment of his sentence because it rejects exactly that into which his theory of the "exception" is transformed in Agamben's *State of Exception*: a legal hubris.[8] Yet it is by understanding minority as "a borderline concept" in its relation to the state, and therefore also as a potential *constituens* thereof, that I will invest its relation to power with a *chiasm* that truly takes its paradoxical manifestations in life and in cinema into account.

But what do I mean by chiasm? It is a clash, a conflict, or simply a paradox between two competing potentialities. The chiastic relation between "minority" and the "state," between borderline and power so to speak, is one in which demise and constitution cross each other to form a structure. It is best developed and deployed by Hannah Arendt's *dialectics of exceptionality*, which thus provides me with my third definition of "minority." But let me underline that Arendt arrives at her depiction of the plight of minorities in the middle of *The Origins of Totalitarianism*,[9] after a presentation of multiple minor characters (the fallen French nobility, the exceptional Jew, the *déclassé*, the *indésirable*, the outlaw, the stateless people, the superfluous men, etc.) who could easily be described by their position at the borderline of class, state, the nation, capital, race, religious homogeneity, and let us add sexuality, or simply by their minority position, as "exceptions."[10] That such borderline position, that such minority position, is equated as she does first with powerlessness, does not necessarily condemn these "superfluous people" to the continuous plight of marginality only. Paradoxically it also locates them in the very position where state and power are constituted. The paradox between the demise of minorities and their position as *constituting structures of power* is described through her patient exposition of the layers of the circular reinforcement of the Nazi regime by the colonialists, through the "boomerang effects"[11] of colonialism in the Western metropolis; or more precisely through her description of the urge strongly felt after 1919 "to introduce colonial methods into European affairs."[12] The paradox (or chiasm) she describes is a history of the reinforcement of totalitarianism by imperialism.

That paradox uncovers a connection, a *nexus* I would say, between power-lessness and power, between marginality and state, between potentialities that exclude each other *per definitionem*: minorities are therefore not only the result of the death of the nation, they are at the beginning of its rise too. Minority is not only looked at as a performative position of subversion, dissidence, inter-rogation, distanciation, and confrontation of the state,[13] as Homi Bhabha wants us to believe, for minority is also a position from where power is constituted. And thus appears a true *circulus vitiosus* that Arendt sees at work in the implo-sion of the European nation-state, and for the discovery of which she is still celebrated by Seyla Benhabib who calls it "brilliant" while contending that "it remains historically as well as philosophically underexplored."[14] In other words, if it is easy to state with Homi Bhabha that the "dehistoricized figure of Man," say of Western man, "is gained at the cost of those "others"—women, natives, the colonized, the indentured and enslaved—who, at the same time but in other spaces were becoming the people without history";[15] if it is possible to see that the Western nations were built at the expense of minorities, it is equally essential to remember that the constitutive *minoritization of the West* has always been on the way precisely because of a necessary "drive into the center"[16] of all minorities that is not achieved without violence. Yet isn't it in such a conflict between minority's exceptions[17] that one should also look to find the charting line between those who participated in colonial films at the dawn of German cinema, and those who make a cinema of minorities in Germany today?

"Rooted in a pejorative term for foreigners," one reads in *Germany in Transit*, published by Deniz Göktürk, David Gramling, and Anton Kaes, "Kanaken Kultur, or Kanak culture, became the lingua franca of a transethnic cultural politics common to Italian-German, Serbian-German, and other immigrant youth communities beyond the Turkish-German milieu."[18] The editors con-tinue to elaborate on their vision that reveals the blueprint of Homi Bhabha's coalition of minorities: "The circulation of transnational hip hop through cul-tures of solidarity, as well as the slowly increasing representation of immi-grants in German television and other media, contributed to the emergence of so-called Kanak chic."[19] And finally taking an example from cinema, they as-sert: "*Head On* might represent another pivotal moment in Turkish Germany's itinerary from invisibility to chic."[20] Based on the book's premise of "cultures of solidarity," should it be possible to write similar stories for women's cinema in Germany, for German queer cinema, or for the cinema made by Afro-German filmmakers, as a path from curse to chic? Is the code word "cultures of solidarity" enough to cover the deep-seated conflicts that are rooted in the history of films made by and around people who have been at the borderline of the German state? Can a history of the German minority cinema of today, even when written through the sole analysis of the "Kanak chic," truly afford to run on the course of total amnesia by forgetting the murdered minorities of the German past, thus by overlooking films like *Jud Süss* (1940) and their depiction of Jews—the *minorité par excellence*?

There are other questions to ask, more importantly: Doesn't the "Kanak chic" of today owe something to those black actors, "poor devils" as Joseph Goebbels calls them in his journal, who survived the war only because they were enlisted in colonial films in Babelsberg? What about the relation between "Kanak chic" and the exoticas of expressionism: doesn't the "orientalization of Germany"[21] that is dramatized in Fatih Akin's *Im Juli* (1999) owe something to Karlheinz Martin's romance *Die Perle des Orients* (1921)? Cinema is a construct that reflects upon a particular time of a nation's imagining of itself; still, does the unfulfilled film career of a Sam Mefire in today's Germany, as depicted in the documentary *Dreckfresser* (2000) by the Nigerian filmmaker Branwen Okpako, have anything to find in the long career of Louis Brody who appeared in such racist stripes as *Quax in Africa* (1947)? What these questions reveal is the difficulty of transforming the complex history of minorities in German cinema into a linear narrative that goes from invisibility to visibility, from dusk to dawn so to speak, for after all minorities already appeared in the very first German films, and in very successful ones like *Die Herrin der Welt* (1919) of John May, or even *Der müde Tod* (1921) of Fritz Lang. But what these questions also reveal is the need to address the relation of minority and nation in Germany more rigorously. Thus they reveal the need to first elaborate a theoretical field, and then develop a methodology of analysis that takes the paradoxical condition of minorities in Germany into account, before seeing through the chiasmic history of German minority cinema. After all, how else can one account for the fact that arguably more films on celluloid were made involving and about minorities in Germany between 1919 and 1950 than between 1979 and 2000?

Because today's minority cinema tactically overlooks its paradoxical relation to films like *Sumurun* (1920) by Ernst Lubitsch, its "orientalization of Germany" does not search for any precedent in orientalizing films of the German past. Both the films of Akin and the perception they propel invent their own past through a procedure that can be described as having three moments:

first, they relate themselves to an obviously non-German cultural history of "transnational hip hop" that itself is de-historicized. Second, they trace their history back to media that are located beyond classical cinema, or to use the phrase of *Germany in Transit*, they capitalize on an "increasing representation of immigrants in German television and other media." Third, they construct a German pan-migrant "culture of solidarity" as their socio-cultural background: "He set his story," writes *Die Zeit* about Akin's *Kurz und schmerzlos* (1998), "in the context of a brotherly friendship between a Turk, a Serb, and a Greek in his own backyard of Hamburg Altona. Between red-light bars, Turkish sofas, and Serbian weddings, the living image of a city district developed."[22] Thus a constitutive relation is established not only with French beur cinema (in reference to Matthieu Kassovitz's acclaimed films *Métisse* (1993) and *La Haine* (1995)), but also with the early films of Martin Scorsese, and this only to present the vision of a cinema that *gives birth to itself*: "Scorsese and the other Italian-Americans needed 70 years to begin making their films. The French Algerians needed 30 years for their cinema beur. We are faster. We're starting now," says Fatih Akin (ibid.). A *global vision* of transnationally connected minorities is constructed, from which emerges the project of a German minority cinema that turns its back on German film history.

Yet, two main axes can be drawn in German postwar film's relation to minorities: the first axis is spearheaded by the New German Cinema, and particularly by the films of Rainer Werner Fassbinder (*Katzelmacher*, 1969; *Angst essen Seele auf*, 1974) and Werner Herzog (*Aguire, der Zorn Gottes*, 1972; *Fitzcarraldo*, 1982). It continues with films like *Otomo* (1999) by Frieder Schlaich and even *Clando* (1996) by the Cameroonian filmmaker Jean-Marie Teno or his historical documentary *Le Malentendu colonial* (2004). The second axis, which includes German minority cinema proper, certainly consists of films like *40 Quadratmeter Deutschland* (1986) by Tevfik Baser and easily ends with Fatih Akin's whole cinematography. The New German cinema and German minority cinema represent two distinct manifestations of Germany's struggle with the representation of its minorities. If through Shahbaz Noshir's *Angst isst Seele auf* (2003), a creative adaptation of Fassbinder's film, German minority cinema has established a connection with, and even an attempt at appropriation of the New German Cinema's discourse on minorities, its relation to the general archive of German cinema still remains one of erasure. Without doubt, such erasure is a product of Germany's conflicted relation to its own past with minorities (Third Reich, colonialism, *Gastarbeiter* migration, etc.); but it is also a repetition of the truly conflicted relation between *all* contemporary German filmmakers with the German film archive. After all, Herzog, Fassbinder, Schlöndorff, and all the other filmmakers of the post–World War II generation also had to navigate through the complexity of the German film archive to claim a position of their own. Herzog's productive rediscovery of Murnau's films in *Nosferatu* (1979), Fassbinder's inspiration in Douglas Sirk's films, and Schlöndorff's current restoration of Babelsberg are indications of such cinematographic re-appropriations.

Jean-Marie Teno conceded once to me that he could not have made *Afrique je te plumerai* (1993) had he not gone into the German film archive. The same certainly holds true for *Le Malentendu colonial*, but mostly because it is a film on German colonialism and its legacy. Yet can the archive of German cinema be closed to contemporary German minority filmmakers like Akin, Okpako, or Ataman? From the point of view of the filmmakers and their contemporary critics, the answer to this question is: yes. "They are not only rendering the victim cinema films of the 1980s like Hark Bohm's *Yasemin* obsolete," writes a critique, "but the token Turk as well."[23] If Fatih Akin's cinema is already so estranged from German films of the eighties, and from those films' depiction of minorities, what about its relation to German films of the twenties? One thing is certain: in accepting the principle of a German minority cinema that does not have its origins in the German film archive, in creating a cinema that, rather than searching into the German film archive, finds its conditions of possibility in a transnational "culture of solidarity" between minorities in the globe, thus in creating a "rootless" cinema that does not even need "a token Turk," German minority cinema raises one question: is German minority cinema really structurally so different from German colonial cinema? To answer this question, I will have to move to an analysis of German colonial cinema.

What deeply opposes German colonial cinema to its British, French, and even Belgian variants is its lack of the tangible colonial referent "Africa," "Asia," or "Orient." Germany having lost all of its African and Asian colonies with the Versailles Treaties of 1919, it is impossible to understand German colonial cinema from a "reality" of some German colonies that were there, and ready to be filmed by German filmmakers. Not only was the access of German filmmakers to all the former German colonies prohibited by France or Britain, as Paul Lieberenz says in *Unser Kamerun* (1937); with the exception of a few films like Hans Schomburgk's *Im Deutschen Sudan* (1917), which was partly shot in Togo when it was still a German colony, from the beginning of the German film industry, a peculiar groundlessness became the structural feature of virtually all German colonial films. This should not be surprising, for after 1919 even the cover of scholarship or religion could not open up former German colonies to German filmmakers: among German ethnographic films of the time, *Tanze der Frischbeschnittenen* (1939) by Baumann was shot in Angola; *Geheimbund-Riten der Frauen* (1923) by Schomburgk in Liberia; *Handwerkliche Fertigkeiten der Yoruba* (1927) by Melzian in Nigeria; and the short *Dime* (1927) by J. A. Borgstedt in Ethiopia. As for Christian missionary movies, the long film *Tokosile, die schwarze Schwester* (1932) was shot in South Africa—here too, *not* a German colony. This lacking reference to German colonies as a structurally significant moment in German colonial cinema can be analyzed in two ways: first, negatively, as an indication of the fact that German films lost touch with the reality of the German colonial world, the effect of which can be particularly measured in films shot during the Third Reich. But it can also be analyzed positively, as a fundamental characteristic of German colonial films in toto.

It is the second way I will follow, for after all even French, British, and Belgian colonial films, although shot mostly in French, British, or Belgian colonies, are fully invested in the discourse of colonialism. It is impossible to imagine and resurrect an "Africa" or an "Asia" that lies there in their pictures in its full and untouched authenticity.[24] Because of its evident lack of a tangible referent, German colonial cinema offers a platform where the relation between colonial and minority cinemas can be analyzed in the full range of its paradox. For the question when watching them cannot be if Africa is or was truly like it appears in them. Instead, a more promising question is: How does Schomburgk's *Mensch und Tier im Urwald* (1924) construct "Africa"? And: How does *Im Schatten der Moschee* (1923) by Edmund Linke invent "the Orient"? How these films fabricate a minority is indeed the main question all German colonial films suggest, for their "Other" is clearly located on the borderline of the German nation, as a cinematographic construction. In *Der müde Tod* (1921), Fritz Lang underscores the "authenticity" of his Orient by stating that the artifacts he used came from the Heinrich Umlauff Museum in Hamburg. It is easy, watching Schomburgk's films one after another, to see how he recycles pictures from his previous films in his next film ventures to produce a particular image of the African continent. It is also easy to recognize the studio construction of "Africa" in early films like *Indische Nächte* (1919) by Richard Lowenbein, or to see the fabricated "Africa" of the NS film *Kongo-Express* (1939) by Eduard von Borsody.

The groundlessness of the "Africa" of each of these films, understood as the chosen or forced use of studio pictures to represent a non-German space, certainly has a different cinematographic explanation, depending on the historical situation. For if early German films are noticeable for their relentless use of the studio (imagine *Das Cabinet des Doctor Caligari* (1920) without the studio!), the Third Reich's use of film studios to depict "Africa" is also related to its aggressive use of cinematography to convey its particular brand of racism. Both films nevertheless chart two main axes between which all German colonial films can be arranged according to some easily recognizable trends. On the one end would certainly stand Schomburgk's *Im Deutschen Sudan* (1917), representing travelogues; *Dr. Soft besucht Togo* (1917), one of the few examples of an official newsreel in the German archive; the numerous hunting films (for example, *Urwaldsymphonie*, 1931); the NS "culture films" *(Auf Tierfang in Abessinien*, 1926); and all the subgenres of the colonial documentary. The second axis would be introduced by the exoticas of Fritz Lang (*Die Spinnen* 1 and 2, 1919, and *Harakiri*, 1919), but also *Das indische Grabmal* (1921), by Joe May, with Conrad Veidt, or *Die Jagd nach dem Tode* (1921) by Karl Gerhardt, and would be followed by adventure movies (Paul Lieberenz's *Der Weg in die Welt*, 1936), films of colonial longing (Walter Scheunemann's *Deutsches Land in Africa*, 1930; Erno Metzner's *Kehre wieder, Afrika!*, 1929), and the numerous films of colonial nostalgia, Schomburgk's *Wildnis. Das letzte Paradies*, 1932, for instance, that until *Quax in Afrika* (1947) of Heinz Rühmann kept being produced by German cinema.

In its *principle* German minority cinema shares colonial cinema's lack of a tangible referent: its impossible reference to a "Turkey" that is there in Germany corresponds *structurally* to German colonial cinema's lack of an unadulterated "Orient," "Asia," or "Africa." The rootlessness of German minority cinema appears in the form of transnationalism, while the groundlessness of German colonial cinema stems from an imposed ban on German filmmakers in German colonies after 1919. But this only establishes structural similarities and lays the ground. What still remains unexplored thus far is the paradoxical inscription of colonial cinema in German minority cinema, and vice versa. Yet only the clear establishment of such a connection would solidify the chiasm of constitution and demise, which binds the four axes of German cinema's relation to minorities.

The paradoxical history of minorities in Germany can inform the way German film history is presented. Such a *methodology*, visualized on the present chart, sets four axes of German cinema's relation to minorities, each of which is spearheaded by one or many important genres (exoticas, colonial travelogues for colonial cinema, but also New German Cinema and German minority cinema), then by the major films each of these genres has produced. The films are made by important filmmakers, such as Rainer Werner Fassbinder

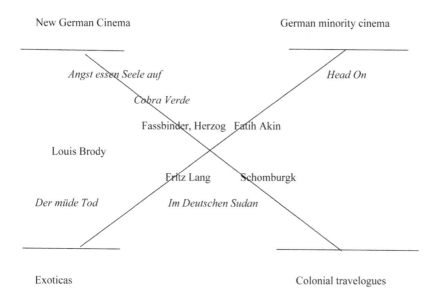

Fig. 12. The chiasm of German colonial and minority cinema

and Werner Herzog for the New German Cinema, Fatih Akin for the German minority cinema, Fritz Lang for exoticas, and Hans Schomburgk for colonial travelogues and ethnographic films.

But none of these layers would be meaningful without the actors, who thus reveal the *nexus of the whole analysis*. I say nexus, *not example*, and definitely *not agency*, for the position of actors underscores a specific horizon that is different from that of the filmmakers, of the films, and of the film genres. After all, the history of German cinema is a history of films, a history of genres, and of filmmakers; but it is also a history of actors. The inscription of German colonial cinema in minority cinema therefore reveals a structure with *multiple horizons*, in the middle of which it unveils a story of lives. For the most original paradox such an analysis reveals is neither related to the genre of films made, nor to the films or the filmmakers who made them. It is the highest irony indeed that from its creation until the end of World War II, the film studios of Babelsberg offered a safe ground on which many non-German, and particularly non-white actors, could be professionally engaged, thus forming the budding ground not only for all German films dealing with minorities, but also for the naked survival of Germany's threatened ethnic minorities, in a country that more and more was sinking into a murderous swamp of racism. Yet the films that were produced there did not only employ many of those imperial subjects who remained in Germany after the end of World War I. At the moment when some non-white performers were fleeing the United States (most notably Paul Robeson who went to England in the 1920s and Josephine Baker who went to France) due to the impediment Hollywood placed on their talents, Babelsberg provided a safe heaven to international actors and added a German paragraph to the career of actors like the Chinese-American Anna May Wong. The undifferentiated use of non-white and white actors with a facial makeup to signify Otherness in the German exoticas may be a departure of Babelsberg's early films from Hollywood where blackface and yellowface were constantly used. Such aesthetic flexibility provided an early professional venue for many a non-white actor, even though today it also reveals the tragedy of those actors who had to play the most stereotypical parts in some of the most viciously racist films ever made in the history of cinema. One such actor was without doubt Ludwig M'bebe Mpessa, whose artist name is Louis Brody.

Ludwig M'bebe Mpessa was born in Douala on February 15, 1895. He came to Germany very early, at only fifteen. His is an exceptional story, yet very little is known about his life in Cameroon, particularly because he seemed not to belong to the Douala nobility whose children were sent to Germany to attend school. He did many manual jobs before landing a short part in Joe May's film *Das Gesetz der Mine* (1915). The film is said to have disappeared. In later years, M'bebe Mpessa changed his name to Brody-Alcolson, probably in an homage to Al Johnson. Because of his very imposing physique, Brody also frequently starred as a boxer, or as an entertainer in bars and other venues. From 1915 until 1951, he appeared in a staggering number of films, sixty-five films in total. He appeared in many big budget films of his time, including the serial *Die Herrin der Welt* (1920) by Joe May and Fritz Lang's classic of expressionistic cinema, *Der müde Tod* (1921), but he also starred in many of the most degrading "Africa films" of the Nazi film factory and beyond, such as *Die Reiter von Deutsch Ostafrika* (1934), *Jud Süss* (1940), *Carl Peters* (1941), *Ohm Krüger* (1941), *Germanin* (1943), and *Quax in Africa* (1947). Here is how his wife, Erika Diek, also of Cameroonian descent and whom he married in 1938, speaks of his life during the Nazi era:

> My husband was also denationalized at that time. Because Cameroon still was a French colony, he contacted the French Consulate and got the French citizenship immediately. So I also became a French citizen after the marriage. We had to get in touch with the police every week. We had to bear many things in Berlin. When I got pregnant, I was told: 'Our Füh-

rer (leader) doesn't set value on children of that ilk.' When our daughter was at the age of four, I registered her at the kindergarten, I was working during the day. After one week I was't allowed to bring her there anymore, because it was unacceptable for the other kids to play with a *Negro kid*. During the war my husband had a contract in Munich as an actor. We had booked two parallel seats in the train in order to allow the kid to lay to sleep in between. Suddenly the door of the compartment opened and a SA-officer appeared: 'You Negro with your beer-ass, make way for this old lady!' I don't know how I was able to hold my husband back. After all, he was weighing 100 kilograms. He let loose on the SA-officer like a tiger. The man disappeared immediately. I can't think of all the things that could have happened. After a while, my husband said: 'Madam, you can have my seat.' But she refused.[25]

M'bebe Mpessa died in Berlin in February 11, 1951. Because of the paradoxical nature of his life (the most paradoxical aspect of it being that he survived the Nazi regime *by playing in racist movies*), I will choose three films from the archive of films in which he appeared, taking films that are representative of the diverse facets of his career: first, *Der müde Tod* for its inscription in expressionism; second, *Die Reiter von Deutsch-Ostafrika* (1934) by Herbert Selpin for the Nazi years; and finally, *Quax in Afrika* (1947) for the postwar years. Appearing as the character of "the Moor" in the second installment of *Der müde Tod*, "the story of the second light," M'bebe Mpessa probably delivered the most enduring performance of his entire career, for he is none other than an uncredited double of Death, the main character, who himself is doubled by a look-alike, Girolamo, the jealous Italian fiancé of the story. Tasked to kill Girolamo by Monna Fiametta, the unhappy madonna and promised wife of the wealthy Girolamo who is in love with Giovan Francesco, a troubadour coming straight out of a commedia dell'arte, the Moor is introduced into a web of intrigues that culminate in a sword fight during which he mistakenly kills the wrong man, Giovan Francesco. If the most powerful instance in the film is his transformation into the character of Death, *Der müde Tod* is also a true tour de force in which Fritz Lang presents tableaux of the Orient, Italy, and Asia, by indifferently casting the same actors multiple times in different settings to tell the same story. *Der müde Tod* was Lang's first international success, and it had an immense influence on many other filmmakers, particularly Luis Buñuel, Alfred Hitchcock, Douglas Fairbanks and F. W. Murnau, and the traces of its aesthetic can be found particularly in Ingmar Bergman's *The Seventh Seal* (1957).

It is a real disappointment to see the promise of *Der müde Tod* be dashed in the subsequent films in which M'bebe Mpessa appears. *Die Reiter von Deutsch-Ostafrika* is one such film: his part is that of Mustapha, the black servant of a German colonial official in East Africa between 1914 and 1916. His role, although credited, as opposed to his appearance in *Der müde Tod* that wasn't, is totally in line with the German policy of the Nazi years. It is that of the loyal black servant trapped between the German and British front lines, and who expresses his loyalty to the Germans, although these have just lost their colony. "Do you speak German?" he is asked at a moment in the film, to which he answers: "yes"; and the dialogue goes: "Then give him the bag to carry." And his last lines are: "I will not stay with the English." The film, a tableau of most ideological positions of both colonial and Nazi politics, expresses a view prominent in German colonial circles during the thirties: Africans are willing to be recolonized by the Germans and they resent the British. It was indeed produced under the umbrella of the then still influential *Reichskolonialbund*. One would imagine that it is hard to beat the exercise in genuflection M'bebe Mpessa does in *Die Reiter von Deutsch-Ostafrika*, yet the postwar film *Quax in Afrika* (1947) by Helmut Weiss proves such prediction to be wrong. Shot as a second part of two comedies featuring Quax (the other part is *Quax, der Bruchpilot*, 1941), a humorous but self-righteous Heinz Rühmann, M'bebe Mpessa's part is that of a vicious herbalist and king dressed in all the attires of stereotype such as being bare-chested and, wearing a bone in the nose. As a counterpart to Quax whose plane lands in an unspecified African forest and is discovered by Africans, his is the position of the antagonist. Such a racially overloaded counterpart is enhanced by the competition for an African girl called Banani, a competition that he of course loses. Since German colonial racism had multiple chapter, particularly when expressed in film, gone in *Quax in Afrika* is the longing for Africa, which defined the storyline of *Die Reiter von Deutsch-Ostafrika* and took pathetic tones in early films like *Kehre wieder, Afrika* (1929) by Friedrich Paullmann and Ludwig Weichert. Also gone is the competition with those colonial powers under whose tutelage Germany's lost colonies now stood: England and France. The film's political position is that of a Germany that has given up its colonial dream altogether, and defines its Europeanness in opposition to an Other that is "Africa." In that way it is a prelude to *Der Stern von Afrika* (1957), by Alfred Weidemann, in which German flight technology is also displayed on an African landscape, and a Nazi flight lieutenant's prowess during the war is hailed, with the blessing of the Allied force's film censoring board. It would be easy to forget M'bebe Mpessa's acting career, were it not for the fact that it is an exceptional story of real survival—*through film.*

In summary, it is impossible to draw a picture of German minority cinema, from the first appearance of people of non-German descent on the screen until today, without confronting multiple conflicts. While some are rooted in the normal development of cinema that sets younger generations against older ones, many others reveal unavoidable clashes. The most fundamental one is certainly the fact that from the very beginning of German cinema, minorities were involved in the fabrication of pictures *as actors*, but it is only during the 1980s that some of them became the actual makers of their own images *as filmmakers*. Unearthing the shameful archive of colonial cinema transformed this basic paradox into a theory. To set the personality of a M'bebe Mpessa against the career of those leading actors of Turkish descent who are celebrated today can only be done in a paradoxical fashion, for although he participated in an amount of films that surpasses the work of any contemporary German actor coming from a minority, M'bebe Mpessa's contribution to German minority cinema is truly embarrassing today because of the stereotypes he helped create. Uncovering his four decades of acting in films reveals the origins of that cinema in the fabric of German colonial cinema, with those men and women for whom Babelsberg finally became a lifesaving enclave in a crumbling Germany. Such an *archaeology of cinema* cannot be done with the classical methods of film history only, by using the conventional classifications of German cinema, or even the usual definition of minority. It therefore proved necessary to first elaborate a positive concept of minority: as exception. This made it possible to draw four contrastive axes in the large German film archive. The chiasm they revealed became a useful category because it made it possible to navigate between the formal analysis of films, their segmentation into genres, and the self-positioning of filmmakers, to uncover the struggle of individual actors who survived in a Germany that was drowning in Nazi politics and colonial phantasms. In so doing, it revealed how deep the films made by minorities in Germany today are rooted in Babelsberg, for in many ways, their conflict with the ugly German past with minorities is certainly what makes their trajectory become quintessentially German. After all, the story of their paradoxical relation to colonial films mirrors the difficulty of German women filmmakers today when they face the controversial but yet pioneering personality of Leni Riefenstahl. It also mirrors the difficulty of putting *Der Golem* (1920), that early film of expressionistic cinema, alongside such classics like *Das Cabinet des Doctor Caligari* (1920) or *Nosferatu* (1922). And in general, it shows the still difficult relation of all German filmmakers with the early productions of German cinema.

NOTES

1. Gilles Deleuze and Félix Guattari, *Kafka: Toward a Minor Literature. Trans. Dana Polan* (Minneapolis: University of Minnesota Press, 1986), 16–17.

2. See Katrin Sieg, *Ethnic Drag: Performing Race, Nation, Sexuality in West Germany* (Ann Arbor: University of Michigan Press, 2002).

3. Negative and positive are purely logical categories, and not moral ones, as the negative is defined against something else and the positive if found in the "thing itself." For a philosophical analysis with specifics about the difference between a negative and positive definition of a concept, see Martin Heidegger, *Die Grundbegriffe der Metaphysik: Welt—Endlichkeit—Einsamkeit* (Frankfurt am Main: Klostermann, 2004), 3–5.

4. Homi K. Bhabha, *The Location of Culture* (London: Routledge, 1994), 155.

5. Ibid.

6. Carl Schmitt, *Political Theory: Four Chapters on the Concept of Sovereignty,* trans. George Schwab (Chicago: University of Chicago Press, 2005), 5.

7. Ibid.

8. Giorgio Agamben, *State of Exception,* trans. Kevin Attell (Chicago: University of Chicago Press, 2003).

9. Hannah Arendt, *The Origins of Totalitarianism* (New York: Harcourt Brace Jovanovich, 1973), 267.

10. Ibid., 271.

11. Ibid., 223.

12. Ibid., 271.

13. Bhabha, op cit., 155.

14. Seyla Benhabib, *The Right of Others: Aliens, Residents and Citizens* (Cambridge: Cambridge University Press, 2009), 52.

15. Bhabha, op cit., 197.

16. Arendt, op cit., 240.

17. That such conflict of minorities happens sometimes around memory is showed by the so-called conflit de mémoires that in France today opposes proponents of slavery and those of the Holocaust.

18. Deniz Göktürk, David Gramling, and Anton Kaes, eds., *Germany in Transit: Nation and Migration, 1955–2005* (Berkeley: University of California Press, 2007), 427–28.

19. Ibid.

20. Ibid.

21. Ibid., 427.

22. Ibid., 467.

23. Ibid., 464.

24. Siegfried Kraucauer's film theory defines cinema as a dialectical movement of destroying a reality and rescuing it as film. Colonial films certainly correspond to such a view.

25. "Africa in Berlin—A Walk through the City with the German Historic Museum," trans. Andrea Oberheiden (2), http://www.aj-images.com/pdf-artikel/AndreaOberheidenbrodyarticle.pdf. Accessed May 28, 2013.

Bibliography

We would like to thank Susanne Ebermann for her assistance in compiling this bibliography.

ARCHIVAL SOURCES

Archives

Archiv des Berliner Missionswerkes im ELAB
Archive of the Belgian Ministry of Foreign Affairs (Belgique, Ministère des Affaires étrangères, Direction des Archives)
Basel Mission Archives, Mission 21 (BMA)
Bavarian Mission Archives, Neuendettelsau
Benedictine Abbey, Peramiho, Tanzania
Bundesarchiv Berlin (BArch)
    Administration of the German Protectorate Togo (R150F)
    Imperial Government Southwest Africa (R151F)
    Reichskolonialamt (R1001)
    Auswärtiges Amt (R901)
    Behörden des Schutzgebietes Samoa (R1004)
Bundesarchiv-Koblenz (BArch), Germany
Colonial Picture Archive, Frankfurt University Library
Geheimes Staatsarchiv Preußischer Kulturbesitz (GStAPK)
Leipzig Institut für Länderkunde, Leipzig, Germany
Library of Congress (LC), Prints and Photographs
The National Archives, London / Public Record Office (PRO)
National Archives of Australia (NAA)
    Imperial Government German New Guinea (G2)
National Archives of Namibia, Windhoek, Namibia (NAN)
    South West Africa Administration (SWAA)
Rhodes House Library, Oxford
Royal Museum for Central Africa (RMCA; Musée royal de l'Afrique centrale, Tervuren)
Tanzania National Archives (TNA), Dar es Salaam, Tanzania

NEWSPAPERS/JOURNALS

Anzeigen für Tanga (Stadt und Bezirk)
Arbeiten aus dem kaiserlichen Gesundheitsamte (AkG)

Archiv für Schiffs- und Tropen-Hygiene (ASTH)
Bohai Ribao [*Northern Times*]
Deutsche Kolonialzeitung
Deutsches Kolonialblatt
Evangelisches-Lutherisches Missionsblatt
Kiautschou-Post
Kreuz-Zeitung
Medizinal-Berichte über die Deutschen Schutzgebiete (MB)
Ostasiatische Lloyd
Reichtagsakten, 7. Legislaturperiode, 127.11 (1889/90)
Samoanische Zeitung
Shandong Guanbao [*Shandong Gazette*]
Shenzhou Ribao [*National Herald*]
Shuntian Shibao [*Shuntian Times*]
Tsingtauer Neueste Nachrichten
Usambara Post
Xiehe Bao [*Xiehe News*]

BOOKS, ARTICLES, AND FILMS

Abrahams, R. G. *The Political Organization of Unyamwezi.* Cambridge: Cambridge University Press, 1967.

Abun-Nasr, Sonia. *Afrikaner und Missionar. Die Lebensgeschichte von David Asante.* Basel: Schlettwein, 2003.

"Africa in Berlin—A Walk through the City with the German Historic Museum." Translated by Andrea Oberheiden. http://www.aj-images.com/pdf-artikel/AndreaOberheidenbrodyarticle.pdf. Accessed May 28, 2013.

Agamben, Giorgio. *State of Exception. Translated by Kevin Attell.* Chicago: University of Chicago Press, 2003.

Ahrens, Theodor. "Die Aktualität Christian Keyßers." *Zeitschrift für Mission* 14 (1988): 94–110.

Ahrens, Theodor. "Lutherische Kreolität: Lutherische Mission und andere Kulturen." In *Luther zwischen den Kulturen: Zeitgenossenschaft–Weltwirkung*, edited by Hans Medick and Peer Schmidt, 421–51. Tübingen: Vandenhoek & Ruprecht, 2004.

Akinwumi, Adesokan. *Postcolonial Artists and Global Aesthetics.* Bloomington: Indiana University Press, 2011.

Akyeampong, Emmanuel. *Drink, Power, and Cultural Change: A Social History of Alcohol in Ghana c. 1900 to Recent Times.* Portsmouth, NH: Heinemann, 1996.

Albrecht, Monika. "Doppelter Standard und postkoloniale Regelpoetik: Eine kritische Revision Postkolonialer Studien." In *Postkolonialismus und Kanon*, edited by Herbert Uerlings and Iulia-Karin Patrut, 67–111. Bielefeld: Aisthesis, 2012.

Alpers, E. A. "'To Seek a Better Life': The Implications of Migration from Mozambique to Tanganyika for Class Formation and Political Behavior." *Canadian Journal of African Studies* 18, no. 2 (1984): 367–88.

Alpers, Edward A. "The Nineteenth Century: Prelude to Colonialism." *Zamani: A Sur-*

vey of East African History, edited by B. A. Ogot and J. A. Kieran, 229–48. Nairobi: East African Publishing House, 1968.

Alsheimer, Rainer. *Bilder erzählen Geschichte: Eine Fotoanthropologie der Norddeutschen Mission in Westafrika*. Bremen: Universität Bremen, 2010.

Altena, Thorsten, *"Ein Häuflein Christen mitten in der Heidenwelt des dunklen Erdteils." Zum Selbst- und Fremdverständnis protestantischer Missionare im kolonialen Afrika 1884–1918*. Münster: Waxmann, 2003.

Ames, Eric, Marcia Klotz, and Lora Wildenthal, eds. *Germany's Colonial Pasts*. Lincoln: University of Nebraska Press, 2005.

Anderson, Amanda. *The Powers of Distance: Cosmopolitanism and the Cultivation of Detachment*. Princeton: Princeton University Press, 2001.

Anderson, Benedict. *Imagined Communities: Reflections on the Origin and Spread of Nationalism*. New York: Verso, 1991.

Appiah, Anthony. *Cosmopolitanism: Ethics in a World of Strangers*. New York: W. W. Norton, 2006.

Aragon, Lorraine V. "Translating Precolonial into Colonial Exchanges in Central Sulawesi, Indonesia." *American Ethnologist* 23, no. 1 (Feb. 1996): 43–60.

Archibugi, Daniele. *Debating Cosmopolitics*. London: Verso, 2003.

Arendt, Hannah. *The Origins of Totalitarianism*. New York: Harcourt Brace Jovanovich, 1973.

Arnold, David. *Colonizing the Body: State Medicine and Epidemic Disease in Nineteenth Century India*. Berkeley: University of California Press, 1993.

Ashcroft, Bill, Gareth Griffiths, and Helen Tiffin. *The Empire Writes Back: Theory and Practice in Post-Colonial Literatures*. 2nd ed. London: Routledge, 2002.

Asher, Ron, and Christopher Moseley. *Atlas of World's Languages*. Rev. ed. London: Routledge, 2007.

Asiwaju, A. I. "Migration as Revolt: The Examples of Ivory Coast and Upper Volta before 1945." *Journal of African History* 14 (1976): 577–94.

Assmann, Aleida. *Der lange Schatten der Vergangenheit: Erinnerungskultur und Geschichtspolitik*. Munich: Beck, 2006.

Atangana, Karl, and Paul Messi. *Jaunde-Texte. Experimentalphonetische Untersuchungen über die Tonhöhen im Jaunde und einer Einführung in die Jaunde-Sprache*. Edited by Martin Heepe. Hamburg: Friederichsen, 1919.

Atkinson, Paul. Review of *Auto/Ethnography: Rewriting the Self and the Social*, by Deborah Reed-Danahay. *Journal of the Royal Anthropological Institute* 5, no. 1 (March 1999): 152–53.

Aukongo, Stefanie-Lahya. *Kalungas Kind: Wie die DDR mein Leben rettete*. Reinbek bei Hamburg: Rowohlt, 2009.

Austen, Ralph A. *Middlemen of the Cameroons Rivers: The Duala and Their Hinterland, c. 1600–c. 1960*. New York: Cambridge University Press, 1999.

Austen, Ralph A. *Northwestern Tanzania under German and British Rule: Colonial Policy and Tribal Politics, 1889–1939*. New Haven: Yale University Press, 1968.

Ayim, May. *Grenzenlos und unverschämt*. Berlin: Fischer, 2002.

Bade, Klaus J., et al. *Imperialismus und Kolonialmission: Kaiserliches Deutschland und koloniales Imperium*. Wiesbaden: Steiner, 1982.

Bader, Wolfgang, and János Riesz. *Literatur und Kolonialismus*. Frankfurt am Main: Lang, 1983.

Bair, Henry Martin. "Carl Peters and German Colonialism: A Study in the Ideas and Actions of Imperialism." PhD diss., Stanford University, 1968.

Bald, Detlef. *Deutsch-Ostafrika, 1900–1914: Eine Studie über Verwaltung, Interessengruppen und wirtschaftliche Erschließung.* Munich: Weltforum, 1970.

Balibar, Etienne. *We, the People of Europe? Reflections on Transnational Citizenship.* Translated by James Swenson. Princeton: Princeton University Press, 2004.

Ballantyne, Tony, and Antoinette Burton, eds. *Bodies in Contact: Rethinking Colonial Encounters in World History.* Durham: Duke University Press, 2005.

Baltzer, Franz. "Hausbau der Europäer." In *Deutsches Kolonial Lexikon,* vol. 1, ed. Heinrich Schnee, 47. Leipzig: Quelle & Meyer, 1920. Accessed May 13, 2009. http://www.ub.bildarchiv-dkg.uni-frankfurt.de.

Barooah, Nirode K. *Chatto, the Life and Times of an Indian Anti-Imperialist in Europe.* New Delhi: Oxford University Press, 2004.

Barooah, Nirode K. *India and the Official Germany, 1886–1914.* Frankfurt am Main: Peter Lang, 1977.

Batsa, Kofi. *West German Neo-Colonialism and Africa: Documentation of the Neo-Colonialist Policy of West Germany in Africa.* Accra: Spark Publications, 1964.

Bauer, Wolfgang. *China und die Fremden. 3000 Jahre Auseinandersetzung in Krieg und Frieden.* Munich: Verlag C. H. Beck, 1980.

Bauer, Wolfgang, Peng Chang, and Michael Lackner. *Das chinesische Deutschlandbild der Gegenwart: Eine Bibliographie, vol. 2: Karl Marx und Friedrich Engels im chinesischen Schrifttum, 1970–1984.* Stuttgart: F. Steiner Verlag Wiesbaden, 1989.

Beachey, R. W. "The East African Ivory Trade in the Nineteenth Century." *Journal of African History* 8 (1967): 269–90.

Becher, Jürgen. "Die deutsche evangelische Mission. Eine Erziehungs- und Disziplinierungsinstanz in Deutsch-Ostafrika." In *Alles unter Kontrolle: Disziplinierungsprozesse im kolonialen Tanzania (1850–1960),* edited by Albert Wirz, Andreas Eckert, and Kathrin Bromber, 141–69. Cologne: Rüdiger Köppe, 2003.

Bechhaus-Gerst Marianne, Mechthild Leutner, and Hauke Neddermann, eds. *Frauen in den deutschen Kolonien.* Berlin: Links, 2009.

Bechler, Th. *Zur Kriegszeit in Deutsch-Ostafrika, im Kongo und in Frankreich Kriegserlebnisse und Gefangenschaft der Unyamwesi-Missionare der Brüdergemeinde in den Jahren 1914–17.* Herrnhut: Verlag der Missionsbuchhandlung, 1918.

Beck, Ulrich. *Der kosmopolitische Blick, oder: Krieg ist Frieden.* Frankfurt am Main: Suhrkamp, 2004.

Beck, Ulrich, and Edgar Grande. *Das kosmopolitische Europa: Gesellschaft und Politik in der zweiten Moderne.* Frankfurt am Main: Suhrkamp, 2004.

Beez, Jigal. *Geschosse zu Wassertropfen: Sozio-religiöse Aspekte des Maji-Maji-Krieges in Deutsch-Ostafrika (1905–1907).* Cologne: Rüdiger Köppe, 2003.

Behrend, Heike. "Kannibalischer Terror." In *Africa Screams: Das Böse in Kino, Kunst und Kult,* edited by Tobias Wendl, 165–73. Wuppertal: Peter Hammer, 2004.

Beidelman, T. O. *Colonial Evangelism: A Socio-Historical Study of an East African Mission at the Grassroots.* Bloomington: Indiana University Press, 1982.

Benhabib, Seyla. *The Rights of Others: Aliens, Residents, and Citizens.* Cambridge: Cambridge University Press, 2004, 2009.

Bennett, Norman R. *Mirambo of Tanzania, 1840?–1884.* New York: Oxford University Press, 1971.

Bennett, Tony. *The Birth of the Museum: History, Theory, Politics.* New York: Routledge, 1995.

Benninghoff-Lühl, Sibylle. *Deutsche Kolonialromane, 1884–1914, in ihrem Entstehungs- und Wirkungszusammenhang.* Bremen: Im Selbstverlag, Übersee-Museum Bremen, 1983.

Berman, Nina. "Yusuf's Choice: East African Agency During the German Colonial Period in Abdulrazak Gurnah's Novel *Paradise.*" *English Studies in Africa* 56, no.1 (2013): 51–64.

Berman, Russell A. *Enlightenment or Empire: Colonial Discourse in German Culture.* Lincoln: University of Nebraska Press, 1998.

Besier, Gerhard. "Mission und Kolonialismus im Preußen der Wilhelminischen Ära." *Kirchliche Zeitgeschichte* 5, no. 2 (1992): 239–53.

Bhabha, Homi K. *The Location of Culture.* London: Routledge, 1994, 2001; new ed., 2004.

Bhatawadekar, Sai Prakash. "Symptoms of Withdrawal: The Threefold Structure of Hegel's and Schopenhauer's Interpretation of Hindu Religion and Philosophy." PhD diss., Ohio State University, 2007.

Bhatti, Anil. "Utopie-Projektion-Gegenbild: Indien in Deutschland." *Zeitschrift für Kulturaustausch* 37, no. 3 (1987): 388–525.

Biener, Annette S. *Das deutsche Pachtgebiet Tsingtau in Schantung 1897–1914. Institutioneller Wandel durch Kolonisierung.* Bonn: Selbstverlag Matzat, 2001.

Bischoff, Eva. *Kannibale-Werden: Eine postkoloniale Geschichte deutscher Männlichkeit um 1900.* Bielefeld: transcript, 2011.

Biskup, Peter. "Dr. Albert Hahl—Sketch of a German Colonial Official." *Australian Journal of Politics and History* 14 (1968): 342–57.

Black German Heritage & Research Association. http://blackgermans.us/new/about-2/

Bley, Helmut. *Kolonialherrschaft und Sozialstruktur in Deutsch-Südwestafrika 1894–1914.* Hamburg: Leibniz, 1968.

Bley, Helmut. *Namibia under German Rule.* Hamburg: Lit Verlag, 1996.

Blier, Suzanne Preston. *The Royal Arts of Africa: The Majesty of Form.* New York: Adams, 1998.

Blohm, Wilhelm. *Die Nyamwezi, Gesellschaft und Weltbild.* Hamburg: Friederichsen De Gruyter, 1933.

Bollard, A. E. "The Financial Adventures of J. C. Godeffroy and Son in the Pacific." *Journal of Pacific History* 16, no. 1 (1981): 3–19.

Bonner, Phil. "'Desirable or Undesirable Basotho Women?' Liquor, Prostitution and Migration of Basotho Women to the Rand, 1920–1945." In *Women and Gender in Southern Africa to 1945*, edited by Cheryl Walker, 221–50. Claremont, South Africa: David Philip Publishers, 1990.

Bornemann, Fritz. *Der selige P.J. Freinademetz 1852–1908: Ein Steyler China-Missionar; Ein Lebensbild nach zeitgenössischen Quellen.* Rome: Collegium Verbi Divini, 1976.

Bozzoli, Belinda. *Women of Phokeng: Consciousness, Life Strategy, and Migrancy in South Africa, 1900–1933.* Portsmouth, NH: Heinemann, 1991.

Breidbach, Angela, and William Kentridge. *William Kentridge: Thinking Aloud*. Cologne: Walther König, 2006.

Breman, Jan. *Taming the Coolie Beast: Plantation Society and the Colonial Order in Southeast Asia*. Delhi: Oxford University Press, 1989.

Brennan, Timothy. *At Home in the World: Cosmopolitanism Now*. Cambridge: Harvard University Press, 1997.

Brown, Emily Clara. *Har Dayal: Hindu Revolutionary and Rationalist*. Tucson: University of Arizona Press, 1975.

Brubaker, Rogers, and Frederick Cooper. "Beyond 'Identity.'" *Theory and Society* 29 (2000): 1–47.

Buck-Morss, Susan. "Hegel and Haiti." *Critical Inquiry* 26, no. 4 (2000): 821–65.

Büttner, Kurt. *Die Anfänge der deutschen Kolonialpolitik in Ostafrika: Eine kritische Untersuchung an Hand unveröffentlichter Quellen*. Berlin: Akademie-Verlag, 1959.

Büttner, Kurt. *Neokolonialistische Afrikatheorien im wissenschaftlichen Gewand*. Leipzig: Karl-Marx-Universität, 1969.

Büttner, Kurt, and Heinrich Loth. *Philosophie der Eroberer und koloniale Wirklichkeit: Ostafrika 1884–1918*. Berlin: Akademie-Verlag, 1981.

BUGRA (Internationale Ausstellung für Buchgewerbe und Graphik Leipzig). Amtlicher Katalog. Leipzig: BUGRA, 1914.

Bühler, Andreas. *Der Namaaufstand gegen die deutsche Kolonialherrschaft in Namibia von 1904 bis 1913*. Frankfurt am Main: IKO, Verlag für Interkulturelle Kommunikation, 2003.

Bührer, Tanja. *Die Kaiserliche Schutztruppe für Deutsch-Ostafrika: Koloniale Sicherheitspolitik und transkulturelle Kriegführung, 1885 bis 1918*. Munich: Oldenbourg, 2011.

Bundeszentrale für Politische Bildung. "Afrikanische Diaspora." Accessed August 23, 2012. http://www.bpb.de/gesellschaft/migration/afrikanische-diaspora.

Buzard, James. "On Auto-Ethnographic Authority." *Yale Journal of Criticism* 16, no. 1 (2003): 61–91.

Cai, Rong. "Problematizing the Foreign Other: Mother, Father and the Bastard in Mo Yan's *Large Breasts and Full Hips*." *Modern China* 29, no. 1 (2003): 108–37.

Calhoun, Craig. "The Class Consciousness of Frequent Travelers: Towards a Critique of Actually Existing Cosmopolitanism." In *Conceiving Cosmopolitanism: Theory, Context, and Practice*, edited by Steven Vertovec and Robin Cohen, 86–109. Oxford: Oxford University Press/USA, 2003.

Callahan, William A. *China, The Pessoptimist Nation* (Oxford: Oxford University Press, 2010).

Callahan, William A. "Historical Legacies and Non/Traditional Society: Commemorating National Humiliation Day in China." Paper presented at Renmin University, Beijing, April 2004. http://www.dur.ac.uk/resources/china.studies/Commemorating%20National%20Humiliation%20Day%20in%20China.pdf. Accessed May 28, 2013.

Cameron, Dan, Carolyn Christov-Bakargiev, and William Kentridge. *William Kentridge*. London: Phaidon, 1999.

Campt, Tina. *Other Germans: Black Germans and the Politics of Race, Gender, and Memory in the Third Reich*. Ann Arbor: University of Michigan Press, 2004.

Carroll, John. *Edge of Empires: Chinese Elites and British Colonials in Hong Kong.* Cambridge: Harvard University Press, 2005.

Castles, Stephen. "Migrant Settlement, Transnational Communities and State Strategies in the Asia Pacific Region." In *Migration in the Asia Pacific: Population, Settlement and Citizenship Issues,* edited by Robyn Iredale, Charles Hawksley, and Stephen Castles, 3–26. Northampton, MA: Edward Elgar, 2003.

Césaire, Aimé. *Discourse on Colonialism.* Translated by Joan Pinkham. New York: Monthly Review, 2000.

Chakrabarty, Dipesh. *Provincializing Europe: Postcolonial Thought and Historical Difference.* Princeton: Princeton University Press, 2000.

Cheah, Pheng, and Bruce Robbins. *Cosmopolitics: Thinking and Feeling beyond the Nation.* Minneapolis: University of Minnesota Press, 1998.

Chen, Gan. "Zhi Beijing tongxiang guan de gonghan [Official Letter to the Shandong Officials in Beijing]." In *Chenminghou jiangjun: Shishi qishi zhounian jinian ji [General Chen Minghou: Festschrift of 70 Yahrzeit],* edited by Chen Jun and Tong Lirong, 103–4. Beijing: China Literature and History Publishing House, 1997.

Chen, Jun, and Tong Lirong. "Chengong minghou xiansheng zhuan [Biography of Honorable Mr. Chen Minghou]." In *Chenminghou jiangjun: Shishi qishi zhounian jinian ji [General Chen Minghou: Festschrift of 70 Yahrzeit],* edited by Chen Jun and Tong Lirong, 3–52. Beijing: China Literature and History Publishing House, 1997.

Chen, Zhuang Ying. *Asiatisches Gedankengut im Werke Hermann Hesses.* New York: Lang, 1997.

Cohen, Paul A. *Discovering History in China: American Historical Writing on the Recent Chinese Past.* New York: Columbia University Press, 1984.

Cohen, Paul A. *History in Three Keys: The Boxers as Event, Experience and Myth.* New York: Columbia University Press, 1997.

Comaroff, Jean, and John L. Comaroff. *Of Revelation and Revolution: The Dialectics of Modernity on a South African Frontier. Vol. 2.* Chicago: University of Chicago Press, 1997.

Connell, R. W. *Masculinities.* Berkeley: University of California Press, 1995.

Conrad, Sebastian. *Globalisierung und Nation im deutschen Kaiserreich.* Munich: Beck, 2006.

Conrad, Sebastian, and Jürgen Osterhammel. *Das Kaiserreich transnational: Deutschland in der Welt 1871–1914.* Göttingen: Vandenhoeck & Ruprecht, 2004.

Cooper, Frederick. *Plantation Slavery on the East Coast of Africa.* New Haven: Yale University Press, 1977.

Copland, Ian. "Christianity as an Arm of Empire: The Ambiguous Case of India under the Company, c. 1813–1858." *Historical Journal* 49 (2006): 1025–54.

Coquery-Vidrovitch, Catherine. *The History of African Cities South of the Sahara.* Princeton: Markus Wiener, 2005.

Cox, Jeffrey. *The British Missionary Enterprise since 1700.* New York: Routledge, 2008.

Davies, Margit. "Das Gesundheitswesen im Kaiser-Wilhelmsland und im Bismarckarchipel." In *Die deutsche Südsee 1884–1914: Ein Handbuch,* edited by Hermann Hiery, 417–49. Paderborn: Ferdinand Schöningh, 2001.

Dayal, Har. *Forty Four Months in Germany and Turkey. February 1915 to October 1918: A Record of Personal Impressions.* London: P. S. King and Son, 1920.

Declé, Lionel. *Three Years in Savage Africa.* Bulawayo: Books of Rhodesia, 1974.

Dedering, Tilman. "The German-Herero War of 1904: Revisionism of Genocide or Imaginary Historiography?" *Journal of Southern African Studies* 40, no. 1 (1993): 80–83.

Degla, Luc. *Das afrikanische Auge.* Schwülper: Cargo, 2007.

Deleuze, Gilles, and Félix Guattari. *Kafka: Toward a Minor Literature.* Translated by Dana Polan. Minneapolis: University of Minnesota Press, 1986.

Deltombe, Thomas, Manuel Domergue, and Jacob Tatsitsa. *Kamerun!: Une guerre cachée aux origines de la Françafrique, 1948–1971.* Paris: Découverte, 2011.

Department of Labour. Tanganyika Territory. *Annual Labour Department Reports, 1927.*

Dernburg, Bernhard. *Zielpunkte des Deutschen Kolonialwesens: Zwei Vorträge.* Berlin: Mittler & Sohn, 1907.

Derrida, Jacques. *Of Hospitality.* Stanford: Stanford University Press, 2000.

Derrida, Jacques. *On Cosmopolitanism and Forgiveness.* London: Routledge, 2001.

Deutsch, Jan-Georg. "Celebrating Power in Everyday Life: The Administration of Law and the Public Sphere in Colonial Tanzania, 1890–1914." *Journal of African Cultural Studies* 14, no. 1 (2002): 93–103.

Deutsch, Jan-Georg. *Emancipation without Abolition in German East Africa c. 1884–1914.* Oxford: James Currey, 2006.

Deutsch-Ostafrika, Kaiserliches Gouvernement. *Zusammenstellung der Berichte über die in den Monaten August, September, Oktober 1914 stattgefundenen Gefechte der Kaiserlichen Schutztruppe für Deutsch-Ostafrika.* Morogoro: Regierungsdruckerei, n.d. [1914].

Deutsch-Ostafrika, Kaiserliches Gouvernement. *Zusammenstellung der Berichte über die in den Monaten November, Dezember 1914 und Januar 1915 stattgefundenen Gefechte der Kaiserlichen Schutztruppe für Deutsch-Ostafrika nebst Nachtrag über die in den Monaten August bis Oktober stattgefundenen Gefechte.* Morogoro: Regierungsdruckerei, n.d. [1915].

Dharmavir. *Lala Hardayal. Prasiddha Deshbkahta Lala Hardayal ka Jeevan tatha unke Samaya ke Krantikari Andolana.* Delhi: Rajpal and Sons, 1970.

Dharwadker, Vinay. *Cosmopolitan Geographies: New Locations in Literature and Culture.* New York: Routledge, 2001.

Diallo, Aly. *Die Täuschung.* Translated from the French by Gabriele Henschke. Frankfurt am Main: Nexus, 1987.

Ding, Weifen. "Shandong Gemingdang shigao [History of Shandong Revolutionists]." *Shandong wenxian [Shandong Literature]* 3 of vol. 1 (1975): 8–18.

Ding, Weifen. "Shandong Gemingdang shigao [History of Shandong Revolutionists] -continued." *Shandong wenxian [Shandong Literature]* 4 of vol. 1 (1975): 27–37.

Dominik, Hans. *Kamerun. Sechs Kriegs- und Friedensjahre in deutschen Tropen.* Berlin: Stilke, 1911.

Duala-M'bedy, Munasu. *Xenologie: Die Wissenschaft vom Fremden und die Verdrängung der Humanität in der Anthropologie.* Freiburg im Breisgau: K. Alber, 1977.

Duara, Prasenjit. *Rescuing History from the Nation: Questioning Narratives of Modern China.* Chicago: University of Chicago Press, 1995.

Dudink, Stefan, and Karen Hagermann. "Masculinity in Politics and War in the Age of

Democratic Revolutions, 1750–1850." In *Gender in History: Masculinities in Politics and War: Gendering Modern History*, edited by Stefan Dudink et al., 3–12. Manchester: Manchester University Press, 2004).

Dudink, Stefan, Karen Hagermann, and John Tosh, eds. *Gender in History: Masculinities in Politics and War; Gendering Modern History*. Manchester: Manchester University Press, 2004.

Dukes, Jack Richard. *"Helgoland, Zanzibar, East Africa: Colonialism in German Politics, 1884–1890."* PhD diss., University of Illinois at Urbana-Champaign, 1970.

Dumont, Louis. *Introduction to Two Theories of Social Anthropology: Descent Groups and Marriage Alliance*. Edited and translated by Robert Parkin. New York: Berghahn Books, 2006.

Eckert, Andreas. *Die Duala und die Kolonialmächte. Eine Untersuchung zu Widerstand, Protest und Protonationalismus in Kamerun vor dem Zweiten Weltkrieg.* Münster: Lit, 1991.

Eckert, Andreas. *Grundbesitz, Landkonflikte und kolonialer Wandel: Douala 1880 bis 1960.* Stuttgart: Franz Steiner, 1999.

Eckert, Andreas. *Herrschen und Verwalten. Afrikanische Bürokratie, staatliche Ordnung und Politik in Tanzania, 1920–1970.* Munich: Oldenbourg, 2007.

Eckert, Andreas. "Konflikte, Netzwerke, Interaktionen. Kolonialismus in Afrika: Zum Gedenken von Ulrich Haarmann (1942–1999)." *Neue Politische Literatur* 44, no. 3 (1999): 446–80.

Eggers, Maureen Maisha, ed. "Schwarze Community in Deutschland." Heinrich Böll Stiftung, May 2006. http://www.migration-boell.de/web/diversity/48_583.asp. Accessed August 23, 2012.

Eiselen, Tobias. "'Zur Erziehung einer zuverlässigen, wohldisziplinierten Streiterschar für den Missionskrieg.' Basler Missionsausbildung im 19. Jahrhundert." In *Mission im Kontext. Beiträge zur Sozialgeschichte der Norddeutschen Missionsgesellschaft im 19. Jahrhundert*, edited by Werner Ustorf, 47–120. Bremen: Überseemuseum, 1986.

Ellis, Carolyn, Tony E. Adams, and Arthur P. Bochner. "Autoethnography: An Overview." *Forum Qualitative Sozialforschung / Forum: Qualitative Social Research* 12, no. 1 (2010), Art. 10, http://nbn-resolving.de/urn:nbn:de:0114-fqs1101108.

El Loko. "Biografie." Accessed August 23, 2012. http://www.el-loko.de.

El Loko. *Der Blues in mir: Eine autobiographische Erzählung.* Mit Holzschnitten des Autors; Nachwort von Al Imfeld. Oberhausen: Graphium Press, 1986.

El-Tayeb, Fatima. *Schwarze Deutsche: Der Diskurs um 'Rasse' und nationale Identität 1890–1933.* Frankfurt: Campus, 2001.

Emmett, Tony. *Popular Resistance and the Roots of Nationalism in Namibia, 1915–1966* Basel: P. Schlettwein, 1999.

Engombe, Lucia (with Peter Hilliges). *Kind Nr. 95: Meine deutsch-afrikanische Odyssee.* Berlin: Ullstein, 2004.

Enloe, Cynthia. *Bananas, Beaches, and Bases: Making Feminist Sense of International Politics.* Berkeley: University of California Press, 1990.

Eppelsheimer, Natalie. "Homecomings and Homemakings: Stefanie Zweig and the Exile Experience In, Out of, and Nowhere in Africa." PhD diss., University of California, Irvine, 2008.

Erll, Astrid. "Cultural Memory Studies: An Introduction." In *Cultural Memory Studies: An International and Interdisciplinary Handbook*, edited by Astrid Erll and Ansgar Nünning, in collaboration with Sara B. Young, 1–15. Berlin: de Gruyter, 2008.

Esherick, Joseph W. *The Origins of the Boxer Uprising*. Berkeley: University of California Press, 1987.

Esleben, Jörg, Christina Kraenzle, and Sukanya Kulkarni, eds. *Mapping Channels between Ganges and Rhein: German-Indian Cross-Cultural Relations*. Newcastle upon Tyne, England: Cambridge Scholars Publishing, 2008.

Evans, Jones Kwesi (with Kai Schubert and Robin Schmaler). *Ich bin ein Black Berliner: Die ungewöhnliche Lebensgeschichte eines Afrikaners in Deutschland*. Freiburg im Breisgau: Herder, 2006.

Eyoum, Jean-Pierre Felix, Stefanie Michels, and Joachim Zeller. "Bonamanga: Eine kosmopolitische Familiengeschichte." *Mont Cameroun* 2 (2005): 11–48.

Fabian, Johannes. *Out of Our Minds: Reason and Madness in the Exploration of Central Africa*. Berkeley: University of California Press, 2000.

Fabian, Johannes. *Time and the Other: How Anthropology Makes Its Object*. New York: Columbia University Press, 1983.

Fabian, Johannes. "You Meet and You Talk: Anthropological Reflections on Encounters and Discourses." In *The Fuzzy Logic of Encounter: New Perspectives on Cultural Contact*, edited by Sünne Juterczenka and Gesa Mackenthun, 23–34. Münster: Waxmann, 2009.

Fanon, Frantz. *The Wretched of the Earth*. Preface by Jean-Paul Sartre. Translated by Constance Farrington. London: Penguin, 2001.

Farnbacher, Traugott. *Gemeinde verantworten: Anfänge, Entwicklungen und Perspektiven von Gemeinde und Ämtern der Evangelisch-Lutherischen Kirche in Papua-Neuguinea*. Hamburg: LIT, 1999.

Faure, David. *The Structure of Chinese Rural Society: Lineage and Village in the Eastern New Territories, Hong Kong*. Hong Kong: Oxford University Press, 1986.

Field, Michael J. *Mau: Samoa's Struggle for Freedom*. Auckland: Polynesian Press, 1984.

Fine, Robert, and Robin Cohen. "Four Cosmopolitan Moments." In *Conceiving Cosmopolitanism*, edited by Steven Vertovec and Robin Cohen, 137–62. Oxford: Oxford University Press, 2003.

Finsch, Otto. *Samoafahrten: Reisen in Kaiser Wilhelms-Land und Englisch-Neu-Guinea: In den Jahren 1884 und 1885: An Bord des deutschen Dampfers "Samoa."* Leipzig: Ferdinand Hirt & Sohn, 1888.

Firth, Stewart. *New Guinea under the Germans*. Victoria: Melbourne University Press, 1982.

Firth, Stewart. "The Transformation of the Labour Trade in German New Guinea, 1899–1914." *Journal of Pacific History* 11, no. 1 (1976): 51–65.

Fischer, Hans-Jörg. *Die deutschen Kolonien: Die koloniale Rechtsordnung und ihre Entwicklung nach dem Ersten Weltkrieg*. Berlin: Duncker und Humblot, 2001.

Fischer, Hermann. *Augustin Henninghaus: 53 Jahre Missionar und Missionsbischof: Ein Lebensbild*. Kaldenkirchen: Steyler Missionsbuchhandlung, 1946.

Fischer-Tiné, Harald. "Indian Nationalism and the 'World Forces': Transnational and

Diasporic Dimensions of the Indian Freedom Movement on the Eve of the First World War." *Journal of Global History* 2, no. 3 (Nov. 2007): 325–44.

Fonck, Heinrich. *Deutsch-Ostafrika. Eine Schilderung nach 10 Wanderjahren.* Berlin: Voss, 1907.

Foucault, Michel. *Geschichte der Gouvernementalität I: Sicherheit, Territorium, Bevölkerung: Vorlesung am Collège de France (1977–1978).* Translated by Claudia Brede-Konersmann and Jürgen Schröder. Frankfurt: Suhrkamp, 2004.

Frerichs, A. C. *Anutu Conquers in New Guinea: A Story of Seventy Years of Mission Work in New Guinea.* Columbus, OH: Wartburg Press, 1957.

Freud, Sigmund. *Murder, Mourning and Melancholia.* Edited by Adam Phillips and translated by Shaun Whiteside. London: Penguin Books, 2005.

Friedländer, Paul. *The Neocolonialism of the West German Federal Republic: A Documentation.* Berlin: Afro-Asiatisches Solidaritätskomitee in der DDR, 1965.

Friedrichsmeyer, Sara, Sara Lennox, and Susanne Zantop, eds. *The Imperialist Imagination: German Colonialism and Its Legacy.* Ann Arbor: University of Michigan Press, 1998.

Gammage, Bill. *The Sky Travellers: Journey in New Guinea, 1938–1939.* Melbourne: Miegunyah Press and Melbourne University Press, 1998.

Gandhi, Leela. *Affective Communities: Anticolonial Thought, Fin-de-Siècle Radicalism, and the Politics of Friendship.* Durham: Duke University Press, 2006.

Garrett, John. *Footsteps in the Sea: Christianity in Oceania to World War II.* Suva: Institute of Pacific Studies, University of the South Pacific, 1992.

Geary, Christraud. "Art and Political Process in the Kingdoms of Bali-Nyonga and Bamum (Cameroon Grassfields)." *Canadian Journal of African Studies / Revue Canadienne des Études Africaines* 22, no. 1 (1988): 11–41.

Geary, Christraud. "Bamum and Tikar: Inspiration and Innovation." In *Cameroon: Art and Kings,* edited by Lorenz Homberger, 22–67. Zurich: Museum Rietberg, 2008.

Geary, Christraud. *Images from Bamum: German Colonial Photography at the Court of King Njoya, Cameroon, West Africa, 1902–1915.* Washington, DC: Smithsonian, 1988.

Geary, Christraud. "Impressions of the African Past: Interpreting Ethnographic Photographs from Cameroon." *Visual Anthropology* 3 (1990): 289–315.

Geary, Christraud. *Patterns from Without, Meaning from Within: European-Style Military Dress and German Colonial Politics in the Bamum Kingdom (Cameroon).* Discussion Papers in African Humanities, no. 1. Boston: African Studies Center, Boston University, 1989.

Geary, Christraud. *Things of the Palace: A Catalogue of the Bamum Palace Museum in Foumban (Cameroon).* Wiesbaden: F. Steiner, 1983.

Geary, Christraud, and Paul Jenkins. "Photographs from Africa in the Basel Mission Archive." *African Arts* 18, no. 4 (1985): 56–63.

Geary, Christraud, and Adamou Ndam Njoya. *Mandu Yenu: Bilder aus Bamum, einem westafrikanischen Königreich, 1902–1915.* Munich: Trickster, 1985.

Gensichen, Hans-Werner. "Mission und Kolonialismus: Überlegungen zur Morphologie einer Beziehung." *Zeitschrift für Missionswissenschaft und Religionswissenschaft* 77 (1993): 25–34.

Germanistik in Afrika Subsahara. http://www.gas-verband.org/home/index.php/content/view/13/21/lang,de/.

Gerstmeyer, Johannes. "Eingeborenenrecht." In *Deutsches Kolonial-Lexikon*, 3 volumes, edited by Heinrich Schnee, vol. 1: 507–14. Leipzig: Quelle & Meyer, 1920.

Gerwarth, Robert, and Stephan Malinowski. "Hannah Arendt's Ghosts: Reflections on the Disputable Path from Windhoek to Auschwitz." *Central European History* 42 (2009): 279–300.

Gewald, Jan-Bart. *Herero Heroes: A Socio-Political History of the Herero of Namibia, 1890–1923*. Athens: Ohio University Press, 1999.

Geyer, Michael, and Charles Bright. "World History in a Global Age." *American Historical Review* 100, no. 4 (1995): 1034–60.

Giblin, James. *A History of the Excluded*. Athens: Ohio University Press, 2005.

Giblin, James. "Land Tenure, Traditions of Thought about Land and Their Environmental Implications in Tanzania." *Tanzania Zamani* 4, no. 1/2 (1998): 1–56.

Gilman, Sander L. *On Blackness Without Blacks: Essays on the Image of the Black in Germany*. Boston: Hall, 1982.

Gilson, R. P. *Samoa 1830 to 1900: The Politics of a Multi-Cultural Community*. London: Oxford University Press, 1970.

Glassman, Jonathon. *Feasts and Riot: Revelry, Rebellion, and Popular Consciousness on the Swahili Coast, 1856–1888*. Portsmouth: Heinemann, 1995.

Godbout, Jacques T. *World of the Gift*. Montreal: McGill-Queen's University Press, 1998.

Göktürk, Deniz, David Gramling, and Anton Kaes, eds. *Germany in Transit: Nation and Migration, 1955–2005*. Berkeley: University of California Press, 2007.

Goldblatt, Howard. "'The Saturnicon.' Forbidden Food of Mo Yan." *World Literature Today* 74, no. 3 (Summer 2000): 477–85.

Goodman, Bryna, and David S. G. Goodman. "Introduction: Colonialism and China." In *Twentieth-Century Colonialism and China: Localities, the Everyday and the World*, edited by Bryna Goodman and David S. G. Goodman, 1–22. London: Routledge, 2012.

Goss, Jon, and Bruce Lindquist. "Placing Movers: An Overview of the Asian-Pacific Migration System." *Contemporary Pacific* 12, no. 2 (2000): 385–414.

Göttsche, Dirk. "Colonial Legacies and Cross-Cultural Experience: The African Voice in Contemporary German Literature." *Edinburgh German Yearbook* 1 (2007): 159–75.

Göttsche, Dirk. "Cross-Cultural Self-Assertion and Cultural Politics: African Migrants' Writing in German since the Late 1990s." *German Life and Letters* 63 (2010): 54–70.

Göttsche, Dirk. "Deutsche Literatur afrikanischer Diaspora und die Frage postkolonialer Kanonrevision." In *Postkolonialismus und Kanon*, edited by Herbert Uerlings and Iulia-Karin Patrut, 327–60. Bielefeld: Aisthesis, 2012.

Göttsche, Dirk. "Der neue historische Afrika-Roman: Kolonialismus aus postkolonialer Sicht." *German Life and Letters* 56 (2003): 261–80.

Göttsche, Dirk. "Rekonstruktion und Remythisierung der kolonialen Welt: Neue historische Romane über den deutschen Kolonialismus in Afrika." In *Deutsch-afrikanische Diskurse in Geschichte und Gegenwart: Literatur- und kulturwissen-*

schaftliche Perspektiven, edited by Michael Hofmann and Rita Morrien, 171–95. Amsterdam: Rodopi, 2012.

Göttsche, Dirk. *Remembering Africa: The Rediscovery of Colonialism in Contemporary German Literature*. Rochester, NY: Camden House, 2013.

Göttsche, Dirk. "Self-Assertion, Intervention and Achievement: Black German Writing in Postcolonial Perspective." *Orbis Litterarum* 67 (2012): 83–135.

Gouda, Frances. *Dutch Culture Overseas: Colonial Practice in the Netherlands Indies, 1900–1942*. Amsterdam: Amsterdam University Press, 1995.

Graham, James D. "A Case Study of Migrant Labor in Tanzania." *African Studies Review* (1970): 23–33.

Graydon, Michael. "Don't Bother to Wrap It: Online Giftgiver and Bugchaser Newsgroups, the Social Impact of Gift Exchanges and the 'Carnivalesque'." *Culture, Health & Sexuality* 9, no. 3 (2007): 277–92.

Gregory, Brian. Review of *Auto/Ethnography: Rewriting the Self and the Social*, by Deborah E. Reed-Danahay. *Journal of American Folklore* 113, no. 449 (Summer 2000): 328–30.

Grosse, Pascal. *Kolonialismus, Eugenik und bürgerliche Gesellschaft in Deutschland 1850–1918*. Frankfurt am Main: Campus, 2000.

Gründer, Horst. *Christliche Mission und deutscher Imperialismus: Eine politische Geschichte ihrer Beziehungen während der deutschen Kolonialzeit (1884–1914). Unter besonderer Berücksichtigung Afrikas und Chinas*. Paderborn: Schöningh, 1982.

Gründer, Horst. *Geschichte der deutschen Kolonien*. Paderborn: Schöningh, 1985, 2004.

Gründer, Horst. "Mission und Kolonialismus—Historische Beziehungen und strukturelle Zusammenhänge." In *Christliche Heilsbotschaft und weltliche Macht: Studien zum Verhältnis von Mission und Kolonialismus. Gesammelte Aufsätze von Horst Gründer*, edited by Franz-Joseph Post, Thomas Küster, and Clemens Sorgenfrey, 7–19. Münster: Lit, 2004.

Gurnah, Abdulrazak. *Paradise*. New York: New Press, 1994.

Gutman, Matthew C. "Trafficking in Men: The Anthropology of Masculinity." *Annual Review of Anthropology* 26 (1997): 385–409.

Habermas, Jürgen. "Die postnationale Konstellation und die Zukunft der Demokratie." In Jürgen Habermas, *Die postnationale Konstellation. Politische Essays*, 91–169. Frankfurt am Main: Suhrkamp, 1998.

Hagen, Gunther von. *Kurzes Handbuch zum Negerenglisch an der Küste Westafrikas unter besonderer Berücksichtigung von Kamerun*. Berlin: Dingeldey und Werres, 1913.

Hagermann, Karen. "German Heroes: The Cult of Death for the Fatherland in Nineteenth Century Germany." In *Gender in History: Masculinities in Politics and War; Gendering Modern History*, edited by Stefan Dudink, Karen Hagermann, and John Tosh, 116–36. Manchester: Manchester University Press, 2004.

Hagström-Ståhl, Kristina. "Mourning as Method: William Kentridge's *Black Box/ Chambre Noire*." *Arcadia* 45, no. 2 (2011): 339–52.

Hamed bin Muhammed el Murjebi. "Autobiographie des Arabers Schech Hamed bin Muhammed el Murjebi, genannt Tippu Tip." *Mitteilungen des Seminars für Orientalische Sprachen* 3/4 (1902/03): 175–277, 1–55.

Hamid, Abdul. "Sisal—The Tree of Wonder." *Dawn,* July 26, 1955.

Hartmann, Wolfram. "Urges in the Colony: Men and Women in Colonial Windhoek, 1890–1914." *Journal of Namibian Studies* 1 (2007): 49–50.

Hau'Ofa, Epeli. *We Are the Ocean: Selected Works.* Honolulu: University of Hawai'i Press, 2008.

Hausen, Karin. *Deutsche Kolonialherrschaft in Afrika: Wirtschaftsinteressen und Kolonialverwaltung in Kamerun vor 1914.* Zurich: Atlantis, 1970.

Hegglund, John. "Modernism, Africa, and the Myth of Continents." In *Geographies of Modernism,* edited by Peter Brooker and Andrew Thacker, 43–53. London: Routledge, 2005.

Heidegger, Martin. *Die Grundbegriffe der Metaphysik: Welt—Endlichkeit—Einsamkeit.* Frankfurt am Main: Klostermann, 2004.

Heine, Bernd. *Pidgin-Sprachen im Bantu-Bereich.* Berlin: Dietrich Reimer, 1973.

Heller, Peter. *Deutsche Kolonien. DVD 1. Mulattin Else oder Eine deutsche Art zu lieben.* Munich: Multimedia, 2007.

Hempenstall, Peter. *Pacific Islanders under German Rule: A Study in the Meaning of Colonial Resistance.* Canberra: Australian National University Press, 1978.

Hempenstall, Peter J., and Paul Tanaka Mochida. *The Lost Man: Wilhelm Solf in German History.* Wiesbaden: Harrassowitz, 2005.

Hempenstall, Peter, and Noel Rutherford. *Protest and Dissent in the Colonial Pacific.* Suva: Institute of Pacific Studies of the University of the South Pacific, 1984.

Henrichsen, Dag. "'. . . unerwünscht im Schutzgebiet . . . nicht schlechthin unsittlich': 'Mischehen' und deren Nachkommen im Visier der Kolonialverwaltung in Deutsch-Südwestafrika." In *Frauen in den deutschen Kolonien,* edited by Marianne Bechhaus-Gerst and Mechthild Leutner, 80–90. Berlin: Ch. Links, 2009.

Henrichsen, Dag, and Gesine Krüger. "'We Have Been Captives Long Enough. We Want to be Free': Land, Uniforms, and Politics in the History of the Herero in the Interwar Period." In *Mobility and Containment: Namibia under South African Rule, 1915–46,* edited by Patricia Hayes, Jeremy Sylvester, Marion Wallace, and Wolfram Hartmann, 149–74. Athens: Ohio University Press, 1999.

Henriot, Christian. *Prostitution and Sexuality in Shanghai: A Social History, 1849–1949.* Translated by Noël Castelino. Cambridge: Cambridge University Press, 2001.

Hershatter, Gail. *Dangerous Pleasures: Prostitution and Modernity in Twentieth-Century Shanghai.* Berkeley: University of California Press, 1997.

Hevia, James. *Cherishing Men from Afar: Qing Guest Ritual and the Macartney Embassy of 1793.* Durham: Duke University Press, 1995.

Hiery, Hermann J., and Hans-Martin Hinz, eds. *Alltagsleben und Kulturaustausch: Deutsche und Chinesen in Tsingtau 1897–1914* [*Everyday Life and Cultural Exchange: Germans and Chinese in Tsingtau, 1897–1914*]. Wolfratshausen: Ed. Minerva, 1999.

Higate, Paul. "'Soft Clerks' and 'Hard Civvies': Pluralizing Military Masculinities." In *Military Masculinities: Identities and the State,* edited by Paul Higate, 27–42. Westport, CT: Praeger, 2003.

Hildebrandt, M. *Eine deutsche Militärstation im Innern Afrikas.* Wolfenbüttel: Heckners Verlag, 1905.

Hindorf, Richard. *Der Sisalban in Deutsch-Ostafrika (Sisal Cultivation in German East Africa).* Berlin: Reimer, 1925.

Hirsch, Marianne. *Family Frames: Photography, Narrative and Postmemory*. Cambridge: Harvard University Press, 1997.

Hitchcock, Eldred. *The Sisal Industry of East Africa*. London: Beauchamp Printing, 1957.

Hockey, John. "No More Heroes: Masculinity in the Infantry." In *Military Masculinities: Identities and the State*, edited by Paul Higate, 15–26. Westport, CT: Praeger, 2003.

Hofmann, Michael, and Rita Morrien, eds. *Deutsch-afrikanische Diskurse in Geschichte und Gegenwart: Literatur- und kulturwissenschaftliche Perspektiven*. Amsterdam: Rodopi, 2012.

Hollinger, David. *Postethnic America: Beyond Multiculturalism*. New York: Basic Books, 1995.

Horn, Peter. "Die Versuchung durch die barbarische Schönheit: Zu Hans Grimms 'farbigen' Frauen." *Germanisch-Romanische Monatsschrift* 35, no. 3 (1985): 317–41.

Horne, John. "Masculinities in Politics and War in the Age of Nation-States and World Wars, 1850–1950." In *Gender in History: Masculinities in Politics and War; Gendering Modern History*, edited by Stefan Dudink, Karen Hagermann, and John Tosh, 22–40. Manchester: Manchester University Press, 2004.

Howard, Michael C. *Transnationalism and Society: An Introduction*. Jefferson, NC: McFarland, 2011.

Hsia, Adrian. *Hermann Hesse und China: Darstellung, Materialien und Interpretation*. Frankfurt am Main: Suhrkamp, 1974.

Huagong chuguo shiliao huibian (Selected Historical Documents concerning the Emigration of Chinese Workers), ed. Lu Wendi, Chen Yixuan, and Cai Jiali. Beijing: Zhonghua shuju, 1984.

Huang, Fu-teh. *Qingdao: Chinesen unter deutscher Herrschaft 1897–1914*. Bochum: Projekt, 1999.

Hull, Isabel V. *Absolute Destruction: Military Culture and the Practices of War in Imperial Germany*. Ithaca: Cornell University Press, 2005.

Hyam, Ronald. *Empire and Sexuality: The British Experience*. Manchester: Manchester University Press, 1990.

Iliffe, John. "The Effects of the Maji Maji Rebellion of 1905–1906 on German Occupation Policy in East Africa." In *Britain and Germany in Africa: Imperial Rivalry and Colonial Rule*, edited by Prosser Gifford and Wm. Roger Louis, 557–76. New Haven: Yale University Press, 1967.

Iliffe, John. *A Modern History of Tanganyika*. Cambridge: Cambridge University Press, 1979.

Iliffe, John. *Tanganyika under German Rule, 1905–1912*. London; Nairobi: Cambridge University Press; East African Publishing House, 1969.

Jenkins, Paul. "Sources of Unexpected Light. Experiences with Old Mission Photographs in Research of Overseas History." *Jahrbuch für Europäische Überseegeschichte* 1 (2001): 157–67.

Jericho, E. A. *Seedtime and Harvest in New Guinea*. Brisbane: New Guinea Mission Board/UELCA, 1961.

Ji, Manhong. "Lun wan Qing zhengfu dui Dongnanya huaqiao de baohu zhengce [The Late Qing Government's Protective Policy of Overseas Chinese in Southeast Asia]." *Dongnanya yanjiu* [Southeast Asian Studies], no. 2 (2006): 52–56.

Jones, Adam. "Ethnographie als 'Nebenprodukt' der Arbeit der Leipziger Mission in Ostafrika." In *Auf der Suche nach Vielfalt: Ethnographie und Geographie in Leipzig*, edited by Claus Deimel, Sebastian Lentz, and Bernhard Streck. Leipzig: Leibniz-Institut für Länderkunde, 2009.

Joseph, John Earl. *Eloquence and Power: The Rise of Language Standard and Standard Languages*. London: Frances Printer, 1987.

Kapila, Shruti. "Self, Spencer and Swaraj: Nationalist Thought and Critiques of Liberalism, 1890–1920." *Modern Intellectual History* 4, no. 1 (April 2007): 109–27.

Kaplan, Cheryl. "Inside the Black Box: William Kentridge in an Interview." *Db artmag* 31 (2005). Accessed July 15, 2012. http://db-artmag.de/archiv/2005/e/7/1/383.html.

Karl, Rebecca E. "On Comparability and Continuity: China, circa 1930s and 1990s." *Boundary* 32, no. 2 (2005): 169–200.

Karl, Rebecca E. *Staging the World: Chinese Nationalism at the Turn of the Twentieth Century*. Durham: Duke University Press, 2002.

Kaya, Hassan Omari. *Disarticulation and Poor Incentives Programmes in African Economies: The Case of the Sisal Industry in Tanzania*. Berlin: Verlag Schreiber Publishers, 1989.

Kemung, Numuc Zirajukic. *Nareng-Gareng: A Principle for Mission in the Evangelical Lutheran Church of Papua New Guinea*. Erlangen: Erlanger Verlag für Mission und Ökumene, 1998.

Kennedy, Paul M. *The Samoan Tangle: A Study in Anglo-German-American Relations 1878–1900*. Dublin: Irish University Press, 1974.

Kentridge, William. "Learning from the Absurd." Avenali lecture March 15, 2009, at University of California Berkeley. Accessed January 29, 2010. http://townsendcenter.berkeley.edu/webcast_Kentridge.shtml.

Kentridge, William, and Maria-Christina Villaseñor. *Black Box/Chambre Noire*. New York: Guggenheim Museum Publications, 2005.

Keyßer, Christian. *Anutu im Papualand*. Nuremberg: Glocken-Verlag, 1926.

Keyßer, Christian. *Eine Papuagemeinde*. Kassel: Bärenreiter Verlag, 1929.

Keyßer, Christian. *Zake: Der Papuahäuptling*. Neuendettelsau: Freimund Verlag, 1950 [1934].

Khanna, Ranjana. *Dark Continents: Psychoanalysis and Colonialism*. Durham: Duke University Press, 2003.

Kim, David. "The Scandals of Translation: Cannibalism and the Limits of Colonial Authority in the Trial of Iringa, December 1908." *German Studies Review* 34, no. 1 (2011): 125–42.

King, Richard C. "The (Mis)uses of Cannibalism in Contemporary Cultural Critique." *Diacritics* 30, no. 1 (2000): 106–23.

Kispert, Wolf. *Pioniere in Ostafrika*. Teil I. Amboni: Tanga, n.d.

Kistner, Ulrike. "Die kolonisierende Rede: Strukturen eines restringierenden Codes am Beispiel eines Romans von Martin Jaeckel." PhD diss., University of Witwatersrand, 1986.

Klein, Josef. "Sprache und Macht," 16.2.2010. Accessed July 20, 2012. http://www.bpb.de/apuz/32949/sprache-und-macht?p=0.

Klein, Thoralf. "The Basel Mission as a Transcultural Organization: Photographs of

Chinese Christians and the Problem of Agency." In *Getting Pictures Right: Context and Interpretation*, edited by Michael Albrecht, Veit Arlt, Barbara Müller, and Jürg Schneider, 39–56. Cologne: Köppe, 2004.

Klein, Thoralf. *Die Basler Mission in der Provinz Guangdong (Südchina), 1859–1931. Akkulturationsprozesse und kulturelle Grenzziehungen zwischen Missionaren, chinesischen Christen und lokaler Gesellschaft.* Munich: Iudicium, 2002.

Klein, Thoralf. "Mission *und* Kolonialismus—Mission *als* Kolonialismus. Anmerkungen zu einer Wahlverwandtschaft." In *Kolonialgeschichten. Regionale Perspektiven auf ein globales Problem*, edited by Claudia Kraft, Alf Lüdtke, and Jürgen Martschukat, 142–61. Frankfurt am Main: Campus, 2010.

Klein, Thoralf. "Wozu untersucht man Missionsgesellschaften? Eine Antwort am Beispiel der Basler Mission in China," *Jahrbuch für Europäische Überseegeschichte* 5 (2005): 73–99.

Klotz, Marcia, ed. *German Colonialism: Another Sonderweg?* Special issue of *European Studies Journal* 16, no. 2 (Fall 1999).

Knight, Nick. *Rethinking Mao: Explorations in Mao Zedong's Thought.* Lanham, MD: Lexington Books, 2007.

Koponen, Juhani. *Development for Exploitation: German Colonial Policies in Mainland Tanzania, 1884–1914.* Helsinki: Lit Verlag, 1994.

Korn, Fadumo (with Sabine Eichhorst). *Geboren im Großen Regen: Mein Leben zwischen Afrika und Deutschland.* Reinbek bei Hamburg: Rowohlt, 2004 (*Born in the Big Rains: A Memoir of Somalia and Survival.* Translated by Tobe Levin. New York: Feminist Press and City University of New York, 2006).

Kössler, Reinhard. "Genocide, Apologies, and Reparation—The Linkage between Images of the Past in Namibia and Germany." Paper presented at Africa Group for Interdisciplinary Studies (AEGIS) European Conference in African Studies, Leiden, Netherlands, July 11–14, 2007. Accessed August 20, 2012. http://freiburg-postkolonial.de/Seiten/Koessler-Linkages-2007.pdf.

Kouega, Jean-Paul. *A Dictionary of Cameroon English Usage.* Oxford: Lang, 2007.

Kreutzer, Leo. *Goethe in Afrika: Die interkulturelle Literaturwissenschaft der "École de Hanovre" in der afrikanischen Germanistik.* Hannover: Wehrhahn, 2009.

Kron, Stefanie. "Afrikanische Diaspora und Literatur Schwarzer Frauen in Deutschland." In *Dossier Migrationsliteratur—eine neue deutsche Literatur?*, edited by Sibel Kara and Heinrich Böll-Stiftung, February 2009. Accessed August 27, 2012. http://www.migration-boell.de/web/integration/47_2026.asp#6.

Krüger, Gesine. *Kriegsbewältigung und Geschichtsbewußtsein. Realität, Deutung und Verarbeitung des deutschen Kolonialkrieges in Namibia 1904 bis 1907.* Göttingen: Vandenhoeck & Ruprecht, 1999.

Kum'a Ndumbe III. *Ach Kamerun! Unsere alte deutsche Kolonie . . . : Ein Dokumentarstück in zehn Szenen.* Douala: AfricAvenir, Berlin: Exchange & Dialogue, 2005.

Kum'a Ndumbe III. *Hitler voulait l'Afrique: le projet du 3e Reich sur le continent africain.* Paris: Harmattan, 1980.

Kum'a Ndumbe III. "Les traités camerouno-germaniques 1884–1907." In *Africa and Germany: From Colonisation to Cooperation, 1884–1986 (The Case of Cameroon)*, edited by Kum'a Ndumbe III, 42–68. Yaounde: AfricAvenir, 1986.

Kurtz, Joachim. "Selbstbehauptung mit geliehener Stimme: J. G. Fichte als Redner an die chinesische Nation." In *Selbstbehauptungsdiskurse in Asien: China—Japan—Korea*, edited by Iwo Amelung et al., 219–42. Munich: Iudicium, 2003.

Kuß, Susanne. *Deutsches Militär auf kolonialen Kriegsschauplätzen: Eskalation von Gewalt zu Beginn des 20. Jahrhunderts.* Berlin: Links, 2010.

Kwalanda, Miriam (with Birgit Theresa Koch). *Die Farbe meines Gesichts: Lebensreise einer kenianischen Frau.* Frankfurt am Main: Eichborn, 1999.

Laburthe-Tolra, Philippe. *Yaoundé d'après Zenker (1895). Le plan de 1892. L'article de 1895. Reproduction du texte allemand et des 6 planches originales, avec un portrait de l'auteur.* Dijon: Presses Universitaires, 1970.

Lagerwey, John. "Preface." In *Meizhou diqu de miaohui yu zongzu* 梅州地區的廟會與宗族 (Temple Festivals and Lineages in Meizhou), edited by Fang Xuejia 房學嘉, 1–14. N.p.: International Hakka Studies Association. Overseas Chinese Archives and Ecole Française d'Extrême-Orient, 1996.

Lam, Willy Wo-lap. *The Era of Jiang Zemin.* Singapore: Prentice-Hall, 1999.

Langbehn, Volker, ed. *German Colonialism, Visual Culture, and Modern Memory.* New York: Routledge, 2010.

Langbehn, Volker, and Mohammad Salama, eds. *German Colonialism: Race, the Holocaust, and Postwar Germany.* New York: Columbia University Press, 2011.

Larson, Lorne. "A History of the Mahenge (Ulanga) District, ca. 1860–1957." PhD diss., University of Dar es Salaam, 1976.

Lau, Brigitte. "Uncertain Certainties: The Herero-German War of 1904." *Mibagus* 2 (1989): 4–5.

Lauber, Wolfgang. *Deutsche Architektur in Kamerun 1884–1914: Deutsche Architekten und Kameruner Wissenschaftler dokumentieren die Bauten der deutschen Epoche in Kamerun/Afrika.* Stuttgart: K. Krämer, 1988.

Lawrance, Benjamin, Emily Lynn Osborn, and Richard L. Roberts, ed. *Intermediaries, Interpreters, and Clerks: African Employees in the Making of Colonial Africa.* Madison: University of Wisconsin Press, 2006.

Lehner, Sonja. *Schwarz-weiße Verständigung: Interkulturelle Kommunikationsprozesse in europäisch-deutschsprachigen und englisch- und französischsprachigen afrikanischen Romanen (1970–1990).* Frankfurt am Main: IKO, 1994.

Leicht, Bernd. "Kannibalen in Deutsch-Neuguinea: Der 'Andere' im kolonialzeitlichen Diskurs." PhD diss., Universität Heidelberg, 2000.

Lennox, Sara. "Das afrikanische Gesicht, das in deinem Raum spricht: Postkoloniale Autoren in Deutschland: Kum'a Numbe III und Uche Nduka." In *Literatur und Migration (Text+Kritik* special edition), edited by Heinz Ludwig Arnold, 167–76. Munich: text + kritik, 2006.

Lennox, Sara. "Postcolonial Writing in Germany." In *The Cambridge History of Postcolonial Literature*, ed. Ato Quayson, vol. 1, 620–48. Cambridge: Cambridge University Press, 2012.

Leue, August. *Dar-es-Salaam: Bilder aus dem Kolonialleben.* Berlin: Wilhelm Süsserott, 1903.

Leutner, Mechthild, ed. *"Musterkolonie Kiautschou"—Die Expansion des Deutschen Reiches in China; Deutsch-chinesische Beziehungen 1897–1914—Eine Quellensammlung.* Berlin: Akademie, 1997.

Leutner, Mechthild, and Klaus Mühlhahn, eds. *Deutsch-chinesische Beziehungen im 19. Jahrhundert: Mission und Wirtschaft in interkultureller Perspektive.* Münster: LIT, 2001.

Leutner, Mechthild, and Klaus Mühlhahn, eds. "Interkulturelle Handlungsmuster: Deutsche Wirtschaft und Mission in China in der Spätphase des Imperialismus." In Mechthild Leutner and Klaus Mühlhahn, eds., *Deutsch-chinesische Beziehungen im 19. Jahrhundert: Mission und Wirtschaft in interkultureller Perspektive*, 9–42. Münster: Lit, 2001.

Levenson, Joseph R. *Lian Ch'i-ch'ao and the Mind of Modern China.* Berkeley: University of California Press, 1953.

Lewis, G. Malcolm, and David Woodward, ed. *The History of Cartography: Cartography in the Traditional African, American, Arctic, Australian, and Pacific Societies*, vol. 2, book 3. Chicago: University of Chicago Press, 1998.

Li, Gongzhen. "Deguo dui Hua wenhua zhengce de kaiduan [The Beginning of the German Cultural Policy towards China]." In *Zhong De guanxishi wencong [Selected Works on the History of Sino-German Relations]*, edited by Liu Shanzhang and Zhou Quan, 212–28. Qingdao: Qingdao Press, 1991.

Li, Hongsheng. "Chen Gan yu Shandong geming yundong [Chen Gan and Shandong Revolutionary Movement]." In *Chen Gan jinian wenji [A Collection of Articles in Memory of Chen Gan]*, edited by Chen Jun and Tong Lirong, 6–19. Hong Kong: Tian Ma Publishing, 2001.

Liang, Zhixue, and Shen Zhen. "Fichtes Philosophie in China." In *Der Grundansatz der ersten Wissenschaftslehre Johann Gottlieb Fichtes.* Tagung des Internationalen Kooperationsorgans der Fichte-Forschung in Neapel 1995, edited by Erich Fuchs and Ives, Radrizzani, 287–98. Neuried: Ars Una, 1996.

Lindner, Ulrike, et al. *Hybrid Cultures—Nervous States: Britain and Germany in a (Post) Colonial World.* Amsterdam: Rodopi, 2010.

Lindsay, Lisa, and Stephan Miescher, eds. *Men and Masculinities in Modern Africa.* Portsmouth: Heinemann, 2003.

Lissock, Jean Paul. *Mein Freund, der weiße Mann: Von Kamerun nach Deutschland.* Berlin: Frieling, 1997.

Little, Kenneth. *African Women in Towns: An Aspect of Africa's Social Revolution.* Cambridge: Cambridge University Press, 1973.

Liu, Lydia H. *The Clash of Empires: The Invention of China in Modern World Making.* Cambridge: Harvard University Press, 2004.

Liu, Lydia H. *Translingual Practice: Literature, National Culture, and Translated Modernity—China, 1900–1937.* Stanford: Stanford University Press, 1995.

Liu, Xiaohuan, and Xu Zhongli. "Chen Gan yu zhongguo jindai baokan xinwen shiye [Chen Gan and Modern Chinese Journalism and Press]." In *Chen Gan jinian wenji [A Collection of Articles in Memory of Chan Gan]*, edited by Chen Jun and Tong Lirong, 247–64. Hong Kong: Tian Ma Publishing, 2001.

Liua'ana, Ben Featuna'i. "Dragons in Little Paradise. Chinese (Mis-) Fortunes in Samoa, 1900–1950." *Journal of Pacific History* 32, no. 1 (1997): 29–48.

Louie, Kam. Review of *Explosions and Other Stories*, by Mo Yan. *Australian Journal of Chinese Affairs* 29 (January 1993): 195–96.

Lovett, Margot. "On Power and Powerlessness: Marriage and Metaphor in Colonial

Western Tanzania." *International Journal of African Historical Studies* 27, no. 2 (1994): 273–301.

Lüdtke, Alf. "Geschichte und Eigensinn." In *Alltagskultur, Subjektivität und Geschichte: Zur Theorie und Praxis von Alltagsgeschichte*, edited by Berliner Geschichtswerkstatt, 139–53. Münster: Westfälisches Dampfboot, 1994.

Luo, Jincai. "Xiantan 1860 nian yihou wan Qing zhengfu waijiao huaqiao de biaoxian [The Attitude of the Late Qing Government towards Protection of Overseas Chinese after 1860]." *Fujian Luntan* [Fujian Tribune], no. 1 (2008): 38–39.

Luo, Zhitian. *Luanshi qianliu: Minzu zhuyi yu zhengzhi [Undercurrent in Troubled Times: Nationalism and Politic]*. Shanghai: Shanghai Ancient Books Publishing House, 2001.

Lutz, Jessie Gregory. *Opening China: Karl F. A. Gützlaff and Sino-Western Relations, 1827–1852*. Grand Rapids, MI: Eerdmans, 2008.

Lutz, Jessie Gregory, and Rolland Ray Lutz. *Hakka Chinese Confront Protestant Christianity: With the Autobiographies of Eight Hakka Christians, and Commentary*. Armonk, NY: Sharpe, 1998.

Lutz, Jessie Gregory, and Rolland Ray Lutz. "The Invisible China Missionaries: The Basel Mission's Chinese Evangelists, 1847–1866." *Mission Studies* 12 (1995): 204–27.

Lyman, Stanford M. "The 'Yellow Peril' Mystique: Origins and Vicissitudes of a Racist Discourse." *International Journal of Politics, Culture, and Society* 13, no. 4 (2000): 683–747.

Ma, Gengcun. *Tongmenghui zai Shandong [Tongmenghui in Shandong]*. Jinan: Shandong Renmin Publishing House, 1991.

MacCormack, Carol P. "Human Leopards and Crocodiles: Political Meanings of Categorical Anomalies." In *The Ethnography of Cannibalism*, edited by Paula Brown and Donald Tuzin, 50–60. Washington, DC: Society for Psychological Anthropology, 1983.

Madley, Benjamin. "From Africa to Auschwitz." *European History Quarterly* 35, no. 3 (2005): 429–64.

Mair, Lucy. *African Marriage and Social Change*. London: Frank Cass, 1969.

Malinowski, B. "Kula: The Circulating Exchange of Valuables in the Archipelagoes of Eastern New Guinea." In *Peoples of the Pacific: The History of Oceania to 1870*, edited by Paul D'Arcy, 261–70. Burlington, VT: Ashgate / Variorum, 2008.

Mamozai, Martha. *Herrenmenschen: Frauen im deutschen Kolonialismus*. Reinbek bei Hamburg: Rowohlt, 1982.

Mani, B. Venkat. *Cosmopolitical Claims, Turkish-German Literatures from Nadolny to Pamuk*. Iowa City: University of Iowa Press, 2007.

Mani, B. Venkat. "Kosmopolitismus und Weltliteratur: Thesen gegen die Herrschaft der Ego." In *Das Argument: Zeitschrift für Philosophie und Sozialwissenschaften*, 54.4 (2012): 501–9. Special issue on "Kosmopolitismus in der Weltliteratur," edited by Gerhard Bauer and Julia Schöll.

Manjapra, Kris. *Age of Entanglement: German and Indian Intellectuals across Empire*. Cambridge: Harvard University Press, 2014.

Manjapra, Kris. "The Illusions of Encounter: Muslim 'Minds' and Hindu Revolutionaries in First World War Germany and After." *Journal of Global History* 1, no. 3 (Nov. 2006): 363–82.

Martin, B. G. *Muslim Brotherhoods in Nineteenth-Century Africa.* Cambridge: Cambridge University Press, 1976.

Martin, Peter. *Schwarze Teufel, edle Mohren: Afrikaner in Geschichte und Bewusstsein der Deutschen.* Hamburg: Hamburger Edition, 2001.

Martineau, Joel. "Autoethnography and Material Culture: The Case of Bill Reid." *Biography* 24, no. 1 (2001): 242–58.

Marx, Karl, and Frederick Engels. *On Colonialism: Articles from the New York Tribune and Other Writings.* New York: International Publishers, 1972.

Mascarenhas, Adolfo C. "Resistance and Change in the Sisal Plantation System of Tanzania." PhD diss., University of California, 1970.

Maß, Sandra. *Weiße Helden, schwarze Krieger: Zur Geschichte kolonialer Männlichkeit in Deutschland 1918—1964.* Cologne: Böhlau, 2006.

Matzat, William. *Shan Weilian yu Qingdao tudi fagui* [*Wilhelm Schrameier and Land legislation in Qingdao*], translated by Jiang Hong. Taibei: Research Institute of Chinese Land Policy, 1986.

Mauss, Marcel. *The Gift: Forms of Exchange in Archaic Societies.* New York: Norton, 1964.

Mazumdar, Shaswati. *Feuchtwanger, Brecht: Der Umgang mit der indischen Kolonialgeschichte—Eine Studie zur Konstruktion des Anderen.* Würzburg: Königshausen & Neumann, 1998.

Mbaku, John. *Cultures and Customs of Cameroon.* Westport: Greenwood Press, 2005.

McClintock, Anne. *Imperial Leather: Race, Gender, and Sexuality in the Colonial Conquest.* New York: Routledge, 1995.

McColl Millar, Robert. *Language, Nation, and Power: An Introduction.* New York: Palgrave Macmillan, 2005.

McCullers, Molly. "'We do it so that we will be Men': Masculinity Politics in Colonial Namibia, 1915–45." *Journal of African History* 52 (2011): 43–62.

McGetchin, Douglas T., Peter K. J. Park, and Damodar R. SarDesai, eds. *Sanskrit and "Orientalism": Indology and Comparative Linguistics in Germany, 1750–1958.* New Delhi: Manohar, 2004.

McKeown, Adam. "Global Migration 1846–1940." *Journal of World History* 15, no. 2 (2004): 155–89.

McKittrick, Meredith. "Colonialism, Christianity, and Coming of Age in Ovamboland, Northern Namibia." In *Men and Masculinities in Modern Africa*, edited by Lisa Lindsay and Stephan Miescher, 33–51. Portsmouth: Heinemann, 2003.

Mehari, Senait G. *Feuerherz.* Munich: Droemer, 2004. Translated by Christine Lo as *Heart of Fire: From Child Soldier to Soul Singer.* London: Profile Books, 2006.

Mehnert, Ute. *Deutschland, Amerika und die "Gelbe Gefahr." Zur Karriere eines Schlagworts in der Großen Politik, 1905–1917.* Stuttgart: Franz Steiner Verlag, 1995.

Meinhof, Carl. "Handelssprachen." In *Deutsches Kolonial-Lexikon*, vol. 2, edited by Heinrich Schnee. Leipzig: Quelle und Meyer, 1920.

Melkisede, Advent P. "Christ Danced in Sattelberg between 1886–1914." Unpublished master's thesis, Martin Luther Seminary, Lae, Papua New Guinea, November 10, 1973.

Memmi, Albert. *Portrait du colonisé précédé de Portrait de colonisateur.* Paris: Corréa, 1957.

Mepin, Daniel. *Die Weissagung der Ahnen: Roman. Kamerun.* Unkel/Rhein, Bad Honnef: Horlemann, 1997.

Meyer, Birgit. "Christianity and the Ewe Nation: German Pietist Missionaries, Ewe Converts and the Politics of Culture." In *Weltmission und religiöse Organisationen. Protestantische Missionsgesellschaften im 19. Jahrhundert*, edited by Artur Bogner, Bernd Holtwick, and Hartmann Tyrell, 541–69. Würzburg: Ergon, 2004.

Micheler, Stefan. *Selbstbilder und Fremdbilder der "Anderen:" Männer begehrende Männer in der Weimarer Republik und der NS-Zeit*. Constance: UVK, 2005.

Michels, Stefanie. *Schwarze deutsche Kolonialsoldaten: Mehrdeutige Repräsentationsräume und früher Kosmopolitismus in Afrika*. Bielefeld: transcript, 2009.

Miehe, Gudrun, Katrin Bromber, Said Khamis, and Ralf Grosserhode. *Kala Shairi: German East Africa in Swahili Poems*. Cologne: Rüdiger Köppe Verlag, 2002.

Mignolo, Walter. "The Many Faces of Cosmo-polis: Border Thinking and Critical Cosmopolitanism." In *Cosmopolitanism*, edited by Carol A. Breckenridge, Sheldon Pollock, Homi K. Bhabha, and Dipesh Chakrabarty, 157–88. Durham: Duke University Press, 2002.

Mihalyi, Louis. "Characteristics and Problems of Labour in the Usambara Highlands of East Africa during the German Period, 1885–1914." *East Africa*, May (1970): 20–25.

Militärisches Orientierungsheft für Deutsch-Ostafrika. Dar es Salaam: Deutsch-Ostafrikanische Rundschau, 1911.

Miller, Jon. *Missionary Zeal and Institutional Control: Organizational Contradictions in the Basel Mission on the Gold Coast, 1828–1917*. Grand Rapids, MI: Eerdmans, 2003.

Ministry of Lands, Housing and Urban Development. The United Republic of Tanzania. *Report of the Presidential Commission of Inquiry into Land Matters. Volume I. Land Policy and Land Tenure Structure*. Dar-Es-Salaam, Tanzania, 1994.

Mo, Er (Mohre), ed. *qingdao quanshu [The Complete Book of Qingdao]*. Qingdao, 1912.

Mohanty, Sacchindananda. "Face to Face: Towards a Global Citizenship. *The Hindu*," http://www.hindu.com/lr/2005/07/03/stories/2005070300020100.htm.

Morgen, Curt. *Durch Kamerun von Süd nach Nord. Reisen und Forschungen im Hinterland 1889 bis 1891*. Leipzig: Brockhaus, 1893.

Morlang, Thomas. *Askari und Fitafita: "Farbige" Söldner in den deutschen Kolonien*. Berlin: Christoph Links, 2008.

Morlang, Thomas. "'Die Wahehe haben ihre Vernichtung gewollt.' Der Krieg der 'Kaiserlichen Schutztruppe' gegen die Hehe in Deutsch-Ostafrika (1890–1898)." In *Kolonialkriege: Militärische Gewalt im Zeichen des Imperialismus*, edited by Thoralf Klein and Frank Schumacher, 80–108. Hamburg: Hamburger Edition, 2006.

Moses, John A. "The Coolie Labour Question and German Colonial Policy in Samoa, 1900–14." In *Germany in the Pacific and Far East, 1870–1914*, edited by John A. Moses and Paul M. Kennedy, 234–61. St. Lucia: University of Queensland, 1977.

Moses, John A., and Paul M. Kennedy, eds. *Germany in the Pacific and Far East, 1870–1914*. St. Lucia: University of Queensland, 1977.

Mudimbe, Valentin Y. "African Gnosis—Philosophy and the Order of Knowledge: An Introduction." *African Studies Review* 28, no. 2/3 (1985): 149–233.

Mudimbe, Valentin Y. *The Invention of Africa: Gnosis, Philosophy, and the Order of Knowledge*. Bloomington: Indiana University Press, 1988.

Mühlhahn, Klaus. *Herrschaft und Widerstand in der "Musterkolonie" Kiautschou: In-*

teraktionen zwischen China und Deutschland, 1897–1914. Munich: Oldenbourg, 2000.

Mühlhahn, Klaus. "Negotiating the Nation: German Colonialism and Chinese Nationalism in Qingdao, 1897–1914." In *Twentieth-Century Colonialism and China: Localities, the Everyday and the World,* edited by Bryna Goodman and David S. G. Goodman, 37–56. London: Routledge, 2012.

Mühlhahn, Klaus. *Zai mofan zhimindi Jiaozhouwan de tongzhi yu dikang—1897–1914 nian Zhongguo yu Deguo de xianghu zuoyong [Power and Resistance in the "Model Colony" of Kiautschou—interaction between China and Germans 1897—1914].* Translated by Sun Lixin. Jinan: Shandong University Press, 2005.

Mühlhäusler, Peter. *Pidgin and Creole Linguistics.* London: University of Westminster Press, 1997.

Munn, Christopher. *Anglo-China: Chinese People and British Rule in Hong Kong, 1841–1880.* Richmond, Surrey: Curzon, 2001.

Munro, Doug, and Stewart Firth. "German Labour Policy and the Partition of the Western Pacific: The View from Samoa." *Journal of Pacific History* 25, no. 1 (June 1990): 85–102.

Musambachime, M. C. "Protest Migrations in Mweru-Luapula, 1900–1940." *African Studies* 47 (1988): 19–34.

Nekes, Hermann. *Die Sprache der Jaunde in Kamerun.* Berlin: Reimer, 1913.

Nelson, Hank. "Loyalties at Sword-point. The Lutheran Missionaries in Wartime New Guinea: 1939–45." *Journal of Pacific History* 8 (1978): 199–217.

Nelson, Steven. "Collection and Context in a Cameroonian Village." *Museum International* 59, no. 3 (September 2007): 22–30.

Nelson, Steven. *From Cameroon to Paris: Mousgoum Architecture in and out of Africa.* Chicago: University of Chicago Press, 2007.

Nganang, Alain Patrice. *Interkulturalität und Bearbeitung: Untersuchung zu Soyinka und Brecht.* Munich: Judicium, 1998.

Ngoh, Victor Julius. *History of Cameroon since 1800.* Limbe: Pressbook, 1996.

Nigmann, Ernst. *Geschichte der kaiserlichen Schutztruppe für Deutsch-Ostafrika.* Berlin: Mittler & Sohn, 1911.

Nigmann, Ernst. *Die Wahehe: Ihre Geschichte, Kult-, Rechts-, Kriegs- und Jagd-Gebräuche.* Berlin: Mittler & Sohn, 1908.

Njoya, Sultan. *Histoire et coutumes des Bamum rédigées sous la direction du Sultan Njoya.* Mémoires de l'Institut Francais d'Afrique Noire, Centre du Cameroun. Série Populations no. 6. Dakar: pl. A-E, 1952.

Northrup, David. *Indentured Labour in the Age of Imperialism, 1834–1922.* Cambridge: Cambridge University Press, 1995.

Noyes, John K. *Colonial Space: Spatiality in the Discourse of German South West Africa, 1884–1915.* Chur, Switzerland: Harwood, 1991.

Nussbaum, Martha Craven. *For Love of Country?* Boston: Beacon Press, 2002.

Nyada, Germain. "Deutsch-kamerunische Kommunikationssituationen: Unterhaltungen mit den 'Jaunde' im Regenwald (1890–1910)." *Jahrbuch für Europäische Überseegeschichte* 9 (2009): 225–34.

Ogot, B. A., and J. A. Kieran, eds. *Zamani: A Survey of East African History.* Nairobi: East African Publishing House, 1968.

Oguntoye, Katharina, May Opitz, and Dagmar Schultz, eds. *Farbe bekennen: Afrodeutsche Frauen auf den Spuren ihrer Geschichte*. Berlin: Orlanda Frauenverlag, 1986.

Oji, Chima. *Unter die Deutschen gefallen: Erfahrungen eines Afrikaners*. Wuppertal: Peter Hammer, 1992.

Oldendorp, Christian G. A. *Geschichte der caribischen Inseln Sanct Thomas, Sanct Crux und Sanct Jan*, kommentierte Edition des Originalmanuskriptes. In *Abhandlungen und Berichte des Staatlichen Museums für Völkerkunde Dresden*, edited by Gudrun Meier. Berlin: Verlag für Wissenschaft und Bildung, 2000/2002.

Oloukpona-Yinnon, Adjaï Paulin. *Unter deutschen Palmen: Die "Musterkolonie" Togo im Spiegel deutscher Kolonialliteratur (1884–1944)*. Frankfurt: IKO, Verlag für Interkulturelle Kommunikation, 1998.

Olusoga, David, and Casper Erichsen. *The Kaiser's Holocaust: Germany's Forgotten Genocide and the Colonial Roots of Nazism*. London: Faber and Faber, 2010.

Ortner, Sherry B. *High Religion: A Cultural and Political History of Sherpa Buddhism*. Princeton: Princeton University Press, 1989.

Osayimwese, Itohan. "Colonialism at the Center: German Colonial Architecture and the Design Reform Movement, 1828–1918." PhD diss., University of Michigan, Ann Arbor, 2008.

Osteraas, Gary L. *Colonial Enthusiasm in Germany: A Study in the Cultural Background of German Colonialism, 1870–1914*. New York: Columbia University, 1965.

Osterhammel, Jürgen. *China und die Weltgesellschaft: Vom 18. Jahrhundert bis in unsere Zeit*. Munich: Beck, 1989.

Osterhammel, Jürgen. *Colonialism: A Theoretical Overview*. Princeton, NJ: Wiener, 1997.

Pakendorf, Gunther. "Of Colonizers and Colonized: Hans Grimm on German South West Africa." *Social Dynamics* 12, no. 2 (1986): 39–47.

Pandey, Gyanendra. "Voices from the Edge: The Struggle to Write Subaltern Histories." In *Mapping Subaltern Studies and the Postcolonial*, edited by Vinayak Chaturvedi, 281–99. London: Verso, 2000.

Parpart, Jane L., and Marianne Rostgaard, eds. *The Practical Imperialist: Letters from a Danish Planter in German East Africa, 1888–1906*. Leiden: Brill, 2006.

Pascha, Emin, and Franz Stuhlmann. *Die Tagebücher von Dr. Emin Pascha*. Hamburg: Westermann, 1927.

Passarge-Rathjens. "Bamum." In *Deutsches Kolonial Lexikon*, vol. 1, edited by Heinrich Schnee, 126. Leipzig: Quelle & Meyer, 1920. Accessed May 13, 2009. http://www.ub.bildarchiv-dkg.uni-frankfurt.de.

Pech, Rufus. "Deutsche evangelische Missionen in Deutsch-Neuguinea 1886–1921." In *Die deutsche Südsee 1884–1914: Ein Handbuch*, edited by Hermann Joseph Hiery, 384–415. Paderborn: Schöningh, 2002.

Perraudin, Michael, and Jürgen Zimmerer. *German Colonialism and National Identity*. New York: Routledge, 2011.

Pesek, Michael. "Cued Speeches: The Emergence of Shauri as Colonial Praxis in German East Africa, 1850–1903." *History in Africa* 33 (2006): 395–412.

Pesek, Michael. "Islam und Politik in Deutsch-Ostafrika, 1905–1919." In *Alles unter*

Kontrolle- Disziplinierungsverfahren im kolonialen Tanzania (1850–1960), edited by Albert Wirz, Katrin Bromber, and Andreas Eckert, 99–140. Hamburg: LIT, 2003.

Pesek, Michael. *Koloniale Herrschaft in Deutsch-Ostafrika. Expedition, Militär und Verwaltung seit 1880*. Frankfurt am Main: Campus, 2005.

Pesek, Michael. "Praxis und Repräsentation kolonialer Herrschaft: Die Ankunft des Staatssekretärs Dernburg am Hofe Kahigis von Kianja, 1907." In *Die Ankunft des Anderen: Empfangszeremonien im interkulturellen und intertemporalen Vergleich*, edited by Susann Baller, Michael Pesek, Ruth Schilling, and Ines Stolpe, 99–224. Frankfurt am Main: Campus, 2008.

Peter, Chris Maina. "Imperialism and Export Capital: A Survey of Foreign Private Investments in Tanzania during the German Colonial Period." *Journal of Asian and African Studies* 25, no. 3–4 (1990): 197–212.

Peukert, Detlev. *Inside Nazi Germany: Conformity, Opposition, and Racism in Everyday Life*. New Haven: Yale University Press, 1987.

Pilhofer, Georg. *Die Geschichte der Neuendettelsauer Mission in Neuguinea.* Vol. 1, *Von den ersten Anfängen bis zum Kriegsausbruch 1914*. Neuendettelsau: Evang.-Luth. Missionsanstalt Neuendettelsau, 1961.

Pilhofer, Georg. *Die Geschichte der Neuendettelsauer Mission in Neuguinea.* Vol. 2, *Die Mission zwischen den beiden Weltkriegen mit einem Überblick über die neue Zeit*. Neuendettelsau: Evang.-Luth. Missionsanstalt Neuendettelsau, 1963.

Pilhofer, Georg. *Johann Flierl der Bahnbrecher des Evangeliums unter den Papua.* Neuendettelsau: Freimund-Verlag, 1962.

Podesta, Dr. "Entwicklung und Gestaltung der gesundheitlichen Verhältnisse bei den Besatzungstruppen des Kiautschou-Gebietes im Vergleich mit der Marine und unter besonderer Berücksichtigung von Örtlichkeit und Klima in Tsingtau." *Deutsche Militärärztliche Zeitschrift* 38 (1909): 569–601.

Poeschel, Hans. *Bwana Hakimu: Richterfahrten in Deutsch-Ostafrika*. Leipzig: Koehler und Voigtländer, 1940.

Porter, Andrew. *Religion versus Empire? British Protestant Missionaries and Overseas Expansion, 1700–1914*. Manchester: Manchester University Press, 2004.

Posner, Roland. "Kultur als Zeichensystem: Zur semiotischen Explikation kulturwissenschaftlicher Grundbegriffe." In *Kultur als Lebenswelt und Monument*, edited by Aleida Assmann and Dietrich Harth, 37–74. Frankfurt am Main: Fischer, 1991.

Pratt, Mary Louise. "Arts of the Contact Zone." *Profession* 91 (1991): 33–40.

Pratt, Mary Louise. *Imperial Eyes: Travel Writing and Transculturation*. New York: Routledge, 1992.

Prein, Philipp. "Guns and Top Hats: African Resistance in German South West Africa, 1907–1915." *Journal of Southern African Studies* 20, no. 1 (1994): 99–121.

Pugach, Sara. *Africa in Translation: A History of Colonial Linguistics in Germany and Beyond, 1814–1945*. Ann Arbor: University of Michigan Press, 2012.

Qu, Qi. "Xinhai Geming qian Shandong baozhi jianshu 1894–1911 [A Brief Description of Shandong Newspapers Prior to Xinhai Revolution 1894–1911]." In *Shandong shizhi ziliao* [*Historical and Biographical Materials of Shandong*] 1 (1982): 168–78.

Quinn, Frederic E. "Rain Forest Encounters: The Beti Meet the Germans, 1887–1916."

In *Introduction to the History of Cameroon in the Nineteenth and Twentieth Centuries*, edited by Martin Njeuma, 88–105. Hong Kong: Macmillan, 1989.

Radhakrishnan, R. *Theory in an Uneven World.* Oxford: Blackwell, 2003.

Ranger, Terence. *Dance and Society in Eastern Africa, 1890–1970: The Beni Ngoma.* Berkeley and Los Angeles: University of California Press, 1975.

Reckwitz, Andreas. "Toward a Theory of Social Practices: A Development in Culturalist Theorizing." *European Journal of Social Theory* 5, no. 2 (2002): 243–63.

Reed-Danahay, Deborah E. *Auto/Ethnography: Rewriting the Self and the Social.* Oxford: Berg, 1997.

Reinhard, Wolfgang. "Christliche Mission und Dialektik des Kolonialismus." *Historisches Jahrbuch* 109 (1989): 353–70.

Renan, Ernest. "What Is a Nation?" Translated by Martin Thom. In *Nation and Narration*, edited by Homi Bhabha, 8–22. New York: Routledge, 1990.

Rennstich, Karl. "The Understanding of Mission, Civilisation and Colonialism in the Basel Mission." In *Missionary Ideologies in the Imperialist Era, 1880–1920*, edited by Torben Christensen and William R. Hutchison, 94–103. Århus: Åros, 1982.

Richardson, Peter. "The Recruiting of Chinese Indentured Labour for the South African Gold-Mines, 1903–1908." *Journal of African History* 18, no. 1 (1977): 85–108.

Riesz, János. "'Angst überschattet unser Leben': Afrikaner in Frankreich und Deutschland." In *Interkulturelle Texturen: Afrika und Deutschland im Reflexionsmedium der Literatur*, edited by M. Moustapha Diallo and Dirk Göttsche, 19–43. Bielefeld: Aisthesis, 2003.

Riesz, János. "Autor/innen aus dem schwarzafrikanischen Kulturraum." In *Interkulturelle Literatur in Deutschland: Ein Handbuch*, edited by Carmine Chiellino, 248–62. Stuttgart: Metzler, 2000.

Rivinius, Karl J. *Weltlicher Schutz und Mission: Das deutsche Protektorat über die katholische Mission in Süd-Shangtung.* Cologne: Böhlau, 1987.

Robert, Dana L. "Introduction." In *Converting Colonialism: Visions and Realities in Mission History, 1706–1904*, edited by Dana L. Robert, 1–20. Grand Rapids, MI: Eerdmans, 2008.

Robert, Marc. *La restauration du palais des Sultans de Bamoun à Foumban.* Paris: UNESCO, 1980.

Rockel, Stephen J. *Carriers of Culture: Labor on the Road in Nineteenth-Century East Africa.* Portsmouth, NH: Heinemann, 2006.

Rockel, Stephen J. "Wage Labor and the Culture of Porterage in Nineteenth Century Tanzania: The Central Caravan Routes." *Comparative Studies in South Asia, Africa and the Middle East* 15, no. 2 (1995): 14–24.

Rodney, Walter. "Migrant Labour and the Colonial Economy." In *Migrant Labour in Tanzania during the Colonial Period: Case Studies of Recruitment and Conditions of Labour in the Sisal Industry*, edited by Walter Rodney, Kapepwa Tambila, and Laurent Sago, 4–28. Hamburg: Institut fur Afrika-Kunde, 1983.

Roscoe, Paul. "New Guinea Leadership as Ethnographic Analogy: A Critical Review." *Journal of Archaeological Method and Theory* 7, no. 2 (June 2000): 79–126.

Rothberg, Michael. *Multidirectional Memory: Remembering the Holocaust in the Age of Decolonization.* Stanford: Stanford University Press, 2009.

Sabea, Hanan. "Mastering the Landscape? Sisal Plantations, Land and Labor in Tanga

Region, 1893–1980s." *International Journal of African Historical Studies* 41, no. 3 (2008): 411–32.

Sack, Peter, and Dymphna Clark, eds. *German New Guinea: The Annual Reports.* Canberra: Australian National University Press, 1979.

Salme, Sayyida / Emily Ruete. *An Arabian Princess between Two Worlds: Memoirs, Letters Home, Sequels to the Memoirs, Syrian Customs and Usages.* Edited with an introduction by E. van Donzel. Leiden: Brill, 1993. Arab History and Civilization. Studies and Texts, vol. 3.

Sartori, Andrew. "Beyond Culture-Contact and Colonial Discourse: 'Germanism' in Colonial Bengal." *Modern Intellectual History* 4, no. 1 (2007): 77–93.

Schestokat, Karin. *German Women in Cameroon: Travelogues from Colonial Times.* New York: Peter Lang, 2003.

Schinzinger, Francesca. *Die Kolonien und das Deutsche Reich: Die wirtschaftliche Bedeutung der deutschen Besitzungen in Übersee.* Wiesbaden: Franz Steiner, 1984.

Schlatter, Wilhelm. *Geschichte der Basler Mission. Vol. 2: Die Geschichte der Basler Mission in Indien und China.* Basel: Verlag der Basler Missionsbuchhandlung, 1916.

Schmidt, Max. *Aus unserem Kriegsleben in Südwest-Afrika.* Berlin: E. Runge, 1907.

Schmidt, Rochus. *Kolonialpioniere: Persönliche Erinnerungen aus kolonialer Frühzeit.* Berlin: Safari-Verlag, 1938.

Schmidt, Rochus. "Die Mpapua-Expedition—Wissmann, Emin und Stanley." In *Hermann von Wissmann—Deutschlands größter Afrikaner. Sein Leben und Wirken unter Benutzung des Nachlasses dargestellt,* edited by Carl von Perbandt, Georg Richelmann, and Rochus Schmidt, 252–91. Berlin: Schall, 1906.

Schmied-Kowarzik, Wolfdietrich, ed. *Verstehen und Verständigung: Ethnologie, Xenologie, interkulturelle Philosophie* (Justin Stagl zum 60. Geburtstag). Würzburg: Königshausen & Neumann, 2002.

Schmitt, Carl. *Political Theory: Four Chapters on the Concept of Sovereignty. Translated by George Schwab.* Chicago: University of Chicago Press, 2005.

Schmokel, Wolfe W. *Dream of Empire: German Colonialism, 1919–1945.* New Haven: Yale University Press, 1964. Reprint, Westport, CT: Greenwood Press, 1980.

Schrecker, John E. *Imperialism and Chinese Nationalism: Germany in Shantung.* Cambridge: Harvard University Press, 1971.

Schubert, Michael. *Der schwarze Fremde: Das Bild des Schwarzafrikaners in der parlamentarischen und publizistischen Kolonialdiskussion in Deutschland von den 1870er bis in die 1930er Jahre.* Stuttgart: F. Steiner, 2003.

Schulte, Regina. *Sperrbezirke. Tugendhaftigkeit und Prostitution in der bürgerlichen Welt.* Frankfurt am Main: Syndikat, 1979.

Schultze, Otto. "The Policy of the Basel Mission among the Hakkas." *Chinese Recorder* 47 (1916): 743–58.

Schultz-Ewerth, Erich, and Leonhard Adam. *Das Eingeborenenrecht: Sitten und Gewohnheitsrechte der Eingeborenen der ehemaligen deutschen Kolonien in Afrika und in der Südsee. Vol. 1: Ostafrika.* Stuttgart: Strecker & Schröder, 1929.

Schweizer, Peter A. *Mission an der Goldküste: Geschichte und Fotografie der Basler Mission im kolonialen Ghana.* Basel: Chr. Merian, 2002.

Scott, David. "Colonial Governmentality." In *Anthropologies of Modernity: Foucault,*

326   Bibliography

Governmentality, and Life Politics, edited by Jonathan X. Inda, 23–49. Oxford: Blackwell, 2005.

Scott, James. *Weapons of the Weak: Everyday Forms of Peasant Resistance*. New Haven: Yale University Press, 1985.

Seelemann, Dirk Alexander. "Social and Economic Development of the Kiaochao Leasehold (Shantung, China) under German Administration 1897–1914." PhD diss., University of Toronto, 1982.

Seiner, Franz. *Bergtouren und Steppenfahrten im Hererolande*. Berlin: Wilhelm Süsserott, 1904.

Sewell, William H., Jr. *Logics of History: Social Theory and Social Transformation*. Chicago: University of Chicago Press, 2005.

Shih, Shu-Mei. *The Lure of the Modern: Writing Modernism in Semicolonial China, 1917–1937*. Berkeley: University of California Press, 2001.

Shineberg, Dorothy. "The Sandalwood Trade in Melanesian Economics, 1841–65." In *Peoples of the Pacific: The History of Oceania to 1870*, edited by Paul D'Arcy, 359–76. Burlington, VT: Ashgate / Variorum, 2008.

Shorter, Aylward. "Nyungu-ya-Mawe and the 'Empire of the Ruga-Ruga.'" *Journal of African History* 9 (1968): 235–59.

Sieg, Katrin. *Ethnic Drag: Performing Race, Nation, Sexuality in West Germany*. Ann Arbor: University of Michigan Press, 2002.

Siegel, Brian. "Bomas, Missions, and Mines: The Making of Centers on the Zambian Copperbelt." *African Studies Review* 31, no. 3 (1988): 61–84.

Simo, David. *Interkulturalität und ästhetische Erfahrung: Untersuchungen zum Werk Hubert Fichte*. Stuttgart: Metzler, 1993.

Singleton, Michael. "Muslims, Missionaries and the Millennium in Upcountry Tanzania." *Cultures et Développement* 9, no. 2 (1977): 247–314.

Sinha, Mrinalini. "Giving Masculinity a History: Some Contributions from the Historiography of Colonial India." *Gender and History* 11 (1999): 445–60.

Sippel, Harald. "Aspects of Colonial Land Law in German East Africa." In *Land Law and Land Ownership in Africa: Case Studies from Colonial and Contemporary Cameroon and Tanzania*, edited by Robert Debusmann and Stefan Arnold, 3–38. Bayreuth: Bayreuth African Studies Breitinger, Bayreuth University, 1996.

Sissons, D. C. S. *Karayuki-san*: Japanese Prostitutes in Australia, 1887–1916–I." *Historical Studies* 17 (1977): 323–41.

Siu, Helen F. *Agents and Victims in South China: Accomplices in Rural Revolution*. New Haven: Yale University Press, 1989.

Smith, Woodruff D. *The German Colonial Empire*. Chapel Hill: University of North Carolina Press, 1978.

Songtou jiaohui shi 嵩頭教會史. (History of the Congregation in Songtau). Shanghai: Budao Shushe, 1923.

Sontag, Susan. *On Photography*. New York: Picador, 1973.

Spivak, Gayatri Chakravorty. "Can the Subaltern Speak?" In *Marxism and the Interpretation of Culture*, edited by Cary Nelson and Lawrence Grossberg, 271–313. Urbana: University of Illinois Press, 1988.

Spongberg, Mary. *Feminizing Venereal Disease: The Body of the Prostitute in*

Nineteenth-Century Medical Discourse. Washington Square, NY: New York University Press, 1997.

Stadler, Jürgen. *Die Missionspraxis Christian Keyßers in Neuguinea 1899–1920.* PhD diss., Erlangen-Nuremberg, 2004. Nuremberg: VTR, 2006.

Stanley, Brian. *The Bible and the Flag: Protestant Missions and British Imperialism in the Nineteenth and Twentieth Centuries.* Leicester: Apollos, 1990.

Stanley, Henry M. *Through the Dark Continent, or, The Sources of the Nile around the Great Lakes of Equatorial Africa and down the Livingstone River to the Atlantic Ocean.* 2 vols. New York: Dover Publications, 1988.

Steen, Andreas. *Deutsch-chinesische Beziehungen 1911–1927: Vom Kolonialismus zur "Gleichberechtigung."* Berlin: Akademie-Verlag, 2006.

Steinmetz, George. *The Devil's Handwriting: Precoloniality, and the German Colonial State in Qingdao, Samoa, and Southwest Africa.* Chicago: University of Chicago Press, 2007.

Stoecker, Helmuth. *Deutschland und China im 19. Jahrhundert: Das Eindringen des deutschen Kapitalismus.* Berlin: Rütten & Loening, 1958.

Stoecker, Helmuth, ed. *Drang nach Afrika: Die koloniale Expansionspolitik und Herrschaft des deutschen Imperialismus in Afrika von den Anfängen bis zum Ende des zweiten Weltkrieges.* Berlin: Akademie-Verlag, 1977.

Stoecker, Helmuth. *Kamerun unter deutscher Kolonialherrschaft: Studien,* 2 vols. Berlin: Rütten & Loening, 1960–68.

Stoler, Ann Laura. *Along the Archival Grain: Epistemic Anxieties and Colonial Common Sense.* Princeton: Princeton University Press, 2008.

Stollowsky, Otto. *Jambo Sana! Lustige Geschichten, Plaudereien und Schnurren aus dem Leben in Deutsch-Ost und Zanzibar.* Leipzig: Anger-Dachsel, 1921.

Stolz, Thomas, Christina Vossmann, and Barbara Dewein. "Kolonialzeitliche Sprachforschung und das Forschungsprogramm Koloniallinguistik: eine Einführung." In *Kolonialzeitliche Sprachforschung: Die Beschreibung afrikanischer und ozeanischer Sprachen zur Zeit der deutschen Kolonialherrschaft,* edited by Thomas Stolz et al., 7–29. Berlin: Akademie Verlag, 2011.

Straehler. "Strafrecht." In *Deutsches Kolonial-Lexikon.* 3 volumes, edited by Heinrich Schnee, vol. 3: 417–19. Leipzig: Quelle & Meyer, 1920.

Stuhlmann, Franz. *Mit Emin Pascha ins Herz von Afrika.* Berlin: D. Reimer, 1894.

Sun, Yat-sen. *Complete Works of Sun Yat-sen.* Vol. 2. Beijing: Zhonghua Book Company, 1982.

Sunseri, Thaddeus. "Slave Ransoming in German East Africa, 1885–1922." *International Journal of African Historical Studies* 26, no. 3 (1993): 481–511.

Sunseri, Thaddeus. *Vilimani: Labor Migration and Rural Change in Early Colonial Tanzania.* Portsmouth, NH: Heinemann, 2002.

Sylvester, Jeremy, and Jan-Bart Gewald, eds. *Words Cannot Be Found: German Colonial Rule in Namibia: An Annotated Reprint of the 1918 Blue Book.* Boston: Brill, 2003.

Tabi-Manga, Jean. *Les politiques linguistiques du Cameroun. Essai d'aménagement linguistique.* Paris: Karthala, 2000.

Tagore, Rabindranath. *The Home and the World.* London: Penguin Books, 2005.

Tan, Carol G. S. *British Rule in China: Law and Justice in Weihaiwei, 1898–1930*. London: Wildy, Simmons & Hill, 2008.

Tardits, Claude. "The Kingdom of Bamum." In *Kings of Africa: Art and Authority in Central Africa*, edited by Erna Beumers and Hans-Joachim Koloss, 43–55. Maastricht: Foundation Kings of Africa, 1992.

Tchaptchet, Jean-Martin. *La Marseillaise de mon enfance*. Paris : L'Harmattan, 2004.

Tessmann, Günter. *Die Pangwe. Völkerkundliche Monographie eines westafrikanischen Negerstammes. Ergebnisse der Lübecker Pangwe-Expedition 1907–1909 und früherer Forschungen 1904–1907*. Berlin: Wasmuth, 1913.

Theweleit, Klaus. *Male Fantasies: Women, Bodies, Floods, History*. Translated by Stephen Conway. Minneapolis: University of Minnesota Press, 1988.

Thiong'o, Ngugi wa. *Decolonising the Mind: The Politics of Language in African Literature*. London: James Currey, 1994.

Toit, Brian du. "Filiation and Affiliation among the Gadsup." *Oceania* 35, no. 2 (1964): 85–95.

Townsend, Mary E. *Origins of Modern German Colonialism, 1871–1885*. New York: Fertig, 1974 [1921].

"Transnationalism." h-german forum. Accessed January 2006. http://www.h-net.org/~german/discuss/Trans/forum_trans_index.htm.

Tuchscherer, Konrad. *The Lost Script of the Bagam. African Affairs* 98, no. 390 (1999): 55–77.

Uerlings, Herbert, and Iulia-Karin Patrut, eds. *Postkolonialismus und Kanon*. Bielefeld: Aisthesis, 2012.

Upadhyaya, Visvamitra. *Videson mein Bharatiya Krantikari Andolana*. New Delhi: Pragatishila Jana Prakashana, 1986.

Van der Veer, Peter. *Imperial Encounters: Religion and Modernity in India and Britain*. Princeton: Princeton University Press, 2001.

Van Trease, Howard. "German Colonialism in the South Seas: The Acquisition of New Guinea." MA thesis, San Diego State College, 1968.

Vedder, Heinrich. "The Herero." In *The Native Tribes of South West Africa*, edited by C. H. L. Hahn, Louis Fourie, and Heinrich Vedder, 153–210. London: Frank Cass, 1966.

Vertovec, Steven. *Transnationalism*. London: Routledge, 2009.

Vertovec, Steven, and Robin Cohen. *Conceiving Cosmopolitanism: Theory, Context and Practice*. New York: Oxford University Press, 2002.

Vietsch, Eberhard von. *Wilhelm Solf: Botschafter zwischen den Zeiten*. Tübingen: Wunderlich, 1961.

Vieweg, Burkhard. *Macho Porini—Die Augen im Busch: Kautschukpflanzer Karl Vieweg in Deutsch-Ostafrika; authentische Berichte 1910–1919*. Weikersheim: Margraf Verlag, 1996.

Vollbehr, Ernst. *Bunte Leuchtende Welt: Die Lebensfahrt des Malers Ernst Vollbehr*. Berlin: Ullstein, 1935.

von Prince, Tom. *Gegen Araber und Wahehe: Erinnerungen aus meiner afrikanischen Leutnantszeit 1890–1895*. Berlin: Mittler & Sohn, 1914.

von Wissmann, Hermann. *Afrika: Schilderungen und Rathschläge zur Vorbereitung für den Aufenthalt und den Dienst in den deutschen Schutzgebieten*. Berlin: E. S. Mittler, 1895.

von Wissmann, Hermann. *Unter deutscher Flagge quer durch Afrika von West nach Ost, 1880 bis 1883*. Edited by Paul Pogge und Hermann von Wissmann. Berlin: Walther & Apolant, 1889.

Voskamp, Johannes C. *Aus dem belagerten Tsingtau*. Berlin: Berliner Evangelische Missionsgesellschaft, 1915.

Wagner, Herwig. "Beginnings at Finschhafen: The Neuendettelsau Mission jointly with the Australian Lutheran Church." In *The Lutheran Church in Papua New Guinea: The First Hundred Years, 1886–1986*, 31–83, Adelaide: Lutheran Publishing House, 1986.

Waldenfels, Bernhard. *Studien zur Phänomenologie des Fremden*. 4 vols. Frankfurt am Main: Suhrkamp, 1997–99.

Waldschmidt, Julius. "Salima bint Said & Emily Ruete: Ein Frauenleben zwischen Orient und Okzident." In *Unbekannte Biographien: Afrikaner im deutschsprachigen Europa vom 18. Jahrhundert bis zum Ende des Zweiten Weltkrieges*, edited by Ulrich van der Heyden, 238–45. Werder: Kai Homilius, 2008.

Walkowitz, Rebecca L. *Cosmopolitan Style: Modernism beyond the Nation*. New York: Columbia University Press, 2006.

Wallenkampf, Arnold Valentin. *"The Herero Rebellion in South West Africa, 1904–1906: A Study in German Colonialization."* PhD diss. University of California, Los Angeles, 1969.

Walther, Daniel. "Sex, Race, and Empire: White Male Sexuality and the 'Other' in Germany's Colonies, 1894–1914." *German Studies Review* 33, no. 1 (2010): 45–72.

Wang, Ning. "The Mapping of Chinese Postmodernity." *boundary 2* 24, no. 3 (Autumn 1997): 19–40.

Warmbold, Joachim. *"Ein Stückchen neudeutsche Erd'"—Deutsche Kolonial-Literatur: Aspekte ihrer Geschichte, Eigenart und Wirkung, dargestellt am Beispiel Afrikas*. Frankfurt am Main: Haag + Herchen, 1982.

Weber, Brigitte. "Deutsch-Kamerun: Einblicke in die sprachliche Situation der Kolonie und den deutschen Einfluss auf das Kameruner Pidgin-Englisch." In *Kolonialzeitliche Sprachforschung. Die Beschreibung afrikanischer und ozeanischer Sprachen zur Zeit der deutschen Kolonialherrschaft*, edited by Thomas Stolz, Christina Vossmann, and Barbara Dewein, 111–38. Berlin: Akademie Verlag, 2011.

Weber, Samuel. "Bare Life and Life in General." *Grey Room* 46 (Winter 2012): 6–25.

Wei, Lan. "Tao Huanqing xiansheng xingshu [Brief Biography of Mr. Tao Huanqing]." *Xinhai Geming shi congkan [Collected Articles on the History of the 1911 Revolution]* 6 (1986): 78.

Weidert, Michael. "Zur Geneaologie missionarischer Macht. Das Beispiel der katholischen Kolonialmission in Deutsch-Ostafrika." In *Ethnizität und Geschlecht: Postkoloniale Verhandlungen in Geschichte, Kunst und Medien*, edited by Graduiertenkolleg Identität und Differenz, 35–56. Cologne: Böhlau, 2005.

Weiss, Brad. "A Religion of the Rupee: Materialist Encounters in North-West Tanzania." *Africa* 72, no. 3 (2002): 391–419.

Weiß, Max. *Die Völkerstämme im Norden Deutsch-Ostafrikas*. Berlin: Carl Marschner, 1910.

Wendt, Wolfgang, and Fritz Blanz. *Tok Pisin Bilong Papua Niugini: Das Pidgin von Papua-Neuguinea: Wörterbuch zum Sprachkurs*. Neuendettelsau: Evang.-Luth. Kirche in Bayern, 1998.

Werner, Wolfgang. *No One Will Become Rich: Economy and Society in the Herero Reserves in Namibia, 1915–1946*. Basel: P. Schlettwein, 1998.

Werner, Wolfgang. "Playing Soldiers: The Truppenspieler Movement among the Herero of Namibia, 1915 to ca. 1945." *Journal of Southern African Studies* 16, no. 3 (1990): 485–502.

Werther, C. Waldemar. *Die mittleren Hochländer des nördlichen Deutsch-Ost-Afrika. Wissenschaftliche Ergebnisse der Irangi-Expedition, 1896–1897, nebst kurzer Reisebeschreibung*. Berlin: H. Paetel, 1898.

Werther, C. Waldemar. *Zum Victoria Nyanza. Eine Anti-Sklaverei-Expedition und Forschungsreise*. Berlin: H. Paetel, 1894.

White, Luise. *The Comforts of Home: Prostitution in Colonial Nairobi*. Chicago: University of Chicago Press, 1990.

Widmer, Alexandra. "The Effects of Elusive Knowledge: Census, Health Laws and Inconsistently Modern Subjects in Early Colonial Vanuatu." *Journal of Legal Anthropology* 1, no. 1 (2008): 92–116.

Wierlacher, Alois. *Das Fremde und das Eigene: Prolegomena zu einer interkulturellen Germanistik*. Munich: Iudicium, 1985.

Wilde, Charles. "Acts of Faith: Muscular Christianity and Masculinity among the Gogodala of Papua New Guinea." *Oceania* 75, no. 1 (Sept. 2004): 32–48.

Wildenthal, Lora. *German Women for Empire, 1884–1945*. Durham: Duke University Press, 2001.

Wildenthal, Lora, Jürgen Zimmerer, Russell A. Berman, Jan Rüger, Bradley Naranch, Birthe Kundrus, and Maiken Umbach. "Forum: The German Colonial Imagination." *German History* 26, no. 2 (2008): 251–71.

Williams, C. Peter. "The Church Missionary Society and the Indigenous Church in the Second Half of the Nineteenth Century: The Defense and Destruction of the Venn Ideals." In *Converting Colonialism: Visions and Realities in Mission History, 1706–1904*, edited by Dana L. Robert, 86–111. Grand Rapids, MI: Eerdmans, 2008.

Williams, C. Peter. *The Ideal of the Self-Governing Church: A Study in Victorian Missionary Strategy*. Leiden: Brill, 1990.

Williams, C. Peter. "'Not Quite Gentlemen': An Examination of 'Middling Class' Protestant Missionaries from Britain, c. 1850–1900." *Journal of Ecclesiastical History* 31 (1980): 301–15.

Wirz, Albert. "Einleitung: Körper, Raum und Zeit der Herrschaft." In *Alles unter Kontrolle: Disziplinierungsprozesse im kolonialen Tanzania (1850–1960)*, edited by Albert Wirz, Andreas Eckert, and Kathrin Bromber, 5–34. Cologne: Rüdiger Köppe, 2003.

Wirz, Albert. "Missionare im Urwald—verängstigt und hilflos: Zur symbolischen Topographie des kolonialen Christentums, *Kolonien und Missionen: Referate des 3. internationalen kolonialgeschichtlichen Symposiums 1993 in Bremen*, Bremer Asien-Pazifik Studien, vol. 12, edited by Wilfried Wagner. Münster: Lit, 1994.

Wohltmann, F. *Pflanzung und Siedlung auf Samoa. Erkundungsbericht*. Berlin: Verlag des Kolonialwirtschaftlichen Komitees, 1904.

Wright, Marcia. *Strategies of Slaves and Women: Life Stories from East/Central Africa*. New York: Lilian Barber, 1993.

Wu, Fengbin. "Yapian zhanzheng hou cong Shantou chukou de qijue huagong [About the Indentured Overseas Chinese who left from Shantou after the Opium War]." *Nanyang wenti yanjiu* 2 (1988): 74–80.

Xu, Guoqi. *China and the Great War: China's Pursuit of a New National Identity and Internationalization.* Cambridge: Cambridge University Press, 2005.

Yan, Mo. *Sandalwood Death.* Translated by Howard Goldblatt. Norman: University of Oklahoma Press, 2012.

Yan, Mo. *Die Sandelholzstrafe.* Translated by Karin Betz. Frankfurt am Main: Insel Verlag, 2009.

Yan, Mo. *Tanxiang xing.* Beijing: Writers' Publishing House, 2nd ed., 2005.

Yen, Ching-Hwang. *Coolies and Mandarins: China's Protection of Overseas Chinese during the Late Ch'ing Period (1851–1911).* Singapore: Singapore University Press, 1985.

Yéo, Lacina. *Die Rehabilitation "Schwarzafrikas" in ausgewählten literarischen und publizistischen Schriften deutschsprachiger Autoren seit 1960: Paradigma eines deutschen Beitrags zum internationalen postkolonialen Diskurs.* Frankfurt am Main: Lang, 2011.

Yoder, Michael S. "The Latin American Plantation Economy and the World Economy: The Case of the Yucatecan Henequen Industry." *Review* 16, no. 3 (1993): 319–37.

Yuan, Rongsou. *Jiao'ao zhi [Jiao'ao Gazette].* Taipei: Wenhai Publishing House, 1969.

Zantop, Susanne. *Colonial Fantasies: Conquest, Family, and Nation in Precolonial Germany, 1770–1870.* Durham: Duke University Press, 1997.

Zeller, Joachim, and Jürgen Zimmerer, eds. *Völkermord in Deutsch-Südwestafrika: Der Kolonialkrieg (1904–1908) in Namibia und seine Folgen.* Berlin: Links, 2003.

Zenker, Georg. "Yaúnde." In *Yaoundé d'après Zenker (1895). Le plan de 1892. L'article de 1895. Reproduction du texte allemand et des 6 planches originales, avec un portrait de l'auteur,* edited by Philippe Laburthe-Tolra, 36–70. Dijon: Presses Universitaires, 1970.

Zhang, Xiaomin. "Wan Qing zhengfu dui haiwai huaqiaoren de baohu [The Late Qing Government's Protection of Overseas Chinese]." *Sheke Congheng [Social Sciences Review]* 23, no. 3 (2008): 215–17.

Zhe, Chengzhi. "Qingdao tebie gaodeng zhuanmen xuetang [Qingdao Special High School], *Shandong wenxian [Shandong Literature]* 4 of vol. 6 (1980): 37–65.

Zimmerer, Jürgen. *Deutsche Herrschaft über Afrikaner: Staatlicher Machtanspruch und Wirklichkeit im kolonialen Namibia.* Münster: Lit, 2001.

Zimmerer, Jürgen, and Joachim Zeller, eds. *Genocide in German Southwest Africa: The Colonial War (1907–1908) in Namibia and Its Aftermath.* Monmouth: Merlin Press, 2008.

Zimmerman, Andrew. *Alabama in Africa: Booker T. Washington, the German Empire, and the Globalization of the New South.* Princeton: Princeton University Press, 2010.

Zollmann, Jakob. *Koloniale Herrschaft und ihre Grenzen: Die Kolonialpolizei in Deutsch-Südwestafrika, 1894–1915.* Göttingen: Vandenhoeck & Ruprecht, 2010.

Contributors

Editors

Nina Berman is Professor of Comparative Studies at Ohio State University. She is the author of *German Literature on the Middle East: Discourses and Practices, 1000–1989* (University of Michigan Press, 2011), *Impossible Missions? German Economic, Military, and Humanitarian Efforts in Africa* (University of Nebraska Press, 2004), and *Orientalismus, Kolonialismus und Moderne: Zum Bild des Orients in der deutschsprachigen Kultur um 1900* (Metzler, 1997), and articles on various questions related to German minority literature, orientalism, colonialism, German activities in Kenya, and intercultural contact.

Klaus Mühlhahn is Professor of Chinese History and Culture at Freie Universität Berlin. His research focuses on Chinese legal history in the modern period and the history of imperialism and Sino-Western exchanges in the twentieth century. Publications include *Criminal Justice in China—A History* (Cambridge: Harvard University Press, 2009); *Herrschaft und Widerstand in der "Musterkolonie" Kiautschou: Interaktionen zwischen China und Deutschland, 1897-1914* (München: Oldenburg, 2000); *The Globalization of Confucius and Confucianism*, ed. with Nathalie van Looy (Münster: Lit, 2012); *The Limits of Empire: New Perspectives on Imperialism in Modern China*, ed. (Münster: Lit, 2008).

Patrice Nganang is Associate Professor of Literary and Cultural Theory at the State University of New York, Stony Brook. His publications include a study on Bertolt Brecht and Wole Soyinka, *Interkulturalität und Bearbeitung: Untersuchung zu Soyinka und Brecht* (1998), and a theory of contemporary African literature, *Manifeste d'une Nouvelle Litterature Africaine: Pour une Ecriture Preemptive* (2007). He has also published novels, novellas, and collections of poems. His novel *Temps de Chien* (2001) was awarded the Grand Prix de la Litterature d'Afrique Noire and the Prix Marguerite Yourcenar. His work has been translated into German, English, Spanish, Norwegian, and Italian, among others. His latest novels, *Mont Plaisant* (2011) and *La Saison des prunes* (2013) deal with German and French colonialism.

Contributors

Eva Bischoff received a Dr. phil. from the Ludwig-Maximilians University in Munich in 2009. In her dissertation, published by transcript in 2011 as *Kannibale-Werden. Eine postkoloniale Geschichte deutscher Männlichkeit um 1900*, she reconstructs the entanglement between German colonial and metropolitan discourses on masculinity, race, and class. Since 2011, she has taught International History at the University of Trier and is conducting a research project on the history of settler imperialism in the United States and Australia (ca. 1830–70). Her general interests include colonial and imperial history, postcolonial theory, and gender/queer studies.

Dirk Göttsche is Professor of German at the University of Nottingham (UK). He received a Dr. phil. at Münster in 1986 (*Die Produktivität der Sprachkrise in der modernen Prosa*, 1987) and completed his Habilitation at Münster in 1999 (*Zeit im Roman: Literarische Zeitreflexion und die Geschichte des Zeitromans im späten 18. und im 19. Jahrhundert*, 2001). He has published on the German novel, Wilhelm Raabe, Ingeborg Bachmann, Austrian Modernism, modern short prose, and postcolonial and cross-cultural literary studies, including *Zeitreflexion und Zeitkritik im Werk Wilhelm Raabes* (2000); *Kleine Prosa in Moderne und Gegenwart* (2006); *Remembering Africa: The Rediscovery of Colonialism in Contemporary German Literature* (2013); (co-ed.) *Interkulturelle Texturen: Afrika und Deutschland im Reflexionsmedium der Literatur* (2003); (co-ed.) *Ingeborg Bachmann: "Todesarten"-Projekt* (1995); *Kritische Schriften* (2005); *Bachmann Handbuch* (2003); (co-ed.) *Wilhelm Raabe: Global Themes—International Perspectives* (2009).

Andrew Hennlich is assistant professor of Art History at the Gwen Frostic School of Art, Western Michigan University. He is currently preparing a manuscript, *(un)Fixing the Eye: William Kentridge and the Optics of Witness*, based on his doctoral dissertation received at the University of Manchester (2011). Hennlich is also currently editing with Paul Clinton a special issue of the journal *parallax* on the theme of stupidity. He has written more widely on contemporary art for several journals including *esse, etc.*, and *Image & Text*.

Thoralf Klein is Senior Lecturer in Modern History at Loughborough University (UK) and a former visiting fellow of the College of Cultural Studies, Constance (Germany). He has published widely on the social and cultural history of modern China, the history of imperialism and colonialism, Christian missions, and transnational/global history. He published, among others, *Geschichte Chinas von 1800 bis zur Gegenwart* (Paderborn: Schöningh, 2007), *Kolonialkriege: Militärische Gewalt im Zeichen des Imperialismus* (Hamburg: Hamburger Edition, 2006), and *Die Basler Mission in Guangdong (Südchina) 1859–1931: Akkulturationsprozesse und kulturelle Grenzziehungen zwischen Missionaren, chinesischen Christen und lokaler Gesellschaft* (Munich: iudicium, 2002). His current projects examine the Boxer War of 1900/01 as a transnational media event and trace the development of political religion in twentieth-century China.

Yixu Lü is Associate Professor in Germanic Studies at the University of Sydney. She studied Germanistik and History at Peking University and the Universität Regensburg. Apart from her research exploring the German colonial presence in China, her other main fields of interest are the works of Heinrich von Kleist (1777–1811) and Greek myth in German literature. Her publications include *Wissensfiguren im Werk von Heinrich von Kleist*, edited with Anthony Stephens, Alison Lewis, and Wilhelm Voßkamp (Freiburg: Rombach, 2012); *Medea unter den Deutschen: Wandlungen einer literarischen Figur* (Freiburg: Rombach, 2009); *Frauenherrschaft im Drama des frühen 19. Jahrhunderts* (Munich: iudicium, 1993); and articles on German colonial fiction on China and the coverage of the Boxer Uprising in German newspapers.

B. Venkat Mani is Associate Professor of German and affiliated with the Centers of Global Studies, German and European Studies, and South Asia Studies at the University of Wisconsin-Madison. He is the author of *Cosmopolitical Claims: Turkish-German Literatures from Nadolny to Pamuk* (University of Iowa Press, 2007). He has co-edited two special issues, "Translational and Cosmopolitical Approaches to German Studies," with Elke Segelcke, *TRANSIT* 7. 1 (2011); and "What Counts as World Literature?," with Caroline Levine, *Modern Language Quarterly* 74.2 (2013). He has published articles on world literature, cosmopolitanism, postcolonial theory, globalization, migration, language, and the politics of pedagogy. Mani is currently working on a book-length project, "Borrowing Privileges: Bibliomigrancy and the (Un)-Making of World Literature in Germany (1800-2010)," a study on comparative literature and world literature with a special focus on public and private libraries and print cultural history.

Molly McCullers is an Assistant Professor of History at the University of West Georgia and received her Ph.D. from Emory University in 2012. McCullers has published articles on Herero history and masculinity in the *Journal of African History* and the *Journal of Southern African Studies*. She is currently working on a book manuscript, *Division in the Desert: Men, Water, and Decolonization in Apartheid-Era Namibia*, which explores the tensions between apartheid and independence in Southwest Africa and the ways in which these transnational conflicts became enmeshed with local masculinity and water politics in Hereroland.

Michelle Moyd is an Assistant Professor of History at Indiana University, Bloomington. She received her PhD in History from Cornell University in 2008. Her first book, *Violent Intermediaries: African Soldiers, Conquest, and Everyday Colonialism in German East Africa*, will be published in the New African History series at Ohio University Press in 2014. The book explores African soldiers' roles in the German conquest and administration of Tanzania, offering a socio-cultural explanation of their roles in German colonialism in East Africa.

Germain Nyada holds a PhD in comparative literature (French and German) from the University of Bayreuth. His PhD dissertation was published in 2010 as *Kindheit, Autobiografik und Interkulturalität*. Nyada has been teaching assistant at the University of Yaounde I and at the University of Bayreuth, and is currently part-time faculty at Concordia University. Nyada has published several articles on literature, film, and history. His main research interests are autobiography, interculturality, childhood, literary theory, war cinema, and literature, as well as "German Cameroon."

Itohan I. Osayimwese is Assistant Professor of Art History at Brown University. She is a graduate of Bryn Mawr College and Rice University, and received her PhD in Architectural History from the University of Michigan. Her primary research interest is the co-production of modernity and modernism in light of colonial encounters. She has published on architectural-ethnographic travel writing, the ideologically inflected dissemination of professional architectural knowledge to colonial settlers, and the relationship between imperialism and religion in the work of missionary-architects. She has received grants from the Deutscher Akademischer Austausch Dienst, the Social Science Research Council, the Graham Foundation, the Canadian Institute for Architecture, and the Gerda Henkel Foundation. Her work has been published in Volker Langbehn, ed., *German Colonialism, Visual Culture, and Modern Memory* (Routledge, 2010), and several journals.

Michael Pesek is Visiting Professor for African History at Humboldt-University in Berlin, where he studied Performances Studies, Sociology, and African Studies. He received his PhD in 2004, with a thesis about the establishment of German colonial rule in eastern Africa, which was published in 2005 as *Koloniale Herrschaft in Deutsch-Ostafrika: Expeditionen, Militär und Verwaltung seit 1880* (Campus). In 2010, he published a book on World War I in Eastern Africa, entitled *Das Ende eines Kolonialreichs: Ostafrika im Ersten Weltkrieg* (Campus).

Gabriele Richter is a lecturer at Bremen University. She studied theology, religious studies, ethics, and conflict resolution at Hamburg University, Humboldt-University Berlin, Yale University Divinity School, Columbia University, and the Union Theological Seminary (Columbia affiliated). In 2010, she received her PhD from Rostock University in the field of Religious History. Her dissertation analyzes the autobiography of a German missionary in Australian-ruled New Guinea during the 1930s: "The 'Occupation' of a Mission Field: Wilhelm Bergmann's Mission Work in the 1930s in Chimbu (Highland New Guinea) in the Autobiography *Vierzig Jahre in Neuguinea* and Other Sources." She has taught Religious History at Rostock University and Pacific History at University of Papua New Guinea in the Pacific before she came to the Religious Studies department at Bremen University.

Hanan Sabea is an Associate Professor of Anthropology at the American University in Cairo. She received her PhD in Anthropology from Johns Hopkins University in 2001. Her research examines the dynamics of land and labor on plantations in colonial and postcolonial Africa, their implications for remolding state-subject relations, and the production of the histories thereof. She has published articles in *Journal of Historical Sociology, African Studies, Feminist Africa*, and *International Journal of African Historical Studies*.

Andreas Steen is Associate Professor of Modern Chinese History and Culture at Aarhus University, Denmark. He studied Sinology, English Philology, and Modern Chinese Literature at the Free University of Berlin and Fudan University, Shanghai. His main fields of research concentrate on various aspects of China's popular culture, modern Chinese history, and Sino-German relations from the nineteenth century until 1945. Among his publications are *Zwischen Unterhaltung und Revolution: Grammophone, Schallplatten und die Anfänge der Musikindustrie in Shanghai, 1878–1937* (Wiesbaden: Harrassowitz-Verlag, 2006) and the edited volume *Deutsch-chinesische Beziehungen 1911–1927:*

Vom Kolonialismus zur "Gleichberechtigung"—Eine Quellensammlung (Berlin: Akademie-Verlag, 2006).

Daniel J. Walther is the Gerald R. Kleinfeld Distinguished Professor in German History at Wartburg College, where he teaches modern European and world history. He is the author of *Creating Germans Abroad: Cultural Policies and National Identity in Namibia* (Athens: Ohio University Press, 2002) and several articles on the German experience in Namibia and on German colonialism. He is currently working on a study about the interplay between the medical profession and indigenous agency within the context of venereal diseases and prostitution.

Jianjun Zhu is a Lecturer of History at Ocean University of China. She studied history at Nankai University and Shandong University, and received her PhD in international studies from the University of Technology, Sydney in 2009. Her research concentrates on Sino-foreign relations and social change in modern times. Her most recent publications include an article entitled "The Names and Status of German-occupied Kiao-chau" (2009) and a monograph, *Colonial Experience and Modern Chinese Nationalism: Qingdao, 1897–1914* (Renmin Publishing House, 2010).

Index

Abaca, 117
African migrants' writing, 19, 245–56
Afrikanische Germanistik, 12
Agamben, Giorgio, 286
Akin, Fatih, 289, 293
Akwa (Dika Mpondo), 50
alliance, 15–16, 86, 88–90, 92, 131–32, 139–41; revolutionary, 181
Amboni, 116, 124
Amin, Samir, 6
Angola, 291
anthropophagy, 220–21
anti-colonial resistance, 9, 227
anti-colonialism, 16, 189, 196, 245
anti-imperialism, 3, 252–53
Apartheid, 20, 236, 259, 261, 264–65, 267–68
Apia, 147, 151, 153–56
Appiah, Kwame Anthony, 198
Arab plantations, 115, 118, 121–23, 125
Arendt, Hannah, 2, 286–87
army, 2, 60, 67, 96, 231, 233, 261, 263; Bamun 42; German colonial 15, 101; Herero 235
Asia, 2, 3, 6, 9, 16–17, 21, 147, 174, 205–07, 268, 290–92, 295
Askari, 1, 15, 85, 89–91, 93–97, 101–111, 124–125, 213; deserting, 96–97
Atakpame, 74
Ataman, Kutlug, 285, 290
Atangana, Karl (Attang), 60, 64
Aukongo, Stefanie-Lahya, 246, 255
Auschwitz, 268
Australia, 5, 131–32, 138, 141
authenticity, 34, 36, 140, 291
authority, 18, 36, 77, 88, 90, 103, 105–06, 108, 110–11, 115–16, 119–20, 125, 138, 140, 167, 220, 233–37, 254; bomas, 102–03, 110; colonial, 53, 101, 103, 108, 179–80, 183–84, 186–88; elders' authority, 234–37; German, 78, 103, 106, 229; Herero, 229–

30, 236; missions society, 162–63, 166–67, 169, 172–74; state, 15, 101, 103, 106, 108, 110; tribal, 126
autoethnographic texts, 40–41
autoethnography, 31–32, 45
Axenfeld, Karl, 212, 220

Baba, 105
Babelsberg, 288, 290, 293, 297
Bade, Klaus J., 3
Bader, Wolfgang, 3
Baganda, 94
Baker, Josephine, 294
Bale. See Bâre
Balibar, Etienne, 201
Baluna, 133–34
Bamum, culture, 14, 35; military culture, 42; myth, 33; palace, 34, 36, 45; Palace Museum, 45
Bamun Kingdom, 13–14, 31, 45
Bâre, 133, 137
Bare. See Bâre
Barec. See Bâre
Barooah, Nirode K., 203
Basel, 163, 168, 171
Basel Mission. See Evangelical Mission Society of Basel
Baser, Tevfik, 289
Baumann, 291
Bechuanaland, 230, 235
Beck, Ulrich, 198, 200
Beijing, 152–54, 156
Bell, Ndumb'a Lobe, 50
Bena, 212, 219–20
Bendera, 109
Bene, 51
Benhabib, Seyla, 199, 287
Beni, 105
Benninghoff-Lühl, Sibylle, 3
Bergdama, 78
Bergman, Ingmar, 295
Berlin, 8, 16, 43, 45, 88, 148, 151–56,

Berlin (*continued*)
    203, 205, 215, 295; Conference, 33,
    261; Ethnographic Museum, 41; State
    Opera, 261, 263; University of, 216,
    218
Berliner Missionsgesellschaft, 18, 212–
    13, 216, 221
Berner, Max, 212
Beti, 14, 50–55, 57–67; languages, 51–
    64, 67
Beuys, Joseph, 247
Bhabha, Homi K., 162, 166, 221, 251,
    285, 287
Bhatawadekar, Sai Prakash, 12
Bhatti, Anil, 5
Bible, 41, 54, 116, 120, 166
Bible of sisal, 120
Big Man, 131, 133, 137
bigamy, 166
biopower, 214
Bismarck, 147, 228
Black German Heritage and Research
    Association, 12
Black German writing, 245, 256
Bley, Helmut, 3
Bohm, Hark, 290
Boma, 91–92, 101–11
Bomani, 101–2, 106
Borch, Herbert von, 152
Borgstedt, J. A., 291
Borsody, Eduard von, 291
Boxer Uprising, 20, 271, 279, 281
Brennan, Timothy, 198
British East Africa, 77
Brody, Louis. See M'bebe Mpessa, Lud-
    wig
Brody-Alcolson. See Ludwig M'bebe
    Mpessa
Buea, 39
BUGRA, 44–45
Bulus, 77
Buñuel, Luis, 295
bushmen, 50
Büttner, Kurt, 3

Calhoun, Craig, 198
Cameroon, 7, 13–14, 19, 31, 33, 44–45,
    50–51, 53–54, 56, 58–65, 67, 74–75,
    77–79, 126, 163, 246, 153–255, 284,
    289, 294

Cameroon, Donald (Sir), 126
Campt, Tina, 4
cannibalism, 18, 212–14, 217–21, 272
Canton, 153–54
capitalism, 2–3, 6, 11
Captain Glauning, 43
caravan trade, 85–87, 92, 122
Cat opera, 271, 273, 278–82
catechism, 139
Césaire, Aimé, 4, 247
Chagga, 109
chain-gang prisoner, 104
Changle district, 165–167
Chattopadhyaya, Virendranath, 203
Cheah, Pheng, 196
Chen, Gan, 181, 184–86, 188
Chen, Hanyuan, 183
Cheti cha rukhsa. See Erlaubnisschein
China, 7, 9, 16–17, 20, 148, 151–56,
    161, 163–66, 168–69, 171–73, 179–
    82, 184–91, 272–73, 276, 281–82
Chinese authorities, 17, 148, 150, 154–
    55; legation, 154; nationalism, 180;
    workers. See coolies, labor
Christian mission, 3, 17, 161–61, 171–
    73, 215, 260, 291
Christianity, 136, 139–40, 163–65, 169,
    174, 231
Christianization, 215
coastal traders, 86–89, 97
Cohen, Paul, 6
Cohen, Robin, 199
Cold War, 20
collaboration, 7, 12, 18, 41, 64, 121,
    139, 213, 222, 275
collaborators, 7, 18, 102, 213, 263
colonial administration, 16, 18, 43, 62,
    66–67, 110, 149, 151, 153, 173, 179,
    212, 215–17, 220–21, 260; desires,
    rationalities, 15, 115; discourse, 4, 14,
    118, 221, 251, 265; documentary,
    292; encounters, 2, 6, 14, 227; film,
    21, 287–92, 297; governance, 108,
    115, 254; government, 2, 18, 33, 78,
    105, 107, 115, 119, 126, 150, 213,
    214, 222, 237; governmentality, 2,
    115, 126, 214, 222; imagination (Ger-
    man), 31; military outpost (*see*
    boma); mimicry, 42; order, 14, 31, 71,
    107, 115, 117–19; power, 4, 9, 33, 53,

72, 105, 114, 132, 163, 173, 181, 205, 217, 232–33, 248, 282; project, 15, 114, 118, 125–26, 149, 215, 221; territory, 117; travelogues, 292–93
colonialism, 1–7, 9–10, 14, 16–20, 31, 42, 44, 72, 76, 102–3, 110, 130, 134, 161–62, 172, 179–81, 191, 196, 201–4, 206–8, 216, 220–12, 226–28, 232, 237, 245–56, 259–63, 269, 271, 276, 280, 284–86, 289–91; itinerant, 102–10; secular, 172
concentration camp, 231, 261
Confucian values, 275, 277
Conrad, Sebastian, 11
convict labor, 121
coolie, 147–156; Chinese, 147, 149, 151, 156; contracts, 153; employment, 148, 151; ill-treatment of, 153; import, 152; safety, 150, 154; trade, 147; transportation, 147
Cosmopolitanism, 18, 195–209
Cromwell Ranges, 135
cultural production, 31, 44

Dagong bao, 188
Dar es Salaam, 74
death sentence, 212, 216, 218–20
Decker, Johann, 136
Degla, Luc, 246
Deleuze, Gilles, 284
Dernburg, Bernhard, 9, 214, 216, 218
Derrida, Jacques, 198
deterritorialization, 284
Deutsch, Jan-Georg, 8
Deutsch-Asiatische Bank, 155
Deutsch-Ostafrika. *See* German East Africa
Deutsch-Ostafrikanische Gesellschaft (DOAG), 88, 116, 119, 121
Deutsche Handels-und Plantagen-Gesellschaft (DHPG), 151
Deutsche Samoa Gesellschaft, 155
Deutsches Kolonialblatt, 212
Diallo, Aly, 245, 252
Diek, Erika, 294
diplomacy, 43, 196
Dobeo. See Bâre
documentary film, 259, 263
dominant culture, 32, 227. *See also* popular culture

domination, 6, 71, 130, 285
Dominik, Hans, 54
Douala, 33, 38, 53, 294
drum language, 60, 62
Duala, 50, 54,72,74,75
Duala-M'bedy, Munasu, 12

East Africa, 1–2, 7–8, 12, 15, 33, 74–77, 79, 85–86, 88, 93, 95–96, 101–3, 105–11, 114, 116–17, 216, 255, 265, 296
East Germany, 255
Ebon, 75
Eckert, Andreas, 72, 221
economic, 1–3, 7, 9, 11, 15–17, 33, 43, 50, 71, 75–77, 80, 103, 105, 116–18, 122, 126, 150, 154–55, 162, 164, 195, 216; enterprises, 116, 118; existence, 147; exploitation, 33, 116–17, 148; misery, 147; socio, 103, 115, 228; survival, 148, 150–51
Eingeborenendelikt, 217
Eingeborenenrecht, 217
Ekwalla, Jim (King Dido), 50
El Loko, 19, 245–53, 255–56
ELCONG. *See* Evangelical Lutheran Church of New Guinea
El-Tayeb, Fatima, 4
emasculation, 230, 234, 237
emigration, 3, 147, 150, 152
England, 153, 202, 204, 294, 296
Engombe, Lucia, 246, 255
Enlightenment, 20, 199, 259–64, 269
epidemic disease, 214
Eppelsheimer, Natalie, 12
equality, 16–17, 152–53, 155–56, 169, 254
Erlaubnisschein, 109
Etah, Ayissi, 66
Ethiopia, 291
ethnic group, 39, 50–51, 86, 133, 139, 214, 216
ethnic population, 132
ethnicity, 86, 199
ethnographic films, 291, 293
Eton (Ethnic Group), 51, 66
eugenic science, 261
European colonial history, 245
European plantations, 114, 118–19, 121–22, 125–26

Europeanness, 296
Evangelical Lutheran Church of New
   Guinea, 135
Evangelical Mission Society of Basel,
   37–39, 41, 163–73
Evans, Jones Kwesi, 246
Ewondo/Jewondo, 51–67
exhibitions, 44–45
exoticas, 20, 288, 292–94
extraterritoriality, 164

Fabian, Johannes, 117–18, 130
Fairbanks, Douglas, 295
Falkenhausen, Konrad von, 94
Fanon, Frantz, 6, 247, 250, 285
fascism, 2–4
Fassbinder, Rainer Werner, 285, 289–90,
   292
feng shui, 282
Fiji, 147
Fine, Robert, 199
Finsch, Otto, 133
Finschhafen, 132–33, 135, 140
Flierl, Johann, 132–33, 135–36, 139–40
flogging, 149–50, 152, 154–55. See also
   coolie; labor; punishment
Foreign Bureau, 153, 155
Foucault, Michel, 162, 214–15, 221
France, 5, 153, 290, 294–96
Franconia, 132
Freud, Sigmund, 20, 259, 262
Fulbe, 42, 252
Fumban (Bamum capital), 34, 37, 41,
   44

Gaomi 20, 271, 273–76, 278–79, 281
Gaoqi village, 165
gender identities and ideologies, 237
General von Trotha, 230, 238, 261
generational tensions, 235–36
genocide, genocidal, 4, 18, 20, 226–27,
   230–32, 236–37, 263
Gerhardt, Karl, 292
German colonial army. See Schutztruppe
German colonial cinema, 284, 290–93,
   297
German Colonial Office. See Reichs-
   kolonialamt
German criminal code. See Reichsstrafgesetzbuch

German Democratic Republic (GDR),
   253, 255
German East Africa, 8, 15, 18, 80, 88,
   101–3, 109, 114–15, 117, 212–14,
   216–17, 264
German East Africa Company (DOAG).
   See Deutsch-Ostafrikanische Gesell-
   schaft
German ethnographic films, 291, 293
German Foreign Ministry, 152
German Foreign Office, 154
German legal system, 119, 217, 220
German military, 18, 43, 85, 101, 154,
   187, 207, 226, 228, 231–32, 234–38,
   271, 274–75
German minority cinema, 20–21, 288–
   90, 292–93, 297
German New Guinea, 15, 75, 77, 131–
   33, 147–51, 154–55
German protectorates, 153
German Qingdao 179, 180–91
German Reich, 166, 171
German Samoa, 148, 150
Germanistik in Afrika Subsahara, 12
Germany, 5–6, 12, 19–20, 33, 44–45,
   60, 71, 73, 79, 81, 131–32, 139, 141,
   148, 153–54, 156, 163, 182–83, 185–
   86, 190, 195–96, 202, 205–6, 228–29,
   236, 245, 247, 250–56, 259–61, 269,
   284–85, 288–90, 292, 294, 296–97;
   imperial, 18, 203
Gewald, Jan-Bart, 4, 227
Ghana, 163, 201
globalization, 2, 11, 20, 272, 282
Goethe, Johann Wolfgang von, 205,
   250
Göhring, Martin, 37–38, 43
Göktürk, Deniz, 287
Goldblatt, Howard, 272
Gold Coast, 163
gonorrhea, 75, 78–79
governance, 17, 97, 108, 110, 115, 202,
   254
Gramling, David, 287
Grande, Edgar, 198, 200
Grassfields kingdoms, 35, 43
Great Britain, 151, 156, 203
Grossbatanga, 77
Grosse, Pascal, 4
Gründer, Horst, 3

Guangdong Province, 17, 164, 168,
    188–89
Guattari, Felix, 284
Gurnah, Abdulrazak, 1

Hagström-Ståhl, Kristina, 260
Hahl, Albert, 149–50, 155
Hakka, 164, 166, 168
Hamsa ishirini, 108
Han, Weizhai, 183
Han Chinese, 179–80
Har Dayal, Lala, 18, 196, 202–8
Hau'Ofa, Epeli, 130–31
Hausa, 42, 53
Hausen, Karin, 3
Haxthausen, Elmershaus von, 154
Haya-Chief Kahigi of Kianja, 92, 97
Haya kingdoms, 92
Heepe, Martin, 58
Hegel, Georg Wilhelm Friedrich, 5
Hehe, 90–91, 214–16; Chief Mkwawa,
    90–91; Uprising, 216;
Heimat, 106, 251, 254
Heine, Bernd, 53
Heinrich Umlauff Museum, 291
Hemp, 87, 106
Hempenstall, Peter, 132
Herder, Johann Gottfried, 5, 6
Herero, 4, 18–20, 72, 76, 78, 226–38,
    259–61, 263–64, 268; massacre, 250–
    60, 268; national identity, 227; na-
    tionalism, 226–27
Herzog, Werner, 289–90, 293
Hevia, Jim, 6
Hindorf, Richard (German botanist),
    116, 120, 124, 126
Hitchcock, Alfred, 295
Hollinger, David, 198
Hollrung, Max, 135
Holocaust, 2–3, 24, 246, 261, 263,
    284
Hong Kong, 152, 155, 162, 165
Honolulu, 151–52
Horn, Peter, 4
Houghton, 263
Hoveka, Stephanus, 233
Hsia, Adrian, 5
Hull, Isabel V., 4
Huon Peninsula, 131–32
hybridity, 11, 36, 39, 41

identity, 32, 34, 43, 45, 135, 208, 227,
    237, 245, 253, 255–56, 274; African,
    246, 249, 256; construction, 32, 43;
    cultural, 208, 247; national, 45, 227
    immigration, 147, 247, 267; Chinese,
    151, 156
Imperial Colonial Office. *See* Reichs-
    kolonialamt
Imperial German Pacific Protectorates,
    148
Imperial Germany, 18, 203
Imperial Land Decree, 119
imperialism, 2, 130, 161, 164, 169, 171–
    73, 196, 203–4, 206, 208, 287
India, 162–63, 195, 202–3, 205,
    207–8
Indian Muslims, 203
Indian Ocean, 147
indigenization, 63, 169, 174
indigenous; commoners, 73; response,
    72
infrastructure, 17, 85, 116, 249
Institute for Shandong Railway and
    Mining Studies, 186
interkulturelle Germanistik, 12
interkulturelle Hermeneutik, 12
intermediaries, 7–8, 15–16, 85, 97, 101–
    3, 107, 11, 221
interpreters, 59–65
Iringa, 18, 212–21
Iseke, 89–90
Islam, 40, 42, 44, 89, 207–8, 215

Jallianwala Bagh Massacre, 207
James, C. L. R., 6
Japan, 5, 77, 153, 156, 181, 182–84,
    190
Jarry, Alfred, 259
Jesuit, 164
Jia, Pingwa, 271
Jiang, Zemin, 282
Jiaozhou 膠州, 162. *See also* Ki-
    autschou
Jinan, 181, 183–84, 189, 271
Jinan Normal College, 184
Jing, Dingjiu, 183
Johannesburg, 263–64, 267
Johnson, Al, 294
joint enterprise, 139
Journey to the West, 281

jumbe, pl. majumbe, Jumben, 104, 107, 217

Junker, 217

Kaes, Anton, 287
Kahigi. *See* Haya-Chief Kahigi of Kianja
Kaiser, 42–43, 105, 248, 250
Kaiser-Wilhelmsland, 15, 130–31
Kalahari Desert, 230
Kam, Louie, 272
Kamerun. *See* Cameroon
Kameruner Deutsche, 284
Kanak culture, 287
Kant, Immanuel, 5, 6, 196, 199–200, 205
Kassovitz, Matthieu, 289
Kâte, 16, 132–37, 139–41
Kejia 客家. *See* Hakka
Kekilli, Sibel, 285
Kemung, Numuc, 138–39
Kentridge, William, 20, 259–69
Keppler, Gottlieb, 138
Keyßer, Christian, 16, 131–41
Khanna, Ranjana, 262, 268
Kiaochow Lease Treaty (1897), 183
Kiautschou, 17, 179, 183, 185–88, 190–91
Kieran, J. A., 3
Kihehe, 216
Kilimanjaro, 97, 106
Kim, David, 213
King Malietoa Laupepa, 151
King Mbuembue, 33
King Mlapa 249
King Ndumbe Lobe Bell, 33
King Nsare, 33
Kistner, Ulrike, 4
Kiswahili, 102, 108–10, 216
Kitunde (missionary station), 95
Kouega, Jean-Paul, 51
Kreutzer, Leo, 12
Krishnavarma, Shyamaji, 202
Kristeva, Julia, 285
Kum'a Ndumbe III, Alexandre, 3, 50, 246, 255
Kund, Richard, 50
Kutako, Hosea, 233–36

Labor, 8, 15–16, 71, 73–74, 76, 101,

104–5, 115, 117–25; forced, 155, 254, 261; imported, 121; indentured, 1, 147; indigenous, 71, 147; migrant, 76, 120, 122; recruitment, 149–50, 154; reserve, 147; scarcity of, 151; shortage, 8
Laburthe-Tolra, 62
land rights, 119
Lang, Fritz, 288, 291–95
language deficiencies, 67
Larson, Lorne, 107
law, 123, 126, 147, 149, 152, 185, 188, 198, 205–7, 212, 216–18, 220, 247, 254, 261, 274. *See also* Colonial Law; German Civil Law Code
Leipzig Museum of Ethnography, 41
Lettow-Vorbeck, 94, 97
Li, Yueqiu, 181
Liang, Qichao, 181
Liberia, 291
Lieberenz, Paul, 284, 290, 292
Lieutenant Hirtler, 33
Lin Runzhao, 153–55
Lin Shufen, 153
Lingua Franca, 53–55, 65, 287
Linke, Edmund, 291
Lissock, Jean Paul, 245, 255
Liu, Guansan, 181, 184, 188–89
Liu, Lydia, 6
Lome (Togo), 75, 250–51
Lowenbein, Richard, 291
Lu, Ziren, 182, 183
Luan, Xinghe, 181
Luan, Zhijie, 181
Lubitsch, Ernst, 288
Lutheran Church, 135
Lutheran missionary, 16, 106, 132–33

M'bebe Mpessa, Ludwig, 21, 288, 294–97
Magic Flute, 20, 259–64
Maherero, Samuel, 229–30, 233–35, 237
Maji Maji Rebellion, 9, 118, 122, 214, 216, 220
Maji Maji War. *See* Maji Maji Rebellion
majumbe. *See* jumbe, sing
malaria, 132–33, 149
Malukansi, 218
Mamba, 109

Mamozai, Martha, 4
Manchu, 179, 180–81, 188
Manga Bell, Rudolf, 38
Manjapra, Kris, 11
Männerbünde (fraternities), 228
Mao Zedong, 6
Maoshan, 184
Marangu, 109
Marshall Islands, 75, 79
Martin, Karlheinz, 288–89
Martin Luther Seminary, 134
Marx, Karl, 5, 6
Marxism, 5, 6
Masai, 94
masculinity, 18–19, 131, 140–41, 226–38; hegemonic, 227; misogynistic, 229
mashauri. *See* shauri
May, Joe. *See* May, John
May, John, 288, 292, 294
Mazumdar, Shaswati, 5
Mbaa Masi, 107
McColl Millar, Robert, 52
mediator, 130
Mefire, Sam, 288
Mehari, Senait, 246
Meinhof, Carl, 55
Meiniang, 274, 276–79, 282
melancholia, 20, 259, 262–63, 268
Melanesian Islands, 147
Melkisede, Advent P., 134–38, 140
Melzian, 291
Memmi, Albert 247
mentefacts, 130
Mepin, Daniel, 19, 245–46, 253–56
Messi, Paul, 64
meta-fictionality, 279
Methodist Mission, 132
Metropolitan, 9, 14, 16, 19, 32–33, 41–43, 229; culture, 43
Metzner, Erno, 292
microhistory, 221
migration, 79, 118, 122–23, 152, 195, 245–46, 249, 251, 254, 256, 284, 289; Chinese, 147; Gastarbeiter, 289
military, 15, 33, 41, 73, 85–89, 92, 95, 97, 101–3, 105, 107, 111, 162, 166, 183, 196, 203, 205, 208, 212, 215–17, 221, 226–28, 230–32, 235, 238, 263, 281; culture, 31, 232; education, 66–

67, 183; nationalism, 208; service, 14–15, 229, 232; strength, 104; training, 90, 154, 183
millenarism, 89
Miller, Jon, 162
Miller, Phillip, 263
mimicry, 11, 42, 162
Mining Protection Society, 181,184–91
minorities, 20–21, 284, 285–90, 292–93, 297; critical discourse on, 285; definition of, 286, 297; in German cinema, 284; in Germany, 287–88, 292, 297; literature, 284; and nation, 288; and the "state," 286; treaties in 1919, 284
Mirambo, 86–88, 90, 97
Mo Yan, 20, 271–82
mobility, 15, 32, 102, 114–15, 123
Moisel, Max, 42
Mongo Ewondo. *See* Ewondo
Monopoly, 50, 133
monotheistic religion, 215
moral hygiene, 219
Morning Bell, 181
Moses, John A., 152
mourning, 259, 262, 264
Mozart, Wolfgang Amadeus, 20, 259, 264
Msaba, 109
Mudimbe, Valentin, 5
Mugunda, Aaron, 234
Murnau, F. W., 290, 295
Musinga, King of Rwanda, 94–95
Muslims, 89, 203
Mwelle (ethnic group), 51

Nachtigal, Gustav, 249
Nama, 4, 72, 78
Namibia, 20, 226, 237
Nareng-gareng, 139
nation-state, 16, 18, 42, 44, 180, 195–96, 198, 200–203, 208, 250, 262, 287
National Socialism, 2
nationalism, 16–17, 180–81, 191, 195–96, 198, 200–201, 203, 205–9, 226–27, 268, 292; anti-colonial, 195–96, 198, 205, 207–09; Chinese 180–81
nationalist, 7, 16–18, 31, 180–81, 196, 200, 202–3, 205, 208, 227; resistance, 227

nativist school, 20, 271
Nauhaus, Carl, 219–21
Nauru, 150
Nazi Germany, 20; politics, 296–97; Nazis, 236, 252; Nazism, 261, 265; regime, 261, 286, 295
Ndjobi-Ewondo. *See* Ewondo
Negri, Pola, 285
négritude, 5
Neke, Hermann, 58
neoimperialism, 3
Neuendettelsau, 132, 139, 141
Neuguinea-Kompanie, 132
New Britain, 132
New Caledonia, 147
New German cinema, 289, 292–93
New Guinea, 15–17, 75, 77, 131–35, 138–41, 147–51, 154–56
New Guinea Company (Deutsche Neuguinea-Kompagnie), 148–49
New Hebrides, 147
New Zealand, 5, 156
Nganang, Patrice, 5, 20, 284
Ngoma, 105–6
Ngoni invasion, 85
Ngumbas, 77
Nguni (societies), 88, 97
Nguru chiefs, 88
Nielsen, Asta, 285
Nigeria, 252, 288, 291
Nigmann, Ernst, 212–13, 216, 218–21
Nkrumah, 6
Northern Times, 186, 187
Northey, Edward, 96
Noshir, Shahbaz, 289
NS "culture films," 292
Ntsama, Mevengué, 66
Nussbaum, Martha, 198
Nyada, Germain, 14
Nyamwezi, 8, 122
Nyungu-ya-Mawe, 88

Oceania, 2, 21, 130, 139
Ogot, B. A., 3
Oji, Chima, 245, 252
Okpako, Branwen, 288, 290
Oloukpona-Yinnon, Adjai Paulin, 5
opera, 259, 261–64, 271, 273, 278–82
Opium War, 164, 165–66
oriental racism, 217

Orientalization of Germany, 288
Ortner, Sherry, 10
Osterhammel, Jürgen, 3, 11, 162
Otruppa, 18–19, 226–27, 230–38
Ovambo, 237
ownership rights, 119

Pacific Islands, 147–48
Pakendorf, Gunther, 4
Pamina, 261, 264
Papua New Guinea, 131–32, 134, 221
Pascha, Emin, 89
patriarchal masculinity, 231, 234; patriarchal society, 229
patriotic education, 281
patronage, 106, 227, 229–230, 232, 237
Paullmann, Friedrich, 296
penal policy, 121. *See also* punishment
People of God, 132
permission slip. *See* Erlaubnisschein
Pesek, Michael, 8, 13–15, 67, 85, 108
Peters, Carl, 88, 294
Pfalzer, Georg, 133, 135
Philippines, 261
photography, 19, 41, 265
Pidgin English, 53, 55, 57, 65
Pietist/Pietism, 162, 167
Pillai, Champakraman 203
plantation, 15, 114–26; culture, 115, 119, 124; European, 114, 117–19, 122, 125–26; German 121, 147–48, 150; owners, 147, 149, 151, 155; sisal, 15, 114–15, 117–19, 125–26
Planters' Association, 154
Plato, 262–63, 267
Poeschel, Hans, 108
political economy, 117
political landscape, 86, 92, 97, 229
polygamy, 165–66, 168
Portuguese East Africa, 96
postcolonial studies, 4, 11–12, 36, 286
postcolonial world, 245, 254
postmodernity, 272
precolonial, 4, 8, 15, 227, 238, 247–48, 251, 254; conditions, 86; culture, 252; idyll, 249
prejudices, 14, 148–49
Prince Qing Yikuang, 153
prostitutes, 14, 71,73–77, 79
prostitution, 14, 73–77

protection treaty, 88, 229, 249
protectorate, 33, 50, 53, 148, 150, 153
Protestantism, 162
Prussian, 91–92, 97, 105, 166, 217
Prussian Landwehr, 91
Pugach, Sara, 12
punishment, 42, 101, 108–9, 123, 149–
50, 152, 155, 218

Qeracharuc, 134–35
Qian, Ding (Prefect of Gaomi), 275–78,
282
Qian, Xiongfei, 274–76, 281
Qing court, 274, 278, 281
Qing Dynasty, 153, 179, 183, 191, 274,
276–78, 280
Qing Government, 148, 164, 166, 179–
80, 183, 186–88, 191
Qingdao, 77, 179–85, 187–91; model,
189; Special High School, 188;
Times, 183
Qorafung, 135
Quadiri Sufi order, 90
Queensland, 147

Rabaul, 132, 150
race, 4, 19, 117, 122, 148, 197, 206–7,
215, 227, 264–65, 286; categories,
285; distinction, 123; hierarchy, 167;
landscape, 126
racism, 4, 11, 217, 229, 246–48, 252–
53, 292–93, 296; movies, 295
Radhakrishnan, R., 204
Realpolitik, 207, 276
Reckwitz, Andreas, 10
rehani, 1
Reichskolonialamt, 212
Reichskolonialbund, 296
Reichsstrafgesetzbuch, 218
Reichstag, 154
Republic of China, 179, 189, 191
Republic of Wine, 272, 280
resistance, 6–7, 9, 13, 17, 60, 71–72, 88,
90, 121–22, 125, 148, 170, 227, 230,
253; anti-colonial, 16, 227; Chinese,
17, 152, 155, 179; coolie, 148; local,
271; social, 18, 213, 222
Revolution of 1911 (China), 169, 179,
181, 188, 189
Rhinoceros, 262–68

Riefenstahl, Leni, 297
Riesz, János, 3
ripped Ewondo. *See* Ewondo
Robbins, Bruce, 196
Robeson, Paul, 297
Rockel, Stephen, 8
Roman Catholic Church, 54
Rong, Cai, 272
RStGB. *See* Reichsstrafgesetzbuch
Ruete, Emily, 246
Ruga-ruga, 15, 85–97
Rühmann, Heinz, 292, 296
Rumaliza, 89–90, 97
Rwanda, 94–95

Said, Edward, 4
Salime, 109
Samba, Martin Paul, 59, 60, 63
Samoa, 16–17, 133, 147–48, 150–56
Samoanische Zeitung, 151
The Sandalwood Torture, 271–75,
280
Sarastro, 261–63
Sattelberg, 133–37, 140–41
Schaurizettel, 109–10
Scheunemann,Walter, 292
Schlaich, Frieder, 289
Schlöndorff, 290
Schmied-Kowarzik, Wolfdietrich, 12
Schmitt, Carl, 286
Schneider, Carl, 135
Schoeller, Rudolph, 116
Schomburgk, Hans, 290–93
Schrade, Carl, 135
Schultz, Erich, 150, 154
Schultze, Otto, 169
Schulz, Emil, 50
Schumann, Robert, 264–65, 269
Schutztruppe, 8, 15, 90–93, 101, 103–
05, 109, 217, 226, 228–29, 231
Schwarz, Eugen, 39, 40
Scorsese, Martin, 289
Sea of Islands, 130
self-government, 168–71, 173
self-representation, 5–7, 13–14, 31–32,
41, 43
Selpin, Herbert, 295
semi-colonialism, 7, 9
Sept. 1912 (Sun Yat-sen's visit to Ger-
man Qingdao), 189

settlement, 124, 135, 151–52, 154, 156, 167, 214–15
Sewell, William, 10
sex, 14, 71, 73, 77,70, 125, 231, 272
sexually transmitted diseases (STDs), 71
Shandong, 20, 179–88
Shang, Zhen, 183
Shanghai, 168, 182
Shantou (Swatow), 149, 151–53
Shark Island, 261
shauri, pl. mashauri, 102–3, 106–9
Shenhou ribao (National Herald), 182
Shoah, 2, 4
Simbang, 132
Simo, David, 5
Singapore, 149
Sino-German College, 188
Sirk, Douglas, 290
sisal, 15, 114–21, 124–26; agave, 114
Sissons, Carol, 8
slavery, 8, 205
Smith, Woodruff, 3
social networks, 7, 102, 125
socialist realism, 273, 277
Solf, Wilhelm, 150–152, 154–55
Songtou 嵩頭 village, 168–70, 173–74
Sontag, Susan, 265
South Africa, 10–11, 18, 20, 226, 231, 233–34, 236–37, 246, 259, 261, 264, 267–69, 291
South Pacific, 147
South West Africa (SWA), 18, 20, 33, 226–29, 231, 235, 259–61, 264, 268; German, 76–78
Southeast Asia, 147
Spivak, Gayatri, 162
Steinmetz, George, 4, 150
Stoecker, Helmuth, 3
Strafim, 134
The Straits Times, 149
Stübel, Dr. O. W., 147
Subaltern Studies, 7, 11, 73
Sultan Njoya, 33, 63
Sun, Baoqi (new Shandong governor), 153, 186, 187
Sun, Bing, 274, 276–80, 282
Sun, Yat-sen, 179, 181, 188–91
Sunseri, Thaddeus, 8
Swahili plantations, 117–18
Swiss, 17, 37, 166

syphilis, 75, 78

Tabora, 87–89
Tâgi, 133
Tagore, Rabindranath, 201
Tamino, 262
Tanga, 94, 115–16, 121, 123–24
Tanganyika (lake), 86, 88
Tanzania, 8, 114
Tao Chengzhang, 183
Tappenbeck, Hans, 50
taxes, 91, 102, 106–7, 122–23, 169
Tchaptchet, Jean-Martin, 65
Teno, Jean-Marie, 289, 290
theatricality, 103, 105, 279
Third Reich, 289, 291–92
Tianjin, 275
Tiananmen Square massacre, 281
Togo, 11, 19, 33, 74–75, 246–51, 290, 292
Tok Pisin, 134
Tongmenghui, 181–84
torture, 274–76, 280
Townsend, M. E., 3
transnational, 2, 7, 9, 11–13, 18, 163, 168, 171, 198–99, 245–46, 254, 287, 289–90, 292; history, 11–12, 18; literature, 245
transnationalism, 292
Trauerarbeit, 20, 259, 262–63, 268–69
Trauma, 19, 214, 246, 251, 267
Treaty ports, 11, 164
Triomf, 263
Truppenbambusen, 231, 235
Truppenspieler (play soldiers), 226, 233, 236
Tsingtauer Neueste Nachrichten, 156, 188

United States, 3–4, 11–12, 16, 162, 196, 201, 203, 261, 294
University of Berlin, 216, 218
Unyamwezi, 87, 91, 93, 95, 97
Unyanyembe, 87, 89–90

Veidt, Conrad, 292
venereal disease, 73, 75, 78–80
Versailles Treaties of 1919
Vuhavi, 219

Wahehe, 216
Waldenfels, Bernhard, 12, 28, 329
Wandala, 53
Wang, Ning, 272, 276
Wanyamwezi, 85–86
Warmbold, Joachim, 3, 23, 329
Waterburg, 261, 263
weapons, 42, 91–92, 94, 110, 137–38,
    206
Weber, Brigitte, 53, 58
Weber, Max, 162
Weichert, Ludwig, 296
Weidemann, Alfred, 296
Weiss, Helmut, 296
Weixian, 184
Werkbund, 44–45
West Germany, 247, 252–52, 255
Western Samoa, 16, 147, 150,
    155–56
Wierlacher, Alois, 12
Windhuk/Windhoek, 78, 234, 263,
    268
Wintgens, Max, 94–95
Wirz, Albert, 221
Wissmann, Hermann, 86–91, 93, 97,
Wong, Anna May, 294
World War I, 3–4, 15, 93, 97, 117, 125,
    207, 246, 250, 294
World War II, 2–4, 236–37, 285, 290,
    293
Wright, Marcia, 104
Wu, Cheng'en, 281
Wuhrmann, Anna, 41
Württemberg, 163
Wuzu gonghe (harmonious
    cohabitation of five ethnicities),
    181

xenophobia, 170, 229

Yabem, 136
Yabim, 133, 136
Yan, Chengzhang, 183
Yang Sheng, 152
Yantai, 181, 184, 186
Yao ruga-ruga, 96
Yaúnde, 51, 53, 54, 56, 58, 59, 61, 64–
    67
Yéo, Lacina, 12
Yishui, 184
Yizhou, 183, 184
Yongzheng emperor, 164
Yuan, Shikai, 154, 271, 274–83
Yuan, Shuxun (Shandong Governor),
    184

Zake, 16, 130–41
Zantop, Susanne, 2, 4
Zanzibari, 86, 89
Zauberflöte. See *Magic Flute*
Zeller, Joachim, 4
Zenker, Georg, 51
Zhang Fuxing, 165, 167, 172–73
Zhangcun village, 165–66
Zhao, Jia, 274–80
Zhen, Shidao, 188
Zhendan Public School, 181, 186–88,
    191
Zhong Qingyuan, 168–71
Zhou, Jingfu, 181
Zhuang, Ying Chen, 5
Zhucheng, 184
Zimmerer, Jürgen, 4, 7,
Zimmerman, Andrew, 11
Zumaiang, 133, 138